Enlightenment at Court
Patrons, Philosophes,
and Reformers in
EIGHTEENTH-CENTURY EUROPE

Enlightenment at Court

Patrons, Philosophes,
and Reformers in
Eighteenth-Century Europe

Edited by

THOMAS BISKUP, BENJAMIN MARSCHKE,

ANDREAS PEČAR,

and

DAMIEN TRICOIRE

Published by Liverpool University Press on behalf of
© 2022 Voltaire Foundation, University of Oxford
ISBN 978 1 80085 507 6
Oxford University Studies in the Enlightenment 2022:08
ISSN 2634-8047 (Print)
ISSN 2634-8055 (Online)

Voltaire Foundation
99 Banbury Road
Oxford OX2 6JX, UK
www.voltaire.ox.ac.uk

A catalogue record for this book is available from the British Library

The correct style for citing this book is
Thomas Biskup, Benjamin Marschke, Andreas Pečar, and
Damien Tricoire, *Enlightenment at court: patrons,* philosophes,
and reformers in eighteenth-century Europe
Oxford University Studies in the Enlightenment
(Liverpool, Liverpool University Press, 2022)

Cover illustration: Le Thé à l'anglaise servi dans le salon des quatre-glaces
au Palais du Temple à Paris, en 1764 / Michel-Barthélémy Ollivier / 1766 /
Wikimedia Commons / User: Léna / Public Domain {{PD-US}}

Printed and bound by CPI Group (UK) Ltd, Croydon, CR0 4YY

Oxford University Studies in the Enlightenment

ENLIGHTENMENT AT COURT
PATRONS, PHILOSOPHES, AND REFORMERS
IN EIGHTEENTH-CENTURY EUROPE

This is the first comprehensive analysis of the royal and princely courts of Europe as important places of Enlightenment. The households of European rulers remained central to politics and culture throughout the eighteenth century, and few writers, artists, musicians, or scholars could succeed without establishing connections to ruling houses, noble families, or powerful courtiers.

Covering case studies from Spain and France to Russia, and from Scandinavia and Britain to the Holy Roman Empire, the contributions in this volume examine how Enlightenment figures were integrated into the princely courts of the *ancien régime*, and what kinds of relationships they had with courtiers. Dangers and opportunities presented by proximity to court are discussed as well as the question of what rulers and courtiers gained from their interactions with Enlightenment men and women of letters. The book focuses on four areas: firstly, the impact of courtly patronage on Enlightenment discourses and the work as well as careers of Enlightenment writers; secondly, the court as an audience for Enlightenment writers; thirdly, the function of Enlightenment narratives and discourses for the image-making of rulers and courtiers; and fourthly, the role the interaction of courtiers and Enlightenment writers played for the formulation of reform policies.

Contents

Contents

List of figures

Acknowledgments

Enlightenment at Court is the result of a long working process, which began in 2017 with a conference funded by the German Research Council (DFG) and the Research Initiative of the State of Saxony-Anhalt "Enlightenment – Religion – Knowledge" (Landes-forschungsinitiative "Aufklärung – Religion – Wissen"). The conference was kindly hosted by the Interdisciplinary Centre for Research on the Enlightenment (IZEA) in Halle, Germany. We would like to thank most warmly all these institutions for their support, which enabled us to gather eminent specialists from several European countries and the USA.

The volume is not identical with the conference, however, and it took much time and effort to turn the project into what we hope has become a multifaceted but coherent book. We are very grateful to General Editor Gregory Brown and the editorial Board of the *Oxford University Studies in the Enlightenment*, as well as the anonymous reviewers for their encouragement, helpful advice, and eye for detail. We wish to thank Ally Lee and the entire team at Liverpool University Press, and we are particularly indebted to Leah Morin for her invaluable work during the copy-editing phase, and to Sarah Davison during production. And finally, we thank our authors for making this volume possible.

Introduction: court and Enlightenment

Thomas Biskup, Benjamin Marschke, Andreas Pečar, *and* Damien Tricoire

In the eighteenth century, people who represented themselves as *philosophes* mostly spoke of royal courts in negative terms. For the philosopher Denis Diderot, who attempted to redeem Seneca in his essay about the reigns of Emperors Claudius and Nero, the court exposed a virtuous philosopher like Seneca to countless temptations. At court one found only "Perfidious courtiers, professional flatterers, the most abject sort of man; rulers like Tiberius and Caligula, who oppress men for whom they should be true fathers, accompanied by a flock of little liars who encourage them to hate and who praise their follies to the skies."[1] Quite similarly, Frederick II "the Great" of Prussia condemned his grandfather, Frederick I:

> The expence which Frederick I was so fond of, was far from being of this kind; it was rather the dissipation of a vain and prodigal prince. His court was one of the most magnificent in Europe; and his embassies were as splendid as those of the Portuguese. He granted very large pensions to his favourites. His buildings were magnificent, and his entertainments grand; his stables wers [*sic*] filled with horses, his offices with cooks, and his cellars with wine. [...] His favourites were loaded with his largesses, while the inhabitants of Lithuania and Prussia perished with famine and pestilence; and this generous prince refused to relieve them.[2]

---

1. "Des courtisans perfides, des adulateurs par état, la race la plus abjecte; des Tiberes, des Caligulas, les oppresseurs des hommes dont ils devaient être les peres, avec le nombreux cortege des menteurs subalternes qui servent leurs haines & et qui encensent leurs folies." Denis Diderot, *Essai sur les règnes de Claude et de Néron*, in Denis Diderot, *Œuvres complètes*, ed. Jean Deprun and H. Dieckmann, 33 vols. (Paris, 1975–), vol.25 (1986), book 1, §105, p.188–89. All translations are our own unless otherwise stated.
2. Frederick II, king of Prussia, *Memoirs of the house of Brandenburg: from the earliest*

1

For Frederick II, who styled himself as the "philosophe de Sanssouci," the court of his grandfather was synonymous with profligacy, vanity, idleness, exploitation, and clientelism—with Asiatic despotism.

Frederick II of Prussia and Denis Diderot had little in common except their disparaging judgments of the court (and of each other), in which they both spoke as *philosophes*. As such, they embraced the same stereotypes about princely courts and courtly society. When Frederick judged the court of his grandfather and Diderot judged the courts of the Roman emperors, they drew on a stock of negative clichés that had been propagated by countless authors. If we understand "Enlightenment" as a kind of language with a common vocabulary, then anti-court rhetoric was one of the typical elements of the language of Enlightenment. If "virtue," "truth," "reason," "common good," and "nature" were part of the basic Enlightenment vocabulary, then princely courts were characterized by their obvious antonyms.

All too often, historians have accepted negative contemporary clichés about princely courts, courtiers, and court society as prima facie evidence of the antagonistic relationship between courts and Enlightenment. In plays and pamphlets, novels and poems, the court is often portrayed as the site of despotism, hypocrisy, superficiality, intrigue, effeminization, foreignness, decadence, corruption, greed, personal ambition, moral degeneracy, fornication, and so forth. Courtiers appear as effeminate and hedonistic sycophants, concerned only with their own interests and not at all with the common good. In these writings, the court serves as a negative contrast to the canon of virtues of classical republicanism, which distinguished itself through strict morals, dutifulness, modesty, authenticity, and readiness to sacrifice for the common good. These dichotomies all have older origins and drew upon ancient texts and Reformation discourses, but in eighteenth-century political discourse they became ubiquitous and gained a prominent place in the "new patriotism" that emerged across Europe.[3]

---

accounts, to the death of Frederick I. king of Prussia (London, J. Nourse, 1751), p.200–201.

3.   Rudolf Vierhaus, "'Patriotismus': Begriff und Realität einer moralisch-politischen Haltung," in *Deutsche Patrioten und gemeinnützige Gesellschaften*, ed. Rudolf Vierhaus (Munich, 1980), p.9–29; Rudolf Vierhaus, *Deutschland im 18. Jahrhundert: politische Verfassung, soziales Gefüge, geistige Bewegungen* (Göttingen, 1987), p.96–109; T. C. Blanning, *The Culture of power and the power of culture* (Oxford, 2006); Christoph Prignitz, *Vaterlandsliebe und Freiheit: deutscher Patriotismus von 1750 bis 1850* (Wiesbaden, 1981); *Patriotismus*, ed. Günter Birtsch (Hamburg, 1991).

Throughout the "age of Enlightenment," however, royal and princely courts remained central to European politics and culture. As the sites where the households of European rulers and the government of early modern Europe's dynastic states converged, they remained at the center of networking and patronage through the early nineteenth century, and, before 1800, few writers, artists, musicians, or scholars could succeed without establishing connections to ruling houses, noble families, or powerful courtiers. Indeed, many took positions at court themselves, including large numbers of *philosophes* and *Aufklärer*, from Voltaire to Lessing, who were, officially or informally, temporarily or permanently, members of royal and princely courts.

What this meant for both courts and Enlightenment, however, has not yet been systematically explored. This is all the more timely as scholarship on Enlightenment is changing. First, dichotomies that were apparently firmly rooted (e.g., "Enlightenment and religion")[4] have been shown to be invalid, and this book is part of the current reconsideration of Enlightenment, which is breaking down these long-standing dichotomies in favor of more sophisticated approaches that highlight nuanced and complex personal, institutional, and conceptual connections. Second, concepts that have long dominated studies of Enlightenment (e.g., "enlightened absolutism," the "bourgeoisie," the "public sphere") seem problematic. Current research within the history of ideas and cultural history shows Enlightenment in more complex intellectual, social, and communicative contexts than before.

Princely courts

Courts were complex spaces of power, patronage, and knowledge, and dynamic centers of the production and consumption of Enlightenment works.[5] In this volume, the term "princely court" is used

4.   Jonathan Sheehan, "Enlightenment, religion, and the enigma of secularization: a review essay," *American historical review* 108:4 (2003), p.1061–80; Ritchie Robertson, "Religion and the Enlightenment: a review essay," *German history* 25:3 (2007), p.422–32; Jeremy Gregory, "Religion: faith in the age of reason," *Eighteenth-century studies* 34:1 (2011), p.435–43; *Themenschwerpunkt: Religion*, ed. Robert Theis (Hamburg, 2009); *Die deutsche Aufklärung im Spiegel der neueren französischen Aufklärungsforschung*, ed. Robert Theis (Hamburg, 1998); Simon Grote, "Review-essay: religion and Enlightenment," *Journal of the history of ideas* 75:1 (2014), p.137–60.

5.   *Bücherwelten–Raumwelten: Zirkulation von Wissen und Macht im Zeitalter des Barock*, ed. Elisabeth Tiller (Cologne, 2014); *I saperi nelle corti: knowledge at the*

to describe the entourage and social milieu of the ruler.[6] The court regularly served as the site where the social lives of the royal family and the leading nobles played out, and the court was where political decision-making processes and governmental activity took place.

In size as well as institutional arrangements, there were enormous differences between courts across Europe: While the Bourbon court at Versailles and the Habsburg court at Vienna were by far the largest courts (numbering thousands of officeholders and members, and attracting noblemen far beyond their own territories), the courts of smaller Central European principalities sometimes numbered no more than a few dozen people. However, even smaller territories, such as Anhalt-Dessau, Ansbach-Bayreuth, or Parma, often boasted disproportionally large courts with hundreds of members.[7] Despite all these differences, however, the term "court," in the first instance, denotes the household staff of a ruler and his (or rarely, her) family, at the top of which stood the senior court offices that were almost invariably reserved for the nobility, such as Master of the Wardrobe or Master of Ceremonies. At the bottom end of the hierarchy, the appointments of chamberlains were handled more flexibly, as were the many positions in the theatrical and musical establishments, libraries, and court clergy, not to mention the various logistical support positions related to the provision of food, drink, fuel, light, clothing, transportation, and so forth. Geoffrey Elton once described a princely court as a "point of contact" between the royal dynasty and court society, between regular members of the court and outsiders, between officials and household servants, between military officers and civilians, between clerics and laypeople, and between

courts, ed. Clelia Arcelli (Florence, 2008); *Savoir et pouvoir au siècle des Lumières*, ed. Jan Borm, Bernard Cottret, and Monique Cottret (Paris, 2011); *Höfe und Experten: Relationen von Macht und Wissen in Mittelalter und Früher Neuzeit*, ed. Marian Füssel, Antje Kuhle, and Michael Stolz (Göttingen, 2018). For definitions of space and intellectual production, see *Lieux de savoir*, vol.1: *Espaces et communautés*, ed. Christian Jacob (Paris, 2007); and *Lieux de savoir*, vol.2: *Les Mains de l'intellect*, ed. Christian Jacob (Paris, 2011).

6. See *Princes, patronage, and the nobility: the court at the beginning of the modern age c.1450–1650*, ed. Ronald G. Asch and Adolf M. Birke (London, 1991); and *The Princely courts of Europe: ritual, politics and culture under the ancien régime 1500–1750*, ed. John Adamson (London, 1999).

7. Jeroen Duindam, *Vienna and Versailles: the courts of Europe's dynastic rivals, 1550–1780* (Cambridge, 2003). For an example of a smaller German court, see Paul Beckus, *Hof und Verwaltung des Fürsten Franz von Anhalt-Dessau (1758–1817): Struktur, Personal, Funktionalität* (Halle, 2015).

aristocrats and artists, scholars, physicians, or intellectuals in the widest sense.[8]

The currency of the court was the favor of and proximity to the ruler and other powerful patrons. Courts were centers of political decision-making, stages for the self-representation of the ruler, as well as clearing houses of patronage, and hubs for communication of all kinds—about political themes as well as social issues. On a massive scale, resources were redistributed, offices granted, and honors conveyed. Offices were employment relationships, based primarily on personal allegiance and loyalty rather than academic qualifications, subject-matter expertise, or job performance. To have a career at court and to acquire influence also required either an influential family or influential patrons and sponsors. Through one's own family name or through the advocacy of important courtiers, one acquired "credit" at court, sometimes in material terms, but especially in social and political terms, and this credit enabled further access and participation.[9] Patronage and credit also came with reciprocal duties for those who benefited from them: allegiance, subordination, and the expectations of favors. With the support of influential patrons one took on not only their "friends" (or "allies"), but also their opponents and enemies. In investigating Enlightenment at court we count as belonging to a court all people who were in such networks and who were granted "credit" (or who at least attempted to acquire it), with the associated consequences.

Although royal and princely courts all held comprehensive lists of officeholders and members (most of which were publicly accessible by the eighteenth century), and the court was defined as a particular sphere of legal jurisdiction, courts were not as clearly demarcated as it seems. Contemporaries often used the term metaphorically, for the center of political decision-making ("the court of Versailles has decided..."). It also remained impossible to differentiate between "court" and "state" throughout the period under consideration, just as it remained difficult to differentiate between a ruler's income and that of the "state."

8. Geoffrey R. Elton, "Tudor government: the points of contact," in Geoffrey R. Elton, *Studies in Tudor politics and government*, 4 vols. (Cambridge, 1983), vol.3, p.3–57.
9. See Norbert Elias, *The Court society* (Oxford, 1983); and Andreas Pečar, *Die Ökonomie der Ehre: Der höfische Adel am Kaiserhof Karls VI. (1713-1740)* (Darmstadt, 2003).

Across Europe there were fundamental differences in how much courts were places of political decision-making, but favor and patronage were important throughout the eighteenth century, and members of courts played a central role in distributing these resources.[10] Even in Britain, where political decisions were increasingly dependent upon a majority of Parliament rather than decisions made at court, the court remained a contact point for the political elites, and it was there that favor was curried and patronage sought. Members of Parliament were especially susceptible to such temptations, which is reflected in contemporary criticisms of their corruption and abuse of power.

Royal and princely courts were not isolated from the rest of society by ceremonies or festivities.[11] Rather, they were closely interlinked with their immediate surroundings as well as with other courts through dense networks of communication that functioned on several official and semi-official levels, ranging from diplomatic dispatches to elaborate "festival literature," from correspondences of courtiers (as well as rulers) to book exchanges, and so on.[12] Even as spaces, courts were closely linked by complex webs to their immediate environment, that is, to the city and non-courtiers, from local craftsmen to printers.[13]

10. Patronage networks at court remained important throughout the eighteenth century, and well into the nineteenth century; recent historiography has pointed out that the narratives of a "decline" of court culture, in which courts became ever more "bourgeois" following the zenith of baroque pomp at the turn of the eighteenth century, have mirrored the narratives of the "rise" of the public sphere. Duindam, *Vienna and Versailles*; Thomas Biskup, "German court and French Revolution: émigrés and the Brunswick court around 1800," *Francia: Forschungen zur westeuropäischen Geschichte* 34:2 (2007), p.61–87.

11. Indeed, they were not really always "festive" at all, as Ute Daniel points out. Ute Daniel, "Höfe und Aufklärung in Deutschland: Plädoyer für eine Begegnung der dritten Art," in *Hofkultur und aufklärerische Reformen in Thüringen: die Bedeutung des Hofes im späten 18. Jahrhundert*, ed. Marcus Ventzke (Cologne, 2002), p.11–31. Certainly they were not the gilded cages described by Norbert Elias, who considered them sites where newly absolutist monarchs domesticated an unruly nobility (Elias, *The Court society*).

12. For a discussion of formal and informal structures and modes of communication at court beyond patronage studies, see *Informelle Strukturen bei Hof: Dresdener Gespräche III zur Theorie des Hofes*, ed. Reinhardt Butz and Jan Hirschbiegel (Berlin, 2009); Volker Bauer, "Strukturwandel der höfischen Öffentlichkeit: zur Medialisierung des Hoflebens vom 16. bis zum 18. Jahrhundert," *Zeitschrift für historische Forschung* 38:4 (2011), p.585–620.

13. *Städtisches Bürgertum und Hofgesellschaft: Kulturen integrativer und konkurrierender Beziehungen in Residenz- und Hauptstädten vom 14. bis ins 19. Jahrhundert*, ed. Jan Hirschbiegel, Werner Paravicini, and Jörg Wettlaufer (Ostfildern, 2012).

As was Enlightenment, European courts were highly international. Many courts employed foreigners, particularly Frenchmen and Italians, on a regular basis (and particularly in positions linked to theater, literature, art, and music), especially Central and Eastern European courts. Foreign *philosophes* were often welcome guests at court. Diplomats as well as the members of ruling dynasties also moved across Europe, bringing their own entourages and ideas along. Here, recent research has highlighted the importance of the cultural transfer of female consorts, who almost invariably moved across borders when marrying into other ruling families.[14] Texts, ideas, patrons, and writers thereby circulated throughout Europe, and courts were exposed to Enlightenment ideas and discourses. The chapters of this book explore cases from British, French, Spanish, German, Swedish, and Russian history and culture, with a concentration on the Holy Roman Empire, the part of Europe with the greatest density and diversity of princely courts.

Princely courts brought about specific behavioral norms, which were referred to as "courtliness." This implied paying great attention to differences of rank, and behaving in a self-restrained and polite manner. "Courtliness" also went hand in hand with a strong disdain for "pedantry," that is of technical jargon and theoretical matters. Court culture valued playfulness: Bons mots and elegant sentences were appreciated, as were poetry, coded allusions, and aphorisms. If they wanted to succeed at court or to reach an aristocratic audience, men and women of letters had to adapt to these norms.

How were princely courts and Enlightenment connected?

The idea that "court" and "Enlightenment" were incompatible is due to scholars' mistaken concepts of these and other terms. "Court," "state," "bureaucracy," "public," and "Enlightenment" were hardly homogeneous or discrete units or agents with their own agendas. Court and Enlightenment appear far less antagonistic when one approaches these phenomena from the perspective of individual actors and when one searches for contact zones; then one sees that Enlightenment writers and members of the court (or people who were both) did come together and work together. From such an individual-based perspective

14. *Queenship in Europe, 1660–1815: the role of the consort*, ed. Clarissa Campbell Orr (Cambridge, 2004); *Queens consort: cultural transfer and European politics, c. 1500–1800*, ed. Helen Watanabe-O'Kelly and Adam Morton (Abingdon, 2017).

there was no "state" or "government," but rather various officials who were frequently in competition and conflict with each other.[15] Royal ministers were often part of court factions, whose composition and influence were constantly changing. In the competition for influence, favor, and patronage in the eighteenth century, it was the nobility who could best assert themselves. Court and state were hardly separate, which is why the implications of conflicts at court went far beyond the court to influence all governmental and social matters. Enlightenment men and women of letters were involved in these conflicts, and their arguments frequently took the side of one court faction or the other. Enlightenment authors' attacks on ministers were typically not attacks on the political system or the state or the *ancien régime* per se, but rather attacks on some courtiers or court factions. Similarly, the persecutions of Enlightenment authors were not necessarily attacks on Enlightenment itself, but rather corollaries of the conflicts between court factions.

In this context the importance of patronage as a mechanism binding Enlightenment writers to the court becomes clear. Social cohesion in the eighteenth century was primarily on the basis of kinship networks and patronage relationships, which stretched from the very top of society (the ruler) to the very bottom. Eighteenth-century authors thereby found themselves in a situation that was not fundamentally different from that of previous centuries; they were dependent upon the protection and support of elite patrons, most of whom were at court or had connections at court. One should not imagine that *philosophes* had no leeway—those who were renowned often had the opportunity to select their patrons, and those who were independently wealthy could also express themselves more freely. Additionally, the level of commitment of (wo)men of letters to their patrons varied considerably (as did the level of commitment of patrons to their clients). Although concepts of modern authorship are often said to have emerged in the eighteenth century, there was no copyright law in most of Europe, which made it virtually impossible for writers to earn a decent living as independent authors, and only through the patronage of elites could one obtain material support in the form of presents, pensions, offices, academy memberships, or even arranged marriage. Conversely, beyond supporting their patrons through publications, *philosophes* often provided any number of

15. Benjamin Marschke, *Absolutely Pietist: patronage, factionalism, and state-building in the early eighteenth-century Prussian army chaplaincy* (Tübingen, 2005), p.16–18.

services for their patrons as librarians, art dealers, censors, diplomats, or spies. If they were supported by the right courtiers, they could also easily publish unauthorized texts, be protected from prosecution, and have their competitors' works prohibited or—even better—prevent them from ever appearing at all.

What did patrons expect in return from their author-clients? First, they expected public support in their struggle for political influence. Because philosophical texts maintained the appearance of impartiality, Enlightenment authors supported their patrons not through obvious panegyrics, as was still common in the seventeenth century, but more discreetly. This has made it difficult for scholars to trace eighteenth-century patronage relationships. Nevertheless, there were opportunities to publicly express support. Men, and sometimes women, of letters could praise their patrons in public, which was done aggressively in letters and in salons and more subtly in print. They could also support the policies of those whose patronage they enjoyed (or hoped for). Finally, Enlightenment authors could indirectly and discreetly support their patrons in public by criticizing their enemies. This method was used abundantly, because to be a *philosophe* was to be a critical authority. To appear impartial, Enlightenment writers could couch their criticism in anti-court rhetoric, which often appeared in pamphlets, and has been (mis)interpreted by many historians as an expression of fundamental antagonism toward the court and the *ancien régime*.

Besides distributing patronage, courtiers were also an audience for writers and artists. We can take as an example the *Correspondance littéraire*, a handwritten newspaper that was sent in the diplomatic mail and therefore exclusively to ruling houses.[16] It was tailored to the intellectual interests of high-ranking members of court, and, because the court was an important and paying audience, court culture found its way into Enlightenment texts. As is mentioned above, the ideal of gentlemanly (*honnête*) literature and the rejection of pedantry came from the courts, and they ensured that successful Enlightenment writers (outside of Scotland and Germany) were rarely based at universities. The court valued elegant, playful, and coded writings, which mobilized the good taste, expertise, and spirit of those with a basic education, and the court rejected writings that

16. Kirill Abrosimov, *Aufklärung jenseits der Öffentlichkeit: Friedrich Melchior Grimms Correspondance littéraire (1753–1773) zwischen der "république des lettres" und europäischen Fürstenhöfen* (Ostfildern, 2014).

were too cumbersome, abstract, or removed from reality.[17] Voltaire's writings are a good example of this court culture: He made his career not as a scholar, but as a poet, an inventor of epigrams and bons mots, an author of entertaining and playful history books and tales. He painstakingly avoided any pendantry, even when he wrote about philosophical matters.

A further mechanism that connected court and Enlightenment was the self-representation of rulers and courtiers. At court it was immensely important to maintain one's image to accrue symbolic capital, and appearing in the media could be helpful in doing so. In addition to conspicuous consumption and military glory, the promotion of the arts and sciences was a traditional means for rulers and high-ranking courtiers to gain prestige. The Enlightenment narrative assigned rulers, ministers, and other aristocrats a new role beyond merely patronizing writers and artists—they were also to recognize the moral authority of the *philosophes* and implement initiatives and reforms based on their ideas. This expectation could appear as an unreasonable demand, given how much higher in the social hierarchy aristocrats stood over Enlightenment men and women of letters.[18] The power of the Enlightenment narrative in the eighteenth century is demonstrated in that many courtiers and rulers apparently thought that it could be worth it to play the roles that intellectuals intended for them, because such compliance could bring them praise from the makers of public opinion.

This book gathers new scholarship addressing these different facets of the issue. We are asking how (and to what extent) Enlightenment figures were integrated into princely courts of the *ancien régime*, what kind of relationships (personal or dependent) they had with courtiers, what dangers or opportunities were presented by proximity to court, and what rulers and courtiers hoped to gain from their interactions with Enlightenment men and women of letters. In this book we follow the various connections between princely courts and Enlightenment

17. Therefore, at least in areas where Enlightenment thinkers were less active at universities, the eighteenth century was less a time of great philosophical systems than the seventeenth or nineteenth centuries.
18. One need only think of the rank-conscious duc de Saint-Simon's surprise that some people could consider Voltaire to be important: "une manière de personnage dans la république des lettres et même une manière d'important parmi un certain monde." Louis de Rouvroy de Saint-Simon, *Mémoires complets et authentiques du duc de Saint-Simon sur le siècle de Louis XIV et la Régence*, 40 vols. (Paris, 1840), vol.25, p.151.

writers, question the motives and strategies of various figures, and explore the social and political contexts and consequences. We address mainly four phenomena:

1. The impact of patronage by courtiers on Enlightenment discourses and the careers and works of Enlightenment writers: One of this book's hypotheses is that being clients of courtiers influenced Enlightenment writers' activities, works, and careers much more than has been acknowledged. They spent considerable time promoting and defending, directly or indirectly, the political programs of their patrons. Furthermore, they adapted their texts to a courtly audience that disliked pedantry and appreciated playful and original texts.

2. The influence of the court as audience, and how Enlightenment writers catered to court culture and courtiers' interests (leisure-time interests as well as material/political interests): Enlightenment journalism and polemics were frequently written with their reception at court in mind.

3. The appeal of Enlightenment ideas and discourses as self-representation at court: Many courtiers and rulers wanted to appear "enlightened," and, for this reason, they introduced new sociable practices and spaces, patronized representative art, music, and architecture, and employed Enlightenment narratives and topoi in their own publications and pronouncements. From our point of view, these practices are as much part of Enlightenment as the formulation of the ideas usually associated with it. They influenced the way these princes and courts were perceived not only by contemporaries, but also in the historiography.

4. The symbiosis between court factions and Enlightenment men and women of letters and their influence on the formulation of political programs and policies: Courts were sites where different factions competed for material, social, and symbolic capital and maneuvered to influence decision-making. For this reason, the histories of Enlightenment reform programs cannot be written separately from the histories of princely courts.

Enlightenment at court thus examines European princely courts as places of Enlightenment, that is, as places of encounter for individuals of different ranks involved in Enlightenment, as "resonance chambers" for Enlightenment discourse, and as spaces for formulating and launching Enlightenment projects.

Enlightenment and *ancien régime* societies

The book builds upon recent scholarship that has uncovered the social and communicative connections between Enlightenment authors and the political elite at princely courts. As long as Enlightenment studies were undertaken as a history of ideas, the focus was on authors and their writings, not on aristocratic patronage, court factions, political polemics, or even financial support.[19] This has changed in the last three decades, as Enlightenment has been explored with the tools of social and cultural history. Scholarly academies, intellectual societies, masonic lodges, universities, salons, clubs, coffeehouses have all been thoroughly investigated as places of the Enlightenment.[20] In France, Daniel Roche has established a historiographic school showing the symbiosis between Enlightenment and *ancien régime* elites, who often gathered in institutions founded or sponsored by the monarchy.[21] Indeed, the relationships and the attitudes of Enlightenment figures to monarchy as a form of government and to individual monarchs have long been subjects of Enlightenment studies.[22] To a lesser extent this also applies to the relationships of Enlightenment figures to privileged social groups, such as the nobility or their prominent representatives.[23]

19. For a recent reappraisal of intellectual history, see *Rethinking modern European intellectual history*, ed. Darrin M. McMahon and Samuel Moyn (Oxford, 2014).
20. For scholarly academies, see Sebastian Kühn, *Wissen, Arbeit, Freundschaft: Ökonomien und soziale Beziehungen an den Akademien in London, Paris und Berlin um 1700* (Göttingen, 2011). For intellectual societies, see Holger Zaunstöck, *Sozietätslandschaft und Mitgliederstrukturen: die mitteldeutschen Aufklärungsgesellschaften im 18. Jahrhundert* (Tübingen, 1999). For masonic lodges, see Margaret C. Jacob, *Living the Enlightenment: freemasonry and politics in eighteenth-century Europe* (New York, 1991). For universities, see William Clark, *Academic charisma and the origins of the research university* (Chicago, IL, 2006); and Marian Füssel, *Gelehrtenkultur als symbolische Praxis: Rang, Ritual und Konflikt an der Universität der Frühen Neuzeit* (Darmstadt, 2006). For salons and clubs, see Antoine Lilti, *The World of the salons: sociability and worldliness in eighteenth-century Paris*, translated by Lydia G. Cochrane (Oxford, 2015). For coffeehouses, see Brian Cowan, "Rise of the coffeehouse reconsidered," *Historical journal* 47:1 (2004), p.21–46.
21. Daniel Roche, *Le Siècle des Lumières en province: académies et académiciens provinciaux, 1680–1789* (Paris, 1978); Daniel Roche, *Les Républicains des lettres: gens de culture et Lumières au XVIIIe siècle* (Paris, 1988).
22. *Monarchisms in the age of Enlightenment: liberty, patriotism, and the common good*, ed. Hans Blom, John Christian Laursen, and Luisa Simonutti (Toronto, 2007).
23. E.g., Jean Sareil, *Voltaire et les Grands* (Geneva, 1978); Edward G. Andrew, *Patrons of the Enlightenment* (Toronto, 2006).

New scholarship has thus begun to explore the links between the courts and Enlightenment in greater depth. In recent years, new empirical research has revealed multiple overlapping connections between people at courts and outside courts in the eighteenth century. For example, Antoine Lilti points out that the social milieus of the salons and the court often overlapped.[24] Moreover, salon sociability was characterized less by critical debate than by decorous conversation that reflected and enabled an elitist system of patronage and exclusion (much like court culture). Connections between Enlightenment and the French royal court are also underlined by Dan Edelstein.[25] Studies by Kirill Abrosimov, Kenta Ohji, and others have shown that some of the most original and radical Enlightenment texts were formulated for courtly audiences, that major books of the late Enlightenment (like Raynal's *Histoire des deux Indes*) were written to defend the programs of patrons at court, and that the very idea of the *philosophe* was born at court.[26]

Much remains to be done, however. Unlike the monarchical state in the wider sense, with its wide range of institutions from boards of censors to provincial seats of learning, royal and princely courts as such have relatively rarely been understood as communication spaces critical for Enlightenment studies.[27] The connections between communication at courts, social networks, and Enlightenment ideas and projects have been fairly neglected, and a comparative analysis of different European princely courts and the protagonists of Enlightenment has only partly been attempted. Responsible for this are above all three historiographical concepts that have shaped debates on the relationship of politics and Enlightenment over the last decades: the "public sphere," the "radical Enlightenment," and "enlightened absolutism."

24. Lilti, *The World of the salons*.
25. Edelstein does not develop this systematically; see Dan Edelstein, *The Enlightenment: a genealogy* (Chicago, IL, 2010), p.89–90.
26. Abrosimov, *Aufklärung jenseits der Öffentlichkeit*; Kenta Ohji, "Raynal, Necker et la Compagnie des Indes: quelques aspects inconnus de la génèse et de l'évolution de l'*Histoire des deux Indes*," in *Raynal et ses réseaux*, ed. Gilles Bancarel (Paris, 2011), p.105–82; Damien Tricoire, "Raynal's and Diderot's patriotic history of the two Indies, or the problem of anti-colonialism in the eighteenth century," *The Eighteenth century: theory and interpretation* (forthcoming); and Damien Tricoire, "The fabrication of the *philosophe*: Catholicism, court culture, and the origins of Enlightenment moralism in France," *Eighteenth-century studies* 51:4 (2018), p.453–77.
27. An exception is Otto Dann, "Eine höfische Gesellschaft als Lesegesellschaft," *Aufklärung* 6:1 (1991), p.43–57.

The "public sphere"

Jürgen Habermas's concept of a "public sphere" has played a decisive role in shaping debates on communication and political critique in the eighteenth century.[28] Habermas famously describes a structural transformation from a "representative public" dominated by the staged displays of royal courts, to a "bourgeois public" in salons, associations, and coffeehouses, supported by increasingly available newspapers, periodicals, and books. In keeping with this interpretation, countless historians have viewed the pervasive anti-court (including anti-noble, anti-luxury, and anti-ceremonial) discourses of the eighteenth century as an attack on royal courts by the newly established bourgeois public. Habermas's *Structural transformation of the public sphere*, first published in 1962, appeared in English only in 1989, and this translation unleashed a late flowering of the concept and intense controversy in anglophone and francophone scholarship.

Habermas's concept can be read as analogous to Reinhart Koselleck's *Critique and crisis*, which presented a similar model of transformation from the perspective of the history of ideas.[29] Here, it was not "bourgeois society" but the "state" that allowed a free and secular communication space, protected from religious conflict or orthodoxy. This allowed critical public opinion to unfold at first in semi-private spaces, such as masonic lodges, and then, over the course of the eighteenth century, increasingly in public venues.[30]

The "public sphere" has been criticized conceptually, empirically, and in terms of chronology. Historians of the early modern period have pointed out that, contrary to Habermas's vision of a "representative public," political and religious communication never operated only in a one-way top-down mode. Since the Reformation, rulers had never been able to and did not always want to stop the production, distribution, and discussion of printed matter that challenged social and religious conventions, and the subjects of princely states had

28. Jürgen Habermas, *The Structural transformation of the public sphere: an inquiry into a category of bourgeois society*, translated by Thomas Burger (1962; Cambridge, MA, 1989).

29. Reinhart Koselleck, *Critique and crisis: Enlightenment and the pathogenesis of modern society* (1959; Cambridge, MA, 1988).

30. See Michael Schwartz, "Leviathan oder Lucifer: Reinhart Kosellecks 'Kritik und Krise' revisited," *Zeitschrift für Religions- und Geistesgeschichte* 45:1 (1993), p.33–57.

never been just a mute and uncritical audience of courtly spectacles.[31] Moreover, the existence of a critical "public sphere" long before the eighteenth century raises the question of when a "public" as a critical resonance chamber can be identified—in the seventeenth or even the sixteenth century—and problematizes Enlightenment's supposed role in fostering a critique of existing political and social structures.[32] Critics of Habermas's concept also raised the question of access to the "bourgeois" public sphere; what about the role of the lower and upper classes for the formation of public opinion? Finally, the critical character of the "public sphere" has come to be challenged; was it necessarily critical of the powers that be, or did it provide a forum which also allowed government officials and prominent courtiers, and the writers they supported, to advance their arguments and place their pamphlets?[33]

31. Andreas Gestrich, *Absolutismus und Öffentlichkeit: Politische Kommunikation in Deutschland zu Beginn des 18. Jahrhunderts* (Göttingen, 1994).

32. For England, see David Zaret, *Origins of democratic culture: printing, petitions, and the public sphere in early-modern England* (Princeton, NJ, 2000); Dagmar Freist, *Governed by opinion: politics, religion and the dynamics of communication in Stuart London* (London, 1997); Joad Raymond, *Pamphlets and pamphleteering in early modern Britain* (Cambridge, 2003); Richard Cust, "News and politics in early seventeenth-century England," *Past and present* 112:1 (August 1986), p.60–90; Peter Lake and Steve Pincus, "Rethinking the public sphere in early modern England," *Journal of British studies* 45 (2006), p.270–92; Greg Walker, *Writing under tyranny: English literature and the Henrician Reformation* (Oxford, 2005); Kevin Sharpe, *Selling the Tudor monarchy: authority and image in sixteenth-century England* (New Haven, CT, 2009), p.30–31. For France, see John W. A. Gunn, *Queen of the world: opinion in the public life of France from the Renaissance to the Revolution* (Oxford, 1995); Cédric Michon, "Du bon usage de l'anachronisme en histoire: l'opinion publique à la Renaissance," in *L'Opinion publique en Europe (1600–1800)*, ed. Lucien Bély (Paris, 2011), p.39–67; Bernard Guenée, *L'Opinion publique à la fin du Moyen Age d'après la "Chronique de Charles VI" du Religieux de Saint-Denis* (Paris, 2002); Claude Gauvard, "Qu'est-ce que l'opinion avant l'invention de l'imprimerie?," in *L'Opinion: information, rumeur, propagande*, ed. Claude Gauvard (Nantes, 2008), p.21–59; Hélène Ducini, *Faire voir, faire croire: l'opinion publique sous Louis XIII* (Seyssel, 2003); Jeffrey K. Sawyer, *Printed poison: pamphlet propaganda, faction politics and the public sphere in early seventeenth-century France* (Berkeley, CA, 1990). For the Holy Roman Empire, see Gestrich, *Absolutismus und Öffentlichkeit*; and Johannes Arndt, "Gab es im frühmodernen Heiligen Römischen Reich ein 'Mediensystem der politischen Publizistik'? Einige systemtheoretische Überlegungen," *Jahrbuch für Kommunikationsgeschichte* 6 (2004), p.74–102.

33. This question is discussed by Blanning, *The Culture of power*, p.5–14. For France, see Arlette Farge, *Dire et mal dire: l'opinion publique au XVIIIᵉ siècle* (Paris, 1992);

In Koselleck and Habermas's interpretation, "Enlightenment" is largely equated with the "public sphere," and this is in turn seen as separate from the court or "governmental" sphere, and fundamentally opposed to the political system of the *ancien régime*. Both authors admit that they researched neither the concrete social and political contexts in which public opinion was expressed nor the positions of Enlightenment authors, their interests, or dependencies. Recent scholarship, however, has not only questioned the validity of the Habermas model, but also clearly demonstrated that some courtiers played central roles in the *république des lettres* as audience members, correspondence partners, social critics, financial backers, project managers, and kindred spirits.[34]

The "literary underground" and "radical Enlightenment"

Older Enlightenment studies have regarded a relatively small number of prominent eighteenth-century authors, such as Montesquieu, Voltaire, Rousseau, and Diderot, as the canon. The broadening of the concept of Enlightenment, and the inclusion of vast numbers of authors and writings, institutions and practices, has spawned new differentiations in the last few decades. The most notable (above all in anglophone scholarship) is to divide Enlightenment into radical and moderate wings. Robert Darnton suggested that we should differentiate between two groups of Enlightenment figures: those who were integrated within the cosmos of aristocratic patronage and princely courts, and those who were without the patronage of a court or courtier. Members of this latter group were in his view more radical in their criticisms of established institutions, and, lacking the powerful support networks that were necessary for entry and success in high society, these authors produced an "underground" literature in which the condemnation of the court was a constant feature.

In this interpretation, anti-court literature was largely the work of socially marginalized and/or economically precarious authors ("Grub Street"), who from their positions as outsiders called into question the entire political system and social hierarchy. Darnton attributes to

---

Keith Michael Baker, "Politique et opinion publique sous l'ancien régime," *Annales ESC* 42:1 (1987), p.41–71. Similar: Mona Ozouf, "L'opinion publique," in *The French Revolution and the creation of modern political culture*, ed. Keith Michael Baker, 4 vols. (Oxford, 1987–1994), vol.1, p.419–34.

34. See, as an example, Abrosimov, *Aufklärung jenseits der Öffentlichkeit*.

such literature a role in preparing the way for the French Revolution.[35] Darnton subsequently abdicated the broader implications of his thesis and recanted some of his early conclusions by relativizing the supposed opposition between radical literature and the court. He showed that some court members, like the minister Maurepas, may have played a role in diffusing satires of other court members (such as the royal mistress Mme de Pompadour). Darnton continued to insist, however, that most pamphleteers were excluded from formal or informal structures set up by court members. In his view, the "town" (Paris) was generally a separate world from the "court" (Versailles). This is why, although some court members were involved in the creation of polemics, the pamphleteers often launched fundamental attacks on the social and political system, and Darnton sees their underground literature as a "literary movement" against the *ancien régime*.[36]

Many studies of the "radical Enlightenment," most prominently the works of Jonathan Israel, also postulate an insurmountable incompatibility between courtiers and radical Enlightenment authors on socioeconomic and ideological grounds.[37] In contrast to Darnton, Israel draws on a much more limited, "classic" body of sources, and examines primarily *philosophes* who have long held prominent places in the history of ideas. His portrayal of these *philosophes* as resistance fighters against the *ancien régime*, however, has been criticized as unnuanced, and the differentiation between moderates and radicals as formulaic.[38] Israel

35. Robert Darnton, *The Literary underground of the Old Regime* (Cambridge, MA, 1982); Robert Darnton, *The Forbidden best-sellers of pre-revolutionary France* (New York, 1995); Robert Darnton, "'Philosophical sex': pornography in Old Regime France," in *Enlightenment, passion, modernity: historical essays in European thought and culture*, ed. Mark S. Micale and Robert L. Dietle (Stanford, CA, 2000), p.88–112.

36. See the dismantlings of Darnton's works and his recantations in *The Darnton debate: books and revolution in the eighteenth century*, ed. Haydn T. Mason (Oxford, 1998). Robert Darnton, *The Devil in the holy water, or the Art of slander from Louis XIV to Napoleon* (Philadelphia, PA, 2010); Robert Darnton, *Poetry and the police: communication networks in eighteenth-century Paris* (Cambridge, MA, 2010).

37. Jonathan Israel, *A Revolution of the mind: radical Enlightenment and the intellectual origins of modern democracy* (Princeton, NJ, 2010); Jonathan Israel, *Enlightenment contested: philosophy, modernity, and the emancipation of man 1670–1752* (Oxford, 2006); Jonathan Israel, *Democratic Enlightenment: philosophy, revolution, and human rights 1750–1790* (Oxford, 2012).

38. Regarding the Israel debate, see Annelien de Dijn, "The politics of Enlightenment: from Peter Gay to Jonathan Israel," *Historical journal* 55 (2012),

places moderate Enlightenment figures (including Locke, Voltaire, and Wolff) squarely in the orbit of princely courts, and denies them any will to comprehensively criticize existing political conditions. In contrast, a small group of radicals (Spinoza, Raynal, Diderot, Holbach, Helvétius), who were distant from any court and often politically persecuted, argued for radical political change.[39] In Israel's telling, their political criticism ultimately led to the French Revolution, thereby aiding the breakthrough of the political values and structures of modern Western liberal democracy.

"Enlightened absolutism"

The relationship between Enlightenment and European monarchs has long been discussed under the terminology of "enlightened despotism" or "enlightened absolutism," which appears, at first glance, well suited to understanding the connections between Enlightenment and princely courts. Instead, most of the studies that use these terms characterize Enlightenment and court as incompatible.

First, historians have understood "enlightened absolutism" less as a general structural feature of monarchies in the eighteenth century, and more as an accolade for a few select rulers and their reigns, or for political ministers with exceptional influence. This group of outstanding rulers typically includes the Prussian king Frederick II ("the Great"), the Russian empress Catherine II (also "the Great"), the Holy Roman emperor Joseph II, as well as the leading ministers of Portugal (Pombal), Denmark (Struensee), and the Habsburg monarchy (Kaunitz).[40] In the case of monarchs—and this is especially true for Frederick II and Joseph II—it is generally emphasized that

---

p.785–805; and the exchange between Israel and Lynn Hunt: Lynn Hunt, "Louis XVI wasn't killed by ideas: this is what happens when you ignore the role of politics in intellectual history," *The New Republic*, 14 June 2014, https://newrepublic.com/article/118044/revolutionary-ideas-jonathan-israel-reviewed (last accessed January 19, 2022); Jonathan Israel and Lynn Hunt, "Was Louis XVI overthrown by ideas?," *The New Republic*, 31 July 2014, https://newrepublic.com/article/118811/jonathan-israel-response-lynn-hunts-review (last accessed January 19, 2022).

39. Martin Mulsow presents a similar narrative in *Moderne aus dem Untergrund: Radikale Frühaufklärung in Deutschland (1680–1720)* (Hamburg, 2002).

40. See the chapters in *Enlightened absolutism: reform and reformers in later eighteenth-century Europe*, ed. Hamish M. Scott (London, 1990); *Der Idealtyp des aufgeklärten Herrschers*, ed. Günter Birtsch (Hamburg, 1987). See the contributions of Alexei Evstratov, Tal Soker, and Simon Karstens in this volume.

they rejected life at court, and either largely removed themselves from their courts or even abolished them. Those using the term "enlightened absolutism" thereby take for granted that the embrace of Enlightenment by these monarchs (or their leading officials) went hand in hand with an aversion to the court as a political and cultural center of power.

Second, historians have associated the term "enlightened absolutism" with theories of state-building.[41] Focusing on comprehensive political reforms and initiatives, this interpretation identifies two major developments: On the one hand, the rationalization, bureaucratization, and intensification of rule are seen in the context of a long-term state-building process, and, on the other hand, penal reform, pedagogical initiatives, and religious tolerance are interpreted as the emergence of human rights. Whether the actions of rulers and their officials are interpreted as being based on the logic of state power or on political idealism, the court either plays little role in these interpretations or appears as a bastion of resistance against any reforms.[42]

Nonetheless, recent research has shown that social networks at court as well as patron–client networks played decisive roles in the success or failure of Enlightenment reforms and projects.[43] Substantive controversies about political decisions can hardly be separated from factional and positional struggles at court. Studies

41. Günter Birtsch, "Aufgeklärter Absolutismus oder Reformabsolutismus?," *Aufklärung* 9:1 (1996), p.101–109; Peter Baumgart, "Absolutismus ein Mythos? Aufgeklärter Absolutismus ein Widerspruch? Reflexionen zu einem kontroversen Thema gegenwärtiger Frühneuzeitforschung," *Zeitschrift für historische Forschung* 27:4 (2000), p.573–89; Johannes Kunisch, *Absolutismus: Europäische Geschichte vom Westfälischen Frieden bis zur Krise des Ancien Régime* (Göttingen, 1999), p.31–36; Scott, *Enlightened absolutism*.
42. *Power elites and state building*, ed. Wolfgang Reinhard (Oxford, 1996); *Reformabsolutismus und ständische Gesellschaft: Zweihundert Jahre Preußisches Allgemeines Landrecht*, ed. Günter Birtsch (Berlin, 1998); *Reformabsolutismus im Vergleich: Staatswirklichkeit–Modernisierungsaspekte–verfassungsstaatliche Positionen*, ed. Günter Birtsch (Hamburg, 1996); Alexander de Castro, "Enlightened absolutism and legal culture in Portugal: rise and decline of legal Pombalism in the 18th century (1769–1789)," *Zeitschrift der Savigny-Stiftung für Rechtsgeschichte / Germanistische Abteilung* 133:1 (2016), p.296–364; Timothy D. Walker, "Enlightened absolutism and the Lisbon earthquake: asserting state dominance over religious sites and the church in eighteenth-century Portugal," *Eighteenth-century studies* 48:3 (2015), p.307–28.
43. See the contribution of Simon Karstens in this volume.

of "enlightened absolutism" have long assigned rulers and top-down rule an exaggerated importance, and they tend to obscure or forget that rulers were confronted with the conflicting expectations and competing ideas of different groups.[44] The clearing house for such groups' expectations and ideas remained, throughout the eighteenth century, the princely court. These concerns have led to skepticism of "enlightened absolutism" in recent scholarship.

Furthermore, recent studies have focused on the real-world limits of the reforms and projects of "enlightened absolutism." The latest historiography shows that common examples of drastic reforms in the eighteenth century (often described as "enlightened absolutism") often were less about the rationalization of governance and more about rulers' self-representation.[45] Here, the accomplishments of rulers played ever larger roles in their public images. Many of the activities that historians have long seen as part of a reform agenda were primarily, and sometimes even entirely, image politics, such as the well-known story of Joseph II plowing a field.[46] Other rulers made a name for themselves by introducing penal reforms, promoting the arts and sciences, or pursuing educational or agricultural policies (typically naming new educational institutions, museums, or law codes after themselves).[47] Frequently, the publicity effect of these measures far exceeded the practical effects. Comprehensive change was almost impossible to implement with the limited resources of the eighteenth-century state under the constraints of the multilayered and hierarchical early modern society, but signature policies could quickly contribute to improving the image of a ruler.

Important as the tension between the public promotion of Enlightenment projects and their real-world accomplishments doubtlessly is, however, we should be skeptical that "enlightened absolutist" rulers were forced to choose between two supposedly fundamentally

44. See André Holenstein, "Introduction: empowering interactions: looking at statebuilding from below," in *Empowering interactions: political cultures and the emergence of the state in Europe (1300–1900)*, ed. Wim Blockmans et al. (Burlington, VT, 2009), p.1–34.

45. On Frederick II, see Thomas Biskup, *Friedrichs Größe: Inszenierungen des Preußenkönigs in Fest und Zeremoniell 1740–1815* (Frankfurt am Main, 2012); Jürgen Luh, *Der Große: Friedrich II. von Preußen* (Munich, 2011); and Andreas Pečar, *Die Masken des Königs: Friedrich II. von Preußen als Schriftsteller* (Frankfurt am Main, 2016).

46. Derek Beales, *Joseph II*, 2 vols. (Cambridge, 1987–2009), vol.1, p.338.

47. See the contribution of Paul Beckus in this volume.

incompatible pathways, Enlightenment or reason of state.[48] This would be the logical consequence of viewing Enlightenment as a critical emancipatory project that was formulated as a challenge to the social and political situation of the *ancien régime*, but it would not do justice to the complex networks in which courtiers, writers, musicians, and artists operated and pursued their careers. In contrast, an alternative understanding of Enlightenment, which focuses on the intellectual claims and political ambitions of men (and women) of letters, courtiers, and even rulers, would allow us to see their self-representation not just as a cloak concealing their "real" machinations, but to take it seriously, and place it at the center of inquiry.

What was Enlightenment?

The "bourgeois public," "radical underground literature," or "enlightened absolutism" theses all assume that, in the eighteenth century, new future-oriented impulses were unleashed. These new movements were supposedly in competition with (or in opposition to) the long-established institutions of the *ancien régime*, and ultimately superseded and overcame them. In this juxtaposition of old and new, the court and Enlightenment cannot fit together. These theses see in the princely court and its associated system of values and patterns of behavior an obsolete institution, and they see in Enlightenment the worldview and program of the future.

It is the central claim of this book that Enlightenment studies have not been fully aware of the enormous impact of royal courts on the intellectual and cultural history of this age. Especially the French Enlightenment, or at least its "radical" stream, is still often considered in opposition to the world of the court, although it may have been, on the contrary, especially marked by court culture in comparison to the Scottish and German Enlightenments, where universities played a much greater role.

One reason for the difficulty in acknowledging the role of princely courts in Enlightenment history lies in common definitions of Enlightenment as a movement striving to realize a progressive program supposedly antagonistic to established social and political hierarchies.

---

48. See Volker Sellin, "Friedrich der Große und der aufgeklärte Absolutismus: Ein Beitrag zur Klärung eines umstrittenen Begriffs," in *Soziale Bewegung und politische Verfassung: Beiträge zur Geschichte der modernen Welt*, ed. Ulrich Engelhardt (Stuttgart, 1976), p.83–112.

This is not the definition we have adopted here. Scholars have attempted to define Enlightenment in multifarious ways in the last decades, and this introduction is not the place to recount them all.[49] We understand Enlightenment neither as a political program nor as a social movement, but, instead, as a narrative of the purpose and course of human history and a set of discursive and social practices tightly linked to this narrative.[50] "Enlightenment" means a narrative of human progress as a consequence of the accomplishments of "philosophy" (i.e., in literature, the sciences, and the arts). There are many implications of this narrative.

First, this Enlightenment narrative created a kind of political language, with a common vocabulary and guiding concepts, such as reason, nature, progress, philosophy, and education. This language was also present at princely courts in the eighteenth century (i.e., rulers and members of their courts justified and legitimized their agendas using the language of Enlightenment). This narrative also promoted new forms of communication in the areas of political advising and decision-making, such as the composition of memoranda or policy papers. These memoranda served to justify ideas and initiatives on the grounds of reason and the improvement of society.[51] The circle of people who availed themselves of these forms of communication included people established at court as well as people from outside,

49. A sampling of attempts to define Enlightenment, to illustrate the problem: *What is Enlightenment? Eighteenth-century answers and twentieth-century questions*, ed. James Schmidt (Berkeley, CA, 1996); Linda Kirk, "The matter of Enlightenment," *Historical journal* 43:4 (2000), p.1129–43; *What's left of Enlightenment? A postmodern question*, ed. Keith Michael Baker and Peter Hanns Reill (Stanford, CA, 2001); László Kontler, "What is the (historians') Enlightenment today?," *European review of history / Revue européene d'histoire* 13:3 (2006), p.357–71; J. G. A. Pocock, "Historiography and Enlightenment: a view of their history," *Modern intellectual history* 5:1 (2008), p.83–96; Karen O'Brien, "The return of the Enlightenment," *American historical review* 115:5 (2010), p.1426–35; de Dijn, "The politics of Enlightenment"; James Schmidt, "Enlightenment as concept and context," *Journal of the history of ideas* 75:4 (2014), p.677–85.
50. This largely follows the definition of Edelstein, *The Enlightenment*.
51. For example, about Kaunitz: Lothar Schilling, *Kaunitz und das Renversement des alliances: Studien zur außenpolitischen Konzeption Wenzel Antons von Kaunitz* (Berlin, 1994); Franz A. J. Szabo, *Kaunitz and enlightened absolutism 1753–1780* (Cambridge, 1994); about Sonnenfels: Simon Karstens, *Lehrer–Schriftsteller–Staatsreformer: Die Karriere des Joseph von Sonnenfels 1733–1817* (Vienna, 2011); Eric Brian, *La Mesure de l'Etat: administrateurs et géomètres au XVIIIᵉ siècle* (Paris, 1994).

for whom such memoranda could be a way to make new contacts at court and in the government.

Second, this Enlightenment narrative granted scholars, writers, and artists important social and political roles. Celebrity *philosophes*, especially, received widespread recognition, as they publicly commented on the "improvement" of religious, social, economic, and political conditions, and thereby claimed for themselves a special role as social critics. Writers claimed to be allowed to influence and express public opinion on the strength of their arguments, without being distinguished by their social background or any specific position. They recalled ancient predecessors—Cicero, Seneca, and Marcus Aurelius were popular —whose successors they imagined themselves to be. They laid claim to "reason" and "justice," and accused their opponents of working contrary to these principles.[52] In these debates terms such as "reason," "truth," "impartiality," and "Enlightenment" were unprotected trademarks of those who seized the moral high ground in public debates, regardless of whether they had in mind the common good, their own personal gain, or (most commonly) some combination of the two. These were loaded terms in the eighteenth century, polemical, fighting words used to legitimize one's own positions.[53] Because enlightened men and women of letters often sought to change existing conditions, their initiatives were typically bundled with criticisms of current practice or specific elite people or groups.[54] With their claim to influence and express public opinion, such writers were attractive allies in the struggles among courtiers.

Third, this Enlightenment narrative had consequences for what was discussed in public—and thus also at court—and what was not. Because they claimed to be arguing on behalf of the common good, Enlightenment men and women of letters adopted a rhetoric of personal disinterest. Therefore it should not be surprising that

---

52. Ulrich Oevermann, "Der Intellektuelle: soziologische Strukturbestimmung des Komplementär von Öffentlichkeit," in *Die Macht des Geistes: Soziologische Fallanalysen zum Strukturtyp des Intellektuellen*, ed. Andreas Franzmann, Sascha Liebermann, and Jörg Tykwer (Frankfurt am Main, 2001), p.13–75.

53. Andreas Pečar and Damien Tricoire, *Falsche Freunde: War die Aufklärung wirklich die Geburtsstunde der Moderne?* (Frankfurt am Main, 2015), p.27–35; and Michael Sauter, "The Prussian monarchy and the practices of Enlightenment," in *Monarchisms in the age of Enlightenment*, ed. H. Blom, J. C. Laursen, and L. Simonutti, p.217–39.

54. Andreas Pečar, "Der Intellektuelle seit der Aufklärung: Rolle und/oder Kulturmuster?," *Das achtzehnte Jahrhundert* 35 (2011), p.187–203.

they—in a change from earlier centuries—praised their sponsors and high-ranking patrons less overtly for their protection and did so in different ways.[55] Conversely, Enlightenment rhetoric regarding elites was often marked by admonishment and instruction in the use of reason and the importance of the common good. Individual self-interest and, to an even greater extent, political interests as a court faction were assigned to the opposition and condemned. Indeed, some of the most vociferous controversies among Enlightenment figures revolved around accusations that they sought favor at court. Most prominently, Rousseau condemned Enlightenment writers for this and praised instead the freedom of those who had chosen to live the *Vita contemplativa* in isolation from the world.[56] The playwright Charles Palissot de Montenoy also pointed to the discrepancy between the claims of *philosophes* to be independent, and their integration in patronage networks.[57]

Fourth, this Enlightenment narrative implied a Manichean paradigm. The language of Enlightenment portrayed rivals (for example, at court) as enemies of reason, truth, and Enlightenment, and assigned them clichéd motivations such as fanaticism, will to power, greed, or corruption. All too often scholars have accepted uncritically such polemics by Enlightenment writers, rather than looking more closely at the connections between the authors and the conflicting parties. More recent research has shown that such polemics and dichotomies do not do justice to the complex interrelationship of literary production and princely courts. Jeremy Popkin and Simon Burrows have pointed out that many of the pamphleteers regarded as "radical" were in fact in the service of high-ranking courtiers.[58] Heated debates in print coincided frequently with political or personal conflicts within court society, and, indeed, should be seen as an important aspect of these conflicts among early modern elites. Rather than questioning the fundamental legitimacy of the *ancien régime*, many of these pamphlets had actually been commissioned to retroactively legitimize the transition of power from one court faction to another.

55. On the contemporary idea of the independence of the Enlightenment scholar via noble patronage, see Roger Chartier, "Der Gelehrte," in *Der Mensch der Aufklärung*, ed. Michel Vovelle (Frankfurt am Main, 1996), p.122–68.
56. This has led to the assertion that Rousseau himself was not part of Enlightenment; see Graeme Garrard, *Rousseau's Counter-Enlightenment: a republican critique of the philosophes* (Albany, NY, 2003).
57. Charles Palissot de Montenoy, *Les Philosophes: comédie* (Paris, Duchesne, 1760).
58. See the contribution of Damien Tricoire in this volume.

Even those pamphlets that were really aimed at powerful members of court—like the famous, sometimes pornographic texts attacking Queen Marie-Antoinette of France—only had a limited distribution, due to effective suppression by the police, and their impact was weak.[59]

Rather than seeing them as incompatible, we should recognize that the idea of the *philosophe*, and thus the central tenet of the Enlightenment narrative, was invented at the royal court. Already in the late seventeenth century at the court of Louis XIV, a group of authors around Bossuet styled themselves as *philosophes* and thereby claimed to be advocates of morality and social utility. La Bruyère especially made a decisive contribution to the persona of the *philosophe* as the intellectual who was to reform society based on his reason. Arguing for a society based on personal merit, where vicious and unproductive courtiers would turn into wise economic agents, good fathers, upstanding judges, patriotic officers, great orators, and—of course—*philosophes*, La Bruyère harshly criticized the court while remaining part of it and being strongly influenced by it. After all, his ideal of the *honnête homme* and of playful literature, which pervaded Enlightenment *philosophie*, was a courtly one. Indeed, it can be argued that one of the reasons for the success of Enlightenment narratives in France was the centrality of the French court and the vitality of French court culture.[60]

The ideal of the *philosophe* soon became popular beyond the French royal court. For example, in the early eighteenth century, the English aristocrat Shaftesbury praised in his *Characteristicks* the role of the *philosophes* as teachers of virtue in words similar to those in La Bruyère's *Caractères*.[61] The precise details of a virtuous society and the means to achieve this ideal were of course a matter of intense discussion. As scholarship has increasingly shown in the past decades, Enlightenment ideas were very diverse and even contradictory. There were differences between European countries, and above all within each country.[62] However, what matters here is that many intellectuals

59. Jeremy Popkin, "Pamphlet journalism at the end of the Old Regime," *Eighteenth-century studies* 22:3 (1989), p.351–67; Simon Burrows, *Blackmail, scandal, and revolution: London's French libellistes, 1758–1792* (Manchester, 2006).

60. Tricoire, "The fabrication of the *philosophe*."

61. Anthony Ashley Cooper, earl of Shaftesbury, *Characteristicks of men, manners, opinions, times*, ed. Philip Ayres, 2 vols. (1711; Oxford, 1999); Jean de La Bruyère, *Les Caractères, ou les Mœurs de ce siècle* (1688; Paris, 1994).

62. *The Enlightenment in national context*, ed. Roy Porter and Mikuláš Teich (Cambridge, 1981).

across Europe used the language and the *imaginaire* of Enlightenment to present the relevance of their ideas. Despite all their differences, Enlightenment actors drew on the narrative of improving humankind through the arts and sciences. These discourses gained popularity at princely courts.

Contributions to this volume

The structure of the book follows four major threads: patronage; public sphere; self-representation; and projects and reforms. The first part of the book examines how writers worked for courtiers and the impact these patronage relationships had on their works. Andreas Pečar and Damien Tricoire explore the case of Diderot, who has been assumed to have maintained his philosophical independence and thus supposedly defended ideas at the roots of liberal democracy. Pečar and Tricoire study how Diderot developed an ideal of the *philosophe* at court, and they situate him in the patronage networks of his time. Although it is well known that Diderot was protected by Catherine II, publications on Diderot do not take into consideration the extent to which he worked for high-ranking courtiers, the ways he adapted his behavior, the impact on his writings, or the advantages that he accrued from this.

Clarissa Campbell Orr presents the careers and writings of the musicologist Charles Burney (1726–1814) and his novelist daughter Frances (1752–1840). Campbell Orr explores how the ideals of Jean-Jacques Rousseau had an impact at the British court of George III (r.1760–1820) and his consort, Queen Charlotte of Mecklenburg-Strelitz (1744–1818). Her chapter studies Frances Burney's ambivalence as an Enlightenment writer and a courtier. Her fame as a writer (and that of her father as a musicologist) enabled her to gain a prestigious office at the British court, and Campbell Orr shows how Burney profited from her new position but at the same time found it hard to reconcile it with her role as an independent writer.

The second part of the book focuses on the public sphere, and the chapters examine closely the impact of court culture and the interests of courtiers in Enlightenment writings and vice versa. Damien Tricoire examines a corpus of unauthorized publications from the 1770s, comprising famous texts like the *Anecdotes sur Madame Du Barri* and the *Mémoires secrets de la république des lettres*, which are usually ascribed to Pidansat de Mairobert. Examining how these periodicals and pamphlets were connected with courtiers, Tricoire shows how the authors of the so-called "Mairobert corpus," far from having a consistent ideology, repositioned themselves following political changes at court. This casts into doubt the thesis according to which there were autonomous writers, an independent public sphere, and radical opposition to the court-centered political system in eighteenth-century France.

Tal Soker aims to give a more complex picture of the public sphere than that presented in the Habermas theory. He analyzes a controversy in Berlin around the relative merits of the French and Italian musical styles and their relation to the German style. A close reading of the pamphlets reveals that, for their authors, engaging in a debate was not about the matter at hand, but rather a means to discredit rival musicians and raise their own profiles. This contest for symbolic capital took place in a courtly context, as the authors endeavored to forge connections with key figures at court and to obtain positions at court.

The third part of the book explores the impact of the Enlightenment narrative on the self-representation and sociability of rulers and high-ranking courtiers. Paul Beckus compares two German princes, Franz of Anhalt-Dessau and Frederick August of Anhalt-Zerbst, who both enacted roughly the same reform policies but have been judged very differently by contemporaries and historians. Beckus shows that the reason for these different assessments was the divergent representational strategies of the two princes. In contrast to Frederick August, Franz successfully presented himself as the father of his principality and as the epitome of an enlightened prince, living apart from the corrupt world of the court. His famous landscape garden at Wörlitz, where he received Enlightenment writers and artists, was instrumental to this representational strategy.

Luise Maslow studies how Enlightenment ideas could be represented in a courtly garden. Maslow looks at how Wilhelmine, margravine of Bayreuth, used a natural landscape with strangely shaped rocks to create spaces for an alternative court life. The garden included spaces dedicated to scholarly and musical activities, and its lack of formal features or axial arrangements precluded conventional court ceremonial. Paths led through the bizarre rock formations, which forced courtiers to abandon formal posture and clothing. The garden thus embodied the renewal of society through philosophy, and helped ensure Wilhelmine's acceptance in philosophical circles.

Alexei Evstratov examines how the Russian imperial court used Enlightenment media and narratives to represent Catherine II's exercise of power. Her frequent change of favorites made her the subject of many eighteenth-century pamphlets, some of them pornographic. It is less frequently mentioned that some of her favorites abandoned her and fell in love with ladies in waiting. As this chapter demonstrates, the empress used these events of a supposedly private nature to enhance her imperial image. To do so, Catherine drew on a range of narratives praising clemency. This chapter analyzes dramatic performances, literary texts, sermons, legal documents, and ego documents, in order to explore how the unrequited love of a woman was linked with a discourse (inspired by Montesquieu) about clemency in a well-ordered monarchy.

Andreas Önnerfors examines another intersection between courtly and Enlightenment sociability: freemasonry. He focuses on the royal court of Gustav III of Sweden (1772–1792), where the position of freemasonry has been disputed. Some researchers have not acknowledged Gustav's involvement with the masons at all, while others have reduced the masonic influence to his brother, Duke Charles. In light of sources that have only recently been made accessible, Önnerfors elucidates the position of freemasonry at the court of Gustav as an integral part of court sociability and as a centerpiece of his monarchical self-representation.

The fourth part of the volume examines the connections between court politics and Enlightenment projects and reforms. Dealing with Leibniz and the introduction of natural science in Russia in the first half of the eighteenth century, Kirill Ospovat's chapter explores the links between natural science, politics, and religion. Ospovat shows that "natural philosophy" was very much part of court culture and was associated with literary and poetic practices, as well as theology. He examines the intellectual and political context of the foundation of the Russian Academy of Sciences, and shows how natural science was considered a means to improve the morality and discipline of the Russian people.

Gijs Versteegen studies how the discourse at the Spanish court regarding education was adapted to new Enlightenment pedagogy. In the history of education, the emphasis is often placed on criticism of the traditions of the court, contrasting traditional aristocratic education in areas such as dance, fine manners, and polite conversation against new proposals that were supposed to contribute to the common good, social utility, or patriotic values. However, this dichotomy between Enlightenment and courtly discourses is difficult to maintain when studying in detail the discourse on education. The court was not criticized per se; rather the criticism was often directed at the decadence of some courtly customs. Versteegen explores in depth the writings of Gaspar Melchor de Jovellanos, one of the foremost Spanish Enlightenment writers connected to the court.

Simon Karstens investigates the influence of the court on enlightened reforms in the Habsburg monarchy. Research on the subject thus far has concentrated on the different attitudes toward Enlightenment of the four rulers between the 1740s and 1790s, as well as a few of their ministers, and has seen imperial successions as breaking points. By focusing instead on the continuities of court networks, Karstens can demonstrate that, even in an area as sensitive (and important to Enlightenment concepts of justice, control, and welfare) as police reform, interdependencies between courtiers and ruler were central to the formulation of policy, the articulation of which in the language of Enlightenment proved remarkably resilient over decades.

I

Courtly patronage

Diderot the courtier? Philosophers and the world of the court in Enlightenment Europe

Damien Tricoire *and* Andreas Pečar

Introduction

Can philosophers be courtiers? Can they maintain close contacts with high-placed members of the court, seek to increase their prestige, profit from their patronage, and recommend other people to these court figures? Can they, like every other member of a courtly faction, be dependent on political conjunctures at court and on the career of their patrons?

For some scholars, the answer is no, and the history of Grimm and Diderot amply demonstrates this. According to the historiography on the Enlightenment, the more philosophers became courtiers, the more they moved away from their duty as philosophers. For Jonathan Israel, Grimm was a true *philosophe* so long as he remained primarily in the company of other *philosophes*, for example in Holbach's salon. Grimm's journey to St. Petersburg, the offices and honors that Catherine II conferred on him (he became Gentleman of the Bedchamber to the empress), and then his ennoblement by the emperor are certain evidence of his desertion of philosophy. According to Israel, Grimm became "a courtier," "an agent of princes," and an idolizer of "enlightened despotism."[1] His careerist self-abasement corresponded

This chapter was written in French and translated into English by Adam L. Storring (Oxford), whom we thank warmly. The French version has been published in *Romanische Studien* (2020), special issue: *Friedrich Melchior Grimm, philosophe et homme de réseaux dans l'Europe des Lumières*, ed. Jonas Hock and Kirill Abrosimov.

1. Jonathan Israel, *Democratic Enlightenment: philosophy, revolution, and human rights 1750–1790* (Oxford, 2012), p.439. The same interpretation is given by Gerhardt Stenger, "Diderots Beitrag zu Raynals Geschichte beider Indien: das erste Donnergrollen der Französischen Revolution," in *Denis Diderot und die Macht / Denis Diderot et le pouvoir*, ed. Isabelle Deflers (Berlin, 2015), p.121–34 (132).

to a fundamental opposition to Diderot's political agenda: "Diderot's former friend [...] had, since the early 1780s, rejected the political part of Diderot's radical legacy."[2] Starting from the moment when Grimm became part of the world of the court, he was no longer a true Enlightenment *philosophe*.

According to Israel, Diderot personifies, in contrast, the ideal of the radical *philosophe*. His experience at the court of Catherine II supposedly disillusioned Diderot and led him to throw himself into a fundamental struggle against "enlightened despotism."[3] Diderot appears as a sort of revolutionary *avant la lettre*. Israel is far from being the only one to present such an interpretation. Scholarly biographies of Diderot do not hesitate to talk of his "revolutionary stoicism."[4] The title of the celebrated biography published by Gerhardt Stenger presents Diderot as a "freedom fighter."[5] The edited volume published recently by Isabelle Deflers under the title *Denis Diderot und die Macht* presents a similar image. This revolutionary spirit is said to be notably visible in the *Encyclopédie*, Diderot's participation in Raynal's *Histoire des deux Indes*, and his admiration for the American Revolution.[6]

Partially at least, this interpretation of Diderot rests on certain passages which have been taken out of their textual and social context and declared representative of the worldview of the *philosophe*. This is the case with the incendiary letter that Diderot wrote to Grimm in 1781—a letter that he never sent, but which is in the published edition of his correspondence. This letter reflects the opposing opinions of Grimm and Diderot regarding Raynal. The dispute flared up when Raynal decided to publish the new edition of the *Histoire des deux Indes* no longer anonymously but under his real name. In this letter, probably intended, like many of his writings, to be kept at the

2. Jonathan Israel, *Revolutionary ideas: an intellectual history of the French Revolution from "The Rights of man" to Robespierre* (Princeton, NJ, 2014), p.236–37.
3. Israel, *Democratic Enlightenment*, p.619–26. See also Gerhardt Stenger, *Diderot: le combattant de la liberté* (Paris, 2013), p.306; Jacques Proust, "Diderot et l'expérience russe: un exemple de pratique théorique au XVIIIᵉ siècle," *SVEC* 151–55 (1976), p.1777–1800; Isabelle Deflers, "Diderots Auseinandersetzung mit dem 'aufgeklärten Despotismus' Friedrichs II.," in *Diderot und die Macht*, ed. I. Deflers, p.61–82 (76–78).
4. Paolo Quintili, "Le stoïcisme révolutionnaire de Diderot dans l'*Essai sur Sénèque* par rapport à la contribution à l'*Histoire des deux Indes*," *Recherches sur Diderot et sur l'Encyclopédie* 36 (2004), p.29–42.
5. Stenger, *Diderot*.
6. Michel Kerautret, "Diderot et la Révolution américaine," in *Diderot und die Macht*, ed. I. Deflers, p.101–19.

bottom of a drawer, Diderot interprets Grimm's criticism of Raynal as a sign of treason against the *philosophes*. Grimm had allegedly become an *anti-philosophe*: "My friend, I [do not] recognize [you] any more. You have become, perhaps without realizing it, one of the best veiled, but one of the most [lacuna] *anti-philosophes*. You live with us, but you hate us."[7]

In this letter, Diderot affirms that a philosopher must openly face his persecutors. To hide is to take an anti-philosophical attitude. Diderot thus contrasts the courtier who hides with the philosopher who makes serving truth his duty, and he tries to demarcate himself clearly from Grimm. In his *Apologie pour l'abbé Raynal*, Diderot considers that a philosopher should be ready to suffer for the sake of truth: "How have we escaped from barbarism? Because, happily, men were found who loved truth more than they dreaded persecution."[8] One who truly loves liberty defies danger. According to Diderot, Raynal's decision to reveal publicly that he was the author of the *Histoire des deux Indes* is the sign that his friend is a true philosopher, whereas Grimm's plea for an anonymous publication is proof that the latter is a courtier. Nevertheless, it must be remembered that the total opposition that Diderot presents here was no more than a reaction to the violent reproaches that Grimm had made against Raynal. According to Grimm, Raynal was no more than a "coward" and a "fool" for having revealed his identity. In response to these reproaches, Diderot presented Raynal as a philosopher taking on the torch of those who had fought for truth under Tiberius, Caligula and Nero:

> Where is the folly, where is the cowardice, in disregarding both their power and their impotence? Whether the enemy of philosophy is a dangerous or an insignificant person, [philosophy] will not cease to pursue him until he has ceased to be vicious and nasty. This is the opinion that was held by philosophers of the most opposed schools under Tiberius, Caligula, and Nero, and these philosophers were not fools.[9]

Prudence should invite us to consider carefully the context of this letter, and to reflect on the reasons why Diderot did not send it to Grimm. Some scholars, however, take a quite different approach.

7. Denis Diderot, *Correspondance*, ed. Georges Roth and Jean Varloot, 16 vols. (Paris, 1955–1970), vol.15, p.213–14. All translations are by Adam L. Storring unless otherwise stated.
8. Diderot, *Correspondance*, vol.15, p.211.
9. Diderot, *Correspondance*, vol.15, p.212.

They hold up this letter to demonstrate the incompatibility of the roles of courtier and philosopher, at least for the true philosopher.[10] Diderot therefore appears as the very incarnation of the indomitable *philosophe*: radical, going it alone if necessary, doing battle for the abstract ideas of liberty and equality.

This image of Diderot is based, however, on a selection of particular sayings and a setting aside of the communicative and social contexts in which the works of that author were written. Diderot thus becomes part of the prehistory of the American and French Revolutions, for which he appears as an intellectual precursor.[11] If one places Diderot back in the debates and patronage networks of his time, however, another image of that author emerges: that of a *philosophe* who was a client of major figures of the French and Russian courts, courted them, worked for them, and secured considerable personal advantage from these activities.[12]

---

10. Israel, *Democratic Enlightenment*, p.439–41.
11. René Tarin, *Diderot et la Révolution française: controverses et polémique autour d'un philosophe* (Paris, 2001).
12. In this chapter, we define the court as the entourage of the king and do not distinguish it from the highest sphere of the state, since these worlds coincided largely in the eighteenth century. Several modern historians have sought to determine the moment when the state distinguished itself from the household of the prince, but these attempts are problematic because they transpose a principle of the contemporary world into the modern world. See notably the thesis of Geoffrey Elton according to which there was a "Tudor revolution in government" under Henry VIII: Geoffrey R. Elton, *The Tudor revolution in government* (Cambridge, 1953). This thesis was refuted by David Starkey, "Court history in perspective," in *The English court from the Wars of the Roses to the Civil War*, ed. David Starkey (London, 1987), p.1–24 (11–19). Starkey's critique provoked a controversy in the *Historical journal*: Geoffrey R. Elton, "Tudor government," *Historical journal* 31:2 (1988), p.425–34, and David Starkey, "A reply: Tudor government: the facts?," *Historical journal* 31:4 (1988), p.921–31. Wolfgang Reinhard and Mark Hengerer propose theses similar to that of Elton: Wolfgang Reinhard, *Geschichte der Staatsgewalt: eine vergleichende Verfassungsgeschichte Europas von den Anfängen bis zur Gegenwart* (Munich, 1999), p.125–209; Mark Hengerer, *Kaiserhof und Adel in der Mitte des 17. Jahrhunderts: eine Kommunikationsgeschichte der Macht in der Vormoderne* (Konstanz, 2004), p.153–368. For a criticism of this separation between government and court, see Andreas Pečar, *Die Ökonomie der Ehre: Der höfische Adel am Kaiserhof Karls VI. (1713–1740)* (Darmstadt, 2003), p.13–19. Norbert Elias developed ideas similar to those of Elton, Reinhard, and Hengerer in making a distinction between the new elites of the state under Louis XIV and the old courtly nobility: Norbert Elias, *The Court society* (Oxford, 1983), ch.7. This thesis was criticized by Jeroen Duindam, *Myths of power: Norbert Elias and the early modern court* (Amsterdam, 1995); and Leonhard Horowski, *Die Belagerung des Thrones: Machtstrukturen und Karrieremechanismen am Hof von Frankreich 1661–1789* (Ostfildern, 2012).

Beyond the specific case of Diderot, this chapter seeks to contribute a reinterpretation of what is called the "radical" Enlightenment. What is at stake is the degree of independence of authors critical of the court. Robert Darnton depicts the pamphlets directed against high-ranking figures as "Grub Street literature," that is to say writings published by independent authors, often miserable and frustrated, with motives at the same time commercial and counter-cultural. Jeremy Popkin and Simon Burrows have, however, called this interpretation into question. According to them, eighteenth-century authors could hardly be independent from courtiers. Moreover, there are hints that writings directed against high-ranking figures at court, far from being the expression of a counter-culture, themselves emanated from court factions. They were political instruments in the hands of powerful people.[13] In recent years, researchers have taken these insights further, and we have increasingly started to see the overlaps between the Enlightenment and the world of the court.[14]

Through this chapter, we seek to contribute to these new perspectives. Our aim is not to deny that Diderot had his own philosophical agendas. Diderot may have been sincerely committed to the struggle against injustice and oppression. However, in our view, we should acknowledge that he also pursued a major personal goal—the social advancement of his family—and that, in order to achieve it, he was dependent on courtiers. We maintain that his relationships to people of much higher

13. Robert Darnton, "The Grub Street style of revolution: J.-P. Brissot, police spy," *Journal of modern history* 40:4 (1968), p.301–27; Jeremy Popkin, "Pamphlet journalism at the end of the Old Regime," *Eighteenth-century studies* 22:3 (1989), p.351–67; Simon Burrows, *Blackmail, scandal, and revolution: London's French libellistes, 1758–1792* (Manchester, 2006).

14. From the 1970s, Darnton called into question the idea that relations between the state and the encyclopedists were antagonistic: Robert Darnton, *The Business of Enlightenment: a publishing history of the Encyclopédie, 1775–1800* (Cambridge, MA, 1979), p.538–39. In his interpretation of the Enlightenment, Dan Edelstein also underlined the overlaps between the world of the court and that of the *philosophes*: Dan Edelstein, *The Enlightenment: a genealogy* (Chicago, IL, 2010), p.89–90. Above all, detailed studies of the networks of patronage between courtly figures and *philosophes* have started to come out in recent years: Kenta Ohji, "Raynal, Necker et la Compagnie des Indes: quelques aspects inconnus de la génèse et de l'évolution de l'*Histoire des deux Indes*," in *Raynal et ses réseaux*, ed. Gilles Bancarel (Paris, 2011), p.105–82; Kirill Abrosimov, *Aufklärung jenseits der Öffentlichkeit: Friedrich Melchior Grimms Correspondance littéraire (1753–1773) zwischen der "république des lettres" und europäischen Fürstenhöfen* (Ostfildern, 2014). Leonhard Horowski has provided a comprehensive study of the factions at the court of France. He does not emphasize the *philosophes*, but repeatedly mentions their integration into the networks of courtly patronage, Horowski, *Die Belagerung des Thrones*, p.317–67.

rank have often been misrepresented as "friendship" in scholarship, whereas it would be more appropriate to term them "patronage relationships." Diderot's activities for members of the French and the Russian courts went much further than usually recognized, and had a major impact on his work as a *philosophe*. Furthermore, we claim that Diderot understood very well the patronage logic, was largely successful in securing protection from the *Grands*, and indeed enabled his family to climb the social ladder in a tremendous way.

In the first section, we will examine the *Essai sur les règnes de Claude et de Néron* in order to consider to what degree Diderot considered the position of philosopher compatible with that of courtier. In the following sections, we will situate Diderot and his writings in the context of the courtly elites of the second half of the eighteenth century. We will study his integration into patronage networks and briefly examine how Diderot's "radical" writings should be seen in this context.

The philosopher at court: the *Essai sur les règnes de Claude et de Néron*

It is not possible, within this chapter, to present all the facets of the *Essai sur les règnes de Claude et de Néron*, published in 1782, or of the first version of that essay published in 1778 under the title *Essai sur la vie de Sénèque le philosophe*. The text can be read on several different levels. It contains a critique of Rousseau, who had recently died, and praise for American independence. To understand Diderot's relationship to the world of the court, it is above all Diderot's appreciation of Seneca that demands our attention.

Diderot's essay is firstly a declaration of admiration for, indeed an identification with, Seneca and the ancient Greek and Roman philosophers. Diderot expresses himself thus: "O Seneca! You are and you will be forever, with Socrates, with all the illustrious unfortunates, with all the great men of antiquity, one of the sweetest links between my friends and me, indeed between educated men of all ages and their friends." Or again: "But, in the absence of success, one cannot deny to you, to me, and to several other writers who have preceded me in the same career, and whose work has not been useless to me, the glory of having tried."[15]

---

15. Denis Diderot, *Essai sur les règnes de Claude et de Néron*, in Denis Diderot, *Œuvres complètes*, ed. Jean Deprun and H. Dieckmann, 33 vols. (Paris, 1975–), vol.25 (1986), p.39–40.

These quotations, taken from the preface, allow several reflections:

1. Diderot does not see the *philosophes* as a group born in the eighteenth century. He emphasizes their ancient roots. According to him, philosophers are a constellation of savants fighting for virtue, a community both ancient and modern.
2. According to Diderot, those who take the path of virtue are unfortunate. In antiquity as in modern times, the struggle for virtue and truth is hopeless. Misfortune is part of the social role of the philosopher.
3. If happiness does not characterize philosophers, then glory is their attribute. The struggle for virtue makes them immortals even if they do not attain their objective. Indeed, the philosophers of later times cherish their memory and take up the torch.
4. Diderot is therefore doing his duty as a philosopher when he defends the reputation and glory of his predecessor Seneca against unjustified criticism. Perhaps Diderot also hopes that, in the distant future, other philosophers will cherish his memory as he cherishes that of Seneca.
5. Diderot cites Seneca as a witness to describe the relationship of the philosopher with the world. He turns to Seneca's letter 108, in which the latter sings the praises of his old master Attalos: "I found him more than a king, because he judged kings at the tribunal of his censure."[16] The philosopher is conceived as the master of kings and of the powerful. The weapon of the philosopher is language, and the art of rhetoric. Since this art was no longer cultivated after the fall of the Roman Republic, however, the art of speaking saw a decline in the epoch of Seneca. Therefore, according to Diderot, "tyranny imprints a character of baseness on all sorts of production." In place of a "tone of frankness," the "tone of finesse," "flattery," and "duplicity" reigned under Claudius and Nero.[17]

This introduction might lead us to think that Diderot postulated an incompatibility between the philosophical life and the service of a monarch. However, careful reading reveals a different appreciation.

---

16. Diderot, *Essai*, book 1, §12, p.51.
17. Diderot, *Essai*, book 1, §10, p.50.

Firstly, Seneca was not only a philosopher and the tutor of Nero but also a high political dignitary. Diderot specifies that he was *quaestor*, *praetor*, consul, senator, and member of the imperial court. Diderot never criticizes Seneca's courtly career, nor his political ambition, quite the contrary.[18] For Diderot, Seneca's political engagement was the means to enable him to realize his philosophical principles.[19] The world of the court can certainly be the place for philosophical action so long as philosophy does not renounce its principles.[20]

Certainly, Diderot presents the court as a place of temptation for the philosopher.[21] For his detractors—both for contemporary critics and for posterity—Seneca was the classic example of a philosopher who let himself be seduced by the court, money, and power. However, Diderot does not make this judgment. On the contrary, his essay is a passionate apology of Seneca. When Diderot mentions sensitive points in the life of Seneca—for instance the fact that the Roman philosopher was aware of Nero's plan to assassinate his mother—he takes Seneca's side.[22] According to him, Seneca had no other choice. More than that, he supposedly wanted to maintain his position at court in order to prevent worse things for Rome and to moderate the criminal passions of the tyrant.[23] Certainly, Seneca ultimately failed to achieve these goals, but Diderot does not reproach him. For him, the one responsible is Nero.

Diderot's apology of Seneca is directed at the "censors" who denounce Seneca as a hypocritical courtier.[24] For Diderot, this is about saving the honor not only of Seneca but also of philosophers

---

18. Diderot, *Essai*, book 1, §46, p.90–98.
19. Diderot, *Essai*, book 1, §46, p.90–97.
20. Diderot, *Essai*, book 1, §48, p.99: "Il y a des circonstances où la conduite du courtisan et du philosophe peuvent être la même; alors le courtisan est sage et le philosophe est prudent; le motif seul distingue leurs procédés. Quel qu'il soit, le courtisan ne devient pas philosophe, non plus que le philosophe ne devient courtisan."
21. Diderot, *Essai*, book 1, §29, p.74. See also book 1, §12, p.53–54: "Que penserait-on d'un ministre qui aurait rassemblé et gardé toute sa vie autour de sa personne des hommes de cette trempe, un Attale, un Socion, un Fabinus Papirius, un Démétrius? Les philosophes les plus savants, les plus rigides et les plus considérés de son temps, voilà les amis constants de Sénèque." In this extract, Diderot presents Seneca as a minister who gathered *philosophes* around himself, and not as a *philosophe* himself.
22. Diderot, *Essai*, book 1, §79, p.149–50.
23. Diderot, *Essai*, book 1, §86, p.160, and above all §74, p.140.
24. "Censeurs": Diderot, *Essai*, book 1, §102, p.182–83.

of his own times. He makes a parallel between the critics of Seneca and the enemies of modern philosophers: "We must agree that the enemies of our philosophers are sometimes marvelously reminiscent of the detractors of Seneca."[25] One of the contemporary authors he sees in the line of Seneca is none other than the anonymous author of *La Morale universelle*, that is to say the baron d'Holbach, his acolyte.[26] He thus conceives of virtue as a timeless principle propagated by philosophers both ancient and modern. Seneca is a paragon of philosophical virtue, who chose martyrdom rather than abandon his fight for truth.

According to Diderot, anyone who slanders Seneca actually seeks to undermine the very principles of virtue and thus of philosophy. This is the objective of "perfidious courtiers, professional flatterers, the most abject sort of man; rulers like Tiberius and Caligula, who oppress men for whom they should be true fathers, accompanied by a flock of little liars who encourage them to hate and who praise their follies to the sky."[27] This quotation must be examined in detail. For Diderot, not all courtiers are the enemies of philosophers, but only "perfidious courtiers." Diderot opens this paragraph with a request addressed to François Alexandre Frédéric, duc de La Rochefoucauld-Liancourt, a courtier who, under Louis XVI, would be Grand Master of the Royal Wardrobe. He presents this aristocrat as a descendant of the moralist La Rochefoucauld and as a virtuous courtier:

> Young lord, you who take none of the vices of the court to which your rank and birth have called you; you who are made to believe in the virtues, since your soul is filled with them, you will not permit that the frontispiece where we have seen the seductive mask of virtue on the face of vice should reappear at the start of the ingenious and profound work of your ancestor; you will crush this insulting bust below which one reads *Seneca*, and you will not suffer that he should insult forever the most worthy of mortals.[28]

Diderot taxes the moralist La Rochefoucauld with the title of "detractor of human virtues" and also calls him a "Jansenist

---

25. Diderot, *Essai*, book 1, §119, p.210.
26. *La Morale universelle, ou les Devoirs de l'homme fondés sur sa nature* had been published by Holbach in 1776 in Amsterdam.
27. Diderot, *Essai*, book 1, §105, p.188–89.
28. Diderot, *Essai*, book 1, §105, p.188.

courtier" and "slanderer of human nature."[29] He thus situates La Rochefoucauld in the line of the ancient detractors of Seneca, and makes him the heir of Cassius Dio.[30] In the camp of Seneca's supporters, he names Tacitus, Pliny the Elder, Quintilian, Tertullian, Otto of Freising, and the humanist Calvinist Simon Goulart.[31] He also links together long quotations drawn from accounts of his *Essai sur la vie de Sénèque* published in 1779 in the *Mercure de France*, the *Journal de Paris*, the *Journal de littérature*, the *Année littéraire*, and the *Journal encyclopédique*. For him, this is about showing how his contemporaries, in commenting on his work, take a position for or against Seneca.[32] Those who, following the example of Marmontel, cherish the memory of Seneca, are counted by Diderot among the philosophers. The address to the young duc de La Rochefoucauld shows that the holders of the high offices of the court can also gain this title if they engage in the battle for virtue and defend the honor of ancient philosophers like Seneca.

It must be remembered that Diderot was not an antiquarian. For him, ancient events illustrates a fundamental and indeed current question: Can one be a courtier and still contribute to the common good? Diderot does not limit his examination in the *Essai* to ancient history; he takes a stand in the political conflicts of his own times. Thus, without naming him explicitly, Diderot calls Maupeou "the most contemptible and the most despised of men."[33] Turgot, in contrast, "has shown himself in our days more intrepid than the stoic demands."[34] He equally praises Necker and Malesherbes, whom he presents as exceptional individuals, comparing them with celebrated Athenian political figures who had fought for liberty and suffered persecution:

> Ancient history, which keeps us supplied with important figures without end, attracts our eyes so rarely to the multitude that we do not imagine it in past times to have been as uncouth, as perverse as in our days. Little by little, we believe that one did not cross a street in Athens without being elbowed by a Demosthenes or a Cimon. And the future may indeed believe, unless the philosophical spirit is

---

29. Denis Diderot, *Leçons de clavecin et principes d'harmonie*, in Diderot, *Œuvres complètes*, ed. J. Deprun and H. Dieckmann, vol.19 (1983), p.188 (6th dialogue).
30. Diderot, *Essai*, book 1, §99, p.177–78.
31. Diderot, *Essai*, book 1, §121, p.217–21.
32. Diderot, *Essai*, book 1, §101–107, p.179–92.
33. Diderot, *Essai*, book 2, §78, p.362.
34. Diderot, *Essai*, book 2, §73, p.354.

ultimately introduced in history, that one could not cross a street in Paris without elbowing a N[ecker], a M[alesherbes], or a T[urgot].

Necker, Malesherbes, and Turgot were three courtiers and ministers under Louis XV and/or Louis XVI. In 1782, however, all three had lost their positions or had voluntarily stepped down. For Diderot, the success or failure of such figures indicated whether "the philosophical spirit" was ultimately in the process of imposing itself or not. His diagnosis was pessimistic. All that he could do for these three ministers was to maintain their glorious memory. Diderot thus prophecies for them a posthumous glory that will contrast with the oblivion into which their detractors will fall.[35]

Not only the example of Seneca but also that of the three ministers shows that, for Diderot, participation in the world of the court could be compatible with the mission of a philosopher. Describing the case of the three ministers, Diderot makes himself the advocate of the active life, a topos of the republican epoch: "without doubt, a life in retirement is softer, but a busy life is more useful and more honorable."[36] More than this, Diderot reiterates in the *Essai* his praise for Catherine II, whom he describes as a "wise and great sovereign of the North"—very far from the cliché according to which he vigorously kept his distance from the empress after his stay in St. Petersburg. Diderot's fawning praise in the *Essai* for high-ranking contemporary figures thus invites us to examine to what extent Diderot was himself a courtier.

Diderot the "Russian" courtier

To call Diderot a courtier might be considered a provocation. Diderot's biographers portray him as the opposite of a courtier. According to Johanna Borek, "Diderot does not want to be a courtier, and he is not a man of the court."[37] In his own country, Diderot supposedly kept himself completely detached from the world of the court: Voltaire, D'Alembert, and Diderot were supposedly "in disgrace with the establishment of their own country," Arthur Wilson writes.[38] His

---

35. Andreas Pečar and Damien Tricoire, *Falsche Freunde: War die Aufklärung wirklich die Geburtsstunde der Moderne?* (Frankfurt am Main, 2015), p.37–45.
36. Diderot, *Essai*, book 2, §73, p.354.
37. Johanna Borek, *Denis Diderot* (Reinbek, 2000), p.122.
38. Arthur M. Wilson, *Diderot* (Oxford, 1957), p.443.

strained relations with Choiseul at the end of the 1760s are interpreted as a clash between the party of the *philosophes* and "power."[39] In St. Petersburg, Diderot allegedly looked out of place at the imperial court.[40] According to his biographers, he encountered a strong hostility from the courtiers there and was apparently the victim of intrigues.[41] Uninterested in material questions, he supposedly rejected the favors of Catherine II.[42] As the story goes, he returned from Russia disillusioned, discouraged, even embittered, and the profound disappointment that he felt regarding Catherine II is supposed to have pushed him to formulate democratic ideas in the *Observations sur le nakaz*.[43] The empress is said to have been so enraged on receiving Diderot's manuscript, after his death, that she had it destroyed as quickly as possible.[44]

This interpretation of Diderot keeping his distance from the establishment is partly explicable by the fact that documentation on the editor of the *Encyclopédie* is often meagre. The main problem for all studies of Diderot, including as client and courtier, is that his correspondence has not survived except in fragments. Only 780 letters have come down to us, as against 15,300 for Voltaire. And yet his biographers also acknowledge a series of facts which contradict their interpretation. They mention the interventions of Malesherbes on behalf of the *Encyclopédie*,[45] the purchase of Diderot's library by Catherine II and the monetary gifts that followed in subsequent years,[46] Diderot's purchases of paintings for the court of St. Petersburg,[47] and indeed the sycophantic praise that Diderot addressed again and again to the empress.[48] That Diderot played a diplomatic role for the French court during his stay in St. Petersburg is mentioned in

39. Borek, *Diderot*, p.96.
40. Wilson, *Diderot*, p.633.
41. Raymond Trousson, *Diderot* (Paris, 2007), p.270–71; Wilson, *Diderot*, p.643; P. N. Furbank, *Diderot: a critical biography* (London, 1992), p.376.
42. Wilson, *Diderot*, p.514, 644; Stenger, *Diderot*, p.632; Trousson, *Diderot*, p.270–71.
43. Wilson, *Diderot*, p.643, 651; Stenger, *Diderot*, p.306, 647; Borek, *Diderot*, p.121, 125; Israel, *Democratic Enlightenment*, p.623.
44. Wilson, *Diderot*, p.650; Borek, *Diderot*, p.127; Israel, *Democratic Enlightenment*, p.622.
45. Borek, *Diderot*, p.79; Stenger, *Diderot*, p.137, 231.
46. Wilson, *Diderot*, p.466, 513, 697, 710; Borek, *Diderot*, p.10, 108; Stenger, *Diderot*, p.307, 702–703; Trousson, *Diderot*, p.180–81, 191–93; Furbank, *Diderot*, p.300.
47. Wilson, *Diderot*, p.546, 601; Stenger, *Diderot*, p.308; Trousson, *Diderot*, p.211; Furbank, *Diderot*, p.314.
48. Stenger, *Diderot*, p.308; Furbank, *Diderot*, p.301–302, 380.

passing by certain biographers.[49] Among the biographies, Arthur Wilson's (published in 1957) is one of the most voluminous, and informs us about the services rendered by Diderot for personalities like Sartine[50] and his efforts with statesmen to obtain financial advantages for his family. However, these aspects of Diderot's career do not fundamentally influence Wilson's narrative.[51]

It must be emphasized that biographers do not totally ignore these actions by Diderot, but they do not seem to understand the underlying courtly logic that informed them, and this in spite of the fact that Diderot himself expressed it several times in his correspondence. They largely ignore that Diderot was acting in the context of patronage relationships. This is seen in the treatment of Diderot's relations with Golitsyn, who is presented as a "friend."[52] Prince Dimitri III Alexeievitch Golitsyn was the scion of one of the greatest Russian families. Ambassador in Paris, then in The Hague, he may be counted among the leading personalities of Europe in the 1760s and 1770s. At first glance, there are good reasons for qualifying this important figure as a "friend" of Diderot: Indeed, the philosopher himself uses this word and its related terms.[53] This would, however, be to ignore the significance of this term for the early modern period. The term *amitié* was at that time employed to express loyalty in a patronage relationship.[54] Indeed, careful reading shows that Diderot uses the term "friend" to designate superiors who are giving him particular protection. He writes thus in an address to Catherine II: "You have here a court and your courtiers, and these courtiers have noble, elevated, honest, generous souls [...]. They are all [...] my friends."[55]

A similar misunderstanding is found in the way the biographers interpret Diderot's ostentatious refusal to accept presents of great value in St. Petersburg, namely as a sign of his disinterest in material things. Here again, the biographers rely on what Diderot himself says in some letters. The philosopher, always quick to underline his detachment

49. Wilson, *Diderot*, p.636; Stenger, *Diderot*, p.625; Furbank, *Diderot*, p.384–85.

50. Wilson, *Diderot*, p.401–402, 553, 555, 581. See also Trousson, *Diderot*, p.230–31.

51. Wilson, *Diderot*, p.655, 677–78, 682.

52. Wilson, *Diderot*, p.512; Borek, *Diderot*, p.113; Stenger, *Diderot*, p.406, 584; Trousson, *Diderot*, p.251.

53. Letter to Falconet, May 15, 1767, in Diderot, *Correspondance*, p.730–40 (730).

54. Christian Kühner, *Politische Freundschaft bei Hofe: Repräsentation und Praxis einer sozialen Beziehung im französischen Adel des 17. Jahrhunderts* (Göttingen, 2013).

55. Letter to Betskoy, November 29, 1766, in Diderot, *Correspondance*, p.709–13 (709).

with regard to money[56] and his incorruptibility,[57] affirms in a letter to his mistress Sophie Volland that he did not ask anything more than a "trifle" from the empress, which supposedly shows that he is not "venal": "By Jove, you must believe what I tell you of that extraordinary woman [Catherine II], for my praise has not been bought, and does not issue from a venal mouth."[58] In a letter to his wife, however, Diderot explains the entirely courtly logic underlying his modest demands. We learn first that Diderot has received the equivalent of 12,600 *livres* from the empress, of which, after all the expenses, a good 5000–6000 *livres* will remain. Above all, Diderot explains that he has negotiated to obtain ultimately the equivalent of 200,000 *livres* for the project of a new encyclopedia. He therefore enjoins his wife to prepare to move soon to a more prestigious home. Finally, he explains not without some pride that he has been wise in asking little of the empress at the moment of his departure. He had consulted experienced courtiers such as the baron Noltken, the Swedish ambassador, on the wisest means of gaining the empress's favor, or, in Diderot's own words, of "binding her hands." According to the logic of a courtier, all work for a sovereign must be presented as disinterested, and all the favor of a sovereign must be freely given. Diderot thus explained to his wife that, in demanding little, he counted on obtaining much. To assure her that this would be the case, he related his conversation with the Swedish ambassador, who confirmed the idea that, faced by such "gallant" behavior, the empress "will do her duty":

> Baron Noltken, one of those whom I had consulted, came a few days later to learn how the petition had been received. "Very well," I said to him. He replied: "I was sure of its effect." And he added: "You have done your duty as a very gallant man, a completely disinterested man, and I am sure that the empress will do her part.—But Baron …—I understand; you have spoken to the empress in all seriousness. You have told her what you really think. But it is impossible that she should take you at your word. She was struck by your reasons because they are good ones. She will not want to take the character of truth from the good things that you have said to her,

56. Letter to Falconet, May 15, 1767, in Diderot, *Correspondance*, p.730–40 (734); to Princess Dachkova, January 25, 1774, in Diderot, *Correspondance*, p.1208–10 (1208).
57. Letter to the Volland ladies, March 30, 1774, in Diderot, *Correspondance*, p.1214–15 (1214); to the Volland ladies, late April or early May 1774, in Diderot, *Correspondance*, p.1229–32 (1230).
58. Letter to the Volland ladies, April 9, 1774, in Diderot, *Correspondance*, p.1222.

but when you have spoken, she will act. That is what I would do in her place, and what she will do. She may delay more or less the marks of her favor, but they will come, do not doubt it.[59]

It was in accordance with this logic that Diderot asked of the sovereign an object of only symbolic value. The "trifle" that Catherine II accorded to Diderot was, however, far from being without value: It was a ring with her image engraved on the stone. Diderot often spoke of asking for no more than a teaspoon from Catherine, but, in a letter to his wife, he confesses to having asked for an "engraved stone."[60]

Despite what his biographers say, Diderot was well aware that he was a courtier. Certainly, he proclaimed the contrary loud and clear.[61] In certain of his letters, however, Diderot does not hide his position. He describes "paying court" to Catherine II,[62] to Princess Ekaterina Romanovna Dachkova,[63] and to General Ivan Ivanovitch Betskoy.[64] In a missive to Falconet, he describes himself as a panegyrist: "It is for [Catherine] to do the greatest things; it is for us to celebrate them."[65] Moreover, he describes his position as official agent of

---

59. To Mme Diderot, April 9, 1774, in Diderot, *Correspondance*, p.1222–27 (1226). The same logic underlies the "gift" that Diderot made of his manuscripts to Catherine II, as he explains to Sophie Volland: December 10, 1765, in Diderot, *Correspondance*, p.568–72 (570–71).
60. To Mme Diderot, April 9, 1774, in Diderot, *Correspondance*, p.1222–27 (1225).
61. To Falconet, June or July 1767, in Diderot, *Correspondance*, p.741–48 (746–47): "Mais dans une cour, moi dans une cour? Moi que vous connaissez pour la droiture, la simplicité, la candeur incarnées! Moi qui n'ai qu'un mot! Moi dont l'âme est toujours sur la main! Moi qui ne sais ni mentir, ni dissimuler! [...] Avez-vous bien pensé à cela?"
62. To Falconet, November 15, 1769, in Diderot, *Correspondance*, p.998–99: "faire ma cour à une souveraine à qui je dois le repos dont je jouis"; to the Volland ladies, March 30, 1774, in Diderot, *Correspondance*, p.1214–15 (1215).
63. To Falconet and Mlle Collot, December 29, 1770, in Diderot, *Correspondance*, p.1052–53 (1053).
64. To Golitsyn, in Denis Diderot, *Œuvres complètes de Diderot*, ed. J. Assézat, 20 vols. (Paris, 1875–1877), vol.20 (1877), p.87–88.
65. To Falconet, May 15, 1767, in Diderot, *Correspondance*, p.730–40 (731–32). Diderot refused, however, to write a work of pure propaganda celebrating the great actions of Catherine II. He preferred to dedicate to her a work in his eyes essential for the progress of humanity: a new encyclopedia, which Diderot repeatedly describes in his correspondence as "erecting a pyramid" to the immortal glory of Catherine II. To Betskoy, November 29, 1766, in Diderot, *Correspondance*, p.709–13; to Falconet, April or May 1767, in Diderot, *Correspondance*, p.727–30 (729–30); to Falconet, May 15, 1767, in Diderot, *Correspondance*, p.730–40 (731–32).

the empress in Paris, playing a role complementary to that of the ambassador:

> My friend, there must be an ambassador who is an *honnête homme* and is known as such; and moreover, an indifferent person who is thought incapable, under any circumstances, of risking the happiness of another man, and who joins his testimony to that of the ambassador regarding the good things that the latter cannot fail to say of his court. The goodness, the gentleness, the affability, the veracity of Prince Golitsyn weakens them, and I finish them off.[66]

Diderot used his library as a place of representation for Catherine II, which "attracts," by its prestigious objects, "the center and the four corners of the city."[67] He waited with great impatience in 1766–1767 to receive for the library a bust of the empress executed by the student of Falconet, Marie-Anne Collot.[68] When he finally received it in May 1768, however, he was greatly disappointed: The marble had been ruined by water during the trip, which did not stop Diderot from putting the bust on a pedestal, transformed into a sort of altar, before which, so he said, his wife, his daughter, and he would sometimes say their prayers in the morning.[69] Diderot therefore asked for a second bust of Catherine, and the ambassador Golitsyn promised to send him one in bronze this time.[70] Moreover, Diderot received gold medals celebrating the glory of Catherine II.[71] Since Diderot could not read Russian, he asked Grimm for a book describing the medals struck in Russia.[72]

---

66. To Falconet, May 15, 1767, in Diderot, *Correspondance*, p.730–40 (735).
67. To Falconet, August 15, 1767, in Diderot, *Correspondance*, p.748–52 (749).
68. To Falconet, November 12, 1766, in Diderot, *Correspondance*, p.704–707; to Betskoy, November 29, 1766, in Diderot, *Correspondance*, p.709–13 (711); to Falconet, August 15, 1767, in Diderot, *Correspondance*, p.748–52 (749); to Sophie Volland, September 19 or 20, 1767, in Diderot, *Correspondance*, p.762–66 (766); to Sophie Volland, October 11, 1767, in Diderot, *Correspondance*, p.787–89 (788).
69. To Falconet, May 1768, in Diderot, *Correspondance*, p.817–28 (821).
70. To Falconet, May 1768, in Diderot, *Correspondance*, p.817–28 (822); to Falconet and Mlle Collot, July 18, 1768, in Diderot, *Correspondance*, p.838–39; to Falconet, July 11, 1769, in Diderot, *Correspondance*, p.948–51 (950); to Falconet, September 7, 1769, in Diderot, *Correspondance*, p.971–72.
71. To Falconet, September 6, 1768, in Diderot, *Correspondance*, p.848–77 (859); to Grimm, September 1776, in Diderot, *Correspondance*, p.1274–77 (1276).
72. To Grimm, October 13 or 14, 1776, in Diderot, *Correspondance*, p.1279–80 (1280).

Diderot was also good at speaking the language of the courtier. A detailed analysis of the exaltations of the glory of Catherine that are scattered throughout his correspondence lies beyond the scope of this chapter, but his correspondence with Falconet is particularly garnished with praise for the empress and professions of loyalty for her, perhaps because Diderot thought that his letters were communicated to the empress.[73] Diderot does not cease to affirm his commitment and indeed his devotion to Catherine. In his letters to the empress, to Betskoy and to Falconet, he uses typical phrases expressing the loyalty of a client to their patron. Not only is he "the most humble, most obedient and most devoted servant" of her imperial majesty,[74] but, according to him, "fathers, mothers, brothers, sisters, children, babies, friends, acquaintances throw themselves [at the] feet" of Catherine.[75] He writes fictive dialogues in which he says the best things about the empress.[76] He describes himself on his knees before the empress, strangled with emotion: "Great princess, I prostrate myself at your feet, I stretch out both my arms toward you; I would like to speak, but my soul tightens, my head becomes confused, my ideas are weighed down, I wait like a child, and the true expressions of the sentiment that fills me expire on the edge of my lips."[77] To give such assertions more weight, Diderot denies that he was trying to flatter her.[78] However, he clearly followed baroque encomiastic norms. Diderot the materialist calls for the blessings of God for the empress and her ministers,[79] and he claims to rejoice in Catherine's military victories "as a man, as a philosopher, and as a Russian, for I have become one through the ingratitude of my own country and through your bounties."[80] He compares the indulgence of the

---

73. It is most clear that he thinks this in the letter, in which he says that he cannot immediately make the trip to St. Petersburg because of his love for his mistress: to Sophie Volland, mid-November 1767, in Diderot, *Correspondance*, p.808–809.

74. To Catherine II, September 13, 1774, in Diderot, *Correspondance*, p.1255–59 (1259).

75. To Catherine II, December 17, 1774, in Diderot, *Correspondance*, p.1259–61 (1259).

76. To Catherine II, December 17, 1774, in Diderot, *Correspondance*, p.1259–61 (1259–60).

77. To Betskoy, November 29, 1766, in Diderot, *Correspondance*, p.709–13 (709).

78. To Catherine II, September 13, 1774, in Diderot, *Correspondance*, p.1255–59 (1259).

79. To Falconet, September 6, 1768, in Diderot, *Correspondance*, p.848–77 (855).

80. To Catherine II, September 13, 1774, in Diderot, *Correspondance*, p.1255–59 (1255).

empress with that of God,[81] and writes verses calling Catherine the "faithful image [...] of the divinity."[82] According to Diderot, Catherine is infinitely superior to Frederick II of Prussia because, while she has his genius, he does not have her kindness.[83] Thanks to her sovereign, Russia will become a country of pilgrimage for all those researching the Enlightenment, just as, in antiquity, people visited Egypt and Greece.[84] Diderot also supports Russian anti-Polish propaganda, calling the Poles "fanatics."[85]

It is not the place here to present in detail the numerous services rendered by Diderot to his principal patron, the empress. Diderot was a loyal and active client. His biographers tend to underline his scant eagerness to accept Catherine's offer to finish the *Encyclopédie* under her aegis in 1762,[86] but that was before Diderot became the empress's client. From 1767 onward, he repeatedly asked Catherine for the favor of being able to produce a new edition of the *Encyclopédie* under her protection. This time, it was the turn of the court of St. Petersburg to decline the offer.[87] Diderot nonetheless served Catherine enthusiastically: During these years, he worked to procure artisans, brass engravers, sculptors, illustrators, actors, philosophers, professors, and even artillery specialists for the court of Russia, and it is certain that this occupied him intensively, the more so as it often obliged him to enter into arduous negotiations.[88] The acquisition of

81. To Catherine II, February 22, 1774, in Diderot, *Correspondance*, p.1210–12 (1211).
82. To Betskoy, November 29, 1766, in Diderot, *Correspondance*, p.709–13 (710–11).
83. To Catherine II, February 22, 1774, in Diderot, *Correspondance*, p.1210–12 (1211).
84. To Catherine II, September 13, 1774, in Diderot, *Correspondance*, p.1255–59 (1257).
85. To Falconet, September 6, 1768, in Diderot, *Correspondance*, p.848–77 (858).
86. To Voltaire, September 29, 1762, in Diderot, *Correspondance*, p.449–50.
87. To Falconet, March 1767, in Diderot, *Correspondance*, p.724–26 (726); to Damilaville, June or July 1767, in Diderot, *Correspondance*, p.737–40 (743–46).
88. To Vialet, July 1766?, in Diderot, *Correspondance*, p.656–59 (658); to Betskoy, August 1766, in Diderot, *Correspondance*, p.685–91 (685); to Mlle Jodin, January 1767, in Diderot, *Correspondance*, p.720–22; to Falconet, April or May 1767, in Diderot, *Correspondance*, p.727–30 (728); to Falconet, May 15, 1767, in Diderot, *Correspondance*, p.730–37 (735); to Falconet, June or July 1767, in Diderot, *Correspondance*, p.741–48 (746–47); to Falconet, August 15, 1767, in Diderot, *Correspondance*, p.748–52 (748, 751); to Falconet, May 1768, in Diderot, *Correspondance*, p.817–28 (823); to Falconet, March 20, 1771, in Diderot, *Correspondance*, p.1062–64; to Betskoy, June 15, 1774, in Diderot, *Correspondance*,

paintings, sculptures, engravings, and books on behalf of the empress must also have cost him a significant amount of his time. Diderot made a tour of the collections, tried to convince collectors to sell, conducted negotiations during the accessions, and advised the artists who produced plans for the empress.[89] Moreover, one of Diderot's tasks was to ensure that nothing should damage the image of the empress in France. In at least one case, he negotiated to suppress an offensive manuscript.[90]

After his return from St. Petersburg, Diderot, entirely satisfied with his trip, declared to his wife: "[T]he sovereign has charged me with a multitude of commissions, of which there are many which will use my talent and my time."[91] Among these tasks—which included working on a catechism, theater plays, a mathematical treatise, and a plan for the founding of a university[92]—the most important was without doubt the publication of a major work of propaganda, the *Plans et statuts des différents établissements ordonnés par sa majesté impériale Catherine II*. This book presented the educational, charitable, and health-care institutions created by Catherine as the realization of a program of enlightened

p.1244–47 (1244); to Grimm, mid-December 1776, in Diderot, *Correspondance*, p.1284–89; to Catherine II, August 25, 1781, in Diderot, *Correspondance*, p.1319.

89. To Sophie Volland, July 20, 1765, in Diderot, *Correspondance*, p.500–505; to Falconet, August 15, 1767, p.748–52 (749–50); to Falconet, May 1768, in Diderot, *Correspondance*, p.817–28 (818); to Falconet, March 6, 1769, in Diderot, *Correspondance*, p.936–37 (936); to Falconet, May 26, 1769, in Diderot, *Correspondance*, p.944–47 (945); to Falconet, November 15, 1769, in Diderot, *Correspondance*, p.998–99 (999); to Falconet, March 15, 1770, in Diderot, *Correspondance*, p.1006–1007; to Falconet, March 20, 1771, in Diderot, *Correspondance*, p.1062–64; to Falconet, April 17, 1772, in Diderot, *Correspondance*, p.1106–1107; to François Tronchin, July 17, 1772, in Diderot, *Correspondance*, p.1114–19 (1116–17); to Grimm, September 1776, in Diderot, *Correspondance*, p.1274–77 (1275); to Grimm, October 13 or 14, 1776, in Diderot, *Correspondance*, p.1279–80 (1279).

90. To Falconet, May 1768, in Diderot, *Correspondance*, p.817–28 (820, 828); to Falconet, September 6, 1768, in Diderot, *Correspondance*, p.848–77 (862).

91. To Mme Diderot, April 9, 1774, in Diderot, *Correspondance*, p.1222–27 (1224).

92. To Betskoy, June 9, 1774, in Diderot, *Correspondance*, p.1240–41; to Betskoy, June 15, 1774, in Diderot, *Correspondance*, p.1244–47; to Catherine II, December 6, 1775, in Diderot, *Correspondance*, p.1265–68.

reforms.[93] Contrary to what is often suggested,[94] Diderot's work was not restricted to finding an editor. Diderot reworked the manuscript, negotiated with the editor, and oversaw the publication of the work at The Hague both in a sumptuously illustrated quarto edition and in a cheaper format.[95] The text, written in Russian by Betskoy, then translated into French by Nicolas-Gabriel Clerc, was largely inspired by several memoranda written by Diderot in St. Petersburg for the empress. Where the original memoranda proposed reforms, the *Plans et statuts* presented them as accomplished facts. Diderot took part in this sleight of hand for the glory of the sovereign.[96] It is also quite possible that he had participated in the preparation of the work in St. Petersburg. This would at least explain why he received a diploma from the orphanage of the imperial capital in gratitude for his service, although no other work done by him for that institution is known.[97]

Was Diderot a clumsy courtier, incapable of dissimulation? Were Diderot's contacts with the Russian courtiers cold and distant? Did they reflect the division between two worlds, that of the radical Enlightenment and that of princely courts? His correspondence suggests the complete opposite. As we have seen, Diderot knew not only how to ask cleverly for favors but also how to pay compliments worthy of an *honnête homme*.[98] Above all, the correspondence reveals an astonishing intimacy between him and some of the highest-ranking figures of the empire who formed the Betskoy/Golitsyn faction, composed of intimates of the empress. Diderot was part of a circle that he called in his letters "the round table," or "the Pantagruelian devotees,"[99] which indicates

---

93. Ivan Ivanovitch Betskoy, *Plans et statuts des différents établissements ordonnés par sa majesté impériale Catherine II* (Amsterdam, Marc Michel Rey, 1775).

94. Stenger, *Diderot*, p.636.

95. To Betskoy, June 9, 1774, in Diderot, *Correspondance*, p.1240–41; to Betskoy, June 15, 1774, in Diderot, *Correspondance*, p.1244–47.

96. Georges Dulac, "Diderot éditeur des *Plans et statuts* des établissements de Catherine II," *Dix-huitième siècle* 16 (1984), p.323–44. That Diderot played an active role in the propaganda celebrating the educational institutions founded by Catherine can also be seen from a letter in which he asks Betskoy to send him all the "things" "which can demonstrate to my compatriots the excellence of the education that you give to your young ladies." To Betskoy, June 9, 1774, in Diderot, *Correspondance*, p.1240–41 (1241).

97. Wilson cannot explain the presentation to Diderot of a diploma from the orphanage: Wilson, *Diderot*, p.639.

98. See the messages that he asked Clerc to pass on to the great figures of the court. To Clerc, April 8, 1774, in Diderot, *Correspondance*, p.1216–18.

99. To Clerc, June 15, 1774, in Diderot, *Correspondance*, p.1242–44 (1243); to Betskoy,

that eating and drinking played no small part in their activities. Thus, a "Pantagruelian" note has survived, addressed to Golitsyn.[100] In this circle, informality reigned, as shown by the fact that Diderot enjoins Clerc to kiss Anastasia Ivanovna Sokolova, a favorite of the empress, "as I kissed her when we were making merry, on the neck, [...] next to the ear, as this gave her pleasure."[101] Diderot had, moreover, always emphasized that he had been magnificently well received by the great figures of the court. One finds in his correspondence no trace of the supposed intrigues of the courtiers against him. On the contrary, he states that he spent five months at court "without having laid myself open to the malignant."[102]

If Diderot suffered a disillusionment in St. Petersburg, he hid it well. In fact, no source provides clear proof that this was the case. The idea that Diderot lost all illusions regarding enlightened despotism is based only on the writings that the philosopher produced for posterity, such as the *Observations sur le nakaz*. Israel claims that Diderot criticized Catherine in private, but does not cite any document to support these claims.[103] The correspondence speaks another language altogether. Both after his arrival in Russia[104] and on his return from St. Petersburg, Diderot more than ever sang the praises of the empress, whether in his letters to Mme Necker[105] or in his correspondence with Sophie Volland, which was not intended to be public.[106] He affirmed to all who would listen that, if the empress lived long enough, she would change the face of Russia for the better.[107] In the following years, Diderot continued to serve the empress and to benefit from her largesse.

March 21, 1774, in Diderot, *Œuvres complètes de Diderot*, vol.20, p.88–91.

100. To Golitsyn, May 21, 1774, in Diderot, *Œuvres complètes de Diderot*, vol.20, p.1236–37.

101. To Clerc, April 8, 1774, in Diderot, *Correspondance*, p.1216–18 (1217).

102. To the Volland ladies, end of April or beginning of May 1774, in Diderot, *Correspondance*, p.1229–32 (1230).

103. Israel, *Democratic Enlightenment*, p.619, 625.

104. To Mme Diderot, October 9, 1773, in Diderot, *Correspondance*, p.1189–92; to Mme Caroillon de Vandeul, October 23, 1773, in Diderot, *Correspondance*, p.1194–96; to Mme Diderot, end of October 1773, in Diderot, *Correspondance*, p.1196–97; to Princess Dashkova, December 24, 1773, in Diderot, *Correspondance*, p.1203–1205.

105. To Mme Necker, September 6, 1774, in Diderot, *Correspondance*, p.1251–55.

106. To the Volland ladies, April 9, 1774, p.1221–22; to the Volland ladies, end of April or beginning of May 1774, p.1229–32.

107. To Mme Diderot, end of October 1773, in Diderot, *Correspondance*, p.1197; to the Volland ladies, March 30, 1774, p.1214–15; to Mme Necker, September 6, 1774, p.1251–55.

Furthermore, there is no evidence that Catherine was enraged on reading the *Observations sur le nakaz* after Diderot's death. Certainly, she speaks of them with contempt,[108] but to argue on this basis that she was furious is a step further than the sources permit. Moreover, the fact that no version of the manuscript was found in Russia does not necessarily prove that the empress ordered its destruction, still less that she threw it into the fire herself, as certain biographers have fondly imagined.[109] Ultimately, Catherine was probably aware of the content of the *Observations* from the version written at The Hague, without this leading her to end her generosity to Diderot. Indeed, Golitsyn, at whose palace Diderot lodged at The Hague, had Diderot's chest opened in order to inspect the manuscript. Why would Golitsyn have done this if not to inform the empress of the content of a manuscript potentially detrimental to her public image?[110] In any case, it seems that the Russian court was not unduly worried by this work, as no sanctions followed.

The empress's patronage greatly increased both Diderot's symbolic and his financial capital. He sought and obtained nomination to the St. Petersburg Academy of Fine Arts.[111] It is no exaggeration to say that the story of Diderot and his family is that of a spectacular social rise made possible by the protection of the great figures of the Russian and, as we shall see, the French court. It is impossible to estimate even approximately the total financial favors of the empress. Indeed, it is highly probable that what is preserved in the correspondence gives no more than a partial picture. However, adding up what we know from the letters that have been preserved, Diderot received, alongside the bust of Catherine, the gold medals, and the ring, 15,000 *livres* for his library,[112] a pension of at least 1000 *livres* for the year 1765–1766 in his role as librarian, gifts of 50,000 *livres*,[113] then 3000 roubles (converted into 12,600 *livres*),[114] and 2000 *livres*,[115] probably to pay off a debt of unknown size that

108. Wilson, *Diderot*, p.650.
109. Borek, *Diderot*, p.127; Israel, *Democratic Enlightenment*, p.622.
110. Wilson, *Diderot*, p.655.
111. To the Imperial Academy of the Arts in St. Petersburg, February 5, 1767, in Diderot, *Correspondance*, p.724.
112. Wilson, *Diderot*, p.466.
113. Wilson, *Diderot*, p.513.
114. To Mme Diderot, April 9, 1774, in Diderot, *Correspondance*, p.1221–27 (1221–22).
115. To Catherine II, June 29, 1779, in Diderot, *Correspondance*, p.1303–1304.

Diderot had contracted from Naryshkin.[116] Catherine paid the costs of the journey in full, in spite of the fact that she had given the philosopher the 3000 roubles mentioned above for this purpose.[117] She rented a vast, modern, and sumptuous apartment on the rue de Richelieu for Diderot and his wife.[118] She apparently paid the dowry of his daughter, and thus permitted her to contract a very advantageous marriage.[119] She perhaps assumed the costs of his burial, greatly increased because his daughter and son-in-law did not skimp on pomp, and also because it was necessary to convince the curate of the prestigious parish of Saint-Roch to bury the atheist in consecrated ground.[120] Certainly, Diderot's hopes of receiving 200,000 *livres* to produce a new encyclopedia never materialized. In spite of this, thanks to his patroness, Diderot became affluent enough to finish his life in a certain luxury.

Diderot and the French court

But there is more: Thanks to the patronage brought by members of the French court, Diderot made his daughter and son-in-law immensely rich. The philosopher's links with French statesmen are less well known, and Diderot is often presented as an opponent of the Versailles establishment. Yet nothing could be less true. Certainly, toward the end of the 1760s, Diderot missed no opportunity to dent the image of Choiseul, principal minister of the French king. Choiseul, scion of a great aristocratic family, made a military and diplomatic career in the late 1750s and in the 1760s through the patronage of the marquise de Pompadour. Choiseul was minister of Foreign Affairs from 1758 to 1761 and again from 1766 to 1770, minister of War from 1761 to 1770, and minister of the Navy and Colonies from 1761 to 1766. He was assisted by his cousin Praslin, who was minister of Foreign Affairs from 1761 to 1766, and minister

116. To Catherine II, February 22, 1774, in Diderot, *Correspondance*, p.1210–12 (1212).
117. Diderot pretends to reproach Catherine for shaking his confidence in doing him this favor, which is a delicate way of thanking her. To Catherine II, September 13, 1774, in Diderot, *Correspondance*, p.1255–59 (1256). The sum given by Catherine before his departure was 3000 roubles, which Diderot converted into 12,600 *livres*. To Mme Diderot, April 9, 1774, in Diderot, *Correspondance*, p.1221–27 (1221–22).
118. Wilson, *Diderot*, p.710.
119. Borek, *Diderot*, p.108.
120. Stenger, *Diderot*, p.703.

of the Navy and Colonies from 1766 to 1770. Choiseul was the most
influential minister until his fall in 1770, when Maupeou, Terray,
and Aiguillon took the reins of power.[121] Diderot was thus attacking
a figure of the first rank on the European scene. However, what
may appear to reflect a principled opposition to "power" was
in fact most probably linked to his position as a paid agent
of Catherine II. Indeed, tensions between the courts of France
and Russia mounted during this period, as Choiseul used his
secret services to support the Polish opposition against Russian
interference, the Confederation of Bar. Choiseul and his partisans
sought to damage the image of the empress.[122] The accusations
of hostility toward the Enlightenment that Diderot made against
Choiseul[123] should probably be seen in this context. These attacks
have sometimes been taken at face value by historians. In fact,
Choiseul was the patron of numerous philosophers with whom
Diderot had close relations. If Diderot painted a very negative
image of Choiseul, it is certainly not because the latter displayed
a marked obscurantism, at least no more than the empress whom
the philosopher so praised. Moreover, the Choiseul circle repaid
Diderot in kind, and supported among others Palissot, who wrote
plays ridiculing several philosophers' pretentions to leadership and
their claims to be incorruptible and disinterested.[124]

Diderot's hostile relations with Choiseul until the latter's fall in
1770 did not prevent the editor of the *Encyclopédie* from maintaining
close relations with Choiseul's clients Malesherbes and the physiocrats
Dubucq and Sartine. The first traces of these contacts go back to
the end of the 1750s and are preserved in a 1759 letter addressed to
Turgot, a friend of Malesherbes. Turgot and Malesherbes were two
nobles de robe whose careers are so well known that there is no need to
retrace them here. It is sufficient to recall that Turgot owed his career
to Mme de Pompadour and to Choiseul,[125] and that he was briefly
minister of the Navy in 1774. In his 1759 letter, Diderot asked for

121. On Choiseul, see Guy Chaussinand-Nogaret, *Choiseul: naissance de la gauche*
(Paris, 1998).
122. To Falconet, May 26, 1769, in Diderot, *Correspondance*, p.944–47 (945).
123. To Falconet, May 15, 1767, in Diderot, *Correspondance*, p.730–37 (730); to
Falconet, May 1768, in Diderot, *Correspondance*, p.817–28 (827–28); to Falconet,
September 6, 1768, in Diderot, *Correspondance*, p.848–77 (854).
124. Chaussinand-Nogaret, *Choiseul*, p.124–28.
125. On the links between Choiseul and Turgot, see Chaussinand-Nogaret, *Choiseul*,
p.181–85. In the 1770s, by contrast, the party of Choiseul, now stripped

Turgot's support with Malesherbes both in order to avoid a condemnation of the *Encyclopédie* and for "a relative." Diderot also asked
Turgot to write two articles for the work.[126]

At the same time, Diderot maintained relations with the lieutenant-
general of the police of the kingdom, Bertin d'Antilly.[127] In the
mid-1760s, Diderot "found protection with M. Dubucq," as he put it.[128]
Jean-Baptise Dubucq was then first clerk of the Ministry of the Navy
and responsible for the Colonial Bureau. He was therefore Choiseul's
closest collaborator in the ministry, and his relative by marriage.[129]
Diderot sought Dubucq's protection primarily to obtain a position for
the nephew of his mistress, Sophie Volland, a certain Fayolle. In the
following years, Diderot courted Dubucq intensively in order to settle
Fayolle's difficulties.[130]

Above all it was Antoine de Sartine, another protégé of Choiseul,
who played the role of Diderot's patron. From 1759 to 1774, Sartine
was lieutenant-general of the police of the kingdom and, starting in
1763, director of the Royal Library. He was therefore the policeman
and censor of the literary world, and had a network of spies in his
pay. In the historiography, Sartine appears as a "friend." Diderot
himself uses the term in order to underline that he is more than a
usual protector: "M. de Sartine is not my protector, he is my friend
of 35 years. He has written to me twice during my absence from
France."[131] One episode reveals, moreover, that Diderot did not
conceive of his relations with this courtier as a relationship between
equals. In 1762, Diderot discovered that a man he employed to copy
his manuscripts was a spy (*mouche*) of the police. According to his
own version of events, he went to complain to Sartine, but the latter
merely laughed in his face.[132] If Sartine and Diderot had been friends

---

of his positions and exiled, fought with the party of Turgot: Jean-François
  Labourdette, *Vergennes: ministre principal de Louis XVI* (Paris, 1990), p.134–36.
126. To Turgot, January 21, 1759, in Diderot, *Correspondance*, p.87.
127. To Grimm, June 5, 1759, in Diderot, *Correspondance*, p.102–106 (104).
128. To Sophie Volland, October 20, 1765, in Diderot, *Correspondance*, p.541–43.
129. On Dubucq, see Chaussinand-Nogaret, *Choiseul*, p.208–14.
130. Letters to Sophie Volland, October 20, 1765, December 18, 1765, December
  30, 1765, January 27, 1766, September 13, 1767, mid-November 1767, October
  8, 1768, November 4, 1768, November 12, 1768, November 22, 1768, June
  30, 1769, July 15, 1769, August 31, 1769, September 11, 1769, in Diderot,
  Correspondance, p.541–43, 572–73, 578–80, 587–90, 757–61, 808–809, 894–98,
  907–11, 912–14, 918–23, 947–48, 952, 967–70, 972–75.
131. To Betskoy, June 15, 1774, in Diderot, *Correspondance*, p.1244–47 (1247).
132. To Sophie Volland, September 19, 1762, in Diderot, *Correspondance*, p.439–41.

in the modern sense of the term, such behaviour would certainly
have brought their relations to an end. According to the modern
conception of friendship, it is unacceptable for a friend to spy on
another. Yet their relations do not seem to have been undermined in
the medium term, which reveals Diderot's dependency on Sartine.

From 1765, Diderot's correspondence shows him working in the
service of Sartine, without us learning exactly what he was getting
in return.[133] Diderot used his relations with Sartine to prevent the
censoring of his works and those of his friends, as can be seen from
the example of the *Dialogues* of Galiani, which he edited in 1769.[134]
He asked Sartine to intervene against the financial demands of the
booksellers publishing the *Encyclopédie*.[135] Were these requests for
services between friends? In fact, Diderot did give something in
exchange, which has not really been noted by any biographer:[136] He
worked as censor for the lieutenant-general of the police. In 1768,
Sartine "secretly" sent him a manuscript by Mercier de La Rivière on
which the clerks of the Royal Library had not been able to come to a
unanimous decision: *L'Ordre naturel et essentiel des sociétés politiques*. The
description that Diderot gives to Falconet suggests that he exercised
the function of unofficial censor, as it was his opinion that enabled the
publication of the book:

> A further word on M. de La Rivière [...]. M. de La Rivière is
> publishing a work on which the faint-heartedness of the magistrate,
> increased by the diverse judgments of his censors, did not know what
> view to take. The affair was referred secretly to me on the fourth floor
> [*à mon quatrième étage*]. I read, I approve, and the book comes out.[137]

Thus, through his work for the censorship institution, Diderot had
at least facilitated the publication of this important physiocratic
work. Did he consistently use his position to moderate the censor? It
seems that he did not, and that Diderot acted more as a man of his
party. Indeed, in March 1770, the tone regarding *La Réfutation des*

133. To Sophie Volland, May 20, 1765, in Diderot, *Correspondance*, p.492.
134. To Sophie Volland, September 11, 1769, in Diderot, *Correspondance*, p.972–75
     (973–74); to Sartine, October 13, 1769, in Diderot, *Correspondance*, p.982.
135. To Sartine, October 13, 1769, in Diderot, *Correspondance*, p.982.
136. To our knowledge, only Wilson reports Diderot's activities on behalf of Sartine,
     but he presents them euphemistically as advice to a friend, which Sartine
     sometimes had recourse to all the more willingly because he knew that Diderot
     was in favor of the freedom of the press anyway: Wilson, *Diderot*, p.555.
137. To Falconet, September 6, 1768, in Diderot, *Correspondance*, p.848–77 (851).

Dialogues de l'abbé Galiani by the abbé Morellet is a completely different one. This was a work that attacked the *Dialogues* that Diderot had himself published the previous year. Certainly, Diderot specified that, "as censor, I see nothing here that might prevent publication."[138] At the same time, he suggests that it would be better if the work were not published.[139] Morellet should merely put his critical reflections in a letter and send it to Galiani. According to Diderot, this would be better for Morellet himself, since his work could only harm his career after the criticisms he had received in making himself the advocate of the government against the shareholders of the Compagnie des Indes. Diderot here adds a thinly veiled threat in suggesting between the lines that he would not want to be obliged to take an aggressive tone toward Morellet:

> The abbé Galiani does not need, in order to be great, the abbé Morellet to measure himself against him. The only thing that the critic could do with his work would be to make it into a good letter, which he would send to the one in Paris whom he calls his friend. He would have less to lose than to gain by this sacrifice, since this work will pass without making the least sensation, in spite of the name and celebrity of the author, of which only the light veneer of a black man will remain. After having hurt one foot in the affair of the Compagnie des Indes, he should not hurt the other foot in the wheat business, as that would risk no longer being able to walk. [...] I would not want to take such a harsh tone except with my enemy [...] [B]ut, on reflection, I am persuaded that the abbé Morellet will not publish his patched rags.[140]

This hostile attitude certainly contributed to delaying the publication of Morellet's work, which came out only in 1774.[141]

We know another case in which Diderot used his position as censor to prevent the publication of a work to which he was hostile. In June 1770, Palissot submitted to the Royal Library a play entitled *Le Satirique*, which openly ridiculed Diderot. The editor of the *Encyclopédie* reacted violently to the manuscript, which Sartine communicated to him. Certainly, Diderot affirms "that if [he] had been the censor

---

138. To Sartine, March 10, 1770, in Diderot, *Correspondance*, p.1004–1005 (1005).
139. Here again, the biographers pass over this in silence, quoting only Diderot's statement that nothing justifies the prohibition of the book. See for example Furbank, *Diderot*, p.320, following Wilson, *Diderot*, p.555.
140. To Sartine, March 10, 1770, in Diderot, *Correspondance*, p.1004–1005 (1005).
141. Wilson, *Diderot*, p.555.

of the *Satirique*, [he] would [have] smiled at all these injuries" and "would not [have] removed any."[142] Indeed, according to Diderot, these attacks would rebound on the author, who would find the doors of Parisian high society slamming in his face:

> As for me, I do not have a very sensitive skin, and will be more ashamed of a failing on my own part than of a hundred vices which I do not have, and which I may be unjustly reproached for. I reiterate to you that, if I had been the censor of the *Satirique*, I would have smiled at these injuries, would not have had any removed, and would have regarded them as pinpricks more painful in the long term for the author than for me. [...]
>
> What is the moral of his comedy? It is that one must close the door to every man of spirit without principles and without probity. We will apply this rule to him, and what awaits him is contempt.[143]

At the same time, he is not sparing in insults toward the author, and calls above all for royal censorship. Indeed, Diderot maintained that Sartine could not authorize a text insulting a leading light like himself, who was revered throughout all of Europe, without damaging his own reputation. Again, Diderot alludes to the influence that he and his friends have on public opinion:

> It is not for me, sir, to advise you, but if you could see to it that it is not said that someone has twice, with your permission, insulted in public one of your fellow citizens who is honored in all parts of Europe, whose works are devoured far and wide, whom foreigners revere, send for, and reward, who will be cited and who will contribute to the glory of the French name when you are no more and he also, whom travelers make a point of visiting when they are here, and whom they are honored to have known when they have returned to their own country. I believe, sir, that you will act wisely. Tricksters must not be allowed to besmirch the greatest magistracy, nor should posterity, which is always just, reserve for you a portion of the blame that belongs only to them. Why should they be permitted to associate you with their infamies?[144]

These arguments seem to have convinced Sartine, who protected his client and forbade the play, which could not be shown until 1782.[145]

142. To Sartine, June 1770, in Diderot, *Correspondance*, p.1017–19 (1017).
143. To Sartine, June 1770, in Diderot, *Correspondance*, p.1017–19 (1017–18).
144. To Sartine, June 1770, in Diderot, *Correspondance*, p.1017–19 (1018–19).
145. Wilson, *Diderot*, p.581.

The sources do not tell us whether Diderot, beyond his influence over the censorship, obtained other advantages, notably of a financial nature, from his services rendered to Sartine. What is certain is that around 1770 he intensively paid court to a whole series of influential figures in order to obtain a dowry that would allow his daughter to marry advantageously. Around 1768, he began to frequent the extremely rich banker Necker, who had taken control of the Compagnie des Indes,[146] and to defend him against Morellet, the physiocratic writer in the service of the minister of the Navy, Choiseul-Praslin.[147] In 1772, we find Diderot working behind the scenes for Necker. Thus, in early September 1772, he invited Grimm to join him at the Necker residence in Saint-Ouen to discuss an "affair so serious" and apparently so delicate that Diderot could not be more explicit in a letter that might fall into the wrong hands.[148] The following missive is filled with code words which unfortunately cannot all be deciphered now.[149] What is clear from these letters, however, is that Diderot and Grimm were plotting in the service of Necker, who had political ambitions. In this period, moreover, Diderot also paid court to Mme Necker.[150]

His potential son-in-law, Caroillon de Vandeul, was greedy for the dowry, so Diderot solicited money not only from Necker but also from Jean-Baptiste Devaines, who had important responsibilities in the administration of finances, from the intendant-general of Finance Trudaine, and from Aiguillon, the minister of Foreign Affairs, who had come to power after the fall of Choiseul in 1770.[151] Diderot seems to have obtained some substantial advantage from the latter for his son-in-law, for Caroillon de Vandeul showed himself very satisfied with an interview that Diderot had arranged.[152] Aiguillon, moreover, maintained a foreign policy more favorable to Russia than that of Choiseul. Aiguillon's patronage explains a fact that is well known but nevertheless curiously neglected and left unexplained by Diderot's

---

146. Ohji, "Raynal, Necker et la Compagnie des Indes," p.112–15.
147. To Mme Necker, December 1768, in Diderot, *Correspondance*, p.926–28; to Mme de Maux, around August 10, 1769, in Diderot, *Correspondance*, p.961–62; to Sophie Volland, August 23, 1769, in Diderot, *Correspondance*, p.965–67 (967).
148. To Grimm, September 2, 1772, in Diderot, *Correspondance*, p.1122–23 (1123).
149. To Grimm, October 7, 1772, in Diderot, *Correspondance*, p.1133–35.
150. To Mme Necker, October 15, 1772, in Diderot, *Correspondance*, p.1139; to Mme Necker, end of October 1772, in Diderot, *Correspondance*, p.1141.
151. To his sister Denise, August 27, 1771, in Diderot, *Correspondance*, p.1080.
152. To Grimm, April 29, 1772, in Diderot, *Correspondance*, p.1109; to Grimm, October 18, 1772, in Diderot, *Correspondance*, p.1140.

biographers: In St. Petersburg, Diderot not only showed himself devoted to Catherine II, but also served as an unofficial diplomat in the service of the French minister of Foreign Affairs.[153]

In 1774 there was a dramatic new turn of events. The new king, Louis XVI, surrounded himself with a completely new team that included old clients of Choiseul (but not Choiseul himself). For Diderot, this political upheaval was a good omen: Several of his long-time protectors returned to lead important ministries. Turgot became finance minister and Devaines his first clerk. From the support of the latter, Diderot hoped to derive great benefit,[154] a hope that was not realized. The year 1774 also saw the promotion of Sartine, who was named minister of the Navy and Colonies. Diderot wrote to Betskoy and Clerc that the production of the Russian encyclopedia, which could not fail to involve a lawsuit on the part of the French booksellers, would now be easier.[155] Above all, Diderot seized the moment of the promotion of his patron to ask him to give his son-in-law the extremely lucrative privilege of supplying lumber from the forests of Lorraine, Burgundy, and Franche-Comté to the shipyards of Toulon. In his letter, having recounted the old bonds of patronage that connected him to Sartine, Diderot emphasized that, despite his "long-standing relations with the minister of Finance" (Turgot) and his "intimacy with his first clerk" (Devaines), "[his] little fortune remains the same" (an understatement of his financial position).[156] Rather than deny any interest in questions of money, which, in the context of a request of such importance, would not have been entirely credible, Diderot claims that he is trying to obtain a very great financial favor, but only for "his children." For himself, he despises wealth. He thus presents himself as a father devoted to the interests of his daughter and his son-in-law, and not as a greedy courtier:

> During the whole period of your magistracy, you have protected me from the evil that people sought to do to me. This makes me think

153. Wilson thinks that Diderot "found himself caught up in the diplomatic maneuverings of great powers, perhaps very much against his will." Wilson, *Diderot*, p.635–36.
154. To M. and Mme Caroillon de Vandeul, September 3, 1774, in Diderot, *Correspondance*, p.1248–50.
155. To Clerc, June 15, 1774, in Diderot, *Correspondance*, p.1242–44 (1243); to Betskoy, June 15, 1774, in Diderot, *Correspondance*, p.1244–47 (1247).
156. To Sartine, July 12, 1775, in Diderot, *Correspondance*, p.1264–65 (1265).

that, if the opportunity to do me good were to present itself during your ministry, it would not be disagreeable to you. The issue is explained in the memoir that I take the liberty of enclosing with this letter. It is regarding the navy's forests in Lorraine, Franche-Comté, and Burgundy serving the port of Toulon, for which the contract with an entrepreneur expires on the first of January 1776.

My children, people of the forests [*gens des forêts*], and my son-in-law, Caroillon de Vandeul, who has signed this submission, beg you to give them preference over their competitors, on the same conditions. [...] While I have no ambition for myself, I [have it] for my children. Through an inexplicable quirk of the brain, although I consider riches to be more contrary to well-being than modest wealth, and although I manage very well for myself with that, I cannot be content with it for them, and I would like them to be rich. Yes, sir, very rich![157]

It is unfortunately not known whether Sartine acceded to this request. In any case, Diderot continued to approach Sartine in the following years. In 1779, he asked for the position of *commissaire* or *sous-commissaire* at Cayenne (a very important post in the civil administration) for the nephew of Sophie Volland.[158]

During the first years of the reign of Louis XVI, however, it was above all to Necker that Diderot paid court. This probably explains why Diderot did not obtain much from the physiocrats, and indeed adopted a tone hostile to some of them.[159] Necker was then the great rival of Turgot. In his letters to Necker from this period, Diderot employed the appropriate compliments for courtly society, but adapted for the style of philosophical discourse. He did not hesitate to claim that the memoir on wheat that Necker had directed against the physiocrats was the most interesting thing he had ever read.[160] Diderot was eager to "court" Mme Necker, that is to gain her favors.[161]

In 1776, Necker succeeded in taking the place of Turgot. He exercised the functions of finance minister until 1781. Betting on Necker now paid off handsomely for Diderot. He was more than ever Necker's man. To his friend Grimm, Diderot explained that this implied a break with Turgot: "[O]ne does not quarrel with Monsieur

157. To Sartine, July 12, 1775, in Diderot, *Correspondance*, p.1264–65 (1264–65).
158. To Sartine, October 3, 1779, in Diderot, *Correspondance*, p.1304–1305.
159. To Dupont de Nemours, December 9, 1775, in Diderot, *Correspondance*, p.1269.
160. To Necker, June 10, 1775, in Diderot, *Correspondance*, p.1261–64.
161. To Mme Necker, September 6, 1774, in Diderot, *Correspondance*, p.1251–55.

Necker to remain on good terms with Monsieur Turgot."[162] In his letters to the Neckers, Diderot celebrates the minister as a philosophic "genius," a reformer of mores who gave "sublime moral lessons." According to Diderot, Necker embodies nothing less than "justice, truth, courage, dignity, reason, genius."[163] The philosopher equally celebrates Mme Necker as the incarnation of "charity" and "pity," and as an image of Providence.[164] He adapts to Mme Necker's religiosity. In his correspondence with her, he professes Christian sentiments, begging his patroness to pardon the impertinences that he permits himself in his letters.[165] Diderot's correspondence sheds light on some of his social activities, such as when he begged Mme Necker to excuse him for not having attended a dinner given by the landgrave of Hesse-Darmstadt. Indeed, it was through the mediation of his patrons that Diderot was introduced into this aristocratic high society.[166] Diderot drew great profit for his relatives from his relations with the Neckers. Indeed, he made himself the protector of those whom he recommended to the charity of his patroness.[167] In particular, he asked the finance minister in 1777 for the extremely lucrative position of "partisan" for his son-in-law,[168] and it seems that his request was crowned with success.[169] In spite of this, Diderot was not a particularly loyal client when the political winds shifted for Necker. In the spring of 1781, when the finance minister was the object of violent attacks which led to his fall a short time later, Diderot preferred not to take up the quill to defend him, as he explained to Mme Necker.[170]

162. To Grimm, November 17, 1776, in Diderot, *Correspondance*, p.1281–82.
163. To Mme Necker, March 1st, 1781, in Diderot, *Correspondance*, p.1312–13.
164. To Mme Necker, December 1777, in Diderot, *Correspondance*, p.1296–97; to Mme Necker, March 1st, 1781, in Diderot, *Correspondance*, p.1312–13.
165. To Mme Necker, December 1768, in Diderot, *Correspondance*, p.926–28.
166. To Mme Necker, end of October 1772, in Diderot, *Correspondance*, p.1141.
167. To Mme Necker, December 1777, in Diderot, *Correspondance*, p.1296–97, along with an undated note: Diderot, *Œuvres complètes de Diderot*, vol.20, p.84.
168. To Necker, April 1st or 2, 1777, in Diderot, *Correspondance*, p.1289; to Necker, April 3, 1777, in Diderot, *Correspondance*, p.1289.
169. Alexandre Stroev and Georges Dulac, "Diderot en 1775 vu par Grimm: deux lettres inédites à la princesse Golitsyna et au comte Roumiantsev," *Dix-huitième siècle* 25 (1993), p.275–93 (282).
170. To Mme Necker, March 1st, 1781, in Diderot, *Correspondance*, p.1312–13.

The impact of courtly relationships on Diderot's writings

These patronage relations—or at least the search for protection—had a direct and manifold influence on Diderot's philosophical work: an impact that we can only touch upon here. This influence was not limited only to writing in praise of his patrons. It seems that often the positions Diderot took up were not unrelated to theirs. It was not rare that philosophical discussions and political confrontations were intertwined, requiring a certain party loyalty. One sees this particularly after the fall of Choiseul, as the rivalry between Necker and Turgot burst into the open. In the discussion on commercial agricultural policy, Diderot clearly took the position of his patron Necker and Ferdinando Galiani, a regular at the salon of Mme Necker, against that of the physiocrats.[171]

In particular, one can say that Diderot's work from the mid-1760s was written more and more in a courtly context. In addition to the *Encyclopédie*, finished in 1772, Diderot in the last phase of his literary career worked primarily on two big literary undertakings: He contributed to Grimm's *Correspondance littéraire* and to Raynal's *Histoire des deux Indes*. It is important to remember that the *Correspondance littéraire* was a journal destined for princely courts.[172] Thus, many of Diderot's most daring texts were produced in a courtly context, which has been curiously neglected by many researchers.[173] It was in the context of courtly culture—a playful culture that hated academic pedantry—that Diderot could engage in his literary jokes. In what was called the "bourgeois" theater, in contrast, Diderot demonstrated a moralizing, even clumsy, didacticism.[174] Diderot's art criticism—his famous *Salons*—was also

171. See the letters Diderot sent to Sartine (June 1775) and Necker (June 12, 1775) on the subject: Diderot, *Correspondance*, p.1261–65; Herbert Dieckmann, *Inventaire du fond Vandeul et inédits de Denis Diderot* (Geneva, 1951), p.62–63. On the ideas debated, see Gilbert Faccarello, "Galiani, Necker and Turgot: a debate on economic reform and policy in eighteenth-century France," in *Studies in the history of French political economy: from Bodin to Walras*, ed. Gilbert Faccarello (London, 1998), p.120–95.
172. On the *Correspondance littéraire*, see Abrosimov, *Aufklärung jenseits der Öffentlichkeit*.
173. Kirill Abrosimov reminds us of this: Abrosimov, *Aufklärung jenseits der Öffentlichkeit*, p.11.
174. Damien Tricoire, "The fabrication of the *philosophe*: Catholicism, court culture, and the origins of Enlightenment moralism in France," *Eighteenth-century studies* 51:4 (2018), p.453–77.

destined for a courtly public and, in a more general way, his activities in this area were linked to his position as artistic agent in the service of the empress.

As for the *Histoire des deux Indes*, few researchers have recognized that its genesis and content must be interpreted in the context of the patronage relations between the authors and court personalities. The *Histoire des deux Indes* is generally considered the "bible" of the radical *philosophes* who were violently opposed to colonialism and the *ancien régime*. However, this historiographical work was originally a book commissioned at the behest of Choiseul, although he scarcely profited from it after his fall in 1770. Raynal was paid by the Ministry of the Navy for this work. After the fall of Choiseul, in conformity with the patron–client structures of which the authors were a part, the *Histoire des deux Indes* served to glorify Necker and his work of colonial reform.[175] It is therefore no coincidence that (far from a supposed opposition to colonialism) we find in the *Histoire des deux Indes* not only a political position that corresponded with that of the patrons of Raynal and Diderot, but also a panegyric to the Neckers from the quill of Diderot, in a passage concerning the reform of hospitals:

> This plan [to look after the sick] is not impracticable, nor will it be expensive when better laws and a more vigilant, enlightened, and above all humane administration presides over these establishments. The attempt is being made today successfully under the eyes and through the care of Mme Necker. While her husband works on a grander scale and reduces the number of the unfortunate, she occupies herself with the details that may relieve those who remain. [...] Foreigners, who have become part of the [French] nation through the most meritorious of all naturalizations, that is by the good that you have done, generous couple, I dare to name you, although living, although surrounded by the esteem of a great place, and I do not fear to be accused of adulation. I believe that I have sufficiently proved that I know neither how to fear nor how to flatter the vice of the powerful, and I have thus acquired the right to render great homage to virtue.[176]

175. Damien Tricoire, "Raynal's and Diderot's patriotic history of the two Indies, or the problem of anticolonialism in the eighteenth century," *The Eighteenth century: theory and interpretation* 59:4 (2018), p.429–48.

176. Guillaume-Thomas Raynal, *Histoire philosophique et politique des établissemens et du commerce des Européens dans les deux Indes*, 10 vols. (Geneva, Pellet, 1780), vol.3, p.265.

Diderot thus showed himself to be a party man and a flatterer. Yet, at the same time, he denies being a toady and affirms his position as an impartial judge, as a philosopher assailing vice and not afraid of the powerful. The fact that he had fought important figures with his quill should be the guarantee of his philosophical independence. The game of rivalries between statesmen in which Diderot participated is here skillfully set aside. Contemporaries, however, were not fooled. The *Histoire des deux Indes* was seen as the product of a particular party. It was probably the fall of Necker in May 1781 that led to the condemnation of the work by the *parlement* of Paris.[177]

Conclusion

The passages in the *Essai* favorable to Catherine II, and the flattering allusions that one finds there in favor of Turgot, Malesherbes, and Necker, reflect a fundamental aspect of Diderot's career: It was thanks to the patronage offered by the empress and these French statesmen— to whom one must add Sartine and Aiguillon—that Diderot and his family enjoyed a meteoric ascent in society. A bourgeois son from a provincial city without great means, Diderot succeeded in lavishing on his wife and his daughter phenomenal symbolic, social, and financial capital.

Patronage relations had a profound impact on the works published in his lifetime, and this should be the subject of a full study. Certainly, we must not take this too far and consider all the works of Diderot to have been inspired by court intrigue. It is clear, however, that the opposition between Grimm and Diderot that certain researchers like to claim on the basis of a letter that was probably intended to remain in a drawer must on close examination be treated with caution. The history of Diderot the courtier invites us to reexamine the so-called radical Enlightenment. The story of *philosophes* fighting the Versailles elites is mainly supported by texts written for posterity and was established during the Revolution. This story is anachronistic.

177. Necker was dismissed on May 19, 1781. One week later, the *Histoire des deux Indes* was condemned: *Arrest de la cour de parlement qui condamne un imprimé, en dix vol. in-8°, ayant pour titre: Histoire philosophique et politique des etablissemens et du commerce des Européens dans les deux Indes, par Guillaume-Thomas Raynal;* [...] *à être lacéré et brûlé par l'exécuteur de la haute-justice. Extrait des registres du parlement du 25 mai 1781* (Paris, P. G. Simon, 1781). On this question, see Ohji, "Raynal, Necker et la Compagnie des Indes," p.109.

The ideal proposed by Diderot was the philosopher-minister or the philosopher-king, or rather the minister and sovereign guided by the philosopher. In this way, the role he wanted the philosopher to play was similar to that claimed for centuries by the court clergy. It is certainly no coincidence that Diderot chose to identify himself with Seneca, who was exactly the figure that the Jesuits of the royal court had praised as a model in the seventeenth century.[178]

The philosophers of the Enlightenment, at least those who achieved success, were part of the elites of their age, and the examples presented above show that the context of the court is essential for interpreting many of their works. The myth of independent authors writing for the market, and of the radical Enlightenment, often obscures their real situation. It is high time to write the history of the Enlightenment at court.

178. See notably the celebrated treatise of the Jesuit Nicolas Caussin, who was for a short time confessor of Louis XIII: *La Cour sainte, tome second: contenant les vies et les eloges des personnes illustres de la cour, tant du vieil que du nouveau testament, divisées en cinq ordres: les monarques et princes, les reines et dames, les cavaliers, les hommes d'Estat, les hommes de Dieu* (Paris, J. Dubray, 1653), p.572–97.

Celebrity, status, and gender at the late Hanoverian court: the careers of Charles Burney (1726–1814) and Frances Burney (1752–1840)

CLARISSA CAMPBELL ORR

The careers of the musicologist Charles Burney (1726–1814) and his novelist daughter Frances (1752–1840) can serve as a lens through which to explore how the ideals of the Enlightenment, and especially of Jean-Jacques Rousseau, had an impact at the British court of George III (r.1760–1820) and his consort Queen Charlotte of Mecklenburg-Strelitz (d.1818). The lives of both authors draw attention to different aspects of Enlightenment culture and their relationships to princely courts. My working assumption in the case of Charles Burney is that his encyclopedic history of music makes him an essential part of the English Enlightenment, given that it was conceived in the spirit of the early-seventeenth-century polymath Francis Bacon. However, Roy Porter, among the first to argue in favor of an English Enlightenment, failed to discuss Charles Burney as an outstanding exemplar of the encyclopedic. He needs to be written into its history on these grounds alone.

Frances Burney is not so obviously a contributor to enlightened *inquiry*, but her achievement as a woman of letters was only made possible thanks to the Enlightenment interest in moral improvement or, more precisely, the questioning of established social structures in the light of universal moral standards. This had brought about a wider inquiry about the relationship between nature and nurture, which had raised the question of whether women might possess talents usually thought to be exclusively masculine; in other words, it had helped create the role of the *female author*. This brought its inherent challenges because it raised questions about suitable *subjects* for female authorship, and this mattered in a highly commercialized economy where the royal court and literary leaders alike were suspicious of mere commercial success. The British court of George III and Queen Charlotte wanted to endorse writers who stood for something more moral and solid than fame or mere celebrity, and this made it hospitable, paradoxically perhaps, to the ideas of Jean-Jacques Rousseau.

The attractiveness of Rousseau's ideas to courtiers was not an obvious matter, because Rousseau was a fervent critic of the whole system of court life. He destabilized the idea of a court, and showed that dynasties and courtiers might modify their ways by trying to live more "authentically" in the unpromising soil of the court. Radical as they were, his ideas on morality and education struck a chord with the royal family and with some of their dynastic relatives in Hesse, Denmark, and Saxe-Coburg. There were also courtier families, such as the Harcourts, who were friends of the king and queen in later life, but who when young had been disciples of Rousseau and had eschewed court service. At the same time Rousseau's sentimental anti-materialism also offered a critique of Deism, which was useful to courts like that of George III and Charlotte, who welcomed critiques of philosophic materialism, even though Rousseau was not an obvious ally.[1] It is only when one considers Rousseau's ability to offer a new take on why a spiritual dimension to life was plausible that his relationship both to the royal court and to the nature of British literary life comes together.

The Enlightenment narrative in England

Among the many recent definitions of the Enlightenment, the editors of this volume have found that the arguments made by Dan Edelstein in *The Enlightenment: a genealogy*[2] offer a fruitful way forward for thinking about the Enlightenment and the changes it brought about. Instead of looking at political and social contexts such as the Dutch Republic or Britain for the origins of the Enlightenment or Enlightenments, Edelstein takes a narratological approach. He examines how French *philosophes* characterized themselves, using terms such as *l'esprit philosophique*, many of which derived from the academies founded by the

---

1. This element of Rousseau's critique of elements within the mid-century French *philosophes* is discussed at greater length in Clarissa Campbell Orr, "Queen Charlotte as patron: some intellectual and social contexts," *The Court historian* 6:3 (2001), p.183–212.
2. Dan Edelstein, *The Enlightenment: a genealogy* (Chicago, IL, 2010).

monarchy, and were rooted in the Quarrel of the Ancients and the Moderns. Edelstein's central thesis is that the French *philosophes* did not invent new ideas, but that they crafted a new narrative about the social and political role of knowledge: They expected knowledge (termed *philosophie*), and thus the *philosophe*, to play a critical role in bringing about social and political progress.

This narratological approach is also fruitful in the English case. In Britain too, there was a discussion about whether modern society was technically, artistically, and morally superior to the ancient world. The French *Querelle des Anciens et des Modernes* is mirrored in the English Battle of the Books. As a result of such discussions, "progress" and "improvement" were key words in English eighteenth-century culture. Like in France, scientists, artists, novelists were commonly expected to foster social, political, and moral progress. However, Edelstein's thesis, according to which the narrative about the role of knowledge in bringing about progress was a French invention that resulted from discussions within the academies, should be put into question. English Enlightenment ideas about progress and knowledge were not simply an import from France, but had local roots. Edelstein's findings are not exactly paralleled in the English case, for two main reasons.

First, the relationship between academies and the monarchy was different in England and in France, and this meant that the English Quarrel of the Ancients and the Moderns was not a discussion about the achievements of the monarchy as it had been originally in late-seventeenth-century France. English men and a sprinkling of English women who thought in a "philosophic" way were resistant to monarchs trying to manage culture through academies; they did not want Charles II to act like his cousin Louis XIV. Instead, Charles II took the opportunity to confer kingly approval on the "Society of London for Improving Natural Knowledge," which was initiated by a society of gentleman enthusiasts, and from 1663 called itself, with his permission, "Royal." However, when the English criticized the way the monarchy could corrupt the parliamentary safeguards against absolutism, which had been developed after the Restoration, they often did so using the vocabulary and genres utilized by the Ancients and Moderns.

Secondly, the English Enlightenment was not just about scientific or literary discourses, the role of writers and moralists, and their sense of themselves; it was also about political and cultural events and how they should be interpreted, and these events were interpreted differently from in France. The Enlightenment in

England was inseparable from seventeenth- and eighteenth-century British history: first, the Restoration of the monarchy and the Church of England in 1660, after the Republican or Commonwealth experiment (1643–1660), and then the modification of this monarchy in the Glorious Revolution of 1688, when Charles II's brother and heir James II was deposed. A parliamentary monarchy evolved, and religious toleration of Trinitarian Christians, with the exception of Roman Catholics, was introduced.[3] The parliamentary model of monarchy which resulted, together with the entrepreneurial energy, religious freedom, and relative social mobility of England, was commonly admired by French *philosophes* such as Voltaire, in his *Letters concerning the English nation* (1733). At the same time, many English men and women had perceptions of these events that were not identical with Voltaire's: It was widely believed that God had brought about recent political upheavals. Religion pervaded the English Enlightenment culture much more than the French one. Thus there was Newtonianism,[4] a blend of science and theology, as well as Newtonian science.[5] In the natural sciences, Isaac Newton had described the laws of physics and astronomy, which revealed that the laws of motion were not precise. Just as every four years a leap year with an extra day was required in the astronomical calendar, so it was believed that historical events were providentially managed. The change of winds which had allowed the ships of William and Mary to land in England in November 1688 and James II's decision to leave the country rather than stay and fight were considered examples of this providential intervention. English liberties were divine, and most Enlightenment writers celebrated them. By contrast, in France, religious interpretations of political history came under critique, and political authors sought for a new way to legitimize the monarchy—or called for important political reforms.

3. Catholicism was widely understood as a persecuting faith, which justified confiscation of church lands during the original establishment of Anglican worship and freedom of thought in the reign of Elizabeth I, so religious toleration had its limits, as Britons feared a restitution of these lands if Catholicism were reinstated.

4. Caroline Robbins, *The Eighteenth-century Commonwealth man* (Cambridge, MA, 1959).

5. Margaret C. Jacob, *The Newtonians and the English revolution: 1689–1720* (New York, 1990); J. R. Jacob, *Robert Boyle and the English revolution: a study in social and intellectual change* (New York, 1977). Edelstein discusses these differences in *The Enlightenment*, p.104–15.

In England, the main worry about the Restoration of the monarchy was its potential to corrupt the system through money and the power of patronage. Polemics about this corruption by the monarch were built on seventeenth-century classical republicanism as revived by James Harrington in *Oceana* (1656)[6] and others on into the next century—a tradition virtually inexistent in France. Parallel with these efforts to contrast an idealized gentry republic with a monarchy, Jonathan Swift and Alexander Pope were major figures in creating a still unrivaled age of satire. Literary historians and historians of political thought have given rich interpretations of their works of literature. Swift's invention of the court of Lilliput in *Gulliver's travels* (1726), where tiny figures compete by climbing a greasy pole or run races to win colored ribbons, remains in the political language.[7] Pope's *Dunciad* (1728–1743, three differing editions) was a mock-heroic epic which feared that the commercialization of culture in a censorship-free market would create an age of "dunces" ruled over by a thinly disguised version of the intellectually vivacious Queen Caroline as its queen.[8] Swift, Pope, Joseph Addison, and Richard Steele between them created the new literary genre of social and moral commentaries in short essay format, first published in magazines such as *The Tatler* and *The Spectator*. Their gentler ridicule informed as well as guided polite society. In particular their popularization of science helped turn Francis Bacon, Isaac Newton, and John Locke into cultural icons, contrasting English empiricism with French Cartesian rationalism.

The English royal court and the Enlightenment

What was the role of the royal court in the spread of new ideas about moral, social, and political improvement, and about the role of the arts and letters in it? Until now, scholarship has offered only partial insights into this matter. Ragnhild Hatton's biography of George I, which discussed his cultural patronage, was published as early as 1978,[9] but her discussion of the first Hanoverian as an enlightened monarch was not followed up with similar efforts

---

6. James Harrington, *The Commonwealth of Oceana and a system of politics*, ed. John G. A. Pocock (Cambridge, 1992).
7. F. P. Lock, *The Politics of Gulliver's travels* (Oxford, 1980).
8. See also Pat Rogers, *Pope and the destiny of the Stuarts* (Oxford, 2005).
9. Ragnhild Hatton, *George I: elector and king* (London, 1978).

regarding successive monarchs or consorts.[10] This was in part because until 2011, when Andrew C. Thompson's monograph appeared,[11] there were no satisfactory biographies either of George II or of his consort Caroline of Ansbach. For decades historians had been more focused on the parliamentary elements of Britain's mixed monarchy and the possibility these could be corrupted by money, using the combined efforts of the monarch and his ministers. Right through the nineteenth century a powerful consensus operated that Britain owed her freedom from political revolution to the way Parliament limited the power of the monarchy and permitted the emergence of the party system. So—to simplify a broad consensus—understanding parliamentary politics was the main historical task. There was less interest from the academic profession in the monarch and the court, which was even described as a declining institution as recently as 1993.[12] For the postwar period, other historical questions were paramount in academic history, such as whether the English Civil War resembled a class struggle, and how far historians could practice history from below, looking away from the elites. The consumer revival of the late sixties and seventies then sparked interest in the birth and character of the first consumer society. One facet of consumerism was opened up by historians exploring Britain's parliamentary history: John Brewer for example showed how consumer objects such as textiles and teapots became souvenirs of party allegiance, and how political crowds had a carnivalesque quality, creating tableaus rooted in popular theater.[13]

So it was a long and winding road to kindle interest in both the court and the Enlightenment in England, which required various gaps to be filled, a process that has gradually emerged within the last two decades.[14] Taking recent developments first, Andrew C. Thompson's 2011 biography of George II dealt expertly with his courtly and German roles, while Matthew Dennison's subtle exploration of George II's wife Caroline's enthusiasm for Enlightenment culture

---

10. Hatton, *George I*, p.290.
11. Andrew Thompson, *George II: king and elector* (New Haven, CT, 2011).
12. R. O. Bucholz, *The Augustan court: Queen Anne and the decline of court culture* (Stanford, CA, 1993).
13. John Brewer, *Party ideology and popular politics at the accession of George III* (Cambridge, 1976).
14. The foregoing survey is of necessity brief and somewhat oversimplified. For a recent magisterial discussion of postwar historical practice see John H. Elliott, *History in the making* (New Haven, CT, 2012).

in his 2017 biography also acts implicitly as a thoughtful critique of the 2017 Yale Centre for British Art exhibition, entitled *Enlightened princesses*.[15] This was a well-intentioned attempt at characterizing three Hanoverian consorts as "enlightened princesses" (Caroline, wife of George II; Augusta, wife of the latter's son and heir, Frederick, prince of Wales, who predeceased his father in 1751; and Charlotte, consort of George III, 1761–1818). In its zeal to integrate them into the English Enlightenment, this project failed to offer an account of its character or chronology, virtually suggesting Caroline initiated an English Enlightenment, and giving as much attention to a consort who was queen for only ten years, as it did to Charlotte's stint of fifty-seven years. This long time span incorporated huge changes in politics, society, and intellectual developments.

It is understandable that curators will think about the visitor experience, which for the *Enlightened princesses* exhibition was managed to show how parallel themes, such as medicine and education, each engaged the princesses' attention, but anyone who went on to read the elegantly and beautifully designed book of the exhibition is offered little sense of change over time. Discussion of place is also oddly managed: Almost nothing is said about Hanover, in spite of the fact that these German-born princesses were also electresses[16] in the Holy Roman Empire, and the Hanoverian personal union doubled the status of its monarchs. In the chapter on Germany, the main focus is on Prussia, but Halle Pietism is confused with Prussian *Aufklärung*. Dennison's subtler analysis of Queen Caroline in his 2017 biography reveals her as adapting the Hanoverians' earlier devotion to Leibniz to an English-based devotion to Newtonianism, rather than virtually initiating the Enlightenment.[17]

In short, studying British monarchs themselves has not on the whole been a prelude to exploring their courts. Monarchy itself as an institution, and the ways in which loyalty had been fostered after the change of dynasty in 1714, had also been ignored until Hannah

---

15. *Enlightened princesses: Caroline, Augusta and Charlotte and the making of the modern world*, ed. Joanna Marschner, David Bindman, and Lisa L. Ford (New Haven, CT, 2017). This was reviewed by Julie Farguson, "Enlightenment and modernity? German princesses in Georgian Britain," *The Court historian* 23:1 (2018), p.62–65.

16. With the exception of course of Augusta, who was only ever a dowager princess of Wales.

17. Matthew Dennison, *The First Iron Lady: a life of Caroline of Ansbach* (London, 2017).

Smith's revisionist study of 2006, because the character of Britain
as a parliamentary monarchy, and the fascination with Jacobite
disloyalty, had been of greater significance to the profession.[18] Elaine
Chalus's work on politics as family politics paved the way for a
better integration by historians of court and social politics, and thus
a portrayal of the monarch as the center of social networks. Filling
court appointments was a strategic element of this role, and clearly
some positions, such as that of royal physician, were more linked to
Enlightenment preoccupations than others.[19] Ironically these gaps
in knowledge of the court existed despite the emerging prosopog-
raphies of the royal household and both houses of Parliament, which
provide essential data on individuals linked to the British court
and government.[20] Here I suggested that historians needed to look
at the three-way link between the monarch, Parliament, and court
society in order to understand Hanoverian political culture in its
broadest sense.[21] It was a patron–client society from top to bottom, so
knowledge of the institutions, professions, and societies that fostered
the Enlightenment needs to be based on an understanding of these
mechanisms.

Another hindrance to seeing the English, Scottish, and British
Enlightenments fully in relation to Continental Europe and its courts
was that the link between Britain and Hanover was very underex-
plored until the first decade of the twenty-first century. The remedy
to this was substantially advanced with *The Hanoverian dimension
in British history: 1714–1837* (2007), in which Thomas Biskup, who
also contributes to this volume, underlined the significance of the
University of Göttingen, founded by George II, as a link with the
court in London.[22]

18. Hannah Smith, *Georgian monarchy, politics, and culture: 1714–1760* (Cambridge, 2006); Andrew Hanham, "'So few facts': Jacobites, Tories and the Pretender," *Parliamentary history* 19:2 (2002), p.233–57.
19. Elaine Chalus, *Elite women in English political life c.1754–1790* (Oxford, 2005).
20. The History of Parliament Trust, "The History of Parliament: British political, social and local history," http://www.historyofparliamentonline.org/ (last accessed January 21, 2022); R. O. Bucholz, "The database of court officers: 1660–1837," http://courtofficers.ctsdh.luc.edu./ (last accessed January 21, 2022).
21. Clarissa Campbell Orr, "New perspectives on Hanoverian Britain," *Historical journal* 52:2 (2009), p.513–29.
22. Thomas Biskup, "The University of Göttingen and the personal union 1737–1837," in *The Hanoverian dimension in British history: 1714–1837*, ed. Brendan Simms and Torsten Riotte (Cambridge, 2007), p.128–60.

Roy Porter and Mikuláš Teich's path-breaking *Enlightenment in national context* further back in 1981 had therefore begun an essential corrective to accounts of the Enlightenment as mainly a French phenomenon by introducing the importance of national variation, and arguing for a fresh approach to the unique character of an English Enlightenment. However, although it argued that there was an Enlightenment in England, and that arguably it predated the French, it did not immediately lead to exploring its courtly context, or to polemics about the role of the court.[23] After Teich and Porter's challenge to the received wisdom that the French Enlightenment came first and their insistence that national context was significant and formative, historical attention moved toward looking at Enlightenment and gender, but retained a comparative national focus, notably in the international project resulting in Sarah Knott and Barbara Taylor's anthology *Women, gender and the Enlightenment*.[24] The revival of court studies moved in parallel with this. I began to follow the example of medievalists in looking at female agency at courts in two essay collections, which opened up the role of the female consort during the period between 1660 and 1837, while Helen Watanabe-O'Kelly led an EU-funded project based in four centers to research cross-cultural transfer between courts in a longer timescale, embracing the Renaissance and the Reformation.[25]

The court and the later Hanoverians

Following my 2007 attempt to characterize the late Hanoverian Enlightenment and its relationship to the reign of George III and Queen Charlotte, I would now emphasize these characteristics:[26]

23. *The Enlightenment in national context*, ed. Roy Porter and Mikuláš Teich (Cambridge, 1981).
24. *Women, gender and the Enlightenment*, ed. Sarah Knott and Barbara Taylor (Basingstoke, 2005).
25. *Queenship in Britain 1660–1837: royal patronage, court culture and dynastic politics*, ed. Clarissa Campbell Orr (Manchester, 2002); *Queenship in Europe, 1660–1815: the role of the consort*, ed. Clarissa Campbell Orr (Cambridge, 2004); Faculty of Medieval & Modern Languages at the University of Oxford, "Marrying cultures: queens consort and European identities 1500–1800," www.marrying cultures.eu (last accessed January 21, 2022).
26. Clarissa Campbell Orr, "The late Hanoverian court and the Christian Enlightenment," in *Monarchy and religion: the transformation of royal culture in eighteenth-century Europe*, ed. Michael Schaich (Oxford, 2007), p.317–44.

- It accepted a Newtonian framework for understanding physical science, and followed both Newton and Locke in insisting on experimental methods and not speculative philosophy.
- It followed Francis Bacon in encouraging comprehensive and descriptive accounts of natural history.
- It also followed Bacon and his Central European admirers in believing the ruler should encourage encyclopedic projects, such as dictionaries, laboratories, zoological gardens, and research centers, which needed collaboration.
- It believed the Book of God's word (Holy Scripture) paralleled the Book of God's works, but that Scripture was not a literal description of nature.
- Following John Locke's challenge to the belief in innate ideas, which in turn raised the question of nature versus nurture, it facilitated the emergence of women in the literary marketplace. Women flourished as novelists and providers of moral guidance; they often held conservative views of women's role in the family, but they were now freer to express them.

George III himself was interested in astronomy and built an observatory in the royal park at Bushey, Richmond, for the siblings William and Caroline Herschel. The "discovery" of Australia was a by-product of his sponsorship of a naval vessel to survey the Transit of Venus in 1769. The king gave pensions both to Samuel Johnson, the creator of the *Dictionary*, and to Rousseau. As well as his *Dictionary*, Johnson created a sense of a canon of modern English literature through his work as a literary historian and critic. Charles Burney is integral to the English Enlightenment through his encyclopedic survey of the history of music, *A General history of music* (4 vols., 1776–1789). This was dedicated to Charlotte in words by Samuel Johnson.

These Enlightenment trends for comprehensive surveys or reference works coincided with the age of wonder, which marveled at the apparently "magical" phenomena of new scientific frontiers such as electricity and magnetism.[27] Education was another subject much debated at court. For instance, although the queen disapproved of the morals of Mme de Genlis (Caroline-Stéphanie-Félicité Ducrest de Saint-Aubin, comtesse de Genlis, 1746–1830), governess of the Orleans branch of the French royal family, she did approve of her plays and stories for children, which showed that apparently magical

27. Richard Holmes, *The Age of wonder* (London, 2009).

phenomena such as the northern lights had a perfectly intelligible explanation. Frances Burney's court diaries show how much scientific developments were a matter of daily discussion among courtiers, covering such topics as volcanic action. Finally, the personal friendship of the king and queen with Sir Joseph Banks, president of the Royal Society, whose travel destinations included Tahiti and Iceland, made the court an important hub for the dissemination of the second major wave of geographic discovery.[28]

Rousseau's challenge to the Enlightenment

In his *Essay on the origins of inequality* of 1755, Rousseau suggested several reasons why early forms of human society had fostered differential status. One of them is inequality of performance talent. We must remember that Rousseau had actually been a very successful courtier, having had his opera *Le Devin du village* (*The Village sorcerer*) produced to acclaim at Versailles, and having been invited to be presented to the king. (Charles Burney later produced the piece for the English stage.) Rousseau was also still in good standing with the colleagues who had embarked collectively to create a new encyclopedia, and was given responsibility for the articles on music. In his *Essay*, having grappled with the stages by which originally solitary human beings came to form families and connected social groups, he argues:

> They accustomed themselves to assemble before their huts round a large tree; singing and dancing, the true offspring of love and leisure became the amusement, or rather the preoccupation, of men and women thus assembled together with nothing else to do. Each one began to consider the rest, and to wish to be considered in turn; and thus a value came to be attached to public esteem. Whoever sang or danced best, whoever was the handsomest, the strongest, the most dexterous, or most eloquent, came to be of most consideration; and this was the first step towards inequality, and at the same time towards vice. From these first distinctions arose on the one hand vanity and contempt and on the other shame and envy: and the fermentations caused by these new leavens ended by producing combinations fatal to innocence and happiness.[29]

28. John Gascoigne, *Joseph Banks and the English Enlightenment: useful knowledge and polite culture* (Cambridge, 1994).
29. Cited from Jean-Jacques Rousseau, *The Social contract and discourses*, ed. G. D. H. Cole (London, 1973), p.81.

So began the whole sorry descent into a society intent on living in the eyes of others—a society of self-love and competition, not modest self-esteem.

Rousseau knew that courts devoured talent, always eager for the next sensation, the next star, the next celebrity. His own subsequent works became a leaven working its way through notions about the value of knowledge, of encyclopedism, patriotism, family, the reliability of the heart over the head, the education of children, breastfeeding, religious doctrines and institutions, the architecture and lifestyle of *la vie simple*, including simpler forms of dress, and what constituted politeness and authenticity. In short, he questioned all the norms of society, including the intense competitiveness of courts and modern cities, *and* the project of the Enlightenment to date, which was critical of some of these elements. His influence was unevenly felt, but the courts where it had the clearest impact included some related to that of George III and Queen Charlotte, including the court of George's cousin Duke Ernest in Saxe-Gotha-Altenburg, that of Charlotte's brother Karl in Mecklenburg-Strelitz, that of her niece Queen Luise of Prussia, and the Danish court, where the consort for two generations was an English princess.[30]

It became clear that Rousseau refused to be obliged to anyone or to be anyone's protégé. This struck at the heart of the *ancien régime*, a patron–client society, where one advanced to a great extent by pulling strings and seeking favors (i.e., by being a patron or a protégé). In the 1750s, Rousseau vowed to stop wearing a wig and fancy ruffled shirts and a watch, and to earn his living as a music copyist—a very skilled clerical trade, but not a profession. When Rousseau came to England in 1766, he was prepared to accept a pension from the king (although the matter then dragged on inconclusively for weeks).[31] Someone less in tune with the king's values than Rousseau would be hard to find.

Rousseau's personal "reform" later resonated with others of similar disinclination. Frances Burney bridled very early on during her stint as Second Keeper of the Robes to Queen Charlotte, when she was told

---

30. See Clarissa Campbell Orr, "Marriage in a global context," in *Queens consort, cultural transfer and European politics, c.1500–1800*, ed. Helen Watanabe-O'Kelly and Adam Morton (Abingdon, 2017), p.109–31. Space limitations preclude a comparative discussion.

31. For a meticulous reconstruction of Rousseau's stay in England, see John Edmonds and John Eidinow, *Rousseau's dog: a tale of two great thinkers at war in the age of Enlightenment* (London, 2006).

that she would be given a new dress when the royal family came to visit Oxford and stay at Nuneham Courtenay, home of the Harcourt family (who had previously been great disciples of Rousseau).[32] She reacted by pointing out, in injured pride, that she already had several new ones. There were always people who were not obvious courtier material, and Rousseau's ideas gave them permission to "be themselves"—the kind of catalyzing permission to say "no" that had previously been enabled by religious imperatives. To understand this, some further features of the English court and of the national context of the English Enlightenment need brief discussion.

The English court as a career structure

The paradox for writers of either sex is that there was no professional career structure as such for them in Great Britain. There was no Academy of Letters or Royal Society to provide recognition, training, or pensions for the humanities. But the eighteenth-century intelligentsia was full of clergy who were also antiquarians, natural scientists, poets, and playwrights. This facilitated all kinds of literary and scientific endeavor, as well as the fulfillment of religious duties. In parallel, the thriving world of commercial publishing meant that, by 1800, women were publishing 50 percent of fiction, and the prince regent suggested fiction themes to Jane Austen, so there was some recognition.[33] Moreover, women were permitted to apply to the charitable Literary Fund if they found themselves in financial difficulty, so women's financial difficulties were recognized as on an equal footing to men's.

By contrast, there was a career that was pensioned and salaried, open to both sexes, and that was being a courtier. Royal households needed professionals of all kinds: lawyers, financial managers, doctors, and surgeons, so men could have a dual role. The only scholarly "job" at court was that of royal historiographer. It was not obviously open to women, although by the 1770s women were making advances as historians. However, monarchs also needed loyal supporters who kept them company on the hunting field or at the card table, whose role was social rather than political. For men this could be combined with military or naval service, and also with

32. Campbell Orr, "Queen Charlotte as patron."
33. James Raven, *British fiction 1750–1770: a chronological check-list of prose fiction printed in Britain and Ireland* (Newark, DE, 1987).

being a member of Parliament (MP) who would vote with the current royal ministry. Their female equivalents could accompany royal women when taking a drive or provide uncontroversial sociability in the evenings or on visits. This could also boost the position of courtier families through social bonds.

George III was often able to rely on families over three generations. For instance, the North family served his parents and provided his first stable "prime" minister, Lord Frederick North, as well as courtiers for the prince of Wales's first separate household. The main feature of the English peerage was that it was not only a service nobility, but also constituted by its presence in both houses of Parliament an institutional check on royal power. Legislation only became law if a draft proved acceptable to both houses of Parliament. The importance of this parliamentary sovereignty was so great that, until the start of the twenty-first century, the role of the court was largely overlooked, while historians concentrated on the long story of how Parliament became more and more responsive to the popular electorate while the monarch's executive power declined.

Thus, although being a courtier could be a stepping-stone on the way to political engagement, some peerage families did not seek roles as ministers. In reality, power was shared between the sovereign and Parliament, between the sovereign and various royal households, including those of aunts, uncles, and siblings, and between Parliament and the court. This was reinforced by multiple connections within landed families. There were a variety of three-way relationships.[34] Ministers holding high public office wore court dress in Parliament and attended a royal levee on being appointed. Did this make them servants of the monarch, or answerable to Parliament? It was not yet clear.[35] The political philosopher Montesquieu recognized that Parliament did not fully separate the legislative and executive functions of government. Pragmatically this enabled government to proceed, because the monarch exercised multiple means of patronage, enabling ministers to persuade enough MPs to vote for their monarch's political measures. There were mutual interests in making this work, despite the criticisms of corruption.

Strictly speaking, only Anglicans held office in Parliament or in the royal households, with Catholics being especially disadvantaged. George III and his wife wanted to appoint only Trinitarian Christians

34. Campbell Orr, "New perspectives on Hanoverian Britain."
35. Brewer, *Party ideology and popular politics.*

(and not Deists) with sober morals to both political office and courtier positions. Pragmatism meant that the king had to appoint to high office politicians like the rakish, gambling Charles James Fox in 1782, but he would not appoint such a person to his personal household. He could show approbation of the devout and sober by attending their weddings or smiling at levees on those leading regular lives. For example, C. J. Fox's younger brother, Henry Frederick, was a career army officer who married a daughter of Lady Louisa Clayton, who had enjoyed a lifelong career as Lady of the Bedchamber to George III's redoubtable Aunt Amelia. Lady Louisa was also the sister of the royal governess, Lady Charlotte Finch.

The Enlightenment fostered at court by George III was a Christian one, based on the Baconian parallel between the Book of God's works—created nature—and the Book of God's word—revealed truth contained in Scripture, but understood through a liberal, not a literal, interpretation of sacred books. The advocacy of such encyclopedic surveys, following the ideas of Francis Bacon, and not a social critique of court society, was essential to the English Enlightenment. This Baconian characteristic, and the idea of a parallel between God's word (Scripture) and works (created nature), was also characteristic of Göttingen University in the Electorate, founded by George II and one of the most modern in Europe.[36] In court circles there was a strong connection to the technological thrust of the Lunar Society in industrial Birmingham, focused on the development of steam power, an important link being the queen's Genevan reader, Jean-André DeLuc. The society was also the cradle of luxury goods, such as Wedgwood's pottery and Matthew Boulton's ormolu vases, both of which found an eager patron in Queen Charlotte. DeLuc was a field geologist and friend of Rousseau, and he urged the queen to accept that the latter's heterodoxy in the Christian faith was due to his unfortunate friendships with Paris-based Deists such as Denis Diderot.[37]

Bearing in mind these functions of the landed elite and the trends within the English Enlightenment, let us return to the relative fluidity of English society. Could the court accommodate persons who wanted to be as individualistic as Rousseau? Was this easier for men or for

36. Campbell Orr, "The late Hanoverian court"; John Gascoigne, *Science in the service of empire* (Cambridge, 1998).
37. For a brief but excellent introduction to Rousseau's paradoxical position in the Enlightenment see Robert Wokler, *Rousseau: a very short introduction* (Oxford, 2001).

women? How did status and gender come into play? And did contemporary celebrity help or hinder social advancement?

Charles Burney's ambitions

The Burneys were of indeterminate social status. Charles Burney started life as downwardly mobile. His grandfather Charles McBurney was carefully climbing from being a steward to a peer to buying land for himself and living like a gentleman; the latter's son James then stepped off the ladder, running away to follow a musical career, marrying an actress in the bargain. After his father disowned him, instead of studying medicine, he had to finance his elopement by marketing his accomplishments in music, dancing, and painting.[38] He either performed them or taught them, doing whatever came to hand to support his wife and nine surviving children. On being widowed he married a woman with a bit more money, and settled down as a portrait painter in Shrewsbury, where five more children were born, including Charles, future musicologist. Eventually he was apprenticed to Thomas Arne, composer of the opera *Alfred* that included the song "Rule! Britannia." It does not make for a very elevated "backstory" to eighteenth-century minds.

When Charles Burney drafted his memoirs, he emphasized how he had known all kinds of people from the top to the bottom of later Georgian society:

> ascending from those of the most humble cottagers, & lowest mechanics, to the first nobility, and most elevated personages in the kingdom, [...] overgrown Norfolk farmers, generous, friendly & hospitable Merchants, Men of business & Men of Pleasure, Men of Letters, Artists, Men of Science, Sportsmen & country Squires, dissipated and extravagant voluptuaries, Gamesters, Ambassadors, Statesmen, & even sovereign princes I have had an opportunity of examining, in almost every point of view.[39]

By the opening of George III's reign, Charles Burney was in high demand in London as a teacher among the "quality." Having spent nine years in King's Lynn, Norfolk, he made an initial impact in the capital by deploying his daughter Esther's talents as a keyboard

38. Charles Burney, *Memoirs of Dr. Charles Burney 1726–1769*, ed. Slava Klima, Garry Bowers, and Kerry S. Grant (Lincoln, NE, 1989), p.9–10.
39. Burney, *Memoirs of Dr. Charles Burney*.

prodigy. Her immediate *éclat* led to social contacts which further enabled him to pull strings on behalf of his children to get them onto the early rungs of their careers. Basically, public performance by women was deplored—ladies only ever sang or acted in private, and a child prodigy would not grow into a gentlewoman. As a novelist Frances Burney would later explore the problems of public, female musical performance in *The Wanderer* (1814).

What Burney *père* had, though, was tremendous drive, and a burning desire to do better than be a teacher of music, even a socially well connected and increasingly prosperous one. He pulled off the trick of becoming a serious musical professional when he was awarded a doctorate from Oxford for his musicianship in 1769.[40] He now had some attributes of unquestionably respectable, professional status, and this lustre began to rub off onto his family. He consolidated this by developing his research into the history of music, and made the most of his travels in search of material by writing them up, winning literary esteem as a writer who gave a new fillip to travel writing, with two studies of the contemporary European music and social scene (*Eighteenth-century musical tour in France and Italy*, 1771, and *Eighteenth-century musical tour in Germany and the Netherlands*, 1773), which incorporated the contemporary travels. This was an encyclopedic project ranging from ancient times to the present, and the queen allowed him to dedicate it to her. The first volume was published in 1780, and the following year Burney had himself painted by his friend Joshua Reynolds, triumphantly wearing his doctoral robes and holding his doctoral diploma: He had unquestionably become a man of letters—much more elevated than a performer and tutor. However, he still taught music to make a living, and in that year he was organizing a new secondary school.[41]

Some of Frances Burney's siblings and half-siblings entered or married into the recognized professions. James had joined the navy and served on some of Captain Cook's voyages. His talent for seamanship was unequivocal, but his insubordination hindered formal promotion. Even so he ended his career as a rear-admiral. Five half-brothers served in the Bengal Army in India. The girls would be judged on their choice of marriage partner and their moral conduct before, during, and after marriage; the main lapses of character in a woman would be of a sexual character—either being too flirtatious or, worse still,

40. Roger Lonsdale, *Dr. Charles Burney: a literary biography* (Oxford, 1965), p.77–79.
41. Lonsdale, *Burney*.

actually having lovers. If publicly known, this would have disqualified them or even been grounds for dismissal from service with the queen.

Thus, for these daughters, their safest and best hope was to find a professional man to marry, such as a clergyman, a doctor, or an officer. To equip them for good marriages Burney *père* took Frances and Susanna to France in 1764, so that they acquired the essential ladylike attribute of fluency in French. Because so much of his income was absorbed in running costs, he was aware that all of the children of both marriages would have to "shift for themselves, as I have done."[42] Susanna, Frances's closest confidante, married a fellow officer of brother James, Captain Molesworth Phillips, who was James Cook's second in command on the third voyage of discovery to Oceania; Charlotte married Clement Francis, the personal surgeon (thus, not regarded so highly as a physician) of the governor-general of Bengal, Warren Hastings. These alliances helped stabilize the upward trajectories of the Burney family away from the "cultural trades" into the respectable learned sector at middling level. But Frances, still unmarried, remained an anomaly. Single women in the public eye had to be extremely careful of the company they kept: They could not lead such socially eclectic lives as Frances's father had done.

To avoid drawing attention to herself and demonstrate independence from her father, Frances had published her first novel *Evelina* (1778) anonymously. It quickly sold well. Once the secret of her authorship was out, she became not just recognizable, but famous. After the even greater success of her second novel, *Cecilia* (1782), a confident satire on fashionable life, she commented to Susanna that "you would suppose me something dropt from the Skies. Even if Richardson or Fielding could rise from the Grave, I should bid fair for supplanting them in the *popular Eye*, for being a *fair female*, I am *accounted quelque chose extraordinaire*."[43]

Being a commercially successful writer brought problematic status to both sexes, especially to women. The royal family did not mind Frances being a celebrity: When she attended the theater with them, they teased her for blushing when she was pointed out.[44] It reflected well on their literary taste and moral discernment that they admired

42. Lonsdale, *Burney*, p.61.
43. Margaret Anne Doody, *Frances Burney: the life in the works* (Cambridge, 1988), p.150 (original emphasis).
44. Frances Burney, *Court journals and letters*, ed. Peter Sabor *et al.*, 6 vols. (Oxford, 2011–2019), vol.2, p.123.

such an unflinchingly "proper" author. However, this very *éclat* meant that Burney's own circles of sociability were broadened. She began to have more contacts and invitations; people inside and outside royal circles clamored to meet her. Once she joined the queen's household, she would lose this capacity for social initiative.

Furthermore, Burney was not the kind of female writer who was automatically sisterly toward others, or their patrons. When Burney began her court appointment there was already one female writer in court circles, Charlotte's French reader, Marie Elisabeth de La Fite (1737–1794), who was a well-established woman of letters. Her husband had been a chaplain at the court of the prince of Orange in The Hague; thus his patron was George III's cousin once removed.[45] With a group of like-minded colleagues, the La Fites ran an anti-Deist periodical. Burney was not disposed to be friendly, and mocked La Fite's heavily accented English when she described her to Susanna.[46] She had great fun describing to Susanna the effusive meeting between La Fite and the German novelist Sophie von La Roche, who greeted each other like bosom friends although they had never met in person before—only through corresponding.[47] Burney's first impressions of Mme La Roche were therefore unfavorable:

> could I have conceived her Character to be unaffected, her manners
> have a softness that would be excessively engaging […] [she] has
> a voice of touching sweetness, Eyes of Dove-like Gentleness, looks
> supplicating for favour, & an Air & demeanour the most tenderly
> caressing. I can suppose she has thought herself all her life the Model
> of the Favourite of her own Favourite Romance…[48]

The comment to Susanna about how La Roche saw her own life through the lens of a novel is actually a very barbed one. The phrase "she has thought herself all her life the Model of […] her own Favourite Romance" echoes a line in Richard Graves's misogynistic satire of 1751, *The Heroines, or Modern memoirs*. Graves had written: "

> Not so of modern whores the illustrious train
> Renowned Constantia, Pilkington and Vane,
> Grown old in sin, and dead to amorous joy,

---

45. Daniel de La Fite's patron was George III's cousin, Willem V (1748–1806).
46. Burney, *Court journals and letters*, vol.1, p.262.
47. Burney, *Court journals and letters*, vol.1, p.166.
48. Burney, *Court journals and letters*, vol.1, p.167.

No acts of penance their great souls employ,
Without a blush behold each Nymph advance
The conscious heroine of her own romance,
Each Harlot triumphs in her Loss of Fame,
And boldly prints—& publishes her shame.[49]

The "heroines" are the three autobiographical writers, the bigamist and courtesan Constantia Philips, the rackety Lady Vane, who left her adoring but impotent husband, pursuing a number of amours, and the maligned poetess Laetitia Pilkington, whose social acceptability was compromised deliberately by her own estranged husband so that he could claim that some of their children were not fathered by him—so he was not financially liable for their upkeep.

Frances Burney's court appointment: interchangeable Burneys?

It must be stressed that Frances Burney had not aspired to an appointment in the queen's household (in contrast to Diderot's courtly ambitions, which are discussed in the previous chapter). The king had wanted to reward Charles Burney for his scholarship on the history of music, but no suitable musical vacancies were then available. Leonard Smelt, a military engineer who had been involved in the education of some of the older princes, and was highly thought of by the king, had suggested that Burney's daughter might be given a place at court instead. It is as if these cultured but not easily classifiable men and women were somehow interchangeable. So, in 1786 Frances was made Second Keeper of the Robes, to replace Johanna von Hagedorn (d.1789), who had been with the queen since their arrival in England in 1761. The mediator was Mary Granville Delany, a gentlewoman and descendant of a very old Anglo-Norman family, who had been a personal friend of Handel along with her brother Bernard, and had provided Charles Burney with information on English music. She had assured the queen that this celebrity novelist was a perfectly proper writer.

Frances Burney's success as a novelist was emblematic of the breakthrough made by women in the new profession of writing. By the 1770s it was clear that women were moving into more visible positions in several branches of the arts, including drama, painting,

49. Felicity Nussbaum, *The Brink of all we hate: English satires on women 1660–1750* (Lexington, KY, 1984), p.149.

and history.[50] The problem for novelists was both their extreme self-consciousness over this success and their still ambiguous respectability. For men as well as women, writing for money retained overtones of prostituting their talents for the pen in the commercial hurly-burly of Grub Street. It was not what either ladies or gentlemen "did." For a start, many publications were financed through advance subscription, so even a high-minded conduct book involved touting one's wares for money. With fiction of any type it was always assumed that a woman was drawing on her own experience; ergo, a female novelist was assumed to have experienced her characters' passions— perhaps several times over, with a different lover. However, Burney's female heroines are not in the mould of Rousseau's Héloïse; Evelina suffers from social anxiety and fear of her vulgar relatives, not unsuitable passion. Still more pertinent to the theme of the dangers to gentility created by public performance was Burney's last novel *The Wanderer* (1814), featuring a genteel French émigré forced to earn her living as a professional harpist. Few writing women ditched their patrons as swiftly as Burney did, thereby reinforcing her respectability, when her patron Hester Thrale married Gabriel Piozzi, the Italian music teacher of her own children, as her younger, second husband. Although Burney was not the only one who thought Thrale had revealed her passions too brazenly and put herself above her children's welfare. Given that Burney's father was still teaching music, the fact that his daughter had a patron, who on being widowed had eloped with the live-in music teacher, cut very close to the bone.[51]

Mme de La Fite pressed Burney to embark on a literary correspondence with Mme de Genlis, whose "brand" of religion was more a sentimental kind of Deism than the sacramental Trinitarian theology approved by George III. Mme de Genlis was an admirer of the queen and included a flattering portrait of her in a novel of 1797. However, the queen herself warned Burney off this association, because it was known that, despite her manner and advocacy of virtue, Mme de Genlis had been the mistress of the duc d'Orléans. Women, especially single women, always had to be careful of the company they kept.

What did the queen envisage Frances Burney would do? She was certainly not giving her that "room of her own" with freedom to write

50. *Brilliant women: 18th-century bluestockings*, ed. Elizabeth Eger and Lucy Peltz (London, 2008).
51. Doody, *Frances Burney*.

eulogized later by Virginia Woolf. She did envisage Burney would be a literary advisor of suitable reading material for the princesses. There were also duties to perform in connection with robing the queen for formal appearances—but these were always played down in Burney's letters to her father, as she wanted to emphasize that her appointment was more literary than it actually was. In particular, she claimed that, when she was Second Keeper of the Robes, all the manual part of her office was excluded, but Burney's own descriptions to her sisters show that, though she did not hold the office of a dresser, she had set hours and set tasks, and that she readied the queen for the drawing room but did not actually attend it.[52]

Meanwhile Burney's own subject during this time when she was not publishing was herself, continually recorded in her diary, but sometimes written up as much as a year later. There was the epic battle to be free of the control of the senior dresser, Juliane Elisabeth von Schwellenberg (1728–1797), and so create some initiative and time for herself. This self-narration resonates with the autobiographical turn of Rousseau in his *Confessions* and *Rêveries*.

The social ambiguity of the eating parlor within the royal household

A further challenge for Burney was that her position was in itself socially ambiguous. She and Juliane Elisabeth von Schwellenberg had two roles to play: On the one hand was their attendance on the queen, but on the other hand there was their role within the royal household as co-hostesses of the equerries and the vice-chamberlains, plus other regulars at court, such as educators of the royal children, and various scholars and clerical visitors. The etiquette of her position was a minefield of small decisions and awareness of social nuances. The basic rules of court life were that no one should turn his or her back on the king, or enter any room where anyone in the royal family was without being summoned, nor eat in the royal presence. The equerries accompanied the king when he went hunting during the day, and played backgammon with him in the evening or formed part of the audience for evening music. Thus these regulars needed somewhere to eat, or drink tea and coffee, and sit until summoned to the king or queen.

---

52. *Memoirs of Dr. Burney, arranged from his own manuscripts, from family papers and from personal recollections*, ed. Frances Burney, 3 vols. (London, 1832), vol.3, p.85.

By custom and due to the domineering character of Juliane Elisabeth von Schwellenberg, she had become the arbiter of these occasions, and expected Burney to assist her, as Hagedorn had done before her. As Burney scornfully pointed out to her sister, this was not because Schwellenberg had any noteworthy gifts for sociable conversation, but because as a German she had no native contacts of her own, whereas "I have such as no-one, I believe, ever had before" in that situation.[53] In contrast, Burney already had a social life before joining the court, but at the same time her temperament and vocation as a writer also required regular periods of solitude.

The society who frequented the equerries' eating room came from subtly different layers of peerage and gentry families. The four equerries Burney encountered in her first year were Robert Manners, Fulke Greville, Philip Goldsworthy, and William Price. They each had a slightly different background to their careers at court: The first was the younger son of a younger son of the philoprogenitive second duke of Rutland; the second was a younger son of the first earl of Warwick of the second creation; the third was grandson on his mother's side of Huguenots in the luxury trades, with an aunt who had married money and left it to him, and a father who was a consular official. The last came from Welsh gentry, his brother being the "Picturesque" theorist Uvedale Price, an improving landowner who moved in Bluestocking circles and found a sinecure for his tutor Benjamin Stillingfleet, the man of the real-life blue stockings. Thus Burney was considered socially suitable to be a hostess for courtiers who were much more certain of their social background in landed circles than she was.[54] Yet when she was summoned to the queen's presence, it was by a bell—a mark of servitude, she initially believed. When she was dismissed the queen used the formula "Now I will let you go," customarily directed to her higher-ranking ladies. Burney at first bridled silently at this usage, as it made her feel like the queen owned her, until she discovered it was a mark of honorable standing.[55]

One difficulty about obeying the implicit and explicit court rules was exacerbated by the geography of court life. At Kew, the White House where the family lodged was not really a palace—it had originated as a merchant's villa. The family lived quite informally between themselves, but for all levels within their entourage the small

53. Burney, *Court journals and letters*, vol.1, p.19, 54.
54. I am grateful to Nigel Aston for exploring these issues with me.
55. Burney, *Court journals and letters*, vol.1, p.83.

scale of the residence multiplied the opportunities for unexpectedly encountering a royal and being unable to adjust one's body language quickly enough.

Burney was not a team player within the household, nor a literary "sister," though fitfully she tried hard to be. She did need some privacy and solitude, to process all that was happening in her life. Lady Llanover (and/or her assistant, the writer Geraldine Jewsbury), editor of Mary Granville Delany's correspondence, did have some insight into her situation, although it was never that sympathetic, and drenched in mid-Victorian snobbery:

> Miss Burney's situation certainly was anomalous, for though as a dresser she *had* a *fixed* (though subordinate) position, as a successful novel-writer she had an undefined sort of celebrity won by her talents; and though as the daughter of a music-master she had previously *no individual* position whatever, there was in her case more personal interest manifested on account of her being the daughter of so excellent a man as Dr. Burney, who was much respected [...] She had a *particularly* large share of *vanity*, a *particularly* lively *imagination*, and between both, she made numerous mistakes in the course of her various representations of her *four characters*,–of the *timid* nobody; the wonderful *girl* who had written "Evelina"; the Queen's dresser; and the *amiable* and *devoted daughter* "Fanny Burney."[56]

Colonel Philip Goldsworthy, MP and equerry, had grasped the essence of court service, despite his own family's recent elevation to landed estate, and brought to it a wry sense of humor—not a quality with which Burney was liberally endowed:

> all one's labours, riding, and walking, and standing, and bowing— what a life it is? Well! it's honour! that's one comfort; it's all honour! royal honour!—one has the honour to stand till one has not a foot left; and to ride till one's stiff, and to walk till one's ready to drop,—and then one makes one's lowest bow, d'ye see, and blesses one's self with joy for the honour.[57]

During the Renaissance, writers such as Baldassare Castiglione (1478–1529) had posed the question of whether honor stemmed from

56. *The Autobiography and correspondence of Mary Granville, Mrs Delany*, ed. Augusta Hall, Lady Llanover, 6 vols. (London, 1860–1861), vol.6, p.361–62 (original emphasis). For Mary Delany (1700–1788), see Clarissa Campbell Orr, *Mrs. Delany: a life* (New Haven, CT, 2019).
57. Burney, *Court journals and letters*, vol.1, p.106.

the military valor of nobles, or from the cultivated talents of men without title but endowed with a humanist education. The anxieties of both Burneys were ultimately rooted in the literary discussions of works such as Castiglione's *Book of the courtier* (1528). This Renaissance tension between birth and talent was still unresolved in the age of late Enlightenment and sensibility. The commercialization of cultural life in the eighteenth century combined with concern for propriety had created manifold opportunities for the multitalented, but also multiple anxieties. In the final analysis, these bore down more heavily on women than on men.

II

Public sphere

"Hey France, your coffee is f***ing off!" Or how to interpret unauthorized literature in late *ancien régime* France: courtly patronage and the so-called "Mairobert corpus" (1774–1777)

Damien Tricoire

"Public sphere" and "underground literature"

"Hey France, pay attention, your coffee is f***ing off!"[1] With these words, according to the *Anecdotes sur Madame la comtesse Du Barri* (1775), the royal mistress pointed out to Louis XV that his coffee, which he liked to prepare himself, was boiling over. This vulgar outburst shows the king without any majesty, being addressed in offensive terms as in a dialogue between carriage drivers that could not even be reproduced in a vaudeville. For this reason, it has become a symbol in scholarship of the way "underground literature" desacralized royal power, attacked the court elites, and paved the way for the French Revolution.[2]

Such an interpretation seemed wholly convincing to historians for decades. Two theses have proven especially influential among them, and indeed initiated scholarly interest in pamphlets that were not penned by the "great names" among the *philosophes* and precisely for this reason had been largely neglected before the 1970s: the "public sphere" and the "underground literature" theses. The former could first be seen in Reinhart Koselleck's *Critique and crisis*, which described

---

1. "Eh! La France, prends donc garde, ton caffé f... le camp!": *Anecdotes sur Madame la comtesse Du Barri* (London, n.n., 1775), p.219. *Foutre le camp* was a very vulgar expression in the eighteenth century (it is still quite vulgar) and means the same as "to fuck off" (*foutre* means "to fuck").
2. Robert Darnton, *The Forbidden best-sellers of pre-revolutionary France* (New York, 1995), p.137–66; Robert Darnton, "La France, ton café fout le camp!," *Actes de la recherche en sciences sociales* 100 (December 1993), p.16–26.

the formation of a new historical-philosophical consciousness in reaction to the "absolutist state" through the "Enlightenment process" and the concomitant formation of "bourgeois society."[3] However, it was Jürgen Habermas who penned the most influential formulation of the "public sphere" thesis in his monograph *The Structural transformation of the public sphere*. Habermas made a sharp distinction between a "representative" and a "bourgeois" public sphere. The former was courtly and dominated by the representation of monarchical power, the latter the place of relatively free and critical judgment. Constituted above all in the eighteenth century, the bourgeois public sphere produced "public opinion" that made politics a public matter. In his model, Habermas thus sharply separated the world of the royal court from the world of critical authors, and interpreted the publication of unauthorized literature (books published without a royal privilege from the Librairie du roi) as an expression of the growing importance of the "bourgeois public sphere."[4]

For historians, this model proved attractive because it enabled an escape from an overly simple idea that had dominated scholarship about the origins of the French Revolution since the nineteenth century: that Enlightenment *philosophes* created public opinion.[5] Habermas's model invited historians to adopt a sociological approach and to look beyond the great authors.[6] However, it was criticized in the late twentieth century.[7] For example, while Keith Baker took over several of Habermas's core assumptions (the idea that the public sphere emerged in the middle of the eighteenth century, that it was characterized by a new publication drive, that it reacted to absolutism and destroyed it, and that it paved the way for the French Revolution), he held that not only "bourgeois" criticism but also the French

3. Reinhart Koselleck, *Critique and crisis: Enlightenment and the pathogenesis of modern society* (1959; Cambridge, MA, 1988).

4. Jürgen Habermas, *The Structural transformation of the public sphere: an inquiry into a category of bourgeois society*, translated by Thomas Burger (1962; Cambridge, MA, 1989).

5. This idea found its most complete expression in Daniel Mornet, *Les Origines intellectuelles de la Révolution: 1715–1787* (Paris, 1933).

6. Alain J. Lemaître, "Repères historiographiques," in *L'Opinion publique dans l'Europe des Lumières: stratégies et concepts*, ed. Bertrand Binoche and Alain J. Lemaître (Paris, 2013), p.15–22.

7. For a summary of the debates on Habermas's thesis: Bertrand Binoche, "Les historiens, les philosophes et l'opinion publique," in *L'Opinion publique*, ed. B. Binoche and A. J. Lemaître, p.7–14; Lemaître, "Repères historiographiques."

"government" itself contributed to the emergence of the "public sphere." Because "the government" was unable to contain the flow of pamphlets published by the opposition, Baker writes, it was forced to answer them and thus acknowledged a new principle of political legitimation, "public opinion."[8] In the wake of Baker—though sometimes strangely criticizing him for having neglected the government's role in the emergence of the "public sphere"—a range of studies have shown that several *ancien régime* ministers tried to mobilize "public opinion."[9] While Habermas's model has been criticized in various ways, most historians still think that the idea of "public opinion" and practices linked with it gained a new quality in the eighteenth century.[10]

The "underground literature" thesis is tightly linked to the idea of the "public sphere." It was crafted by Robert Darnton, who played a major role in initiating a more thorough exploration of unauthorized literature in the 1970s. Like the scholars who explored the "public sphere," Darnton was above all interested in enlarging our view of the origins of the French Revolution by looking beyond the "great authors" and revalorizing printed material that was popular in its

8.   Keith Michael Baker, "Politique et opinion publique sous l'ancien régime," *Annales ESC* 42:1 (1987), p.41–71. See also: Mona Ozouf, "L'opinion publique," in *The French Revolution and the creation of modern political culture*, ed. Keith Michael Baker, 4 vols. (Oxford, 1987–1994), vol.1, p.419–34. See also Veysman's studies of the ways Enlightenment *philosophes* conceived of "public opinion": Nicolas Veysman, *Mise en scène de l'opinion publique dans la littérature des Lumières* (Paris, 2004).

9.   Julian Swann, "Ministres et opinion publique," in *L'Opinion publique*, ed. B. Binoche and A. J. Lemaître, p.41–60, esp. 43. John W. A. Gunn has also shown that pro-governmental authors and ministers played a critical role in initiating practices of conquest of "public opinion": John W. A. Gunn, *Queen of the world: opinion in the public life of France from the Renaissance to the Revolution* (Oxford, 1995), esp. p.246–328.

10. Arlette Farge, *Dire et mal dire: l'opinion publique au XVIIIᵉ siècle* (Paris, 1992); Joan B. Landes, *Women and the public sphere in the age of the French Revolution* (Ithaca, NY, 1988); Gunn, *Queen of the world*; Cédric Michon, "Du bon usage de l'anachronisme en histoire: l'opinion publique à la Renaissance," in *L'Opinion publique en Europe (1600–1800)*, ed. Lucien Bély (Paris, 2011), p.39–67; Bernard Guenée, *L'Opinion publique à la fin du Moyen Age d'après la "Chronique de Charles VI" du Religieux de Saint-Denis* (Paris, 2002); Claude Gauvard, "Qu'est-ce que l'opinion avant l'invention de l'imprimerie?," in *L'Opinion: information, rumeur, propagande*, ed. Claude Gauvard (Nantes, 2008), p.21–59; Hélène Ducini, *Faire voir, faire croire: l'opinion publique sous Louis XIII* (Seyssel, 2003); Jeffrey K. Sawyer, *Printed poison: pamphlet propaganda, faction politics and the public sphere in early seventeenth-century France* (Berkeley, CA, 1990).

time but was not part of the literary and philosophical canon. He thus interpreted unauthorized publications as "underground literature" that greatly contributed to the destabilization of the *ancien régime*, especially of Catholicism and the idea of sacred kingship. According to him, many of these pamphlets not only denounced particular members of the court, but also put the whole political system into question. They were penned by frustrated writers who were without the patronage of aristocrats and politicians, and who developed strong rancor against the court elite as a whole.[11]

Both theses thus had in common that they saw in unauthorized literature the product of independent writers who were opposed to the *ancien régime* elites. As eighteenth-century studies were— and still probably are—largely dominated by the search for the origins of secular, liberal, and democratic modernity and the French Revolution, these interpretations found tremendous resonance. They were propagated among others by Roger Chartier's influential essay *The Cultural origins of the French Revolution* (published in 1981 in French and 1991 in English),[12] and they are still popular in recent scholarship.[13]

However, doubts soon arose. Already in 1989, Jeremy Popkin gave a totally different account of the blossoming of pamphlets in the decades before the French Revolution. According to him, the *libelles* were not authored by marginal writers attacking the court elites, and thus were not the expression of a radical Enlightenment opposed to the *ancien régime*. They were rather the commercial products of journalistic entrepreneurs and instruments of leading court figures protecting them.[14] In 2006, Simon Burrows cast Darnton's interpretation further into doubt. Without exploring the subject in any depth, he agreed with Popkin that many of the *libelles* were probably written under the patronage of leading court figures. He showed that their content was usually not as radical as Darnton had supposed; for example, only few were pornographic.

11. Robert Darnton, "The Grub Street style of revolution: J.-P. Brissot, police spy," *Journal of modern history* 40:4 (1968), p.301–27; Darnton, *Forbidden best-sellers*.
12. Roger Chartier, *Les Origines culturelles de la Révolution* (Paris, 1990).
13. Christophe Cave, "Préface," in *Le Règne de la critique: l'imaginaire culturel des Mémoires secrets*, ed. C. Cave (Paris, 2010), p.7–25 (13–14); Pierre-Yves Beaurepaire, *Echec au roi: irrespect, contestations et révoltes dans la France des Lumières* (Paris, 2015), p.255–57.
14. Jeremy Popkin, "Pamphlet journalism at the end of the Old Regime," *Eighteenth-century studies* 22:3 (1989), p.351–67.

He also suggested that the few radical pamphlets (for example the pornographic writings about Marie-Antoinette) were probably not propagated at all, as they were effectively "suppressed" by the police.[15] Thus, they could not have played an important role in the destabilization of the *ancien régime*.

Burrows thereby interprets well-known pamphlets like the *Anecotes sur Madame la comtesse Du Barri* in a different light. Darnton asserted that this critique of Louis XV's last official mistress was published in 1772, when the king was still alive and the *comtesse* was most influential.[16] The *Anecdotes* appear, then, as the expression of opposition to power and the royal court. Burrows notes that such an interpretation cannot be correct, as the *Anecdotes* were published in 1775, and therefore after the death of Louis XV and the fall of Mme Du Barry. This *libelle* was thus probably instrumental in legitimizing the political change that occurred in late 1774, Burrows suggests.[17] A similar issue could be raised in the case of the *Journal historique de la révolution opérée par Maupeou*, which Darnton terms "one of the most important antigovernment publications during the last years of Louis XV's reign"[18] although, as we will see, it was first published after Louis XVI's accession to power.

Even if some of Burrows's theses should perhaps be more nuanced,[19] recent scholarship invites us to reconsider the intentions and the reception of unauthorized literature and to avoid anachronisms in that these texts are considered pre-revolutionary. Accordingly, the critique of the "underground literature" thesis has left traces in historiography, and in their recent works Darnton and Alain Beaurepaire pay some attention to the connections between unauthorized literature and the courtly world.[20] However, theirs and other publications show

15. Simon Burrows, *Blackmail, scandal, and revolution: London's French libellistes, 1758–1792* (Manchester, 2006).

16. Robert Darnton, *The Corpus of clandestine literature in France: 1769–1789* (New York, 1995), p.116.

17. Burrows, *Blackmail*, p.76.

18. Robert Darnton, *Censors at work: how states shaped literature* (New York, 2014), p.82.

19. For example the *Mémoires de la comtesse de Barré*, an erotic pamphlet on Mme Du Barry, was indeed published in 1772, that is before her fall: *Mémoires authentiques de la comtesse de Barré, maîtresse de Louis XV, roi de France, extraits d'un manuscrit que possède la duchesse de Villeroy: par le chevalier Fr. N.; traduits de l'anglois* (London [Paris?], chez J. Roson, 1772).

20. Robert Darnton, *The Devil in the holy water, or the Art of slander from Louis XIV to Napoleon* (Philadelphia, PA, 2010), p.5; Robert Darnton, *Poetry and the*

that the "public sphere" and "underground literature" narratives are still widely accepted.[21] One problem is surely that we still know little about the patronage relationships underlying the unauthorized texts.[22] Unauthorized pamphlets were published anonymously, and patronage relationships were often informal, so that there is no surviving documentation. For this reason, the scholarship does not explore patronage in any depth.

How can we then study how unauthorized texts were connected to court factions without archival evidence? Beyond following uncertain attributions of pamphlets to parties—attributions that are often themselves contained in pamphlets—another possible method is a precise analysis of the content of the sources to reveal whom the authors supported and whom they criticized. Admittedly, this is no proof that the text in question was commissioned by someone at court. However, it shows that *libelles* did not attack the political system as such, that is the court or the monarchy, but rather expressed support for some court personalities. It enables a different reading of these sources.

The aim of this chapter is to apply this method to a famous ensemble of sources, the so-called "Mairobert corpus." There are three wider issues. First, I seek to contribute to the recent reevaluation of the political role of courtiers. Until the 1990s, historical research on France believed in absolutism. It was thought that early

---

police: communication networks in eighteenth-century Paris (Cambridge, MA, 2010); Beaurepaire, *Echec au roi*, p.252–53.

21. Darnton still holds that the *libellistes* slandered all leading courtiers, and thinks that there was a literary movement fundamentally opposed to *ancien régime* order: Darnton, *The Devil*, p.4–7. Beaurepaire writes that Burrows's thesis, according to which pornographical writings against Marie-Antoinette knew no propagation, does not convince him, but he formulates no argument against it. Beaurepaire, *Echec au roi*, p.257.

22. The scholarship contains a range of information, but no comprehensive studies have been published. The case of pamphleteers working for the duke of Chartres/Orléans (the later Philippe Egalité), including Brissot and Choderlos de Laclos, is the most well known; see George Armstrong Kelly, "The machine of the duc d'Orléans and the new politics," *Journal of modern history* 51 (December 1979), p.667–84; Popkin, "Pamphlet journalism," p.361–62. It is also known that unauthorized literature was published in the Temple under the auspices of Conti; see Nina Rattner Gelbart, "The *Journal des dames* and its female editors: politics, censorship and feminism in the Old Regime press," in *Press and politics in pre-revolutionary France*, ed. Jack Censer and Jeremy Popkin (Berkeley, CA, 1987), p.24–73.

modern French elites conceived of politics as the sole domain of their king and granted him absolute legislative power. Historians also supported the view that the monarchy, especially Richelieu and Louis XIV, had disempowered and "domesticated" the aristocracy and reduced high nobles to the role of walk-on actors adorning the stage of the monarchy, whereas "real politics" happened elsewhere, in the royal privy councils where "bourgeois" ministers had seats. New scholarship has shown that these theses, on which Koselleck, Habermas, and Baker built their theory, are based on misconceptions. In early modern France, even "absolutist" theorists did not assert that the monarch had the right to tax his subjects without their consent. The way the political order was conceived in France was not fundamentally different from the system in England,[23] and, contrary to what the term "absolutism" suggests, the French aristocracy consolidated its power in Versailles after 1661. Who became minister and which policy was implemented were largely decided through contests between court factions in which aristocrats played important, or even leading, roles. Ministers were always dependent on members of the royal family, royal mistresses, and the most influential princely and ducal families.[24] Through an analysis of unauthorized publications, one aim of this chapter is to contribute to this recent reevaluation of the political role of the court by examining the competition between courtiers beyond Versailles.

Second, I seek to contribute to the revision of the way we understand the public sphere in the late *ancien régime*. Not only were massive *libelle* campaigns not new in the eighteenth century,[25] but it is essential to understand that the conditions of pamphlet production had barely changed in all these decades: Very few eighteenth-century

---

23. Nicholas Henshall, *The Myth of absolutism: change and continuity in early modern European monarchy* (London, 1992).
24. Leonhard Horowski, *Die Belagerung des Thrones: Machtstrukturen und Karriere-mechanismen am Hof von Frankreich, 1661–1789* (Ostfildern, 2012); Leonhard Horowski, "Hof und Absolutismus: was bleibt von Norbert Elias' Theorie?," in *Absolutismus, ein unersetzliches Forschungskonzept?*, ed. Lothar Schilling (Munich, 2008), p.143–76.
25. I have shown elsewhere that there was a pamphlet war against Louis XIV in the 1680s and 1690s that is strangely neglected in historiography because it is wrongly ascribed to Huguenots in exile: Damien Tricoire, "Attacking the monarchy's sacrality in late seventeenth-century France: the underground literature against Louis XIV, Jansenism, and the Dauphin court faction," *French history* 31:2 (2017), p.152–73.

writers were truly independent, not even Diderot, as is shown in the first chapter of this volume.[26] There existed no author fees, so that it was impossible to live decently from one's pen. The *lieutenant général de police* was—contrary to what Baker claimed—effective in "suppressing" books when he wanted, that is when books were inimical to someone with whom he was allied or upon whom he was dependent, and were not supported by important court figures who could exert pressure on him. Protection was also essential to avoid imprisonment, or simply to gain a position in any of the *ancien régime* institutions. For these reasons, the world of the printed word was dominated by patronage networks, although these were often unstable.

Such an observation forces us to modify our understanding of the public sphere. All the models mentioned above have in common that they presuppose a dichotomy between the "state" (or the "government," "monarchy," or "court") and the opposition. Yet there was no united elite, either at court or in the city. The royal council was made up of rival aristocrats and ministers. We should stop speaking of "the monarchy," "the authorities," "royal censorship," "the police," "the government," or "the state" as if they were actors with monolithic interests or policies, which authors could oppose or criticize.[27] In the same way, we shall not suggest that there was a coherent group called "the Enlightenment *philosophes*" or "the *encyclopédistes*."[28] Writers were clients of different patrons, and, even if they belonged to the same patronage network, this in no way guaranteed that they would not be rivals. For these reasons, instead of a model assuming a dichotomy between men in power and their critics, I would like to stress the juxtaposition of vertical structures, each one having its head at the royal court. In my view, it was precisely the competition among these courtiers and factions that pushed men and women in power to search for influence through "public opinion." This is not to deny that there was a plurality of public spaces in which the various subjects of the French kings exchanged news and expressed opinions, but the impact of this autonomous public on printed works should not be

---

26. See the contribution of Andreas Pečar and Damien Tricoire in this volume.
27. See also Benjamin Marschke, *Absolutely Pietist: patronage, factionalism and state-building in the early eighteenth-century Prussian army chaplaincy* (Tübingen, 2005), p.16–18.
28. On pluralizing "Enlightenment," see J. G. A. Pocock, "Historiography and Enlightenment: a view of their history," *Modern intellectual history* 5:1 (2008), p.83–96 (83).

overestimated. Thus, we should be skeptical about Enlightenment authors presenting themselves as independent and postulating the existence of an independent "public opinion," even if it is true that this myth was powerful and forced politicians to legitimize their actions in public. The "public space" of the printed word was structured by members of the royal court in a significant way.

Third, even though this question will not really be discussed here, this chapter may be relevant for a broader reconsideration of the causes of the French Revolution. In the light of the empirical work presented here, a direct link between *libelles* and revolution appears far from evident. I have pointed out elsewhere the fact that *libelles* attacking the idea of a sacral monarchy were a much older phenomenon that appeared widely as early as the 1680s.[29] That radical pamphlets barely circulated in the 1770s and 1780s and that the vast majority of pamphlets did not put the political system into question should make us more cautious. Of course, we cannot exclude the possibility that unauthorized texts, although attacking particular individuals, created among some readers the impression that the whole political class was corrupt. However, there are numerous signs that politically informed contemporaries (who constituted precisely the readership of these texts) were much more able to ascribe pamphlets to specific courtiers than we are nowadays. Lastly, this question would need to be the matter of another article, but reconsidering unauthorized literature also means that we have to ask whether leading courtiers perhaps played a much bigger role in the outbreak of the 1789 revolt than is commonly acknowledged.

The "Mairobert corpus"

More specifically, this chapter seeks to contribute to a better understanding of a range of famous sources, widely used in political, cultural, and art history: the so-called "Mairobert corpus." This comprised not only the previously mentioned *Anecdotes sur Madame la comtesse Du Barri* (1775), one of the most famous pamphlets on the royal mistress, but also the *Journal historique de la révolution opérée par Maupeou*, published in five volumes in 1774 and 1775, a unique collection of reports on what happened during the years when Chancellor Maupeou had suppressed the *parlement* of Paris (1771–1774), followed by the two-volume *Journal historique du rétablissement de la magistrature*

---

29. Tricoire, "Attacking the monarchy's sacrality."

(1776) which related the beginning of Louis XVI's reign. In 1777, two
new serial publications were launched, *L'Observateur anglois* (10 vols.,
1777–1784) and, above all, the *Mémoires secrets de la république des
lettres* (36 vols., 1777–1789). These sources present different characteristics. The *Anecdotes* are a biography of Mme Du Barry that aims
to defame her party. *L'Observateur anglois* also has some features of
pamphlet literature; it presents the fictional letters of an Englishman
to one of his countrymen, commenting on French society and politics.
By contrast, the *Journal* and the *Mémoires* would be best termed
"retrospective journalism": They present short notices ordered day by
day, not unlike a newspaper, but treating only past events. The facts
presented are considered reliable by specialists.[30] For this reason, the
Mémoires are arguably one of the most important sources for French
intellectual history from 1762 to 1787. However, the *Mémoires* are not
only a mine where scholars find information for the history of ideas,
but also a series of texts based on the Enlightenment narrative, the
explicit goal of which is to recount the history of the "revolution of
minds" that writers brought about in previous decades. It thus gives
elements of a narrative of intellectual history, and in this sense, it is
itself an important chapter of Enlightenment history.

Notwithstanding the different genres to which these sources belong,
they have long been recognized as presenting one body of work. Two
different features indicate that these texts belong together. First, the
publisher named on the front page is the same, John Adamson, a fake
London printing house. Second, it is well established that many of the
stories told in one source also appear in one or two other texts of the
corpus, often with identical wording, although no systematic study of
this phenomenon exists.[31]

What is the reason for such unity? Scholars suspect both a
common source text and a shared author or auctorial team. It is
commonly assumed that a handwritten newspaper (*journal à la main*)

30. Cave, "Préface," p.15–16.
31. Jean Sgard, "Pidansat de Mairobert: journaliste à deux visages," in *Nouvelles,
gazettes, mémoires secrets (1775-1800)*, ed. Birgitta Berglund-Nilsson (Karlstad,
2000), p.15–26; Jean Sgard, "Les *Mémoires secrets* et l'*Observateur anglais*," in *Le
Règne de la critique*, ed. C. Cave, p.345–56; Christophe Cave, "Les *Anecdotes sur
Madame la comtesse du Barri* et les *Mémoires secrets*," in *Le Règne de la critique*, ed.
C. Cave, p.357–62; Christophe Cave and Suzanne Cornand, "Présentation
générale," in *Mémoires secrets pour servir à l'histoire de la république des lettres en
France, depuis 1762 jusqu'à nos jours*, ed. Christophe Cave and Suzanne Cornand,
5 vols. (Paris, 2009–2010), vol.1, p.xiii–lxxxviii (lxxxiii–lxxxvi).

provided some basic material, at least for the news from the years between 1762 and 1779.[32] The author(s) of the texts, and especially of the *Anecdotes*, make(s) several references to a (or several) handwritten journal(s), without giving any details. In the scholarship, the *Mémoires secrets* are considered to be based on the "journal" of the salon of Mme Doublet, but there is no real evidence.[33] The author is usually assumed to be Matthieu-François Pidansat de Mairobert, until his death in 1779, when he was succeeded by his friend Barthélémy Mouffle d'Angerville. Although the role of Mouffle in the early 1780s is supported by some evidence,[34] the significance of Doublet's salon and the role of Mairobert are far from clear. Their roles have nonetheless been asserted as quasi-certainties.[35] In any case, as I

32. In the Bibliothèque Mazarine, there is a copy of *nouvelles à la main* that seems to be the primordial source of the *Mémoires secrets* and that stops in 1779: Jeremy Popkin, "The *Mémoires secrets* and the reading of the Enlightenment," in *The Mémoires secrets and the culture of publicity in eighteenth-century France*, ed. Jeremy Popkin and Bernadette Fort (Oxford, 1998), p.9–35 (18).

33. Regarding the Doublet salon thesis, see Cave, "Préface," p.8–9. The only evidence is that the *Mémoires secrets* say that Mairobert kept the journal of Mme Doublet, and Mairobert is widely believed to be the author of this source until his death in 1779; see Popkin, "The *Mémoires secrets*," p.13–14.

34. Mouffle's leading role in the *Mémoires secrets* in the 1780s is rather well established. The police confiscated a manuscript of the *Mémoires secrets* in Mouffle d'Angerville's flat in 1781. According to the *Révolutions de Paris* (1790), Mouffle spent six weeks in the Bastille because of that, which is confirmed by archival records: Cave, "Préface," p.9–11.

35. For example in Sgard, "Pidansat de Mairobert"; Sgard, "Les *Mémoires secrets* et l'*Observateur anglais*"; Christophe Cave, "Les *Anecdotes* de Pidansat de Mairobert sur Madame du Barry," in *L'Histoire en miettes: anecdotes et temoignages dans l'écriture de l'histoire (XVIᵉ–XIXᵉ siècles)*, ed. Carole Dornier and Claudine Pouloin (Caen, 2004), p.279–98; Cave and Cornand, "Présentation générale," p.xv–xxiv. Sgard and Cave think that the attribution of the *Mémoires secrets* to Mairobert can be grounded on "Mouffle d'Angerville's testimony," i.e., on the announcement in the *Mémoires secrets* reporting Mairobert's death, which is attributed to Mouffle. However, the passages they refer to do not assert that Mairobert was the editor of the *Mémoires secrets*, only that he kept the journal of the Doublet salon and that Linguet accused him of being the author of the *Mémoires secrets*, which Mairobert contested. Sgard also contends that we can attribute *L'Observateur* to Mairobert with certainty, but does not explain on which evidence he bases this claim: Sgard, "Les *Mémoires secrets* et l'*Observateur anglais*," p.345, 354; Cave and Cornand, "Présentation générale," p.xxi–xxii. The evidence for the attribution of the corpus to Mairobert is actually thin. Mairobert may have contributed to the manuscript journal that probably constituted a basis for the *Mémoires secrets*. We also know that Mairobert left

seek to show here, the issue of authorship may be a secondary one in comparison to that of patronage, which better explains the political positions taken in the corpus.

Even if these sources clearly belong together, Popkin raises a number of issues putting into question the consistency of the corpus: The preface to the *Journal historique* asserts that the authors were "zealous magistrates" opposed to Maupeou—thus *patriotes* in the terminology of the time—whereas the foreword to the *Mémoires secrets* presents this text as a gathering of news about the progress of *philosophie*, and enhances the contributions to progress not only by *patriotes*, but also by two other groups of writers: the *encyclopédistes* and the physiocrats (*économistes*). Whereas the foreword of *L'Observateur anglois* refers to the *Journal historique*, it presents a very different ideology. Moreover, the handwritten journal held to be the basis of the corpus comments in very negative terms on the *Journal historique*, *L'Observateur anglois*, and the *Mémoires secrets*. Popkin concludes for that reason that, at least in the case of the *Mémoires secrets*, "no fixed understanding of the text is possible."[36]

In the 2000s, French literary historians discussed whether the *Mémoires secrets* were a rather neutral gathering of news, or whether there was an implicit political agenda underlying this publication. They have interpreted the *Mémoires secrets* in a way reminiscent of Koselleck, Habermas, and Darnton, that is, as a good example of subversive literature and the emergence of an independent public sphere criticizing "the authorities."[37] This research has shown that much of the polemical content explicit in the *Journal historique*, the *Anecdotes*, and *L'Observateur* is present in the *Mémoires secrets*, but only in a fragmentary and seemingly objective way.[38] Unlike Popkin,

---

his manuscripts to Mouffle: Cave, "Préface," p.9–11. Grimm's *Correspondance littéraire* attributes to Mairobert both the *Lettres de Madame Dubarry*, a book published in 1779 and very similar in content to the *Anecdotes*, and *L'Observateur anglois*, but none of this constitutes conclusive evidence. To conclude, Popkin's 1989 call for caution still seems very salutary: Popkin, "The *Mémoires secrets*."

36. Popkin, "The *Mémoires secrets*," p.12.

37. Cave, "Préface"; Cave and Cornand, "Présentation générale," p.xl; Sarah Benharrech, "Guerre des farines et dénigrement de l'autorité: l'imaginaire burlesque dans les *Mémoires secrets*," in *Le Règne de la critique*, ed. C. Cave, p.115–29; Martial Poirson, "Du spectacle de la société à la société de spectacle: la critique théâtrale dans les *Mémoires secrets*," in *Le Règne de la critique*, ed. C. Cave, p.179–204.

38. Sgard, "Les *Mémoires secrets* et l'*Observateur anglais*"; Cave, "Les *Anecdotes sur Madame la comtesse du Barri* et les *Mémoires secrets*."

at least some of these scholars argue that there is an ideological unity underlying the corpus. Christophe Cave considers not only the *Journal*—which is obvious—but also both the *Anecdotes* and the *Mémoires secrets* as supporting the *parlement*. In the case of the *Anecdotes*, he even sees in the *parlement* the true, though paradoxically absent, hero of the narrative.[39] In a similar fashion, according to Jean Sgard, the author of the corpus was a proponent of a constitutional monarchy of the British type.[40] Some articles study the way certain topics and politicians are presented in parts of the volumes of the *Mémoires secrets*. We thus know that both *L'Observateur* and the *Mémoires secrets* were inimical to Turgot,[41] that Marie-Antoinette's entourage was criticized in a volume published in 1784,[42] that volume 28 (published in 1786) did not appreciate Necker's *Administration des finances*,[43] that volume 36, published in 1789, is friendly to Necker and hostile to Loménie de La Brienne,[44] and that volumes 24 and 25, published in 1784 and 1786, attacked the duc de Chartres.[45] Scholars have also asked whether the *Mémoires secrets* were pro-Enlightenment, and have come to the conclusion that the *Mémoires* seem to hold contradictory opinions on this matter.[46]

From these first hints, it appears clearly that the *Mémoires secrets* are not a neutral source, but were presumably from one or several political perspective(s), though it remains unclear which one(s). The overall picture does not seem to be as coherent as sometimes suggested. Indeed there has been no comprehensive study of the corpus analyzing the political positioning in the different volumes, probably because of the mass of text it would be necessary to explore and its mostly fragmentary character. The aim of this chapter is

39. Christophe Cave, "Instrumentalisation politique de l'esthétique et critique de la politique-spectacle," in *Le Règne de la critique*, ed. C. Cave, p.95–114 (95–96); Cave, "Les *Anecdotes* de Pidansat de Mairobert." There is a similar thesis in Keith Michael Baker, *Inventing the French Revolution* (Cambridge, 1990), p.326 (n.13).
40. Sgard, "Les *Mémoires secrets* et l'*Observateur anglais*," p.347.
41. Sgard, "Les *Mémoires secrets* et l'*Observateur anglais*."
42. Bernadette Fort, "Esthétique et imaginaire sexuel: la femme peintre dans les salons," in *Le Règne de la critique*, ed. C. Cave, p.269–94.
43. Claude Labrosse, "Les *Mémoires secrets* et les gazettes," in *Le Règne de la critique*, ed. C. Cave, p.327–44.
44. Philip Stewart, "Critiquer la politique," in *Le Règne de la critique*, ed. C. Cave, p.83–94.
45. Olivier Ferret, "La vie privée… du duc de Chartres et les *Mémoires secrets*," in *Le Règne de la critique*, ed. C. Cave, p.397–414.
46. Stewart, "Critiquer la politique," p.83–94.

precisely to provide such a study of political positions expressed in the first years of the corpus (1774–1777), in the *Journal historique*, the *Anecdotes*, the first two volumes of *L'Observateur anglois* and the first eight volumes of the *Mémoires secrets*—a set of works published within a few years but comprising over 6000 pages.

In this chapter, I will show that, although it is true that all the texts attributed to Mairobert had a political stance, it is equally true that there was no real overall ideological coherence throughout the corpus. We cannot consider all the texts from the *Journal historique* to *L'Observateur* to be pro-*parlementaire*. Statements on politics were usually coherent within each volume, but changed sometimes sharply across the years. Here I intend to demonstrate that this phenomenon is best explained by changes of patronage. The author(s) of the corpus may have served courtiers and thus adapted their statements to their patrons' expectations. This is not to say that commercial considerations did not play any role. The *Anecdotes*, *Observateur anglois*, and *Mémoires secrets* were business ventures. However, their author(s) clearly adapted to political situations, and aligned their positions with those of mighty courtiers. My research on the corpus ascribed to Mairobert thus supports the revision of the underground literature and "bourgeois" public sphere theses. It also gives insights into probable reasons for the distinct character of the different publications, that is, why something like the *Journal historique* was published in 1774 and why the markedly different *Observateur anglois* and *Mémoires secrets* were launched three years later.

Before delving into text analysis, I would like to make three remarks about terminology and method. First, because patronage by court figures dominated the literary scene, I speak of "unauthorized," not of "underground," literature. That a book was not officially approved by royal censors does not necessarily mean that it was a counter-cultural product or critical of the politicians in power.[47] Likewise, even an officially banned text could be not only tolerated but actively supported by some leading politicians. Royal censorship or the police were frequently political instruments of court members against one another, and a prohibited book was often propagated by courtiers.[48]

---

47. For example, see the Tuscan case, per Sandro Landi, "Censure et formation de l'opinion publique dans l'Italie des Habsbourg," in *L'Opinion publique*, ed. B. Binoche and A. J. Lemaître, p.25–39.

48. The fate of Raynal's *Histoire des deux Indes* is a good example of this phenomenon. The first edition was written under the auspices of the dominant faction at

Second, I will speak from now on in this chapter not of the "Mairobert corpus," but of the "John Adamson corpus," because authorship is open to discussion. The fake publisher "John Adamson" is indeed the only visible and uncontested link between the texts of the corpus. Third, discussing the content of the corpus, I will refer to the reports not according to the date they themselves refer to—as frequently done in scholarly publications on the *Mémoires secrets*–but according to the date of their publication. Of course many reports were recycled from older publications (and perhaps from a handwritten journal), but my hypothesis is that the different volumes of the corpus did not merely reproduce older news, but rather that these were sometimes revised and in any case selected and published in order to fulfill political functions in a precise context. This is also the case of "L'observateur hollandais," a text allegedly from 1773 that the author of *L'Observateur anglois* inserted in his book published in 1777. As we will see, "L'observateur hollandais" differs greatly from the texts of the John Adamson corpus published in 1774, so it is reasonable to assume that it was at least seriously revised for its publication in 1777.[49]

Parlementaire radicalism: Conti, patriotic hero (1774–1776)

Of all the volumes published by "John Adamson," the first ones, that is the *Journal* and the *Anecdotes*, are the most pro-*parlementaire* ones. The explicit aim of the first three volumes of the *Journal historique* is to describe how Maupeou, in a coup, destroyed the legitimate constitutional order and how people reacted to that "revolution." According to the foreword of the first volume (1774), the *Journal* was penned by "zealous magistrates," and the preface to the fourth volume (1775) proclaims its aim to be the propagation of "patriotism."[50] The *Journal*

---

court, that of Choiseul. In 1772, after Choiseul's exile, it was censored by the Royal Council. The second and the third editions primarily supported Necker. Because of that, the third edition was censored by the *parlement* when Necker lost power in 1781: Damien Tricoire, "Raynal's and Diderot's patriotic history of the two Indies, or the problem of anticolonialism in the eighteenth century," *The Eighteenth century: theory and interpretation* 59:4 (2018), p.429–48. The problems Mouffle had with the police in February 1781 might be related to attacks on Necker, but this hypothesis would still need a careful evaluation.

49. Contrary to what some scholars suggest, it thus cannot be treated as a source from 1773: Sgard, "Pidansat de Mairobert," p.18.

50. *Journal historique de la révolution opérée dans la constitution de la monarchie françoise, par M. de Maupeou, chancelier de France* [from vol.6 onward: *Journal historique du*

and the *Mémoires secrets* announce in a news story dated October 26, 1772 that a "Journal politique, historique, critique et littéraire des hauts faits de M. Maupeou" will be published. If this is the same piece of writing as the work published two years later, then the project of the *Journal* was formed in the context of the return of the princes to the royal court. If this story is true, opponents of Maupeou decided then to stop publishing pamphlets and to gather material for a journal instead.[51] It is well established that, before this date, Louis Adrien Le Paige published numerous pamphlets in the clandestine press of the prince de Conti in the "enclosure of the Temple" (*enclos du Temple*), a quasi-extraterritorial enclave in Paris where approximately 4000 people lived.[52] Since early 1771, Conti, a prince of royal blood, had been exiled from court for his struggle in favor of the dissolved *parlement* and against Maupeou. By this time, he had already had a long career as a *frondeur*. In the 1750s, he had been the head of the Secret du roi, the secret service, but in 1756–1757, because he had been ousted by Mme de Pompadour, he had entered into negotiations with Protestants in southern France and the government of William Pitt the Elder to prepare an armed uprising (that ultimately never took place). Conti was also in all those years the patron of Jansenism and of the Paris *parlement*, of which he was a member as a prince of the blood. The princes de Conti had performed these two roles since the second half of the seventeenth century, independently of their personal convictions.[53]

That Conti named the jurist Le Paige *bailli* of the Temple and actively supported or commissioned the pamphlet campaign against Maupeou is thus not surprising. The author of the *Journal* ascribes

rétablissement de la magistrature], 7 vols. (London, John Adamson, 1774–1776), vol.1, foreword; *Journal*, vol.4, foreword.

51. *Journal*, vol.3, p.297–98; *Mémoires secrets pour servir a l'histoire de la republique des lettres en France: depuis MDCCLXII jusqu'a nos jours, ou Journal d'un observateur*, 36 vols. (London [Amsterdam?], John Adamson, 1777–1789), vol.24, p.207. Popkin suggests that this news announces the future *Journal*: Popkin, "The *Mémoires secrets*," p.19.

52. Rattner Gelbart, "The *Journal des dames*," p.38.

53. John Woodbridge, *Revolt in pre-revolutionary France: the prince de Conti's conspiracy against Louis XV, 1755–1757* (Baltimore, MD, 1995); Jean Haechler, *Le Prince de Conti: un cousin embarrassant* (Paris, 2007), p.263–83; Damien Tricoire, "D'une Fronde à l'autre: pouvoirs et contestations aristocratiques du Grand Condé à Philippe Egalité," in *Etat, pouvoirs et contestations dans les monarchies française et britannique et dans leurs colonies américaines*, ed. Deborah Cohen (Paris, 2018), p.4–22.

without hesitation this role to Conti, when he states that "most of the prohibited publications are printed in the Temple."[54] In particular, he sees Conti's patronage behind the *Correspondance secrète et familière du chancelier de Maupeou avec Sorhouet* (1771), a pamphlet that he praises highly and from which he excerpted several *notices*. Conti protected Le Paige, who was being sought by the new *parlement*, and arranged for his client to be cleared of all accusations.[55] However, the *libelle* campaign itself, as well as its end in late 1772, reveals that anti-Maupeou literature was not the fruit of a spontaneous reaction of public opinion, but rather an instrument in the hand of the princes. Indeed, when (almost all) the princes reconciled with Maupeou and returned to the royal court, the pamphlets, even those already announced, almost completely ceased to appear.[56] Had these publications been independent from the princes, the "traitors to the cause" would surely have been blamed in numerous brochures.

Did the *Journal* and the *Anecdotes* emanate from the Conti milieu? Interestingly, some sentences seem to betray that the author of the *Journal* lived or worked near Conti, perhaps even in the Temple. He recounts how Conti, upon the news that Louis XV was dead, probably asked Louis XVI for permission to visit the new king and express his condolences: "[Y]esterday he was still here," that is, in his Parisian residence of the Temple.[57] Above all, their content gives us more evidence that the *Journal* and the *Anecdotes* were probably written under Conti's auspices. Although both publications are inimical to Maupeou and pro-*parlementaire*, they develop a narrative that is centered not on the *parlement*, whose exiled members largely disappear from view, but on the royal court. This happens explicitly in the case of the *Anecdotes*, whose topic is the corruption of the court by the royal mistress, and implicitly in the *Journal*. In both, the exiled judges appear as victims rather than as actors. To be sure, the *remontrances* of provincial *parlements* and writings emanating from *parlementaire* circles are reported in detail in the *Journal*. However,

---

54. *Journal*, vol.3, p.281.
55. *Journal*, vol.3, p.30–31, 276; *Journal*, vol.5, p.219. The new *parlement* also suspected Conti was the instigator of this pamphlet: *Journal*, vol.3, p.271–72, 276, 278, 281; *Journal*, vol.5, p.219, 223.
56. The author of the *Journal* interprets exactly in this way the "suspension de toutes les brochures": *Journal*, vol.4, p.47.
57. *Journal*, vol.6, p.6.

the people acting on the political scene are above all members of the royal court. Most of them are the objects of attacks, besides the royal mistress and the king, especially Maupeou, Terray, Aiguillon, La Vrillière, Richelieu, and Mme Louise.

Although exiled by the king because he protected the *parlement* and opposed Maupeou and Du Barry, neither the *Journal* nor the *Anecdotes* are favorable to Choiseul. Actually, the *Journal* pays very little attention to him. In the first five volumes, he is very seldom mentioned.[58] In the part of the *Anecdotes* relating how Mme Du Barry—or rather the men whom the narrator presents as the real driving force behind her—gained power, Choiseul is not neglected, of course. However, he is not characterized in a positive way; he is described as a plotter who was only powerful because he succeeded in making the king believe that he had talent.[59]

The first three volumes of the *Journal*, published together in 1774, provide a coherent narrative: They open with Maupeou's "revolution" and recount in great detail the fight of the princes of the blood to reestablish the *parlement* and the persecutions that they had to endure.[60] The princes are termed the "leaders of the nation" ("chefs de la nation"), and the pro-*parlementaire* "patriotic" party is assimilated with the party of the princes of the blood ("parti des princes et des patriotes," "chefs patriotes").[61] The end of the narrative is also centered on the princes, but in the opposite way: It finishes with their defection in late 1772. This is no coincidence: The aim is to show how ministerial despotism succeeded in corrupting even the patriotic leaders. This narrative also makes up the main thread that runs through the *Anecdotes*, and it is made explicit in the preface of the *Lettres originales de Madame la comtesse du Barry* (1779), a recycling of the *Anecdotes* based on the model of epistolary novels. The foreword lists in a crescendo all the signs of the general corruption of the court under the influence of Mme Du Barry; the climax is a harsh accusation against the princes of the blood: "[M]oved by their

---

58. I could find only a few examples: *Journal*, vol.1, p.23; vol.2, p.373–74; vol.3, p.386–87.

59. *Anecdotes*, p.71, 93–94.

60. *Journal*, vol.1, p.83–84, 92, 99–100, 163–64, 222, 236–38, 247–48, 252, 258, 276, 294, 315; *Journal*, vol.2, p.8, 19–20, 37–38, 52, 61, 64–65, 68, 137, 149–51, 181, 189, 194–95, 215–16, 249–50, 265, 288, 301, 319–20, 332, 341–42, 344–47; *Journal*, vol.3, p.32, 42–49, 74–75, 79, 171, 188, 220–21, 224, 238–39, 328, 341, 351, 386, 392–93, 411–14.

61. *Journal*, vol.1, p.368; *Journal*, vol.3, p.171, 386.

personal interest," they "submitted to the tyrants, paid court to the favorite, abandoned the cause of the people, aided the barbarian ministers in their despotic endeavors, and shared with them what remained of the state."[62]

Thus, the story told is that of the moral fall of the princes. In the *Journal* and the *Anecdotes*, the prince de Condé and his son the prince de Bourbon are accused of having sold out to Maupeou, who promised to try his best to convince the king to marry his son Artois with Mademoiselle, Condé's daughter. The author denounces Condé's weakness, moved as he was by ambition. Condé then formed a "triumvirate" with the prince de La Marche (Conti's son, who supported Maupeou from the start of the "revolution") and the prince de Soubise, and thus shared the most important royal offices with the Du Barry clan.[63] Like Condé, the duc d'Orléans, the first prince of the blood and for this reason the natural leader of the opposition against Maupeou, Terray, and Aiguillon in 1771 and 1772, is also denounced as an "extremely weak man" who placed his love for his mistress, Mme de Montesson, above the interests of the nation. According to the *Journal* and the *Anecdotes*, he agreed to submit to royal authority in order to obtain the authorization to marry her. Although the *Journal* tells the story of how, unlike Condé, he was still lobbying for the dissolved *parlement* and refused to recognize the new one, he abased himself before the royal mistress. His dishonor is symbolized by the king and Mme Du Barry patting his paunch and calling him "gros père."[64] The duc de Chartres, Orléans's son (and future Philippe Egalité), plays a more positive role in the narrative. Whereas Orléans is presented as hesitating already in 1771, Chartres showed a strong commitment to the "patriotic" cause. He insults Condé for having been bought by Maupeou and Terray, and he is celebrated by all true patriots. However, in the story told by the *Journal*, after his submission to the king, he also departs from this honorable behavior and flirts ("folâtre") with Mme Du Barry.[65]

62. *Lettres originales de Madame la comtesse du Barry, avec celles des princes, seigneurs, ministres et autres qui lui ont écrit, et qu'on a pu recueillir* (London, John Adamson, 1779), foreword, unpaginated. All translations are my own unless otherwise stated.

63. *Journal*, vol.3, p.341–42, 382–84, 390; *Journal*, vol.4, p.10, 285; *Anecdotes*, p.297–98.

64. *Journal*, vol.3, p.341, 411; *Journal*, vol.4, p.18, 27, 38, 40, 50–51, 61, 284; *Journal*, vol.5, p.37, 285; *Journal*, vol.6, p.99; *Anecdotes*, p.265–66, 281–82, 292–93.

65. *Journal*, vol.2, p.301–302; *Journal*, vol.3, p.113–14, 121–22, 125, 414.

In the midst of this generalized corruption, there is one exception: In the *Journal*, the prince de Conti categorically refuses all compromise.[66] Conti appears as genuinely humble and connected to the common people. He would stroll along the boulevards on foot, chatting colloquially with the average Parisian. In the eyes of the "patriots," he is considered "glorious."[67] To be sure, Conti is almost entirely absent from the *Anecdotes*, but this may have to do with the fact that this pamphlet aimed to denounce the corruption of the court under Mme Du Barry, not to celebrate patriotism. By contrast, in volume 6 of the *Journal* (1776), that is the first of two volumes relating how the *parlement* was restored at the beginning of Louis XVI's reign, Conti appears as a real patriotic hero, indeed the only one. He is shown to be adored and acclaimed by Parisians, a situation to which he reacts with great modesty.[68] The author very much approves of these marks of gratitude displayed by the people as Conti is, under his pen, "the firmest support of the rights of the nation."[69] The author cites without comment a vaudeville entitled "Commands of Henry IV to his grandson Louis XVI": "You shall consult the valiant Conti / He is the only one to act dutifully."[70] Conti is also shown weeping because of the death of his *chef de conseil*, which "does infinite honor to the sensibility of the prince, and makes him even dearer than ever to the nation."[71]

On November 13, 1774, Louis XVI held a *lit de justice* in which he announced his will to restore the *parlement* suppressed by his predecessor. But the edicts he summoned the Maupeou *parlement* to register comprised several decisions that must have dissatisfied the "patriotic party": Louis XVI established a more hierarchical organization enabling the monarchy to have better control of the institution, declared legal the suppression of the *parlement* by Louis XV, did not automatically accept all former members in the new *parlement*, and maintained the court of justice created by Maupeou, transformed into a Grand Conseil. The *Journal* clearly condemns these measures, asserting that "the spirit of Maupeou is wholly present in them."[72]

66. *Journal*, vol.4, p.57; *Journal*, vol.5, p.62.
67. *Journal*, vol.4, p.213; *Journal*, vol.5, p.62.
68. *Journal*, vol.6, p.185, 343–44.
69. *Journal*, vol.6, p.343–44.
70. *Journal*, vol.6, p.74.
71. *Journal*, vol.6, p.82–83.
72. *Journal*, vol.6, p.314–20 (317).

Accordingly, the foreword of volume 6 announces that the "spirit of despotism" is still alive and requests that the young king annihilate it.[73]

Because the restoration of the *parlement* was still imperfect, the *Journal* does not end at this point, but continues to relate the history of the struggle for the full reestablishment of the "ancient constitution." Volume 6 ends with a scene revealing the implicit principle of the narrative developed since the very first volume: In December 1774, the princes and peers of the realm assembled to discuss how to react to the royal edicts of the preceding month, and Conti wins the vast majority for his "patriotic" agenda. The author states that Orléans pleaded for the adoption of a *remontrance* in favor of the complete restoration of the old *parlement* and the suppression of Maupeou's *parlement*. Only Conti's vigorous and profound intervention convinced "all the voters" ("tous les suffrages"), so that the assembly indeed decided to make *remontrances* to the king for the restoration of the *parlement*.[74] Again, Conti appears as the leading patriot, refusing to make any compromise, a position that he indeed reiterated and developed in the following months.[75]

An exploration of the narrative underlying the selection and presentation of seemingly objective news shows that volumes 1 to 6 of the *Journal* and the *Anecdotes* may indeed have been indirectly a reaction to the return of Condé, Bourbon, Orléans, and Chartres to the royal court in late 1772, which Conti's party considered a defection. It is worth noting that the *Journal* was not published right after the return of the princes to the court, when Conti was isolated and his ability to influence the king strongly reduced. The first three volumes of the *Journal* were published around mid-December 1774, that is a few weeks after the restoration of the *parlement* and a few days before or after the assembly of the princes and peers mentioned above.[76] The *Journal* and the *Anecdotes* may thus have been instruments in the political contest between princes of the blood. In these months, indeed, Orléans's strategy could be considered the most effective one for the "patriotic cause." Even if he had negotiated

---

73. *Journal*, vol.6, p.iii–iv.
74. *Journal*, vol.6, p.376–80.
75. Haechler, *Conti*, p.282–83.
76. In the *Mémoires secrets*, the news about the publication of the *Journal* bears the date of December 17, 1774: *Mémoires secrets*, vol.7, p.285–86. The *Journal* itself reports this news; the news dated March 28, 1775 states that the *Journal* was making its first appearance "for several weeks," *Journal*, vol.7, p.229.

with the king, Orléans had never accepted that his return to court would mean that he accepted the new *parlement*. On the contrary, he had claimed to continue leading the struggle for the restoration of the legitimate *parlement*, but now from within the court. With the accession of Louis XVI to the throne, this strategy seemed to pay off. Orléans was much more influential than Conti, not only because he was the first prince of the blood, but also precisely because he was part of the entourage of the new king, contrary to Conti, who was still "in exile."[77] He could thus claim to be the leader of the "patriotic party" with good reason. The *Anecdotes* and the *Journal*'s main function may have been to present another interpretation: According to these writings, Orléans, and to a lesser extent his son Chartres, had been bought by the "triumvirate" Maupeou–Terray–Aiguillon, and the only real patriot was Conti. He was the real leader of the "patriots."

Political moderation: the good government of Maurepas and Turgot (1776)

That Conti is the protagonist of volumes 1 to 6 of the *Journal* and of the *Anecdotes* has been overlooked by scholarship under the influence of the "public sphere" and "underground literature" theses, but is still consistent with the interpretation of the John Adamson corpus as an ensemble of vehemently pro-*parlementaire* writings. It is all the more striking that the political position expressed by the author(s) changes markedly between the sixth and the seventh volume of the *Journal*, both published in early 1776. This appears clearly in the way the author writes about the process leading to the restoration of the *parlement*, the main topic. In his description of the assembly of the princes and the peers of December 30, 1774, he disapproves of the fact that Conti convinced "the majority" of the princes and dukes ("la pluralité"). According to him, Conti's intervention "lacked clarity, exactitude, and order," and showed "the abstract way of thinking" ("génie abstrait") of this prince.[78] In a *notice* published under the date of January 3, 1775, he returns to this assembly and regrets that "the declaration of the prince de Conti, still shapeless, unclear, and full

---

77. The *Journal* does mention Orléans's efforts in favor of the restoration of the *parlement* in 1774, but it suggests that his "extreme feebleness" prevented him from being efficient: *Journal*, vol.6, p.99, 101, 108, 116, 130, 213, 314.
78. *Journal*, vol.7, p.3.

of savage expressions, has been adopted."[79] What the author seems to fault here is exactly what he praised in the preceding volume: the tendency of Conti to stick to abstract principles, that is to the fundamental rights of the nation, his consequent refusal to make compromises, and his tendency to revert to vehement words. In the narrative of the January *parlement* session, the author displays a similar distance to Conti. He attributes the success of Conti's resolution not to its intrinsic qualities, but to the fact that the assembly "believed" it had to respect Conti's position.[80] In the rest of the volume (relating the events until April 1775), Conti plays only a minor role, and the issue of the *parlement* is only one topic among others. Strangely, the author's pro-*parlementaire* fervor seems strongly diminished.

Conti is not the only court member whose image changes between the sixth and the seventh volume. Whereas the king and the queen are ambivalent figures in volume 6, they are clearly positive, though scarcely present, figures in the next one. To be sure, volume 6 underlines in the news from spring 1774—that is the first weeks of the new reign—that Louis XVI rejected luxury and expensive representation, had an open ear to dissenting advice, was against ministerial maladministration, intrigues, and the surveillance of his subjects.[81] The author underlines that several anecdotes "herald that our young monarch is a friend of order, justice, and decency."[82] However, the news from June 26 onward presents a different image; the author denies that Louis XVI reduced expenses for representation, and portrays him as a weak monarch, paving the way for anarchy, like Louis XV. For her part, the queen appears rather ridiculous in volume 6. Furthermore, this volume relates an anecdote that neither the king nor the queen was popular in the capital city, and that they were not received decently by the Parisian people.[83] In the news about the restoration of the *parlement*, the king again had a positive image.[84] All in all, this back and forth between positive and negative features is confusing. By contrast, in volume 7, things are clear: Louis XVI is praised, though he is rather absent, like Marie-Antoinette.[85]

79. *Journal*, vol.7, p.9–10.
80. *Journal*, vol.7, p.70.
81. *Journal*, vol.6, p.7, 11, 18, 22–23, 28, 32–33.
82. *Journal*, vol.6, p.69.
83. *Journal*, vol.6, p.29–30, 34, 77–78, 100, 125–26.
84. *Journal*, vol.6, p.301.
85. *Journal*, vol.7, p.280–81.

More striking is the change in the image of the comte de Provence, the oldest of the king's two brothers. Provence was one of the main opponents to the restoration of the *parlements* in 1774, and volume 6 does not fail to explain this in great detail. However, after the partial restoration of the *parlements*, he supported the moderate line of the government. Although he was at odds with a "patriotic" line, volume 7 of the *Journal* has very kind words for him and praises the speech he held in the *parlement* at the beginning of January 1775, an additional sign of the *Journal*'s new distance from *parlementaire* radicalism.[86] Agents sent by the king to secure support for his policy from the provincial estates, like the duc de Penthièvre (and his daughter-in-law, the princesse de Lamballe), also receive their share of praise.[87] By contrast, Chartres, though one of the most important proponents of a restoration of the *parlement* in the shape it had before Maupeou, disappears almost entirely in volume 7.

All this suggests that the *Journal* suddenly began to support the dominant faction in the French government with the publication of volume 7. And indeed, all major figures of the Maurepas government are portrayed implicitly or explicitly in a positive way in this volume. Whereas Maurepas's access to power was considered a dubious thing in volume 6, and Maurepas himself was criticized for his want of energy,[88] in volume 7 the author expresses the greatest concern when the main minister is ill, and defends him with strong words against "bitter and unjust" criticism, "all too audacious calumnies," and "bitter and punishable satire" stemming from an "infernal imagination."[89] He underlines the "legitimacy of his projects," even if he criticizes Maurepas for still not having put them fully into effect. He justifies his removal of hostile ministers from power.[90] Chancellor Miromesnil is presented as an "austere magistrate" who rejected sharply all who fawned upon him.[91] Malesherbes—who as an important figure of the opposition to Maupeou was already a positive figure in the preceding volumes—is now praised less for his patriotic fervor than for his "spirit

86. *Journal*, vol.6, p.89, 281–98, 376; *Journal*, vol.7, p.9–10.
87. *Journal*, vol.7, p.12, 17–20, 44, 69.
88. The author thinks that Mme Adélaïde, and perhaps Aiguillon, had Maurepas named prime minister. Marie-Adélaïde de France was an aunt of Louis XVI, and an adversary of the *parlement* and the pro-*parlementaire* princes of the blood: *Journal*, vol.6, p.95, 99, 107–108; vol.7, p.29. On Maurepas: *Journal*, vol.6, p.55.
89. *Journal*, vol.7, p.265–66.
90. *Journal*, vol.7, p.33–34, 261, 274–75.
91. *Journal*, vol.7, p.60.

of peace and concord," that is his policy of a "general amnesty" for all judges who supported Maupeou's reforms.[92]

The government member who is by far the most prominent in volume 7, and who receives the most praise, is Anne-Robert Turgot. In volume 6, he plays a rather ambiguous role. Two thirds of the volume describe him quite negatively. He is considered a "supporter of royal authority, although a member of the *parlement*,"[93] which was surely not meant as a positive attribute. The author relates how, named a *contrôleur général des finances*, Turgot is lectured by the first president of the *chambre des comptes* about the danger of "systematic spirit" ("esprit de système"), a typical reproach against physiocrats. The author does not take sides, but shows how the first president received more applause than the finance minister. Some of Turgot's decisions are also criticized.[94] However, in the news about September 1774 onward (i.e., in the last third of volume 6), Turgot is highly praised in the *Journal*. His grain policy is considered beneficial to France, and he is himself "a wise minister who seems to work only for the utility of all."[95] This new support for Turgot becomes stronger in volume 7. It is probably not exaggerated to say that Turgot is the principal protagonist of this volume. The author relates his reform projects in detail, describes how the finance minister had recourse to the expertise of enlightened men, and how he was criticized by corrupt and deluded groups like tax farmers and fanatic churchmen. He comments on panegyrics to Turgot's glory, saying that such praise is not exaggerated, and himself cites encomiastic verses.[96]

Lastly, in most editions, volume 7 is remarkable for what it does *not* tell. The volume ends abruptly in April 1775. While the first three volumes ended with the return of the princes to the royal court, and the next two ended with the death of Louis XV, that is, they presented coherent narratives with a beginning and an end, the *Journal du rétablissement* seems not to have any real end at all. Of course, this could be due to chance. But there might be a political reason behind this choice to stop the news in April 1775; the author might have wanted to avoid the most delicate task of reporting about the "flour

---

92. *Journal*, vol.7, p.361–64, 422; *Journal*, vol.7, p.47, 97, 132, 150, 274–75.
93. *Journal*, vol.6, p.123.
94. *Journal*, vol.6, p.184, 194.
95. *Journal*, vol.6, p.195, 220, 223.
96. *Journal*, vol.7, p.34–35, 39, 41, 46, 75–77, 108, 112–13, 127, 130–31, 145–46, 161, 174, 178, 220, 227.

war," that is the riots triggered by the rise of the price of bread. Indeed, the most important of Turgot's reforms was the liberalization of the grain trade, supposed to bring an increase in production, better supply, and thus lower prices in the long run. The price increase in spring 1775 was commonly interpreted as a consequence of Turgot's reform, which was thought to have encouraged speculation. Stopping abruptly in April 1775, the narrative ends without questioning that France was destined for a great future thanks to Turgot's reforms.[97]

How can such a sudden and remarkable turn toward supporting the Maurepas government and his moderate policy be explained? The remarkable change in the way Turgot is described, which occurs in the last third of volume 6, could have had two different causes, both compatible with the hypothesis that patronage shaped the content of the *Journal*. One possibility is that the *Journal* here reproduces *notices* from a *journal à la main* contemporaneous to the events described. In this case, the author started to write positively about Turgot shortly after the physiocrats' rise to power in August 1774. Another possibility is that the *notices* published in the *Journal* were selected and rewritten in order to fit the situation at the time of publication (sometime in 1776). In my view, this second explanation is more probable. To understand what may have happened, it is critical to remember that Conti became seriously ill in autumn 1775 and died in August 1776.[98] Confronted with the probable loss of his patron in the near future, the author of the *Journal* had to reorient himself. Conti had no heir willing to follow in his footsteps, because his son La Marche had always been radically opposed to the *frondeur* policy of his father. Furthermore, the Temple was given to the duc d'Angoulême, that is the newborn son of the duc d'Artois, Louis XVI's second brother, who was not a friend of radical literature. The logical step was thus for the authors of the *Journal* to turn to the government for support before the death of Conti would leave them without protection from the court.

Turgot and the physiocrats had the task of educating the French to receive willingly the benefits of what they thought of as the natural and

---

97. There is an edition of volume 7 of the *Journal* that contains a report on the *guerre des farines*; see Göttingen University Library, sig. Hist. Gall. un. III/6431. This report is very ambivalent toward Turgot. Most probably, it was added to the *Journal* after the publication of the edition commented upon here. It thus may be a sign of distancing from Turgot after his fall in May 1776. I thank Jeremy Popkin for this information.

98. Haechler, *Conti*, p.285–89; *Mémoires secrets*, vol.8, p.259, 268.

eternal principles of a well-ordered policy. Not only were they the first systematic theorists of "public opinion," but they also made numerous efforts to influence it.[99] The *Journal* may have been a valuable addition to their array of journalistic instruments. This may explain why the author of the *Journal* changed the way he wrote about Turgot in the middle of volume 6, while still praising Conti (who was probably still alive), whereas in volume 7, probably published somewhat later in the same year, he distanced himself from Conti and wholly supported Maurepas and Turgot.

Philosophical struggles: Necker against Turgot (1777)

The change of political position in the John Adamson corpus between the beginning of 1776 (i.e., the last volume of the *Journal*) and 1777 (i.e., the first volumes of *L'Observateur anglois* and the *Mémoires secrets*) in my view suggests that the author was dependent on the patronage of leading court figures. In the following section, I will first analyze the content of *L'Observateur* before turning to the somewhat more complex case of the *Mémoires*.

A comparison between the political positions taken in the seventh volume of the *Journal* and those taken in first two volumes of *L'Observateur* reveals a range of striking differences. To be sure, *L'Observateur* shares some characteristics with all texts of the corpus: It is anti-clerical (in particular hostile to Mme Louise, a sanctimonious aunt of Louis XVI who became a Carmelite), opposed to the "triumvirate" composed of Maupeou, Terray, and Aiguillon, and distanced from Choiseul.[100] However, it now holds a totally different opinion of the *parlements*, quite the opposite of the "patriotic" ideas defended in the first six volumes of the *Journal* and the *Anecdotes*, but also markedly different from the ideas expressed in the seventh volume of the *Journal*. According to *L'Observateur*, the *parlement* was originally a mere court of justice, but the judges usurped more and more authority over time. They supplanted the *Grands* of the realm, marginalized the provincial estates, and helped the kings to get rid of the estates general. The author makes clear that the judges are

99. Gunn, *Queen of the world*, p.246–81; Joël Félix, "L'économie politique et la naissance de l'opinion publique," in *L'Opinion publique*, ed. B. Binoche and A. J. Lemaître, p.87–104 (91–103).

100. *L'Observateur anglois, ou Correspondance secrete entre milord All'eye et milord Alle'ar*, 10 vols. (London [Amsterdam], John Adamson, 1777–1784), vol.1, p.69, 77, 171.

only members of the Third Estate, and their assembly can in no way
pretend to have legitimacy to play the role of the estates general,
that is to participate in legislative power. This theory does not mean
that the author endorses Maupeou's reforms; he still approves of the
restoration of the *parlements*. Rather, the suppression of the *parlement*
in 1771 appears in this perspective as the last step in a long process of
subjugation of the realm, a process in which the *parlement* itself played
a negative role.[101]

On a range of topics, *L'Observateur* is also more radical, even than
the *Anecdotes*, and provides a great contrast to the text published one
year earlier. It attacks the *ducs et pairs* as a group, thinking that their
superior rank is unjustified. It holds that, among them, only four are
"remarkable" in a positive way: the duc de Nivernais for his literary
quality, the duc de Duras and duc de Beauvau for their fidelity to their
friend Choiseul during the "Maupeou revolution," and, above all, the
duc de La Rochefoucauld, more strongly praised for his "intrepid
patriotism."[102] *L'Observateur* denounces the luxury, sluggishness, and
slavish character of the nobility, and its lack of sense of military honor
and patriotism.[103] It attacks the clergy more violently than any text of
the corpus, and praises "modern philosophy" for having opened the
eyes of the public in church and religious matters.[104] It also develops a
devastating critique of municipal authorities and "financiers."[105]

Another major difference between the seventh volume of the
Journal and the first two volumes of *L'Observateur* lies in their opposite
appraisal of the Maurepas government. If Malesherbes is still strongly
praised,[106] Maurepas, Miromesnil, and Penthièvre are now presented
as spineless politicians lacking energy and courage.[107] Above all,
Turgot and the "sect of the economists," that is the physiocrats,
are heavily criticized. Unlike the seventh volume of the *Journal*,
L'Observateur deals with the "flour war" and does it in a clearly
polemic way. According to *L'Observateur*, the responsibility for the
riots of spring 1775 is entirely Turgot's. The "futile" Maurepas had
appointed a finance minister who loved novelties and introduced

101. *L'Observateur*, vol.1, p.102–106.
102. *L'Observateur*, vol.1, p.172.
103. *L'Observateur*, vol.1, p.172–79.
104. *L'Observateur*, vol.1, p.183–230; *L'Observateur*, vol.2, p.17–58, 301–307.
105. *L'Observateur*, vol.1, p.230–39, 245–58.
106. *L'Observateur*, vol.2, p.10–15.
107. *L'Observateur*, vol.1, p.161, 279–80; *L'Observateur*, vol.2, p.259–60.

reforms following a dogmatic system. He now reaped the fruits of this lack of prudence. Whereas he had praised Turgot for his readiness to engage in fair public discussions in the preceding volume, the author now accuses Turgot of persecuting writers who take positions against him, even locking up some of them in the Bastille. While the conflict between Turgot and the tax farmers was considered in the last volume of the *Journal* to have done great honor to the finance minister, the physiocratic publications against tax farmers are now condemned as a tactical error.[108] Jean Devaines, a physiocrat and one of Turgot's closest collaborators, is also very violently attacked in *L'Observateur*.[109]

Are the differences between the last volume of the *Journal* and the two first volumes of *L'Observateur* due to a difference in literary genres? *L'Observateur* is not a gathering of news that pretends to be neutral; it is a pamphlet, or rather a series of pamphlets. However, underlining the difference in genre does not explain much: The question remains as to why the author of the John Adamson corpus chose to publish a rather vociferous *libelle* in 1777.

To understand this, it is important to have a closer look at the courtiers whom *L'Observateur* does not criticize, but rather praises. Indeed, it would be wrong to interpret *L'Observateur* as an example of the "underground literature" attacking the whole system, because some leading political figures are portrayed in a positive light. It is remarkable that, although the late Louis XV is violently attacked, the reigning king and queen are celebrated.[110] Provence and Artois are presented in a neutral way, as is Chartres. They seem largely apolitical figures.[111] Whereas Orléans is reproached anew for his feebleness,[112] Conti and his mother—who were dead when *L'Observateur* was published—are praised for their freedom of thought, their rejection of sanctimoniousness, and their decorum. Conti is characterized by his "intrepid patriotism," which compensates for his faults, that is his immoderate taste for prostitutes and good food and drink. The author attests to his "restless character" ("génie remuant") which was useful for patriotism during the "Maupeou revolution."[113]

---

108. *L'Observateur*, vol.1, p.279–80, 300–303.
109. *Journal*, vol.6, p.187; *L'Observateur*, vol.2, p.190–200.
110. In "L'observateur hollandais," the first part of *L'Observateur*, and a text supposed to have been written in 1773, under the title "Dauphin" and "Dauphine." *L'Observateur*, vol.1, p.35–44.
111. *L'Observateur*, vol.1, p.44–47, 144; *L'Observateur*, vol.2, p.134, 161–63.
112. *L'Observateur*, vol.1, p.139–43.
113. *L'Observateur*, vol.1, p.154–56.

Nonetheless, *L'Observateur* accuses Conti of having been won over by the maréchal-duc de Richelieu in his trial with the présidente de Saint-Vincent, who accused him of rape.[114]

Besides the aforementioned La Rochefoucauld, who is praised twice (though briefly),[115] one political figure is highly acclaimed: Jacques Necker. This Genevan banker is conspicuously absent from all texts of the John Adamson corpus before 1777. In the part of *L'Observateur* that was supposed to have been written in 1773, Necker is termed "the most eminent man [of the merchant estate], who unites theory with practice, and who has all the qualities of the merchant, the politician, and the man of letters."[116] He is credited for having "almost single-handedly" led the Compagnie des Indes to its rebirth and stopped the sinister plans of bad ministers.[117] He is also praised for having published a eulogy of Colbert, in which he defends Louis XIV's finance minister against physiocratic attacks. The author of *L'Observateur* also admires how Necker criticized the finance minister (Terray) indirectly and subtly through his praise of Colbert.[118] It is also said that Turgot persecuted Necker for his book on the legislation regarding the grain trade.[119]

In my view, these admittedly rather short passages are the key to understanding the political positions taken by *L'Observateur* in 1777. Most probably, the author of the John Adamson corpus changed his patron between the publication of the seventh volume of the *Journal* and the first of *L'Observateur*. Necker was indeed Turgot's main rival. He was opposed to the liberalization of agriculture. He was rather neutral on the question of the place of the *parlements* in the French constitution, which might account for the strange mix of pro-*parlement* ideas and strong criticisms of the *parlements* in *L'Observateur*. Necker was favored by Marie-Antoinette, so that the praise for the queen was convergent with his interests. He was clearly not a client of Maurepas.

Why would the author(s) have changed sides in the conflict between Turgot and Necker? The most probable reason is quite simple: In 1777, Turgot was not in power anymore; he had been replaced by none other than Necker. The John Adamson corpus, far from being

---

114. *L'Observateur*, vol.2, p.103.
115. *L'Observateur*, vol.1, p.172; *L'Observateur*, vol.2, p.103–104.
116. *L'Observateur*, vol.1, p.242.
117. *L'Observateur*, vol.1, p.242.
118. *L'Observateur*, vol.1, p.242–43.
119. *L'Observateur*, vol.1, p.300–302.

"underground literature," simply stayed in the orbit of the finance minister, but the person occupying that post had changed.[120]

Necker's patronage might also account for another change in the John Adamson corpus: It became more clearly "philosophical." To be sure, the texts of the corpus had had a positive view of *philosophie* since the first three volumes of the *Journal*. According to the author, the progress of *philosophie* had revealed the despotic character of the principles put forward by Maupeou and his friends. For this reason, he praises Raynal's *Histoire des deux Indes* (while judging that the strong philosophical digressions are not penned by Raynal, which is correct), Georg Jonathan von Holland's refutation of Holbach's *Système de la nature*, and Helvétius's *De l'homme*.[121] The author of the *Journal* underlines the "fondness" of the *encyclopédistes* for the "patriotic party" and defends them against accusations that they insult God in their writings.[122] However, it becomes clear that he writes positively about the *philosophes* only as long as they endorse "patriotism." For this reason, Voltaire is harshly criticized as an opportunist in the *Journal* and the *Anecdotes*.[123] The first six volumes of the *Journal* and the *Anecdotes* also criticize the clergy (and Mme Louise), but above all because they support "despotism" and are against the *parlement*. The *Journal*'s hostility to Jesuits is also more *parlementaire* than "philosophical."[124] Volume 7 of the *Journal* seems to put more emphasis on *philosophie* as such, which is consistent with Turgot's role as a *philosophe* and *encyclopédiste*. For example, it holds that Devaines's virtue as a *premier commis* of the finance ministry is guaranteed by his being a *philosophe*. He underlines that Turgot and the *intendant des Bâtiments du roi* d'Angivilliers were also proponents

120. To be sure, the possibility cannot be excluded that the author was sincerely disappointed by Turgot, especially after the "flour war" of spring 1775. This would mean that he published *notices* about Turgot in 1776 that did not correspond to his own views anymore, but were a mere reproduction of old *notices*, probably from a *journal à la main*. This hypothesis seems to me less convincing, however, because other changes of political position in the "John Adamson corpus" seem to be reactions to the situation of the author at the time of publication, not at the time on which the *notices* comment. There is thus evidence that the author of the *Journal* did not merely reproduce older *notices*, but selected and adapted them to fit the current situation.

121. *Journal*, vol.1, p.365; *Journal*, vol.3, p.125–26; *Journal*, vol.4, p.36–37, 41–45; *Journal*, vol.5, p.115–16.

122. *Journal*, vol.4, p.20.

123. *Anecdotes*, p.114; *Journal*, vol.5, p.289; *Journal*, vol.6, p.58, 211.

124. *Journal*, vol.6, p.95, 105–106, 132, 304.

of this philosophical school, which had been the victim of calumnies under Louis XV.[125] Furthermore, the author does not appreciate the clergy's opposition to Turgot's financial reforms.[126]

Even if the seventh volume of the *Journal* endorses *philosophie* under the physiocrats' influence, *L'Observateur* develops a much more substantial critique of established social hierarchies. It criticizes the high nobility and asserts that the clergy should not have any temporal power. Above all, religious and church matters are some of the main topics in *L'Observateur*. It develops a real satire of the French clergy, attacking *ad nominem* a range of prelates. According to *L'Observateur*, almost all clergymen are ignorant and do not show any zeal for religion. Interestingly, *L'Observateur* is not favorable to Jansenists either. Through a long narrative ridiculing a provincial priest, it suggests that sexual abstinence provokes psychological and social pathologies—one of Diderot's favorite topics. It holds that *philosophie* has opened the eyes of the people on religion and church matters. All this is closer to Diderot and Voltaire, who is praised for his struggle against superstition and the church, than to the *parlementaire* anti-clericalism present in the first volumes of the *Journal*. Furthermore, *L'Observateur* equates "la France littéraire" with the *encyclopédistes*, judging implicitly that almost no other author can pretend to the title of "man of letters," and relates again the struggle of the clergy against Raynal's *Histoire des deux Indes*.[127]

Again, these discursive changes can be explained by the hypothesis of Necker's patronage. The Genevan banker, as someone of low rank and a Protestant, was an outsider in the traditional court elites. To establish his legitimacy as a politician, he resorted to *philosophie* and the *opinion publique*: He both wrote himself and patronized renowned *philosophes* like Diderot and Raynal.[128] This does not mean that the author of *L'Observateur* appreciated colleagues like Raynal and Diderot personally (after all, they might have competed for the favor of the same patron), but surely he did endorse the general orientation of Necker's literary policy.

125. *Journal*, vol.7, p.187–88.
126. *Journal*, vol.7, p.174.
127. *L'Observateur*, vol.1, p.183–230 ("la France littéraire," p.207); *L'Observateur*, vol.2, p.17–58, 301–307.
128. Gunn, *Queen of the world*, p.315–28; Swann, "Ministres et opinion publique," p.56–58; Félix, "L'économie politique," p.104–105; Tricoire, "Raynal's and Diderot's patriotic history." See also the contribution of Andreas Pečar and Damien Tricoire in this volume.

The *Mémoires secrets* as a partisan work

Does the fact that *L'Observateur* was supporting Necker help to understand better the *Mémoires secrets*, whose first eight volumes were also published in 1777? To explain the genesis of the *Mémoires secrets* and the underlying political project, a close look both at the explicit program contained in the foreword and at the implicit principles of news selection and comment is necessary. The preface explains the goal of the *Mémoires secrets*: retracing the history of "the invasion of the republic of letters by *philosophie*."[129] It defines three groups of authors who contributed to this "invasion": the *encyclopédistes*, the *économistes*, and the *patriotes*. It is striking that these three groups are precisely those that the author of the John Adamson corpus successively supported, only in the reverse chronological order. The author does not write here about rivalries or tensions between all these supporters of *philosophie*, and he does not give preference to one philosophical stream over another. The foreword of the *Mémoires secrets* thus announces a comprehensive and rather neutral gathering of news about these groups.

However, it is only seemingly neutral. Like *L'Observateur*, the *Mémoires* are largely hostile to the second stream mentioned above, physiocracy. To be sure, one news story from volume 7 of the *Journal*, which judges that the praise of Turgot contained in a panegyrical poem is not exaggerated, is reproduced, as is in another news story the emphasis that Turgot has good intentions.[130] By contrast, the *Mémoires* attack major physiocrats: Lemercier de La Rivière is criticized for having created a despotic political theory, the abbé Baudeau is ridiculed for writing fake answers to his own publications, Joseph d'Albert (also a close friend of Turgot) is attacked for his opportunism, and Devaines is—like in *L'Observateur*—presented as corrupt. Again like in *L'Observateur*, Turgot himself is held responsible for the riots of the "flour war."[131] As in *L'Observateur*, this critique of the *économistes* goes hand in hand with praise of their enemy, Necker. The *Mémoires* even shower Necker's writings with praise: his eulogy of Colbert, his treaty *Sur la législation des grains*,

---

129. *Mémoires secrets*, vol.1, p.v.

130. On the poem: *Journal*, vol.7, p.39; *Mémoires secrets*, vol.7, p.302. On Turgot's intentions: *Mémoires secrets*, vol.8, p.177.

131. *Mémoires secrets*, vol.3, p.242–43; *Mémoires secrets*, vol.4, p.63; *Mémoires secrets*, vol.8, p.29–36, 54–55, 62.

and his polemics against the physiocrat Morellet. The *Mémoires* criticize Condorcet's polemical answer to Necker as unworthy and Baudeau's as dreadfully boring. The publication of the *Lettre d'un fermier de Champagne*, a pamphlet against Necker that the author of the *Mémoires* attributes to Voltaire, is interpreted as a sign that Necker's enemies have no real arguments and must have recourse to persiflage. Voltaire is also criticized for having taken Morellet's side, while a text attributed to Lauraguais that attacks Morellet and defends Necker is highly praised.[132]

As numerous news stories were recycled, the *Mémoires* bear the imprint of the whole history of the John Adamson corpus. However, there is good reason to think that the news stories were selected to support, or at least not contradict, Necker's agenda. Thus, though dozens of news reports were taken over from the *Journal*, in my view it cannot be said that the *Mémoires* are clearly pro-*parlementaire*. *Parlements* are criticized for censuring philosophical books and sticking to old prejudices[133]—a line of criticism wholly absent from the *Journal*. The pro-*parlementaire Correspondance secrète de Maupeou*, which was very much praised and copiously cited in the *Journal*, is now characterized by its "wickedness" ("méchanceté").[134] All in all, the image is rather ambivalent, as it also was in *L'Observateur* and as was Necker's relationship to the *parlement*.

The description of the members of the royal family and well-known aristocrats in the *Mémoires* is similar to that of *L'Observateur*. Of Marie-Antoinette, it is said that she inspires strong respect and tenderness in anyone who has seen her.[135] Provence, Artois, and Chartres are presented in an apolitical way: The first is mentioned above all for loving his wife, the other two for being bons vivants and libertine.[136] Choiseul's image is as ambivalent as in *L'Observateur*, and indeed as in the rest of the John Adamson corpus; as in *L'Observateur*, Beauvau is praised for his fidelity to Choiseul, and Nivernais for his literary

---

132. *Mémoires secrets*, vol.4, p.331–32, 350–53; *Mémoires secrets*, vol.7, p.50; *Mémoires secrets*, vol.8, p.17–18, 20–22, 87, 125–26, 344–45. The only news report that does not praise Necker is a positive comment on a satire of all figures at the Compagnie des Indes, including Necker: *Mémoires secrets*, vol.4, p.256.

133. *Mémoires secrets*, vol.3, p.71–72, 74, 90; *Mémoires secrets*, vol.4, p.186–87, 246–47, 299–300.

134. *Mémoires secrets*, vol.7, p.161.

135. *Mémoires secrets*, vol.4, p.141.

136. *Mémoires secrets*, vol.4, p.312–13; *Mémoires secrets*, vol.6, p.192–93; *Mémoires secrets*, vol.7, p.23–24; *Mémoires secrets*, vol.8, p.271–72.

talent.[137] Conti's image is much less heroic than in the first six volumes of the *Journal*. He is mentioned repeatedly for his support of Rousseau, but this is not necessarily positive, because the author rejects Rousseau's person and writings. Conti is also the patron of Beaumarchais, who was a "nasty" author according to the *Mémoires*. The author is worried about the prince's health in the news about autumn 1775 and the first half of 1776, but—like *L'Observateur*—simultaneously considers that the reason of his illness is his "manière de vivre," that is his libertinage.[138] In the *Mémoires*, Conti is not even praised for his patriotism, as he was in *L'Observateur*.

In religious matters, the *Mémoires* oscillate between a conventional denunciation of "poisonous writings" attacking Christianity, and the audacious assertion that philosophical writings actually do show that Christian dogmas are not reasonable,[139] so that "it is hard to resist [the arguments of the philosophical writings] without the special grace of a strong and blind faith."[140] The *Encyclopédie* is qualified as a "vast warehouse of all knowledge of mankind," and the duchesse d'Aiguillon praised for having sponsored it.[141] The *Mémoires* do not appreciate Palissot's satire of the *philosophes*. They discuss Raynal's *Histoire des deux Indes* in identical terms as in the *Journal*, and they praise Saige's radical republican writing, *Le Catéchisme du citoyen*.[142] In all, as in *L'Observateur*, the general orientation is clearly "philosophical" and fits into the Necker milieu, although this does not mean that the *Mémoires* do not criticize the behavior of individual *philosophes* like Diderot and Raynal on several occasions.[143]

137. Choiseul: *Mémoires secrets*, vol.1, p.88, 90; *Mémoires secrets*, vol.3, p.169. Beauvau: *Mémoires secrets*, vol.4, p.272–73; Nivernais: *Mémoires secrets*, vol.4, p.205–206.

138. *Mémoires secrets*, vol.1, p.103–104, 106–107; *Mémoires secrets*, vol.2, p.316–17; *Mémoires secrets*, vol.3, p.231, 332; *Mémoires secrets*, vol.4, p.62; *Mémoires secrets*, vol.7, p.161; *Mémoires secrets*, vol.8, p.68, 259, 268–69.

139. *Mémoires secrets*, vol.2, p.130–31, 135–36; *Mémoires secrets*, vol.3, p.51–52; *Mémoires secrets*, vol.4, p.139–40; *Mémoires secrets*, vol.5, p.16–19.

140. "[I]l est difficile de résister, sans la grâce spéciale d'une foi vive et aveugle," *Mémoires secrets*, vol.5, p.192.

141. "[C]e vaste dépôt de toutes les connaissances humaines," *Mémoires secrets*, vol.4, p.41; *Mémoires secrets*, vol.6, p.178–79.

142. *Mémoires secrets*, vol.6, p.169, 291, 329; vol.8, p.140–41, 163. On the *Mémoires secrets* and Saige, see Baker, *Inventing*, p.111. On Saige's *Le Catéchisme du citoyen*: Baker, *Inventing*, p.128–52.

143. *Mémoires secrets*, vol.1, p.69; *Mémoires secrets*, vol.2, p.139–40, 194; *Mémoires secrets*, vol.4, p.364–66, 376; *Mémoires secrets*, vol.5, p.77–78; *Mémoires secrets*, vol.6, p.182–83.

Conclusion

On November 8, 1774, that is a few days before the restoration of the Parisian *parlement*, Maurepas came into the opera house. As the *Journal* relates, "he was applauded with such enthusiasm that he was about to withdraw in order to escape from the applause."[144] By contrast, on June 23, 1773, only the Dauphin and the Dauphine were applauded eagerly; the duchesse de Bourbon, whose husband had been the first of the "exiled" princes of the blood to return to court, received only "lighter applause."[145]

On first view, these episodes, and other news reports that the princes of the blood or Marie-Antoinette were enthusiastically welcomed at the opera house,[146] seem to give evidence that there existed a lively public sphere independent from the royal court. In a public theater, Parisians showed whether they appreciated leading courtiers or not. However, some other details raise doubts about such an interpretation. In the case of Maurepas's arrival at the opera house, the author of the *Journal* specifies that it was Chartres who gave the signal for the applause.[147] Indeed, Chartres was the host, and all the spectators in some way his guests: The opera house was part of the Palais-Royal, his residence in the capital city, and he financed it. There is good reason to think that the public did not act independently of his will—the opera house was one of his political instruments. This had an impact on the content of plays, which were regularly used to celebrate various members of the court. In 1769, for example, the actors shouted on the stage "Long live the king, and long live all the royal family!"[148] Not only in Versailles, but also "in the city," applause was at least partly regulated by the high-ranked people present in the theater. The news reported that the public applauded because the Dauphine did so; in another *notice*, Choiseul put soldiers in the parterre to intimidate those who could be tempted to boo the play of one of his clients.[149] In light of such evidence, it would be incorrect to consider theaters as spaces of an independent "bourgeois" public sphere.

From a close analysis of the content of the John Adamson corpus, we can conclude that this thesis also applies to unauthorized literature.

---

144. *Journal*, vol.6, p.304.
145. "[A]pplaudissements plus légers," *Mémoires secrets*, vol.7, p.16–17.
146. *Mémoires secrets*, vol.6, p.98–99; *Mémoires secrets*, vol.7, p.301–302.
147. *Journal*, vol.6, p.304.
148. *Mémoires secrets*, vol.4, p.266–67.
149. *Mémoires secrets*, vol.1, p.98; *Mémoires secrets*, vol.7, p.10–11.

The about-turns of the author reveal two major myths: the myth that unauthorized books were "underground literature" and expressions of an autonomous "public sphere," on the one hand, and the myth of the primary role of the author in defining the political content of the texts, on the other. Because we can reconstruct the changes in political statements and see that they were concomitant with changes in the political elite, it appears problematic to search for a coherent ideology (for example pro-*parlementaire*) of the author. It seems more appropriate to explain the ideological content of the different volumes of the corpus with changes in courtly patronage. Precisely this means that unauthorized literature was neither the expression nor the constituting element of a "public sphere" in which "government" and "opposition" confronted each other, any more than it was an "underground" product of authors outside courtly patronage and hostile to court elites in general.

The example of the John Adamson corpus shows that historians still have much to do in analyzing unauthorized literature. Until now, we know only bits of the story, and we are very far from having an overview of the patronage networks behind the scenes. Actually, we should apply the method of the author(s) of the *Journal* and the *Mémoires* to political writings: These journalistic works constantly attribute pamphlets to court factions. To this day, for example, studies of Voltaire too often search for an ideological coherence in his oeuvre, forgetting that, as the *Mémoires* and a study on his ideas about the *parlements* remind us, the *philosophe de Ferney*—much like Diderot, as is demonstrated in the first chapter of this volume—also formulated statements to please specific courtiers.[150]

More generally, the history of the John Adamson corpus shows that *ancien régime* society bore the stamp of vertical patronage networks to a greater extent than has been acknowledged in the history of ideas. This was the case not only of writings supporting the *parti patriote*, like the *Journal historique*, but also of texts reverting to the Enlightenment narrative, like the *Mémoires secrets*. Scholars should thus be critical toward the way Enlightenment writers presented themselves on the stage of literary Europe: Writers might not have been the independent moral exemplars or the primary leaders of public opinion they sometimes pretended to be. On the eve of the French Revolution, the prominent social position of princes and court elites seems barely shaken. This shows that the dichotomy between *la cour* and *la ville*

---

150. James Hanrahan, *Voltaire and the parlements of France* (Oxford, 2009), p.220–24.

should be understood as a dichotomy not between an aristocratic and a "bourgeois" space, but between spaces dominated by different court factions. Paris was a town shaped by aristocracy and court elites, and so were many virtual or physical public spaces.

Music, taste, and Enlightenment discourse at the Prussian court: the Marpurg–Agricola controversy over the relative merits of the French and Italian styles

TAL SOKER

De gustibus non est disputandum

Introduction

On matters of taste, as the old proverb goes, there can be no dispute. Yet the eighteenth century was replete with public controversies about taste, its ethical and social implications, and the danger of its degeneration in recent times. In his travelogue of 1773, the wandering British music historian Charles Burney, whose career is examined in Clarissa Campbell Orr's chapter in this volume, described Berlin as the place in which "controversies [...] have been carried on with more heat and animosity than elsewhere." "[I]ndeed," he concluded with tongue in cheek, "there are more critics and theorists in this city, than practitioners; which has not, perhaps, either refined the taste, or fed the fancy of the performers."[1] Burney's verdict is enough to put into question the overt impetus behind eighteenth-century controversies over taste, and insinuate that there was often more to them than mere aesthetics. With that in mind, the present chapter revisits the controversy over the relative merits of the Italian and French musical styles which erupted in Berlin in March 1749 between Friedrich Wilhelm Marpurg and Johann Friedrich Agricola, two young musicians who were drawn to the city in pursuit of their musical career. The controversy

---

1. Charles Burney, *The Present state of music in Germany, the Netherlands, and United Provinces*, 2 vols. (London, Becket, 1773), vol.2, p.232.

soon transcended the realms of music aesthetics and extended to
include other men of letters and court officials. In the aftermath of
this fierce exchange, Agricola was able to obtain the post of court
musician (and later, court composer). Marpurg had to labor under
great financial difficulties for nearly ten more years before securing
a position for himself at court, and at the cost of giving up his hope
of pursuing a professional musical career.

This chapter therefore focuses on the debate and its outcome,
regarding not only the aesthetic arguments, but also the strategies
deployed by its contenders. It takes a closer look at these strategies and
the rhetorical means implemented by the participants, most notably
anonymity and pseudonymity, the oscillation between courtesy and
discourtesy, and the act of aesthetic position-taking as a means
of accruing social and symbolic capital. What appears, at first, to
be a purely aesthetic dispute over the shifting aesthetic priorities
at the Prussian court, I contend, was on a more specific level a
well-calculated campaign in pursuit of personal goals, quite in line
with the strategies employed by the enlightened authors discussed
in other contributions to this volume. Finally, by analyzing the
backdrop, the unfolding, and the ramifications of this controversy
from a sociological point of view informed by Pierre Bourdieu's theory
of the field of cultural production,[2] I hope to elucidate the entangled
social networks in which its actors were embedded, and uncover the
complex clockwork often at play in Enlightenment aesthetic controversies that unfolded in the public sphere. Since the logic of the field
of cultural production and the powers working in it are, in part, as
Bourdieu notes, self-evident to the agents active in it, and therefore
remain unremarked, it is important first to outline those.

The French precedents

Before plunging into the controversy, it is worth reviewing briefly
the French polemics about national styles and tastes which preceded
and followed it. The ongoing debates over the relative merits of the
French and Italian musical styles had their roots in the polemics of
the Quarrel of the Ancients and the Moderns in seventeenth-century
France. These debates first peaked at the turn of the century with the
abbé François Raguenet's *Parallèle des Italiens et des Français en ce qui*

2. Pierre Bourdieu, *The Field of cultural production: essays on art and literature* (New York, 1993).

regarde la musique et les operas (1702).[3] A partisan of Italian opera and theater, Raguenet was eager to spread and strengthen their status in his homeland after returning from Rome, where he served as a companion to Louis XIV's emissary, the cardinal de Bouillon. Two years after its publication, his pamphlet was countered by another, the *Comparaison de la musique italienne et de la musique française* (1704–1705), written by the Jesuit Jean-Laurent Le Cerf de La Viéville in defense of French musical drama. The controversy peaked for a second time following a performance of Giovanni Battista Pergolesi's intermezzo *La serva padrona* (1733) in 1752 by a troupe of traveling Italian comic opera singers at the Académie royale de musique (the Parisian opera). This time it was no Frenchman, but rather the Saxon diplomat intimately connected to the French *philosophes*, Friedrich Melchior von Grimm, who poured oil onto this heated debate. In his pamphlet *Le Petit Prophète de Boehmischbroda* (1753), Grimm sided with the partisans of imported Italian comic opera, which he juxtaposed with prevailing forms of French musical drama. The debate soon fanned out into what came to be known in the annals of music history as the *Querelle des Bouffons*.[4]

It is likely, however, that the exchange between Raguenet and Le Cerf de La Viéville at the turn of the century would not have attracted much scholarly attention in modern times had its interlocutors not been entangled in the social networks of the Académie française, the *Journal des savants*, and the *Memoires de Trévoux*.[5] Moreover, it seems similarly plainly evident that the *Querelle des Bouffons* of the 1750s would never have become the subject of so much scholarly attention had not Jean-Jacques Rousseau intervened with his renowned *Lettre*

3. See Théodora Psychoyou, "Ancients and Moderns, Italians and French: the seventeenth-century quarrel over music, its status and transformations," in *The Ancients and the Moderns: comparative perspectives*, ed. Paddy Bullard and Alexis Tadié (Oxford, 2016), p.133–54.

4. The chronology of the *Querelle des Bouffons*, it should be mentioned, has come under some scrutiny in recent studies. Pergolesi's *La serva padrona* had in fact already been performed in another venue in Paris as early as 1746 without causing much uproar. Furthermore, the arguments contained within Grimm's *Le Petit Prophète de Boehmischbroda* had already been introduced in his *Lettre sur Omphale* which appeared nearly a year earlier in January 1752, shortly before the celebrated performance of *La serva padrona*. For a reappraisal of this dispute, see David Charlton, "New light on the Bouffons in Paris (1752–1754)," *Eighteenth-century music* 11:1 (2014), p.31–54.

5. Georgia Cowart, *The Origins of modern musical criticism: French and Italian music, 1600–1750* (Ann Arbor, MI, 1981), p.51–59.

sur la musique française (1753). Subsequently, other *philosophes*, most notably Denis Diderot and Jean D'Alembert, were also drawn into the debate.

Recently Richard Taruskin succinctly deemed the *Querelle des Bouffons* a "coded episode" or an "Aesopian discourse" within the "ongoing battle between political absolutism and Enlightenment that raged throughout the eighteenth century."[6] Whereas the "modern style," that is, Italian comical intermezzo, could be read as "modern philosophy," the French traditional *tragédie lyrique* stands for Taruskin as a metonym for the *ancien régime*, its anachronism and monopolistic structures. This interpretation, however, should be treated with caution, especially if we consider the direct personal backdrop against which this controversy unfolded. By mid-century, the most powerful musical figure on the French musical scene was the composer and music theorist Jean-Philippe Rameau. With his stage works being performed regularly at the Académie royale de musique and his theoretical writings being endorsed by members of the Parisian Académie and the Académie française, Rameau's career reached its zenith. He was a worthy successor of Louis XIV's *surintendant* and *compositeur de la musique de la Chambre du roi*, Jean-Baptiste Lully, and, though the king did not grant him the same far-reaching monopolistic advantages over French theater, Rameau was the new champion of the *tragédie lyrique*. Rousseau, who had previously been an admirer of Rameau's stage and theoretical work, changed fronts and joined the Italian party after the two men fell out in 1745 in reaction to a harsh critique of a performance of Rousseau's *opéra-ballet Les Muses galantes* (1743, music now lost), uttered by the older master. Rameau, who discerned the personal critique implied by Rousseau's *Lettre sur la musique française*, countered it with two pamphlets of his own, a patriotic defense of French opera under the title *Observations sur notre instinct pour la musique* (1754) and a critical review of Rousseau's articles on music in the *Encyclopédie* under the title *Erreurs sur la musique dans l'Encyclopédie* (1755).[7] In the end,

6.   Richard Taruskin, *The Oxford history of Western music*, 6 vols. (Oxford, 2005), vol.2, p.438–44.
7.   This argument is supported by the chronology of the publications. As pointed out by Cynthia Verba, Rousseau's aesthetic conversion did not occur until the publication of Grimm's first pamphlet in 1752. Furthermore, his articles for the Encyclopédie, which were drafted in 1740, were still heavily indebted to Rameau's theories of harmony, and his incomplete "Lettre sur le drame musical en France et en Italie" from around 1750 was not yet entirely hostile to French

although Rameau's popularity continued unabated in the following years, his reputation among intellectuals started to fade.[8] Rousseau, by contrast, enjoyed the fruits of the successful performances of his own intermezzo *Le Devin du village* (1752), both at and outside court. Although inspired by the spirited debates of the time, *Le Devin du village* was written in a style recalling the popular vaudevilles, that is, the *opéra-comique* of the first half of the century, rather than anything Italian.[9]

Musical taste in the German public sphere

It was not until 1722 that the music critic Johann Mattheson published an annotated German translation (along with the French original) of Raguenet's pamphlet of 1702 in his journal *Critica musica*.[10] The publication of *Critica musica*, the first music periodical published in German, however, marked the beginning of a new age in the history of music criticism in Germany. Preceded by Mattheson's

---

opera. See Cynthia Verba, *Music and the French Enlightenment: reconstruction of a dialogue, 1750–1764* (Oxford, 1993), p.10. Furthermore, as noted by Thomas Christensen, Rameau's arguments against Rousseau's articles were mostly trivial, taking into account that they were initially based on his own theories, and can therefore be interpreted as one of the ramifications or as a sideshow of the pamphlet war of the *Querelle des Bouffons*, rather than as dealing directly with theoretical issues. Thomas Christensen, *Rameau and musical thought in the Enlightenment* (Cambridge, 1993), p.249–50.

8.   On the entangled relationships between Rameau, Diderot, and D'Alembert, see Verba, *Music and the French Enlightenment*, p.51–90, and Thomas Christensen, "Music theory as scientific propaganda: the case of D'Alembert's *Elémens de musique*," *Journal of the history of ideas* 50:3 (1989), p.409–27.

9.   David Charlton, "The melodic language of Le Devin du village and the evolution of opéra-comique," in *Rousseau on stage: playwright, musician, spectator*, ed. Maria Gullstam and Michael O'Dea (Oxford, 2017), p.179–208 (183–85).

10.   François Raguenet and Johann Mattheson, "Eine Vergleichung zwischen den Italiänern und Franzosen betreffend die Music und Opern: Vorbericht," *Critica musica* 1:4 (August 1722), p.[105]–18, *Critica musica* 1:5 (September 1722), p.[121]–47, and *Critica musica* 1:6 (October 1722), p.[153]–66. There were, for sure, some sporadic historical antecedents dealing with the question of national styles prior to the turn of the century, most notably in Athanasius Kircher's influential *Musurgia universalis* (1650). Another intriguing example with regard to the social significance of the Italian diaspora at German courts was offered by Johann Kuhnau, the predecessor of Johann Sebastian Bach as *Thomaskantor* in Leipzig, in his satirical (and bluntly anti-Italian) novel *Der musicalische Quack-Salber* (1700). Mattheon himself, it should be noted, had already touched upon this theme earlier in his *Das neu-eröffnete Orchestre* (1713).

early German moral weekly *Der Vernünftler* (1713–1714), which only sporadically incorporated articles about music, the goal of *Critica musica* was to establish a separate venue for the nascent public sphere for musical discussions, or, to use Mattheson's own term, the "science of harmony" ("harmonische Wissenschaft").[11]

Some quarter-century later, when the debate migrated to Berlin, the Prussian capital was in the midst of a musical golden era which had begun with the ascension of Frederick II to the throne in 1740 and would abruptly end with the outbreak of the Seven Years War in 1756. In these years Berlin witnessed the reinauguration of its court opera (1742) and the beginnings of a tradition of concerts held in the chambers of the king, the crown prince, the queen mother, and other members of the aristocracy.[12] In comparison with its more glitzy sister Paris, where public concerts were held regularly as early as 1725, a public sphere for music was slow to emerge. Three private musical gatherings were nonetheless documented in Berlin by 1753: the Akademie which met on Fridays in the house of Joachim Gottlieb Janitsch, bass viol player at the court orchestra; the Musikalische Assemblee held on Mondays by Christian Friedrich Schale, cellist at the court orchestra and chamber musician to the king; and Das Concert held on Saturdays at Agricola's home.[13] According to Matthias Röder, the cultural worlds of court entertainment and Berlin's nascent concert life were still closely intertwined, and these music societies, meeting mostly in private homes, were primarily modeled after musical soirées at court. It was only in the decades

11. Holger Böning, *Der Musiker und Komponist Johann Mattheson als Hamburger Publizist: Studie zu den Anfängen der Moralischen Wochenschriften und der deutschen Musikpublizistik*, 2nd ed. (Bremen, 2014), p.284. On the genesis of the music periodical in the context of the German Enlightenment see Imogen Fellinger, "Mattheson als Begründer der ersten Musikzeitschrift ('Critica Musica')," in *New Mattheson studies*, ed. George J. Buelow and Hans Joachim Marx (Cambridge, 1983), p.179–97.

12. Though Frederick II made himself famous for spectacularly bringing opera back to Prussia, his father and predecessor, Frederick William I, had reintroduced musical theater at court in 1734. See Benjamin Marschke, "Die russische Partei, ein Pietist auf dem Thron, und ein Hof-Komödiant: Wandel und Wendepunkte am Hof Friedrich Wilhelms I.," in *Mehr als Soldatenkönig: neue Schlaglichter auf Lebenswelt und Regierungswerk Friedrich Wilhelms I.*, ed. Frank Göse and Jürgen Kloosterhuis (Berlin, 2020), p.73–86 (85).

13. Adolph Friedrich Wolff, "Entwurf einer ausführlichen Nachricht von der Musikübenden Gesellschaft zu Berlin," *Historisch-Kritische Beyträge zur Aufnahme der Musik* 1:5 (1755), p.385–413 (386–87).

following the Seven Years War that these were developed into an independent musical public sphere in such institutions as Johann Friedrich Reichardt's Concerts Spirituels (borrowing its name from its Parisian forerunner) and Johann Friedrich Carl Rellstab's Konzert für Kenner und Liebhaber.[14]

There were, of course, other aspects in which Berlin differed from Paris, or, for that matter, from other European capitals relevant to the current investigation into its musical public sphere. First, whereas in France it was the foreign Italian intermezzo that was pitted against the vernacular French *tragédie lyrique*, as expressed in the works of Lully and later Rameau, in Berlin the genre of *opera seria*, exemplified in the works of composers affiliated with the Berlin school, was sung in Italian.[15] Second, the comic style, that is, the intermezzo, was not perceived in Prussia as having any subversive potential. Quite on the contrary, already in 1745 Frederick II inaugurated a theater for the performance of intermezzos in the city palace in Potsdam.[16] In contrast to the performance which preceded the *Querelle des Bouffons* four years later in Paris, Pergolesi's *La serva padrona* was performed on March 15, 1748 by Domenico Cricchi and his Italian troupe in Potsdam without causing any uproar.[17]

14. Matthias Röder, "Music, politics, and the public sphere in late eighteenth-century Berlin," doctoral dissertation, Harvard University, 2009, p.89–90.
15. Recently Christoph Henzel has coined the term *Berliner Klassik*, in analogy with Viennese classicism, to describe the canonization of the Berlin school of composers, a process which continued, mainly in northern Germany, into the nineteenth century. See Christoph Henzel, "Die Zeit des Augustus in der Musik: Berliner Klassik, ein Versuch," in *Berliner Aufklärung: Kulturwissenschaftliche Studien*, ed. Ursula Goldenbaum and Alexander Košenina, 7 vols. (Hanover, 1999–), vol.2 (2003), p.7–33. As for opera, the most salient composers pertaining to this group were Frederick II's kapellmeister Carl Heinrich Graun and Johann Adolph Hasse, the Saxon kapellmeister whose works were performed with some regularity at the Prussian court. Although sung in Italian, the lingua franca of *opera seria* in Europe, with the exception of France, where its equivalent *tragédie lyrique* was already well established, it was not uncommon for French classical plays to be adapted and translated into Italian for the Berlin stage.
16. On Friedrich's "progressiveness" in relation to the genre of the intermezzo and its role within his politics of representation, see Sabine Henze-Döhring, *Friedrich der Große: Musiker und Monarch* (Munich, 2012), p.125–44.
17. Mary Oleskiewicz, "Music at the court of Brandenburg-Prussia," in *Music at German courts, 1715–1760: changing artistic priorities*, ed. Samantha Owens, Barbara M. Reul, and Janice B. Stockigt (Woodbridge, 2011), p.79–130 (100).

The onset of the Marpurg–Agricola controversy

Against this backdrop, on March 4, 1749, soon after his arrival in
Berlin and at only thirty years of age, Marpurg launched Berlin's first
music periodical, *Der critische Musicus an der Spree* (1749–1750). Picking
up on the rather trite theme of national styles, he proclaimed in the
opening lines of its inaugural issue:

> The prejudice that beautiful music is only at home in Italy is
> gradually vanishing. The awe of the names ending in *ini* and *elli*
> loses its hold and the Germans, who were formerly occupied with the
> shameful middle parts, are [now] elevated to the front of the princely
> orchestras. One dismisses the boasts of the foreigners and our scribes,
> once so dedicated to reproducing the fantasies of witless Italians in
> clean handwriting, now vie with each other in making the work
> of their countrymen known. We follow herein the French. With
> them one does not ask whether this or that allegro was written in
> the Italian fashion, but rather whether it was written in good taste.[18]

Considering that Berlin's musical life was still in the process of
formation, and that Marpurg was still a rather obscure figure in
the city's musical landscape, his decision to make his *entrée* into
the city's nascent public sphere by reinvigorating the debate on the
relative merits of national styles must have been a conscious and
well-calculated step. Very little is known about his life prior to his
arrival in Berlin. Born in 1718 in his family's manor in Wendemark in
the Altmark, he enrolled in 1737 at the University of Jena. He changed
the following year to the University of Halle, where he studied law
and befriended his fellow student, the classicist and art historian

---

18. "Das Vorurtheil ist doch allmählich bey uns verschwunden, als ob die schöne
     Musick nur in Welschland zu Hause sey. Die Ehrfurcht gegen die erlauchten
     Namen in *ini* und *elli* verlieret sich, und die ehemals mit den schamhaften
     Mittelstimmen beschäftigten Deutschen haben sich bis zum ersten Platz in
     dem Orchestre der Fürsten erhoben. Man giebt den Prahlereyen der Ausländer
     nicht weiter Gehör, und unsere Copisten, die sonsten so bemüht waren, die
     öfters windigen Hirngespinste eines nichts denckenden Italiäners durch die
     saubersten Abschriften fortzupflantzen, streiten itzo miteinander um die Wette,
     die Wercke ihrer Landsleute bekandt zu machen. Wir folgen hierinnen den
     Frantzosen nach. Man untersuchet nicht bey ihnen, ob dieses oder jenes Allegro
     nach dem italiänischen, sondern ob es in dem guten Geschmack geschrieben
     ist." Friedrich Wilhelm Marpurg, "Über den Stellenwert deutscher Musik und
     Musiker," *Der critische Musicus an der Spree* (henceforth *CM*) 1:1 (March 4, 1749),
     p.1–8 (1–2). All translations are my own unless otherwise stated.

Johann Joachim Winckelmann. In a letter to Heinrich Wilhelm Muzel-Stosch, dated March 19, 1767, Winckelmann reported that Marpurg had spent much of the 1740s in France before settling in Berlin.[19] It was during this period that he was supposedly introduced into the higher circles of Parisian society and made the personal acquaintance of its luminaries, most notably Voltaire, D'Alembert, Maupertuis, and Rameau. In his letter, Winckelmann succinctly claimed it was a pasquil that Marpurg published against a certain *marister legens* that led him to flee to France via the Netherlands.[20] Nevertheless, the lack of any palpable evidence concerning this case or the identity of the satirized person casts serious doubt on the veracity of this account. Still more disconcerting is the fact that both the exact date and the length of Marpurg's sojourn remain a matter of conjecture. Moreover, more recently Hans-Joachim Schulze has been able to ascertain Marpurg's presence in Germany for most of this period. Yet the circumstances surrounding this blind spot in Marpurg's biography, which he would still be trying to hush up in his later years, remain unclear to the present day, and the exact date of his actual departure is unknown. While Winckelmann's aforementioned letter suggests that Marpurg spent no less than seven years in France, Ernst Ludwig Gerber notes in his *Tonkünstler-Lexikon* (1790), which was published during Marpurg's lifetime, that the latter spent the period around 1746 in Paris.[21] Two years later, however, on April 6, 1748, Marpurg was again enrolled at a Prussian university, this time in Frankfurt (Oder), and soon afterward he entered the service of the Prussian general Count Friedrich Rudolf von Rothenburg as his private secretary in Berlin.[22]

That notwithstanding, Marpurg's statement above should not be read as a mere recapitulation of ideas already articulated by earlier German music scholars, most notably Johann Mattheson and Johann Adolph Scheibe. A closer reading of these lines, against the backdrop of the situation by the time of their publication, reveals that Marpurg's use of the past tense was not arbitrary. Italian composers, singers, and instrumentalists were indubitably a very sought-after

19. See Hans-Joachim Schulze, "Friedrich Wilhelm Marpurg, Johann Sebastian Bach und die 'Gedanken über die welschen Tonkünstler' (1751)," *Bach-Jahrbuch* 90 (2004), p.121–32 (122–23).
20. Schulze, "Friedrich Wilhelm Marpurg," p.123.
21. Schulze, "Friedrich Wilhelm Marpurg," p.125.
22. Schulze, "Friedrich Wilhelm Marpurg," p.124.

commodity at German courts during the seventeenth and early eighteenth century.[23] This economic migration and the growing diaspora of Italian musicians often resulted in friction with local court musicians. In Dresden, for example, the court orchestra was dissolved in 1720, following a row between a few Italian singers and the German kapellmeister, Johann David Heinichen.[24] While in the 1720s Heinichen would probably not have been appointed kapellmeister in Dresden had he not been trained in Italy, by 1739 the critic and kapellmeister in Copenhagen, Johann Adolph Scheibe, would already declare the educational journey to Italy, the *Italienreise*, obsolete for the training of German musicians.[25] The weakening of Italian hegemony by mid-century can be traced particularly in the instrumental domain.[26] Central in this trend were the cultural politics of Frederick II. Although his *Hofkapelle* was modeled upon its Dresdner forerunner, and he still took pride in the names of the foreign artists and intellectuals gathered at his court, already as crown prince he had shown a clear penchant for German and Bohemian musicians over Italians.[27]

What was bothering Marpurg, therefore, was not the presence of Italian musicians at court. It was much more their enduring effect on the market of musical goods. The auspicious "names ending in *ini* and *elli*" to which he refers in the passage quoted above probably hinted not only at the success of some Italian composers on the market, but

23. See, for example, Reinhard Strohm, "Italian *operisti* north of the Alps: 1700–1750," in *The Eighteenth-century diaspora of Italian music and musicians*, ed. Reinhard Strohm (Turnhout, 2001), p.1–60, and Norbert Dubowy, "Italienische Instrumentalisten in deutschen Hofkapellen," in *The Eighteenth-century diaspora*, ed. R. Strohm, p.61–120.

24. Wolfgang Horn, *Die Dresdner Hofkirchenmusik 1720–1745: Studien zu ihren Voraussetzungen und ihrem Repertoire* (Kassel, 1987), p.51.

25. Johann Adolph Scheibe, "Die Haupteintheilung der Musik wird angezeiget und untersuchet," *Der critische Musicus: neue, vermehrte und verbesserte Auflage* 1:3 (April 2, 1737), p.29–38 (p.36, n.6).

26. Michael Talbot, "Et in Italia ego: musicians and the experience of Italy, 1650–1750," in *Europäische Musiker in Venedig, Rom und Neapel (1650–1750)*, ed. Anne-Madeleine Foulet and Gesa zur Nieden (Kassel, 2015), p.68–86 (69).

27. See for example Frederick's letter to his sister, Wilhelmine von Bayreuth (dated November 29, 1739), in which, albeit admitting the superiority of the Italians as singers, he claimed that, as instrumentalists, the Germans much surpassed the Italians in appeal (quoted in Oleskiewicz, "Music at the court," p.92). This trend only increased during his reign, as attested by the lists of musicians he hired (Oleskiewicz, "Music at the court," p.111–30).

also to the common practice among contemporary German composers of using Italianized versions of their names on the title pages of their works, a practice Marpurg himself did not refrain from in later years.[28] However, immediately after this passage he recapitulates the numerous clichés about the Italians already articulated in the writings of his predecessors, arguing that they tend to digressions, excessive freedom, redundancy to the point of weariness, and that they are incapable of committing to paper their ideas in a plausible manner, composing unmethodically and lacking the theoretical knowledge needed to yield correct compositions.[29] The French, he contends, were hitherto far from perfection themselves, yet they "follow nature" more ardently and therefore should serve as a model for his countrymen, the Germans, who were previously accused by their neighbors of being "sluggish notes-stranglers" ("ungelenckigen Notenwürger"), violin-squeakers ("Violinzwitscher"), flute-howlers ("Flötenheuler"), and "other similar torturers of instruments" ("andere dergleichen Istrumentenhencker"). Nowadays, he concludes triumphantly, the Germans are the equals of the French and Italians.[30]

That notwithstanding, a week later, on March 11, 1749, a spirited riposte to the first issue of Marpurg's periodical was published in Berlin under the title *Schreiben eines reisenden Liebhabers der Musik von der Tyber, an den critischen Musikus an der Spree*. Its author, who disguised himself behind the pseudonym Flavio Anicio Olbrio, was none other than the singer and composer Johann Friedrich Agricola.[31] Born in the town of Dobitschen in the duchy of Saxe-Gotha-Altenburg as the son of a

---

28. The two volumes of the *Raccolta delle più nuove composizioni di clavicembalo: di differenti maestri ed autori per l'anno 1756* (1756–1757), which Marpurg edited for Breitkopf in Leipzig, were published under the name Federico Guglielmo Marpurg and comprise the works of Carlo Filippo Emanuele (Carl Philipp Emanuel) Bach, Carlo Enrico (Carl Heinrich) Graun, and, last but not least, Giovanni Federico (Johann Friedrich) Agricola, all of whom were living composers residing in the Prussian capital and members of the Berlin school.

29. Marpurg, "Über den Stellenwert," p.3. For a survey of anti-Italian rhetoric in German music criticism in the latter half of the eighteenth century see Mary Sue Morrow, *German music criticism in the late eighteenth century: aesthetic issues in instrumental music* (New York, 1997), p.44–51.

30. Marpurg, "Über den Stellenwert," p.3.

31. The pseudonym refers to Anicius Olybrius Augustus, Roman emperor in the fifth century, who was the subject of the opera libretto written by Pietro Pariati and Apostolo Zeno (1707) and adapted by the late 1740s by various Italian composers (Nicola Porpora, Francesco Gasparini, Giovanni Porta, Leonardo Vinci, Egidio Duni, and Niccolò Jommelli).

high court clerk, in 1738 Agricola moved to Leipzig to study law at its university. Simultaneously he became a disciple of the renowned *Thomaskantor* Johann Sebastian Bach. On the advice of Carl Philipp Emanuel, Johann Sebastian's second eldest son, Agricola relocated to Berlin in late 1741, soon after the succession of Frederick II to the Prussian throne the previous year, probably in the hope of becoming part of its burgeoning music life and securing himself a position at court. Although he enjoyed the patronage and artistic guidance of the king's close friend and flute and composition teacher Johann Joachim Quantz (1697–1773) and befriended the royal kapellmeister Carl Heinrich Graun (1704–1759), Agricola failed during the first ten years of his residency in Berlin to secure a steady post as court musician, and had to sustain himself by singing and playing in churches and instructing amateurs.[32]

Agricola must have been well aware that Marpurg's assertions concerning the waning Italian hegemony not only were a fait accompli, but also benefited him as a newcomer in the city. Yet in response Agricola not only took on the role of advocate of the Italians, but also launched a direct assault at the (still anonymous) editor of the newly established journal in that he sought to refute almost each and every one of his arguments. Before we move to a more thorough investigation of how taste featured in this debate, it is worth lingering at this point on the appropriation of the discourse of Enlightenment by both interlocutors in the debate.

Anonymous libel and *Schmähschrift*

Early on in their exchange, Marpurg and Agricola each were at pains to unveil the true name of his opponent without risking the disclosure of his own identity. As recently argued by Gillian Paku, *anonymity* and *pseudonymity* were gestures of wide prevalence in the eighteenth-century public sphere, which helped authors to overcome their initial "lack of name" as well as distance themselves from the contents of their own publications.[33] Marpurg's motivation for publishing his

---

32. Hans-Joachim Schulze, "Johann Friedrich Agricola," in *Die Musik in Geschichte und Gegenwart: Personenteil*, ed. Ludwig Finscher, 2nd ed., 17 vols. (Kassel, 1999), vol.1, p.219.

33. Gillian Paku, "Anonymity in the eighteenth century," *Oxford handbooks online*, http://www.oxfordhandbooks.com/view/10.1093/oxfordhb/9780199935338.001.0001/oxfordhb-9780199935338-e-37 (last accessed January 25, 2022).

journal under an eponymic pseudonym enabled him, on the one hand, to distance himself from its content and, on the other hand, to distance himself from his own dubious past. As a vehicle for starting anew and making a name for himself, this action also helped him to overcome his relative obscurity both at court and in Berlin's nascent musical public sphere.[34] Agricola's motivation for distancing himself from the authorship of his pamphlets was, as will be explained below, of a diametrically opposed nature.

Already in his first riposte of March 11, Agricola started dropping hints about the possible identity of his interlocutor. Musing on the allegory Marpurg drew in the first issue of his journal between the esteem of German musicians and their literal advancement from the back seats of the princely orchestras to the front, Agricola suggests sarcastically: "[W]hose fault is it, that you, sir, must have formerly always been *assigned the role of the viola*, even among the Germans?"[35] Marpurg did not remain idle in the face of this insult. In the following issue of his journal (dated March 25), not only did he deny playing this instrument, but he also accused his opponent of drawing this false conclusion from the Jewish Kabballah.[36] A week later, Marpurg inserted a reader's letter in his defense signed by *Wahrmund* (literally "true-mouth"), probably another one of Marpurg's many pseudonyms, contending that the anonymous challenger of the editor was in fact no Italian at all, but merely a failed composer of church music, who only claimed to compose in the Italian *gusto*.[37] On the following page, writing again as the anonymous editor of the journal, Marpurg cordially thanks his reader for his support, yet distances himself from the heated style and claims to eschew any personal attack against his

---

34. Marpurg's next publications indeed made use of his reputation as the "Verfasser des critischen Musicus an der Spree," a name probably still better known at that time to their intended audience than his genuine name.

35. "Wer kann denn davor [*sic*], wenn Sie, mein Herr, vielleicht ehedem, und zwar selbst unter denen Deutschen nur immer *die Bratsche haben spielen müssen?*" Johann Friedrich Agricola, *Schreiben eines reisenden Liebhabers der Musik von der Tyber, an den critischen Musikus an der Spree* (Berlin, n.n., 1749), p.2 (original emphasis).

36. Friedrich Wilhelm Marpurg, "Schreiben eines reisenden Liebhabers der Musik von der Tyber, an den critischen Musikus an der Spree," *CM* 1:4 (March 25, 1749), p.25–32 (31).

37. Friedrich Wilhelm Marpurg, "Hochzuehrender Herr Criticus," *CM* 1:5 (April 1, 1749), p.33–40 (33).

opponent: "It is the matter of contention which counts for me, not the person."[38] That notwithstanding, two pages later Marpurg picks up on Agricola's musing on the ending syllables of Italian names and gives another hint as to his identity: "How happy must the good Olibrio be, to have invented the suffixes *ix* and *utsch*, just to juxtapose them with *ini* and *elli*. To this wit, my Herr Olibrio, let us drink a glass of wine. Why have you not yet added *ola* to these suffixes? The triad would then be complete. Did you omit it for modesty's sake?"[39] Albeit concealed from their readership, there is clear evidence that, almost from the outset of the debate, at least for some in Berlin the anonymity of the two interlocutors was an open secret.[40] This is attested by a fragmentary satirical play titled *Tarantula / Ein Possenoper, im neusten italienischen / Gusto oder Geschmack* (1749) sketched by Gotthold Ephraim Lessing, who was on friendly terms with Marpurg. Two of Lessing's main characters in these fragments are the singing teacher Olibrio, described as a "foolish musician" ("närrischer Musicus"), and Lominte, an anagram on the name of Agricola's soon-to-be-wife Benedetta Emilia Molteni (thus disclosing how intimately involved Lessing was in the debate).[41]

The recurring hints at Agricola's identity in Marpurg's journal as well as Lessing's preposterous parody predictably enraged Agricola. On July 6, he published his second riposte, some fifty pages in length, about a tenth of which is a punitive review of a collection of five keyboard suites published in Paris a few years earlier by a certain

38. "Es ist mir nur um die Sache, nicht aber um die Person zu thun." Marpurg, "Hochzuehrender Herr Criticus," p.34.
39. "Wie froh muß der gute Olibrio nicht gewesen seyn, da er die Sylben in *ix* und *utsch* erfunden, um sie den in *ini* und *elli* entgegenzusetzen. Auf diesen Fund, mein Herr Oblibrio, gehörte ein Glaß Wein. Warum haben Sie diesen Endungssylben nicht noch die in *ola* hinzugefühet? Das Dreyblatt wäre vollkommen gewesen. Haben Sie es aus Bescheidenheit weggelassen?" Marpurg, "Hochzuehrender Herr Criticus," p.36.
40. Other speculations concerning Marpurg's identity, expressed as early as April 1749, are to be found in the letter exchange between Johann Georg Pisendel in Dresden, Carl Heinrich Graun in Berlin, and Georg Philipp Telemann in Hamburg. See Schulze's remarks in "Friedrich Wilhelm Marpurg," p.129.
41. On July 1, 1749, Marpurg nonetheless published in his periodical an ode penned by Lessing, *Über die Regeln in den Wissenschaften zum Vergnügen und besonders der Dicht und Thonkunst* (signed June 28), in which he expressed his views on theater and poetry, which differed to some extent from Marpurg's own vision for the German theater (see John Pizer, "Lessing and Wieland on music and poetry," *Lessing yearbook* 33, 2001, p.97–114, 100).

"Mr. Marpourg."[42] Concerning the opening movement from the first suite alone—a double rondeau merely two pages long—Agricola notes that there is nothing bold ("nichts gewagtes") in its composition and it contains no extraordinary episodes ("keine seltsame Vorfälle"). "The ideas are very common," he goes on, "the music consists in each section of triplets, of very well-known progressions, and all too frequent sequences and repetitions."[43] In the second couplet of the accompanying rondeau he further points out a "violation of the metre" ("ein Fehler wieder das Metrum"), and concludes his review by noting:

> Mr. Marpourg in this piece very often makes the same error which the critic [on the Spree] so reproves in the [work of the] foreigners [*Welsch*], namely, he reiterates the same idea that he considers to be ingenious, and uses it in everything, and often not the most pleasing inversions of tones, not seldom to the point of disgust.[44]

Agricola's motivation for hiding his true identity from the public differed from Marpurg's need to conceal his real name at this early stage of his career. Launching a personal attack on a peer (whose ideas, as will be argued below, were anything but radical) might have harmed his own public image no less than that of his counterpart. Thus, apart from repeatedly accusing Agricola of not being impartial ("unparteyisch") and of lacking in love for his fatherland by favoring the Italians, already in his first riposte of March 25, Marpurg accuses Agricola of being uncourteous:

42. There is some uncertainty concerning the date of publication of Marpurg's *Pièces de clavecin* in Paris. Although its *privilège* is dated 1741, the publication was first announced in the *Mercure de France* in 1748 (Davitt Moroney, "Couperin, Marpurg and Roeser: a Germanic *Art de toucher le clavecin*, or a French *Wahre Art?*," in *The Keyboard in baroque Europe*, ed. Christopher Hogwood, Cambridge, 2003, p.111–30, 122). Considering the fact that Marpurg left Halle in 1746 and resurfaced in Prussia as late as April 1748, it is more probable that his sojourn to France took place (if at all) shortly before his return to Germany.

43. "Die Gedanken sind sehr gemein. [...] die Musik bestehet in dem einem wie in dem anderen aus Triolen, aus sehr bekannten Gängen, aus allzuöfftern Versezungen und Wiederholungen." Johann Friedrich Agricola, *Schreiben an Herrn === in welchem Flavio Anicio Olibrio, sein Schreiben an den critischen Musikus an der Spree vertheidigt, und auf dessen Wiederlegung antwortet* (n.p., n.n., 1749), p.23.

44. "Herr Marpourg ist in diesem ganzen Wercke, sehr offt in dem Fehler gefallen, welchen der Herr Kunstrichter an den welschen tadelt, nemlich, wenn er auf einen, seinem Bedüncken nach, artigen Einfall gerathen ist, so gebraucht er denselben in allen, auch offt nicht den geschicktesten Verwechslungen der Töne, nicht selten bis zum Ekel." Agricola, *Schreiben an Herrn ===*, p.26.

You [Olibrio] reveal throughout a malicious heart impassioned by, I dare not say, a kind of vindictiveness. This is one of the characters of an invective [*Schmähschrift*]. However, your diatribe goes against all those who endorse the good and loathe the abject. [...] Why have you covered your face with a mask to converse with me? That you should genuinely be an Italian: This has been constantly denied by some good friends, whose forthrightness I do not distrust in the least.[45]

Marpurg's words call to mind the contemporary distinction by Johann Christoph Gottshed between two types of polemical interactions, the invective (*Schmähschrift*) and the polemic (*Streitschrift*), the former being "a defamatory brochure, without the name of its author, [...] in which the good name and ways of an honest man are infringed" while in the latter "one argues about truth, history, learned views, or points of doctrine."[46]

Gottsched concludes his account of these two types of publications by noting their social implications: "Despite differing views, one can be his opponent's friend. Only badly mannered and discourteous men attack the person of their opponent [...] invectives corrupt the fine sciences and the scholarship in general. Peasants might curse each other; porter and carrier insult each other. Learned men must know how to treat each other with respect."[47]

45. "Sie [Olibrio] entdecken durchgängig ein durch eine Art von *Rachgier* erregtes, ich will nicht sagen, niederträchtiges Hertz. Dies ist eines von den Hauptkennzeichen einer *Schmähschrift*. Ihre *Schmähschrift* aber gehet wider alle diejenigen Personen, die das gute billigen, und das verwerfliche verabscheuen. [...] Warum haben Sie eine *Maske* entlehnet, um mit mir zu sprechen? Denn daß Sie würcklich ein Italiäner seyn sollen: dieses suchen mir einige gute Freunde, in deren Aufrichtigkeit ich nicht das mindeste Mistrauen setze, beständig aus dem Sinn zu reden." Agricola, *Schreiben an Herrn ===*, p.26.
46. "eine ehrenrührige Schrift, ohne Namen des Verfassers, [...] darinnen der gute Namen, und die Sitten eines ehrlichen Mannes angetastet werden, [...] streitet man um Wahrheiten, Geschichte, gelehrte Meynungen, oder Lehrpuncte." Johann Christoph Gottsched, *Beobachtungen über den Gebrauch und Mißbrauch vieler deutscher Wörter und Redensarten* (Strasbourg and Leipzig, Johann Amandus Königen, 1758), p.229.
47. "[M]an kann in Meynungen uneins, und doch der Gegner Freund seyn. Nur ungezogne grobe Leute greifen die Personen ihrer Gegner an. [...] Pasquille beschimpfen die schönen Wissenschaften, und die Gelehrsamkeit überhaupt. Bauren möge einander schimpfen; Sack- und Last-Träger einander lästern. Gelehrte Männer müssen einander mit Höflichkeit zu begegnen wissen." Gottsched, *Beobachtungen*, p.229-30.

"Consensus in dissensus" and position-taking in the field of cultural production

At this point it is worth leaving the bones of contention between Marpurg and Agricola to one side, and exploring those issues about which they were in agreement. It is through this "complicity," I will argue below, that the covert motivation for starting this controversy in the first place is unveiled. Firstly, both stressed the urgent need to improve the current state of German singing—the only field in which Italian hegemony at the Prussian court still endured. Their mutual agreement confirms their commitment to this mutual cause, or, as Marpurg puts it: "Maybe taste will evolve, and we could also then exceed the foreigners in this field."[48] This trend changed, however, in the aftermath of the Seven Years War, with the appointment of leading soprano Gertrud Elisabeth Mara (née Schmeling) in 1771. Yet Marpurg's views concerning the current state of singing seems to be anything but subversive or deviant compared to the accepted thinking at the Prussian court. In fact, this valuation of the still inferior state of German vocal practices mirrors Frederick II's views concerning the current state and prospects of German literature in his controversial *De la littérature allemande* (1780). Although this work appeared in print some thirty years later, Andreas Pečar has recently argued that Frederick II might indeed have conceived its content much earlier as an answer to Jakob Friedrich von Bielfeld's *Progrès des Allemands dans les sciences, les belles-lettres et les arts: particulièrement dans la poësie, l'éloquence et le théâtre* (1752).[49] Just like Marpurg, Frederick laments what he perceives as the impoverished state of German literature and language, yet assures his readers that the golden age of his mother tongue is nearing. These parallels show that, rather than differing from the views emanating from the court concerning the current state and prospects for German culture, Marpurg's patriotic depiction was in agreement with the king's own judgment.[50]

---

48. "Vielleicht ändert sich hierinnen einmahl der Geschmack, und können wir auch alsdenn in diesem Stück den Ausländern die Spitze bieten." Marpurg, "Über den Stellenwert," p.5.

49. Andreas Pečar, *Die Masken des Königs: Friedrich II. von Preußen als Schriftsteller* (Frankfurt am Main, 2016), p.166.

50. The same can be said about Marpurg's rejections of Rousseau's thesis in the *Discours sur les sciences et les arts* (1750) concerning the corruptive influence of the arts and sciences on human morality: "This paradoxical view, which attests to the ignorance and folly [of its author], was thoroughly refuted by many

Nonetheless, it was Agricola who nearly a decade later published an
annotated and extended translation of a classical singing treatise
by the Italian castrato Pier Francesco Tosi.[51] In its introduction
Agricola expressed his hope that his efforts would contribute to the
advancement of German singing and prove that his fatherland was as
rich in good voices and singers as any other country. That notwithstanding, Agricola dedicates a considerable part of his two ripostes to
the question of whether the German language is suitable for singing:
"[T]hat the tone of your country, my lord, is as suitable for music
as the tone of mine, has not been doubted by any person."[52] Yet he
immediately appropriates this point and challenges his interlocutor
by asking him to translate into German the text of an aria from
Metastasio's *Olimpiade* (1733), one of the most popular librettos of the
eighteenth century.

A second point of agreement between Marpurg and Agricola was
their mutual investment in the musical aesthetics that prevailed at
the Prussian court and were embodied in the works of the so-called
Berliner Klassik.[53] Both combatants showered words of praise on its
leading living composers, especially on Johann Adolf Hasse, Quantz,
Graun, and Bach brothers Carl Philipp Emanuel and Wilhelm
Friedemann. This point is further stressed with the intervention of a
third player in the controversy. On May 12, 1750, after nearly a year
of quiet, another article against the (still anonymous) editor of the
Critischer musicus appeared, this time in Hamburg.[54] The author of

---

excellent opposing scholars of Mr. Rousseau" ("Diese paradoxe Meinung,
die gerade der Unwissenheit und Dummheit Recht spricht, ist von vielen
treflichen Gelehrten wider den Herrn Rousseau gründlich widerlegt worden").
See Friedrich Wilhelm Marpurg, "Schreiben aus Paris über den Streit daselbst
zwischen den französischen und welschen Tonkünstern: aus dem Französischen übersetzt," *Historisch=kritische Beyträge zur Aufname der Musik* 1:2 (1754),
p.160–66 (162). Here again Marpurg's views mirror those of the king in his *Über
den Nutzen der Künste und Wissenschaften im Staate* (1772); see Pečar, *Die Masken
des Königs*, p.161–63.

51. Johann Friedrich Agricola, *Anleitung zur Singkunst* (Berlin, Winter,
1757). Interestingly, the following year Marpurg published his own *Anleitung zur
Singcomposition* (Berlin, Lange, 1758) to compete with Agricola's treatise.

52. "dass der Ton Ihres Landes, mein Herr, eben so geschickt zur Musik sey als
der Ton des meiningen, daran hat noch kein Mensch gezweiffelt." Agricola,
Schreiben eines reisenden Liebhabers, p.5.

53. See n.15 above.

54. "Folgendes Schreiben an den Herrn Verfasser des Kritischen Musicus an der
Spree ist uns zur Einrückung zugefertiget," *Freye Urtheile u. Nachrichten zum*

this article, often falsely attributed to Agricola, was indeed an Italian, namely, the castrato Filippo Finazzi, who resided in Hamburg.[55] Reiterating some of the arguments already made in earlier pamphlets, the anonymous author of this article referred to the works of three of the period's most prominent composers, and claimed that these composers had, in fact, all been to Italy.[56]

However, as noted above, already mid-century, the symbolic value attached to the *Italienreise* had already lost much of its hold for musicians, especially in northern Germany. In his reply to Finazzi's article, dated August 28, 1750, which also concluded the entire controversy, Marpurg leads us back to the beginning of the controversy (but not before denying his rival any right to make a value judgment by virtue of his being castrated) by reiterating the arguments he presented to Agricola:

> Mr. Hasse has been in Germany more than in Italy. [...] Mr. Graun has indeed been to Italy twice; but the first time he was already more advanced in music than most Italians, and the second time he traveled there in the service of his monarch to recruit singers. I do not deny that Mr. Quantz was also there. But are all these great men now Italians, because they have traveled through Italy once or twice? [...] Grauns, Hasses, Telemanns, Bachs, Pfeiffers, Bendas, Quantz, etc. are to be found only among the Germans. [...] At the present time truly good taste, which is erroneously dubbed Italian, is at home in Germany and the Italians [...] decorate themselves with the feathers of these men and are only inflated and cocky through the melodies and harmonies they have stolen from them.[57]

Aufnehmen der Wissenschaften und der Historie überhaupt 7:38 (May 12, 1750), p.289–95.

55. In letter to Meinrad Spieß, composer and member of the Correspondierende Societät der musicalischen Wissenschaften (dated February 8, 1755), Marpurg reports previously leading an exchange of pamphlets with Agricola Finazzi. For a transcription of this letter see Hans Rudolf Jung and Hans-Eberhard Dentler, "Briefe von Lorenz Mizler und Zeitgenossen an Meinrad Spiess: mit einigen Konzepten und Notizen," *Studi musicali* 32:1 (2003), p.74–196 (166).

56. "So kann ich den Herrn Hasse nicht anderes als Italiäner nennen, weil er mehr in Italien als in Deutschland gewesen. Herr Graun hat sich zweimal in Italien aufgehalten. Herr Quanz ist eine gute Zeit ebenfalls da gewesen." "Folgendes Schreiben," p.294.

57. "Herr Hasse ist mehr in Deutschland als in Italien gewesen. [...] Herr Graun ist zwar zweymal in Italien gewesen; allein das erste mal war er schon in der Musik weiter, als die meisten Italiener, und das andere mal reisete er in den Diensten seines Monarchen dahin, um Sänger und Sängerinnen

It is with this intervention of a *genuine* Italian musician in the controversy that the *complicity* of both interlocutors, Marpurg and Agricola, comes to the fore. They shared a social background, had the same professional aspirations, and came from the same musical tradition. In other words, both were, in effect, deeply invested in and inculcated with the same musical aesthetics. Seen through Bourdieu's lens, as agents of cultural production, both interlocutors reinforced the unity of the field through this "consensus in dissensus" rather than challenging or transforming it.[58]

As agents of cultural production, Marpurg and Agricola had a twofold mission: first, to accumulate as much valued capital as possible in order to improve their relative position in the field, and second, to partake in the struggle for the *monopoly of legitimate aesthetic discourse*.[59] With only a limited amount of social capital (social relationships and networks) and symbolic capital (reputation, educational qualifications, and entitlements) at their disposal, they had to acquire more of these to better their positions on the field and to generate more capital. To achieve this goal, both had to implement their embodied capital and seek legitimation. As Bourdieu notes,

> the structured set of the manifestations of the social agents involved
> in the field—literary or artistic works, of course, but also political
> acts of pronouncements, manifestos or polemics, etc.—is inseparable
> from the space of *literary* or *artistic position* defined by possession of a
> determinate quantity of specific capital (recognition) and, at the same

---

auszusuchen. Daß Herr Quantz auch daselbst gewesen, läugne ich gar nicht. Aber sind denn nun alle diese großen Männer Italiener, weil sie ein= oder zweymal in Italien durchgereiset haben? [...] Graune, Hassen, Telemanns, Händels, Bache, Pfeiffer, Bendas, Quanze u.s.f. haben wir nur unter denen deutschen. [...] Noch zur Zeit gehört der wahre gute Geschmack, den man mißbrauchlisweise den italienischen nennet, in Deutschland zu Hause, und die Italiener [...] spicken sich mit den Federn dieser Männer, und werden bloß durch die ihnen abgestohlenen Melodien und Harmonien aufgeblasen und dreuste [*sic*]." Friedrich Wilhelm Marpurg, *Sendschreiben an die Herren Verfasser der freyen Urtheile in Hamburg, das Schreiben an den Herrn Verfasser des kritischen Musikus an der Spree betreffend* (Berlin, n.n., 1750), p.16.

58. On the structural complicity between opposing powers in the intellectual field, by taking the example of the Barthes–Picard controversy in France around 1965, a twentieth-century "quarrel of the Ancients and Moderns," see Pierre Bourdieu, *Homo academicus*, translated by Peter Collier (Stanford, CA, 1988), p.115–18; and Jeremy F. Lane, *Pierre Bourdieu: a critical introduction* (London, 2000), p.72–73.

59. Bourdieu, *The Field of cultural production*, p.35–36.

time, by occupation of a determinate position in the structure of the distribution of this specific capital.[60]

By forging personal alliances and appropriating an Enlightenment controversy, both Marpurg and Agricola sought to increase their social and cultural capital and thus boost their value in the eyes of potential patrons at and outside the court. What was at stake here, therefore, was not a challenge to the canon or to the sanctioned aesthetics at court, nor a questioning of the social hierarchies coded in it, but rather an attempt to position themselves in relation to it.

Well aware of the fact that they could not risk falling out with any of the leading figures of the aforementioned Berlin school or challenging the prevailing taste at court, both were at pains to forge alliances and appeal to these well-positioned agents and institutions and thus accumulate more social and symbolic capital. They did not enjoy the prestige of the *Italienreise*, which had already lost its appeal for German princes, and it should be noted here that affiliation with the Bach family did not necessarily entail social capital for Marpurg or Agricola.[61] Johann Sebastian Bach was, to a large extent, still a forgotten composer during the eighteenth century, and his music was practiced and appreciated by a meager group of connoisseurs. It was only at the turn of the nineteenth century that the "Bach-cult" established itself in Berlin and paved the way for his acceptance into the German canon.[62] Lacking these other resources, both aspiring young musicians had to look for other means to increase their respective cultural and social capital, by way of "persons, their

---

60. Bourdieu, *The Field of cultural production*, p.30 (original emphasis).
61. On Agricola's connections with Johann Sebastian and Carl Philipp Emanuel Bach, see above. There is no palpable evidence suggesting any personal acquaintance between Marpurg and Johann Sebastian Bach apart from a fleeting remark on a possible meeting in Leipzig in an open letter addressed to Mattheson (dated February 1760), authored and printed in the third (and last) music periodical Marpurg initiated in Berlin, the *Kritische Briefe über die Tonkunst* (vol.1 [Berlin: Brinsel, 1760], p.269). However, in 1752 Marpurg had already collaborated with Carl Philipp Emanuel Bach in the publication of the second posthumous edition of Johann Sebastian's last work, *Die Kunst der Fuge* (BWV 1080). On the capital of travel in the eighteenth century, see n.25 above and Vanessa Agnew, *Enlightenment Orpheus: the power of music in other worlds* (New York, 2008), p.23 and passim.
62. Carl Philipp Emanuel Bach himself was not satisfied with his position as court musician and left Berlin after nearly two decades there for a better-paid post as music director of Hamburg's five churches in 1767.

relationships, liaisons, and quarrels, information about the ideas and problems which are 'in the air' and circulate orally in gossip and rumor."[63]

In the aftermath of the controversy, as Marpurg reported later, following a successful performance of Agricola's intermezzo *Il filosofo convino in amore* in May 1751, the latter was appointed court composer (*Hofkomponist*).[64] In the midst of the Seven Years War, following the death of Frederick II's beloved kapellmeister Graun, Agricola was appointed his successor (but without the permission to carry the title). However, Frederick II seemed not to hold him in as high esteem as Graun, and the two often had artistic disagreements, especially around Agricola's *Amor e Psiche* (1767) and *Oreste e Pilade* (1772). Interestingly, from his new position as court musician, it was now Agricola who turned into the "most vociferous anti-Italian reviewer" in the German press.[65] Marpurg, as mentioned above, associated with figures from Berlin's literature circles, not only Lessing, but also the lawyer, critic, and amateur musician Christian Gottfried Krause, who served as Marpurg's predecessor as secretary for General Friedrich Rudolf von Rothenburg, and the author and scientist (and Lessing's relative) Christlob Mylius, to name but a few.[66] It was only in later years that Marpurg started to nurture closer relationships with prominent musicians at court, either as dedicatees or as contributors to his periodicals, although the genre of the public controversy remained a fruitful means for spreading his name.[67] Impoverished as a consequence of the Seven Years War, his musical career nevertheless reached its abrupt and premature end when in 1763 he was appointed a privy councilor of War (*Geheimer Kriegsrat*) and director of the newly

63. Bourdieu, *The Field of cultural production*, p.32.
64. Friedrich Wilhelm Marpurg, "Lebensläufe: Joh. Friedr. Agricola," *Historisch=kritische Beyträge zur Aufname der Musik* 1:2 (1754), p.148–52 (151).
65. Morrow, *German music criticism*, p.56
66. The dedicatee of the collected edition of the *CM* (dated January 30, 1750) was Marpurg's benefactor and close friend of the king, Rothenburg, who died the same year. The dedicatee of his next publication, the treatise *Die Kunst das Clavier zu spielen*, which was also published in the same year, was Mylius, who probably was his pupil for some time during his stay in Berlin and who, together with Lessing, founded the first German theater periodical in the same year, the *Beyträge zur Historie und Aufnahme des Theaters*.
67. The contents of two of these controversies, with Johann Philipp Kirnberger, the teacher and court musician to Frederick II's sister, Princess Anna Amalia, and with Georg Andreas Sorge, music theorist and organist in Breslau, have already been the subject of music theoretical studies in recent decades.

established Prussian Royal Lottery. It remains unclear, however, which connections and networks brought about his royal appointment. A hint at a possible connection at court is suggested by the dedicatee of his *Anleitung zur Singcomposition*, already mentioned above, "Frau Geheimen Kriegsräthinn, Freyfrau von Prinzen," probably Johanna Benedicte von Printzen, née von Meyer, a known figure on Berlin's musical scene and the wife of the privy councilor of War Friedrich Wilhelm Freiherr von Printzen.[68] It is also in this dedication that Marpurg reflected, using the language of Enlightenment, on the phenomenon of the controversy, echoing Burney's critique above:

> In the present book several issues are handled that would not conform to the taste of certain sons of Parnassus. [...] Do not believe, my gracious lady, that I want to engage you in our controversies. It will suffice that you declare yourself the protective goddess of music, and that the world learns that you find its foundations reasonable and its demands grounded [...] That notwithstanding, however, a faultless rivalry has never harmed the arts.[69]

68. Johanna Benedicte von Printzen was also the dedicatee of one of C. P. E. Bach's *Petites pièces pour le clavecin*, titled *La Prinzette* (Wq. 117/21), which was printed the previous year in the second volume of Marpurg's keyboard anthology *Raccolta delle più nuove composizioni di clavicembalo: di differenti maestri ed autori per l'anno 1756* (1757). See Peter Wollny's "Introduction," in *C. P. E. Bach: the complete works*, vol.1/8.2: *Miscellaneous keyboard works II*, ed. Peter Wollny (Los Altos, CA, 2005), p.xiii–xxvi (xvii).

69. "Es sind in gegenwärtigem Buche verschiedene Gegenstände abgehandelt, die nicht nach dem Geschmacke gewisser Söhne des Parnasses seyn werden. [...] Glauben Sie nicht, gnädige Frau, daß ich Sie in unsere Streitigkeiten verwickeln will. Es wird genug seyn, daß Sie Sich für die Schutzgöttinn [sic] der Tonkunst erklären, und daß die Welt erfähret, daß Sie ihre Grundsätze vernünftig, und ihre Ansprüche gegründet finden [...] Jedoch ein tadelfreyer Wetteifer hat noch niemals den Künsten geschadet."

III

Self-representation

What makes Enlightenment princes enlightened? The representation of Franz of Anhalt-Dessau and Frederick August of Anhalt-Zerbst

Paul Beckus

Introduction

This chapter explores the genesis of the depictions of two eighteenth-century princes in the historiography. The issue is why we consider some princes, like Leopold III Friedrich Franz or "Prince Franz" of Anhalt-Dessau (1740–1817), to have been enlightened, whereas others like Frederick August of Anhalt-Zerbst (1734–1793) are considered to have been the opposite of an enlightened prince. This question is closely related to issues addressed in this volume: What role did Enlightenment rhetoric and imagery play in rulers' self-fashioning in the late eighteenth century? Which criteria did contemporaries use to judge whether a ruler was enlightened or not? What did rulers do to appear enlightened? How have contemporary images influenced the historiography in the long run? To answer these questions, it is important to note that the concept of "enlightened prince" had different meanings in the eighteenth century and later in the historiography: first, as synonymous to the contemporary term *prince éclairé*, and second, as "enlightened absolutism," a historiographical concept.

Prince Franz of Anhalt-Dessau—a prince without a court?

The picture of the enlightened prince is closely linked with the topos of the ruler without a court, which is considered here. "Enlightened absolutism" is used to describe a ruler with a progressive reform agenda.[1] Viewed in this way, enlightened absolutism is the opposite

---

1. *Der Aufgeklärte Absolutismus*, ed. Karl Otmar Freiherr von Aretin (Cologne, 1974); Karl Otmar Freiherr von Aretin, "Aufgeklärter Herrscher oder aufgeklärter

of "baroque absolutism." Baroque absolutism is linked with a concept of monarchical self-representation at court;[2] in contrast, enlightened absolutism is seen as a doctrine of government.

A princely court is understood to have been useful or even necessary in baroque absolutism, but a princely court is often seen as a non-issue in enlightened absolutism, because princely courts were often a focus of criticism by Enlightenment authors. Usually, the ruler himself was not criticized, but rather his immediate entourage, and the court was equated with this entourage. This only changed somewhat in the course of the eighteenth century.[3] Enlightenment philosophers detected a supposed moral turpitude among courtiers, especially a penchant for flattery, deception, and lying. According to critics of the court, honest relationships and forthright moral advice were impossible there.[4] They demanded changes at court and in the government, which enabled a new strategy of self-representation for rulers.

Absolutismus: eine notwendige Begriffserklärung," in *Gesellschaftsgeschichte*, ed. Ferdinand Seibt, 2 vols. (Munich, 1988), vol.1, p.78–87; Günter Birtsch, "Der Idealtyp des aufgeklärten Herrschers: Friedrich der Große, Karl Friedrich von Baden und Joseph II. im Vergleich," *Aufklärung* 2:1 (1987), p.9–47; Günter Birtsch, "Aufgeklärter Absolutismus oder Reformabsolutismus?," *Aufklärung* 9:1 (1996), p.101–109; Rudolf Vierhaus, *Germany in the age of absolutism*, translated by Jonathan B. Knudsen (Cambridge, 1988), p.83; Wolfgang Neugebauer, "Aufgeklärter Absolutismus, Reformabsolutismus und struktureller Wandel im Deutschland des 18. Jahrhunderts," in *Ernst II. von Sachsen-Gotha-Altenburg: ein Herrscher im Zeitalter der Aufklärung*, ed. Werner Greiling, Andreas Klinger, and Christoph Köhler (Cologne, 2005), p.23–39. For criticism of the terms "absolutism" and "enlightened absolutism," see Lothar Schilling, "Vom Nutzen und Nachteil eines Mythos," in *L'Absolutisme*, ed. Lothar Schilling (Munich, 2008), p.13–31; Kirill Abrosimov, *Aufklärung jenseits der Öffentlichkeit: Friedrich Melchior Grimms Correspondance littéraire (1753–1773) zwischen der "république des lettres" und europäischen Fürstenhöfen* (Ostfildern, 2014), p.215–17.

2. Vierhaus, *Germany*, p.65–68; Volker Bauer, *Die höfische Gesellschaft in Deutschland von der Mitte des 17. bis zum Ausgang des 18. Jahrhunderts: Versuch einer Typologie* (Tübingen, 1993), p.5.

3. Wolfram Mauser, "Von der Hofkritik zur Fürstenschelte: Kritischer Diskurs als Akt politischer Selbstbefreiung von Canitz bis Pfeffel," in *Konzepte aufgeklärter Lebensführung: literarische Kultur im frühmodernen Deutschland*, ed. Wolfram Mauser (Würzburg, 2000), p.80–102; *Princes, patronage, and the nobility: the court at the beginning of the modern age c.1450–1650*, ed. Ronald G. Asch and Adolf M. Birke (London, 1991).

4. Mauser, "Von der Hofkritik," p.81–83; Hellmuth Kiesel, *"Bei Hof, bei Höll": Untersuchungen zur literarischen Hofkritik von Sebastian Brant bis Friedrich Schiller* (Tübingen, 1979), p.203–204.

This criticism of courts had been mainstream for centuries, going back to ancient times and the revival of courts in Renaissance humanism.[5] Although criticism of princely courts was widespread in the eighteenth century, it was not innovative, and the elements of the topos were the same as they had been for a century. So authors could publish criticism of the princely court, if specific conventions were observed, and the courtly elites were accustomed to it.[6] Often the criticism of the court came from opposing factions at court, and in the late eighteenth century many Enlightenment authors and their readers were members of princely courts or in the networks of courtiers. What was new in the eighteenth century was that some princes incorporated this criticism of the court in their self-representation: In contrast to the court as a place of corruption, and often appropriating the Rousseauian concepts discussed in Clarissa Campbell Orr's chapter in this volume, they presented a simple private life in the countryside as a common antithesis.[7] For many philosophers in Germany from the eighteenth century, this image was connected with physiocracy and anglophilia.[8] Thus, country life became analogous with veracity, progress, and good government.

Various princes embraced this country lifestyle in the late eighteenth century as an instrument of self-representation.[9] Being an enlightened prince was connected with a princely court that was reduced in size, which was seen as analogous to having more rational and effective government for the common good. Enlightenment authors played

5. Kiesel, *"Bei Hof, bei Höll."*
6. Kiesel, *"Bei Hof, bei Höll,"* p.244–45.
7. Kiesel, *"Bei Hof, bei Höll,"* p.200–201, 253–54.
8. Voltaire and Montesquieu had substantial influence in spreading of the latter element in Germany. Andrew Scott Bibby, *Montesquieu's political economy* (New York, 2016), p.29–32; Jennifer Willenberg, *Distribution und Übersetzung englischen Schrifttums im Deutschland des 18. Jahrhunderts* (Munich, 2008), p.19–30; Peter M. Jones, *Agricultural Enlightenment: knowledge, technology, and nature, 1750–1840* (Oxford, 2016), p.17–24; Michael Niedermeier, "Campe als Direktor des Dessauer Philanthropins," in *Visionäre Lebensklugheit: Joachim Heinrich Campe in seiner Zeit (1746–1818)*, ed. Hanno Schmitt (Wiesbaden, 1996), p.45–65 (46–47).
9. See for example Ina Mittelstädt, *Wörlitz, Weimar, Muskau: der Landschaftsgarten als Medium des Hochadels, 1760–1840* (Cologne, 2015); *Politische Gartenkunst? Landschaftsgestaltung und Herrschaftsrepräsentation des Fürsten Franz von Anhalt-Dessau in vergleichender Perspektive: Wörlitz, Sanssouci und Schwetzingen*, ed. Andreas Pečar and Holger Zaunstöck (Halle, 2015); Thomas Biskup, *Friedrichs Größe: Inszenierungen des Preußenkönigs in Fest und Zeremoniell 1740–1815* (Frankfurt am Main, 2012).

an important role in establishing the image of a ruler. They praised
the humility and simplicity of some courts, and in this way they
created a point of reference for the interpretations of later historians.
However, most Enlightenment philosophers did not have an overview
of the whole court. They visited only secondary palaces, where court
ceremonial was indeed reduced, and were not aware that court
ceremonial still applied in full in the main residence.

Based on this, German historians of the nineteenth century
devised the image of "a prince outside the court" in connection with
Enlightenment absolutism.[10] They followed Enlightenment authors by
emphasizing that enlightened rulers had reduced the costs of the court
and separated themselves from it. They understood this as being the
foundation that enabled these rulers to have genuine friendships. At
the same time, the historiography legitimized the nineteenth-century
monarchy by identifying it with good examples of past rulers.[11]

These tendencies were very much present in the historiography
of Anhalt: Prince Franz of Anhalt-Dessau is known as an advocate
of substantial Enlightenment reform at the end of the eighteenth
century.[12] Local historians saw in Prince Franz the model of an
enlightened ruler, who disliked courtly ceremonial and lifestyle. This
viewpoint was derived from Gustav Adolf Harald Stenzel (1792–1854),
author of an influential handbook of Anhalt history (*Handbuch der
Anhaltischen Geschichte*).[13] He characterized Prince Franz as an "enemy
of formality and court festivals."[14] Moreover, he wrote about Franz

---

10. Regarding Enlightenment absolutism, see Birtsch, "Aufgeklärter Absolutismus,"
     p.101–102.

11. Andreas Pečar, "Vater Franz oder Fürst Franz von Anhalt-Dessau?
     Vorbedingungen zum Verständnis des Fürsten in seiner Residenzstadt Dessau,"
     in *Der Fürst in seiner Stadt: Leopold Friedrich Franz und Dessau*, ed. Andreas Pečar
     and Frank Kreißler (Petersberg, 2017), p.10–17 (10–12).

12. Gustav Adolf Harald Stenzel, *Handbuch der Anhaltischen Geschichte*, 2 vols.
     (Dessau, 1820–1824), vol.1, p.366–94; Gustav Adolf Harald Stenzel, "Leopold
     Friedrich Franz: Herzog zu Anhalt-Dessau," *Zeitgenossen: ein biographisches
     Magazin für die Geschichte unserer Zeit* 2:3 (1817), p.37–82; Friedrich Reil, *Leopold
     Friedrich Franz, Herzog und Fürst von Anhalt-Deßau, ältestregierender Fürst in
     Anhalt, nach Seinem Wirken und Wesen: mit Hinblick auf merkwürdige Erscheinungen
     Seiner Zeit* (Dessau, 1845); Erhard Hirsch, *Die Dessau-Wörlitzer Reformbewegung
     im Zeitalter der Aufklärung: Personen–Strukturen–Wirkungen* (Tübingen, 2003).

13. Stenzel, *Handbuch*, vol.1, p.366–94.

14. Stenzel, "Leopold Friedrich Franz," p.64. In the original: "Ein Feind aller
     Förmlichkeit und der Hoffeste." All translations are my own unless otherwise
     stated.

and his court: "His household was not ostentatious. He did not have a court."[15] In Stenzel's interpretation, the entourage of Prince Franz was a circle of friends, while the central location of courtly life, the residential palace in Dessau, was ignored.[16] It was a formative and very influential image for a long time.[17] Statements by Enlightenment authors were used to support this interpretation. For example, Georg Forster (1754–1794) wrote in 1779 about the prince and his court: "Etiquette is not the strictest; but it embarrasses the prince, who is far too noble to tolerate the compulsion of bootlickers and the farce of fools."[18] Such glorification contributed to the understanding of Prince Franz as a ruler outside the court; however, it was a statement about how Prince Franz held court at the secondary residence in Wörlitz, not how things were in Dessau.

The palace and the garden of Wörlitz played a central role in this interpretation. Prince Franz created in Wörlitz one of the first English gardens in Germany. In addition, the country house in Wörlitz was the first neoclassical building in the Holy Roman Empire.[19] He used it as a location for reduced court ceremony. There he could meet people of lower social status without the regular protocol.[20] The cluster of buildings at Wörlitz embodied for Enlightenment visitors the anglophilia of Prince Franz, his modest country life, and his reform agenda.[21]

Recent historical research shows that this view was incomplete. Wörlitz was a place to represent dynasty members' rank as princes

15. Stenzel, *Handbuch*, p.394. In the original: "Prunklos war sein Haushalt. Einen Hofstaat hatte er nicht."
16. Pečar, "Vater Franz," p.10–15; Paul Beckus, "Franz in seiner Stadt: Dessau als Residenz des Fürsten Leopold Friedrich Franz von Anhalt-Dessau," in *Der Fürst in seiner Stadt*, ed. A. Pečar and F. Kreißler, p.18–29.
17. See the following influential papers: Hermann Wäschke, *Anhaltische Geschichte*, 3 vols. (Köthen, 1912–1913), esp. vol.3; Hirsch, *Dessau-Wörlitzer Reformbewegung*; *Weltbild Wörlitz: Entwurf einer Kulturlandschaft* (Wörlitz, 1996), ed. Frank-Andreas Bechtholdt and Thomas Weiß.
18. "Die Eitiquette am Hofe ist just die strengste nicht; aber sie genirt den Fürsten doch, der viel zu edel denkt, um die erzwungene Bücklinge und Narrenpossen leiden zu können." Georg Forster to his father, May 21, 1779, in *Johann Georg Forster's Briefwechsel: nebst einigen Nachrichten von seinem Leben*, ed. Therese Huber, 2 vols. (Leipzig, 1929), vol.1, p.194–99 (197).
19. Ingo Pfeifer, *Schloss Wörlitz* (Munich, 2000).
20. See Erhard Hirsch, *Dessau-Wörlitz: Aufklärung und Frühklassik*, 2nd ed. (Leipzig, 1987).
21. See the essays in Pečar and Zaunstöck, *Politische Gartenkunst?*

of the Holy Roman Empire.[22] Franz also had a conventional court in Dessau, which was smaller than the courts of powerful rulers, but appropriate for the ruler of a small territory like Anhalt-Dessau.[23] Most of the time, he was at court in Dessau; however, Enlightenment opinion-makers rarely saw this court. Instead, their interpretations rest on their impressions of Wörlitz. Moreover, they only saw what they wanted to see, and they interpreted a representational element like a magnificent palace as unequivocal evidence of a reform-minded prince who was outside the court.[24] This is a decisive point, because, for contemporaries and in the historiography, reforms play a major role in defining an Enlightenment prince. The question arises: What did rulers do to meet this criterion?

Frederick August of Anhalt-Zerbst—an enlightened ruler?

In 1827, just before her death, the widowed Princess Friederike Auguste Sophie of Anhalt-Zerbst (1744–1827) announced a prize question by the Anhalt Agricultural Society (Anhaltische Landwirtschafts-Gesellschaft). The question was: "What influence would His Serene Highness the immortalized Prince Frederick August of Anhalt-Zerbst's agricultural law of 1775 have had on the agriculture of the country, if the spirit of the law had been properly applied?"[25] The response essays were expected to answer this question by analyzing practical examples.[26]

With this announcement, Princess Friederike wanted to rehabilitate the damaged public memory of her deceased husband, the last ruling prince of Anhalt-Zerbst, Frederick August (r.1751–1793). His posthumous image was marred by the *Handbuch* that Gustav Adolf

---

22. Pečar and Zaunstöck, *Politische Gartenkunst?*
23. Paul Beckus, *Hof und Verwaltung des Fürsten Franz von Anhalt-Dessau (1758–1817): Struktur, Personal, Funktionalität* (Halle, 2015).
24. Michael Niedermeier, "Macht, Memoria und Mätressen: herrschaftliche Gartenkunst als politische Besetzung der Landschaft in Schwetzingen und Wörlitz," in *Politische Gartenkunst?*, ed. A. Pečar and H. Zaunstöck, p.35–81 (52).
25. "Welchen Einfluß würde das Culturgesetz, welches Se. Durchl. der verewigt Fürst Friedrich August von Anhalt-Zerbst 1775 bekannt machte, auf die Cultur des Landes gehabt haben, wenn der Geist dieses Gesetzes gehörig Eingang gefunden hätte?" [Ludwig] Albert, "War das Culturgesetz, welches der Fürst Friedrich August 1775 bekannt machte, zweckmäßig?," *Möglinsche Annalen der Landwirtschaft* 20 (1827), p.96–164 (96).
26. Albert, "Culturgesetz," p.114.

Harald Stenzel published in 1820.[27] In this comprehensive survey of Anhalt history, Stenzel contrasted Frederick August with his cousin Prince Franz of Anhalt-Dessau, the Enlightenment hero of the last part of the book.[28] Stenzel saw in Frederick August an incarnation of all bad aspects of the *ancien régime*. He depicted him as an eccentric and half-mad ruler who abandoned government to the hands of his corrupt and tyrannical privy council. Because Frederick August supported the British during the American War of Independence, Stenzel presented him as a slave trader who sold his subjects to the English. Frederick August was also said to have initiated the economic decline of his territory because of his disinterest in the welfare of his subjects. His dynastic line ended with his death, and the principality of Anhalt-Zerbst was absorbed by the other princes of Anhalt.[29] The image of Frederick August crafted by Stenzel has survived in the scholarship to this day.[30] Indeed, it was completed by Reinhold Specht, who diagnosed in Frederick August a sadistic disposition.[31]

With the prize question, Princess Friederike wanted to remind the public that Frederick August had dedicated himself to the welfare of his principality. The Anhalt Agricultural Society unanimously selected the financial councilor Ludwig Albert (1778–1836) as the winner of the contest. Albert was an old official of the duke of Anhalt-Köthen. He had administrated the department of Roßlau in what had been Anhalt-Zerbst for decades, so he knew very well the effects of the agricultural law from his own experience.[32]

Albert's essay is one of the few studies of Frederick August that does not give a one-sided and overwhelmingly negative account of his rule. The text reveals details not only about the reign of the last prince of Anhalt-Zerbst, but also about the perception of Enlightenment princes in general, and about the reign and image of Prince Franz of Anhalt-Dessau in particular. Albert showed that the agricultural

---

27. Stenzel, *Handbuch*.
28. Stenzel, *Handbuch*, vol.1, p.260–71, 366–94.
29. Stenzel, *Handbuch*, vol.1, p.260–71.
30. Paul Beckus, *Land ohne Herr–Fürst ohne Hof? Friedrich August von Anhalt-Zerbst und sein Fürstentum* (Halle, 2018), p.22–34.
31. Reinhold Specht, *Geschichte der Stadt Zerbst*, 2 vols. (Dessau, 1998), vol.1, p.76–91; Reinhold Specht, "Das unrühmliche Ende des Fürstentums Anhalt-Zerbst: ein Beitrag zur preußischen Kriegspolitik und zu dem Soldatenhandel deutscher Fürsten im 18. Jahrhundert," unpublished manuscript, 1958 (Landesarchiv Saxony-Anhalt, Abt. Dessau: LAO 230).
32. Beckus, *Land ohne Herr*, p.272–73.

reforms of Frederick August continued to have positive effects until the early nineteenth century.[33] Additionally, he pointed out that the reforms were begun a few years before Franz of Anhalt-Dessau started his own agricultural reforms, which were much praised by Enlightenment philosophers. That Frederick August was actively reforming his territory raises the question of whether he should be seen as a part of the group of *princes éclairés*, and it raises the question: What makes Enlightenment princes enlightened?

Reforms were crucial in helping to define the notion of an Enlightenment prince for both contemporaries and the historiography. Any prince who wanted to appear enlightened had to promote reforms that were considered enlightened. For this reason, Franz of Anhalt-Dessau's support of agriculture was a prominent part of his monarchical self-representation. The physiocratic and enlightened elites praised Prince Franz as a pioneer in this matter and others.[34] However, it is striking that Frederick August of Anhalt-Zerbst had initiated very similar reforms. Inspired by a law promulgated in 1768 by Maria Theresa (1740–1780) for the kingdom of Bohemia, Frederick August in 1770 issued a law on common pastures that limited the number of livestock. This law was improved and expanded in 1775.[35] He also promoted other agricultural innovations. These were the same measures that Prinz Franz later introduced in Anhalt-Dessau.[36]

The same can be said about other policies. Frederick August supported prominent projects promoted by Enlightenment authors in the late eighteenth century. He realized innovative pedagogical and sociopolitical projects, supported manufacturing, and published laws establishing the toleration of the Jews and Catholics.[37] Another example: Under Frederick August, more teachers were hired for new school disciplines at the *Gymnasium illustre* and the Page Institute (*Pageninstitut*) in Zerbst. Frederick August also opened the latter to the children of commoners.[38] The changes at the Page Institute were immediate reactions to the establishment of the *Philanthropin* in Dessau at the end of the 1770s. The *Philanthropin* was an innovative

---

33. Albert, "Culturgesetz," p.108, 159–60.
34. See Hirsch, *Dessau-Wörlitzer Reformbewegung*, p.65–200; Hirsch, *Frühklassik*, passim.
35. Albert, "Culturgesetz," p.133–38.
36. Beckus, *Land ohne Herr*, p.271–89.
37. Beckus, *Land ohne Herr*, p.278–85.
38. Beckus, *Land ohne Herr*, p.279–81.

school, which was of supra-regional importance for education reforms in Germany and a showcase for Prince Franz.[39]

To be clear, most of these projects and laws were not innovative. Other rulers had already initiated similar reforms. However, it is worth pointing out that in the scholarship it is precisely such reforms that are considered the best indicators that a ruler was enlightened. For instance, the rulers of Anhalt-Bernburg and Anhalt-Köthen were considered enlightened rulers by regional historiography of the twentieth century because they imposed similar reforms.[40]

In contrast, Frederick August of Anhalt-Zerbst appears in the scholarship as a paragon of unsuccessful and unenlightened rule because, from the late 1770s to the mid-1780s, several of his reform projects failed—never mind that such failures were typical of Enlightenment projects.[41] Reinhold Specht dismisses his reform efforts as an attempt to improve financial and human resources for his military.[42] Regarding Frederick August's motivations, he might be right. His argument implies, however, that altruism should be considered the leitmotif of enlightened rule. Such a criterion is highly dubious, because financial interests usually played a major role in reform projects. Many reform ideas of the late eighteenth century went hand in hand with endeavors to centralize administration and increase revenues. When princes spoke about the public good, they also meant the good of their own finances. It was generally assumed that the welfare of the state was inseparable from the welfare of the prince. Princely financial interests were intrinsic to social and pedagogical projects, to religious toleration legislation, as well as to industrial and agricultural reforms.[43]

Here we should note that the maxim of Prince Franz of Anhalt-Dessau was "Join the beautiful with the utilitarian."[44] For example, the prince and his family were the chief beneficiaries when he

39. *"Die Stammutter aller guten Schulen": das Dessauer Philanthropinum und der deutsche Philanthropismus 1774–1793*, ed. Jörn Garber (Tübingen, 2008).
40. Ludwig Arndt, *Friedrich der Große und die Askanier seiner Zeit (Dargestellt hauptsächlich aus der "Politischen Korrespondenz" des Königs), Anhaltische Geschichtsblätter* 13 (1937), ed. Verein für Anhaltische Geschichte und Altertumskunde (Dessau, 1938), p.21–57 (49).
41. Beckus, *Land ohne Herr*, p.277–79.
42. Specht, *Geschichte*, vol.2, p.89.
43. Birtsch, "Idealtyp," p.33–34.
44. "Das Schöne mit dem Nützlichen verbinden," Reil, *Leopold Friedrich Franz*, p.56.

improved agricultural and forestry productivity, because they were the only ones with large-scale landholdings. At the beginning of his reign, the ruler of Anhalt-Dessau possessed 52 percent of the agricultural lands and all of the forests. His property increased in the following decades, because the nine estates that had been held in 1758 by other members of the princely family fell to him by succession and family treaties from 1769 to 1798.[45] The whole export economy of Anhalt-Dessau was oriented toward the production of grain and wool on the leased princely estates, and the intensification of agriculture was meant to support these economic sectors.[46] Other projects, such as the pedagogical reforms or the toleration of Jews, were also intended to increase revenues. Indeed, Franz did nothing to improve the conditions of the Jews. There was already an important Jewish community in Anhalt-Dessau, and he let them pay "protection money" (*Schutzgeld*) as his predecessors already had.[47] Nonetheless, his supposed tolerance has been celebrated in the historiography. The confluence of enlightened reforms and economic interest was not a secret—on the contrary, many enlightened promoters openly articulated this idea.[48] Suffice to say: Specht's evaluation of Frederick August as an unenlightened prince is clearly unconvincing, and striving for economic success is hardly a criterion for exclusion from the society of enlightened princes.

Representation of the reform policy

If Frederick August initiated reforms of the "enlightened" type and his motivation was no different from that of other princes, then it is natural to ask why he has been considered by neither contemporaries

45. Ulla Jablonowski, "Wirtschaftliche und soziale Grundlagen der Dessau-Wörlitzer Aufklärung (etwa 1760 bis 1800)," *Mitteilungen des Vereins für Anhaltische Landeskunde* 1 (1992), p.39–75 (40); Beckus, *Hof und Verwaltung*, p.144, 321.
46. Ulla Machlitt, *Die anhaltisch-dessauischen Domänen in der Periode des Übergangs von der feudalen zur kapitalistischen Produktionsweise (etwa 1700 bis 1800)* (Eisleben, 1971), p.39–44.
47. Frank Kreißler, "'Die Toleranz ist in Dessau ganz zu Hause…': Fürst Franz und die jüdische Gemeinde in Dessau im Spiegel der fürstlichen Verordnungen," in *Das Leben des Fürsten: Studien zur Biografie von Leopold III. Friedrich Franz von Anhalt-Dessau (1740–1817)*, ed. Holger Zaunstöck (Halle, 2008), p.82–93; Paul Beckus, "Zwischen Image und Ökonomie: Fürst Franz und die Juden 1758–1817," in *Politische Gartenkunst?*, ed. A. Pečar and H. Zaunstöck, p.143–57.
48. Beckus, *Land ohne Herr*, p.285.

nor the scholarship to be an "enlightened" prince. My argument is that it was not the reforms as such but rather their public representation that influenced whether rulers were classified as "enlightened" or not. It is futile to search for the inner convictions of the princes in order to describe them as "enlightened" or not, as Kirill Abrosimov reminds us.[49] Instead, it is more fruitful to consider why contemporaries regarded a ruler as "enlightened." Communication strategies probably played the most important role. The figure of the *prince éclairé* was a fiction that shaped communication between Enlightenment philosophers and princes.[50] In this sense, enlightened princes were those who communicated as enlightened princes were expected to do. The implementation of reforms was of secondary importance. This becomes clear if the activities of a supposedly unenlightened prince, like Frederick August, are compared with those of supposedly enlightened rulers. The domestic political projects that Frederick August imposed show that a commitment to reforms, although a necessary requirement, was not sufficient for a ruler to be considered "enlightened."

Franz of Anhalt-Dessau was one of the rulers who understood this. From the beginning of his reign, he worked hard to establish a positive image of himself in the public sphere. Already during his Grand Tour, following the Seven Years War, he strived to become a friend of prominent intellectuals in Italy, England, and France, as well as other Enlightenment philosophers. He read their works, and made contact and corresponded with many of them. In his own country he began to implement projects after the mid-1760s. From the 1770s Prince Franz focused increasingly on projects that were helpful in presenting him to a public broader than mere local authors and neighboring principalities.[51]

The first and most prominent project was the *Philanthropin* in Dessau, which was created by Johann Bernhard Basedow (1724–1790). This school was promoted as a place where a new vision of education would be put into practice. Furthermore, it made noble education accessible for commoners. They were taught to behave in a courtly manner, to ride, and to fence. This approach was not unique and limited to Basedow's *Philanthropin*; it is, as Gijs Versteegen reminds us in his chapter in this volume, mirrored in Gaspar Melchor de

49. Abrosimov, *Aufklärung jenseits der Öffentlichkeit*, p.215–56.
50. Abrosimov, *Aufklärung jenseits der Öffentlichkeit*, p.215–19.
51. Hirsch, *Dessau-Wörlitzer Reformbewegung*; Hirsch, *Frühklassik*.

Jovellanos's educational program in Spain. The creation of the *Philan-thropin* was a great media success for the prince of Anhalt-Dessau, and to this day it has influenced the public image of Franz as a supporter of public education and good father to his country. However, in practice, the *Philanthropin* was a failure after 1784, not least due to lack of support from Franz.[52] Contemporaries and the historiography did not take into account that Franz was interested in improving his own image, rather than improving education. They simply accepted what Franz and some of his agents wrote, and considered the *Philan-thropin* a success. This was a direct result of Franz's communication strategies. He himself controlled the media and the accounts of the project by figures like Basedow and Johann Heinrich Campe (1746–1818). In this way, even when it became clear to contemporaries that the *Philanthropin* was not functioning well, Franz managed to impose in the public sphere a narrative of the decline of the institution that did not damage his reputation. According to Franz, quarrels between the teachers were responsible for the decline of the school, not anything he did.[53]

The same can be observed in the case of the other projects usually associated with Franz's public image as an enlightened prince. The celebrated publishing company the Library of Scholars (Buchhandlung der Gelehrten) disappeared after a few years. The special fund giving financial aid to writers and artists (*Verlagskasse für Gelehrte und Künstler*) was also dissolved shortly after it was created.[54] The Princely Chalcographic Society (Fürstliche Chalkographische Gesellschaft) was a financial and personal disaster that provoked a long disagreement between Franz and his natural son, Count Franz Waldersee (1763–1823), who was the president of the society.[55]

---

52. Garber,"*Die Stammutter aller guten Schulen*"; Hirsch, *Dessau-Wörlitzer Reformbe-wegung*, p.297–306.
53. Niedermeier, "Campe," p.63–65.
54. Ernst Fischer, "'… dem Buchhandel eine andere Richtung zu geben': die Dessauer 'Allgemeine Buchhandlung der Gelehrten' als verlegerisches Avantgar-deunternehmen," in *Bücherwelten im Gartenreich Dessau-Wörlitz*, ed. Wilhelm Haefs (Hannover, 2009), p.113–30; Stephanie Rahmede, *Die Buchhandlung der Gelehrten zu Dessau: ein Beitrag zur Schriftstelleremanzipation um 1800* (Wiesbaden, 2008); Hirsch, *Dessau-Wörlitzer Reformbewegung*, p.355–66.
55. Chalcography is copper engraving. "'… Waren nicht des ersten Bedürfnisses, sondern des Geschmacks und des Luxus*": zum 200. Gründungstag der Chalcographischen Gesellschaft Dessau*, ed. Norbert Michels (Weimar, 1996); Anna-Franziska von Schweinitz, *Waldersee und Vater Franz: vom Unglück der nichtehelichen Geburt* (Wettin-Löbejün, 2017), p.107–53.

However, none of these failures had any repercussions for Prince Franz's image. On the contrary, his public image benefited from all these projects.

This discrepancy between public perception and actual achievements was bridged by Franz's successful strategy of self-representation. Franz succeeded in presenting himself as an enlightened reformer not only by controlling the texts published by famous writers, but also thanks to the creation of the "garden kingdom" of Dessau-Wörlitz, an ensemble of palaces and a park, with Wörlitz at its center. This was the decisive element of his strategy of representation. In Wörlitz, Prince Franz created buildings in neoclassical and neo-gothic style.[56] Around the buildings he laid out an extended English garden, which was linked to the adjacent agricultural landscape. Wörlitzer Park served as a stage for his self-representation as an enlightened ruler. He received like-minded princes, enlightened activists, and other visitors in an informal and seemingly non-courtly atmosphere.[57] He presented Wörlitz as a laboratory for enlightened reforms. For instance, he presented fields with novel crops, a small synagogue on the outskirts of the garden (indicating tolerance), and monuments to educational reformers like Rousseau. In Wörlitz, Franz could represent himself as the plain and humble father of his country. He made his principality resemble a mirror in which Enlightenment philosophers could see their own image reflected.[58]

At the same time, the same place could carry different messages for other audiences. This can be seen in the following case: For most of his reign Franz of Anhalt-Dessau resided at his court in Dessau, surrounded by the usual councilors and courtiers. Dessau was the location of classic courtly representation, and over the years Franz worked at this residence and hosted official events there. Franz primarily represented himself in the typical role of a ruler.[59] He went to Wörlitz on special occasions, and an inner circle of courtiers was his entourage at this less ceremonial place. Franz used Wörlitz to

---

56. Pečar and Zaunstöck, *Politische Gartenkunst?*; *"Seltsam, abenteuerlich und unbeschreiblich verschwenderisch": gotische Häuser um 1800 in England, Potsdam, Weimar und Dessau-Wörlitz*, ed. Heinrich Dilly and Barry Murnane (Halle, 2014); Bechtholdt and Weiß, *Weltbild Wörlitz*; Marie-Luise Harksen, *Erdmannsdorff und seine Bauten in Wörlitz* (Wörlitz, 1973); Hirsch, *Dessau-Wörlitzer Reformbewegung*, p.405–407.
57. See Hirsch, *Frühklassik*.
58. Niedermeier, "Macht," p.52.
59. Beckus, "Franz in seiner Stadt," p.18–29.

represent not only his Enlightenment credentials, but also his rank and dynasty, and Wörlitz was used for court ceremonies. It also displayed references to ancient mythology in order to symbolize the Askanian dynasty's genealogy. Furthermore, neo-gothic buildings embodied the fame and honor of the house of Anhalt. They were used to legitimize control over the rulers' own territory and their status as princes of the Holy Roman Empire.[60] All this was barely perceived by Enlightenment intellectuals and probably immaterial to them. They saw Franz as a model ruler, and they ignored whatever did not fit with this image.

Franz of Anhalt-Dessau addressed several audiences at once through his self-representation. Enlightenment writers themselves were the first and foremost audience. Through their writings and their exchanges among themselves they significantly contributed to the dissemination of the image of Prince Franz as an enlightened ruler. Furthermore, through their publications and correspondence they reached a wider audience, including the aristocratic and court elites of Europe. Members of the nobility were also addressed directly via the classical element of self-representation. The commoners of Anhalt-Dessau were less important as an audience, but their perception of their ruler would not have been unaffected by his positive image in the media.

Frederick August of Anhalt-Zerbst largely disregarded such communication strategies, which would have been necessary to be considered an enlightened prince. It was important to act like a sweet-tempered, accessible, and father-like figure. The prince favored

60. See Johannes Süßmann, "Der Garten als Bauakt: zur Einrichtung 'natürlicher Herrschaft' in der Wörlitzer Landschaftsarchitektur," and Ingo Pfeifer, "Dynastische Repräsentation im Wörlitzer Gartenreich," in *Politische Gartenkunst?*, ed. A. Pečar and H. Zaunstöck, p.15–24 and 25–33; Michael Niedermeier, "Germanen in den Gärten: 'altdeutsche Heldengräber,' 'gotische' Denkmäler und die patriotische Gedächtniskultur," in *Revolutio Germanica: die Sehnsucht nach der "alten Freiheit" der Germanen 1750–1820*, ed. Jost Hermand and Michael Niedermeier (Frankfurt am Main, 2003), p.21–116; Michael Niedermeier, "'Wir waren vor den Hohenzollern da': zur politischen Ikonographie des frühen Landschaftsgartens mit einem Seitenblick auf Fontanes Roman 'Vor dem Sturm,'" in *Gehäuse der Mnemosyne: Architektur als Schriftform der Erinnerung*, ed. Harald Tausch (Göttingen, 2003), p.171–207; Michael Niedermeier, "Im Gartenland der Göttin Venus: Dessau-Wörlitz zwischen Aufklärung, Politik und erotisch-kosmologischer Weltanschauung," in *Schauplatz vernünftiger Menschen: Kultur und Geschichte in Anhalt-Dessau*, ed. Hans Wilderotter (Berlin, 2006), p.157–92.

a different image for himself, which was more traditional and less innovative: He emphasized his position as an imperial prince and above all his role as a military commander.[61] Before he came to the throne, Frederick August joined the emperor's army as a colonel and regimental commander. This period of his life made a deep impression on him. In the following years, the relationship between Frederick August and the emperor was deepened by the painful experiences of the Seven Years War: Anhalt-Zerbst was occupied in 1758 by Prussian troops, and Frederick August had to flee to Vienna.[62] His loyalty to the house of Austria was a second feature of the public image he endeavored to establish, and his claim to prestige because of his military prowess and his affiliation with the Habsburgs dominated his representational strategy.

In Frederick August's image there was no place for those elements that were typical of the representational strategies of enlightened princes. He did not present himself as the father of his subjects, like Franz of Anhalt-Dessau, or as a servant of the state who was inspired by the virtues of classical republicanism, like Frederick II of Prussia (1740–1786).[63] Such self-representation would have been difficult anyway, because he was absent from his country from 1765 to 1793, that is, for most of his reign. Moreover, his everyday behavior was emphatically hyper-masculine and aggressive. He was an ostentatious gambler, drinker, and smoker.[64] For these reasons, it would have been difficult for him to embody the ideal of an enlightened prince. In any case, Frederick August did not even try: Domestic policy was not critical to his image policy. Consequently, the reform projects that he imposed in Anhalt-Zerbst did not influence his public image.

However, Frederick August's self-fashioning as a warlord was also unsuccessful. He was not a highly gifted military commander, and he never commanded an army, although he was ultimately named imperial general of the cavalry and imperial general quartermaster (*Reichsgeneralfeldzeugmeister*).[65] This gap between his representational strategy and reality, which was not unusual for high nobles, made

61. Beckus, *Land ohne Herr*, p.333–36.
62. Beckus, *Land ohne Herr*, p.79–92.
63. Regarding the latter, see Andreas Pečar, *Die Masken des Königs: Friedrich II. von Preußen als Schriftsteller* (Frankfurt am Main, 2016), p.145–82.
64. Beckus, *Land ohne Herr*, p.333–54.
65. Beckus, *Land ohne Herr*, p.111–26.

him vulnerable to criticism. Moreover, he was considered ugly, and he had a humpback that earned him the nickname of the "Humpbacked Prince."[66]

How enlightened writers shaped the perception of rulers in the historiography: the example of Johann Christian Schmohl

All things considered, Prince Frederick August never had a talent for the media. He was never active in making connections with Enlightenment writers. In this way, he let others freely interpret his reign. Because of that, he was barely mentioned in the texts of enlightened writers until the end of the 1770s. Until then, Frederick August did not receive any publicity from these opinion leaders, or, when he did, it was negative. In particular, Johann Christian Schmohl (1756–1783) played a critical role in establishing a negative view of the government of Anhalt-Zerbst in 1781.[67]

Schmohl's *Sammlung von Aufsätzen* contains two accounts of the economic situation in Anhalt.[68] Both of them draw a gloomy picture of Frederick August's reign and reforms. Schmohl defamed a number of Frederick August's councilors and officials, and above all he accused the administration of the department of Coswig and the privy council in Zerbst of being corrupt and incompetent.[69] Schmohl also criticized the prince's agricultural policy and suggested that, because Frederick August was abroad,

66. "Buckliger Prinz." Joseph Demuth, *Das unbekannte und geheimnisvolle Luxemburg: Chronik eines kleinen, grossen Landes*, 10 vols. (Luxembourg, 1982–1989), vol.4, p.34–35.

67. Michael Niedermeier, "Der anhaltische Philanthrop: Schriftsteller und Aufrührer Johann Christian Schmohl und seine spektakuläre Flucht aus Halle im Jahre 1781," in *Europa in der Frühen Neuzeit*, ed. Erich Donnert, 7 vols. (Weimar, 1997–2008), vol.4, p.229–48; Michael Niedermeier, "'Thu Recht und scheue Niemand': Johann Christian Schmohl: sorbisch-patriotischer Bauernsohn, philanthropischer Radikalaufklärer, 'Hochverräter': erneute Spurensuche," in *Dessau-Wörlitz und Reckahn: Treffpunkte für Aufklärung, Volksaufklärung und Philanthropismus*, ed. Hanno Schmitt (Bremen, 2014), p.123–42; Beckus, *Land ohne Herr*, p.34–47.

68. Johann Christian Schmohl, *Sammlung von Aufsätzen verschiedner Verfasser besonders für Freunde der Cameralwissenschaften und der Staatswirthschaft* (Leipzig, Schwickert, 1781).

69. Johann Christian Schmohl, "Briefe an Herrn Pstlzz [...] über den Zustand der Landwirthschaft und des Bauerstandes im Fürstenthum Anhalt," in Schmohl, *Sammlung von Aufsätzen*, p.199–340 (259, 265–66, 270–79).

he did not know anything about the situation in his principality. Schmohl even implied that Frederick August was crazy, and said that his militarism was ridiculous.[70] This was a direct attack on Frederick August's self-fashioning. Members of his privy council were aware that responding to this provocation would further damage the prince's public image; however, they still advised their prince to sue Schmohl and to ban his book, because his critique was too harsh to be ignored. The leading councilor, Ehrenfried of Rheinboth (d.1784), wrote: "Experience confirms that a text, which is prohibited and confiscated, sells all the better, because of the appeal of novelty. Nevertheless, the princely government cannot be nonchalant and accept the publication of such a malicious book."[71] According to them, the reason of state demanded that they stop the publication of this book, so they sued Schmohl, which made the case famous.[72]

Schmohl's critique of Anhalt-Zerbst was not really an anti-court polemic. It was rather a critique of the Anhalt-Zerbst government referring to the topoi of anti-court polemics. All the typical elements of criticisms of courts were used here. Schmohl criticized the fact that Frederick August was not involved in daily politics and was isolated from his subjects. He presented the customary patronage practices as corruption and a betrayal of the common good.[73]

This description of the situation in Anhalt-Zerbst has been quite important for the perception of Frederick August in the histori-ography. Later historians were not aware of Schmohl's motivation and the background to his interpretations. They trusted him when he claimed to be an objective observer and an uninterested protagonist of the Enlightenment, and they thereby overlooked Schmohl's personal interests. Schmohl was a subject of the prince of Anhalt-Zerbst. He studied theology and then jurisprudence and cameralism. Between periods of study, he worked as a teacher at the *Philanthropin* in Dessau

---

70. Schmohl, "Briefe," p.273, 327; Schmohl, "Kameralische Reise durch das Fürstenthum Anhalt," in Schmohl, *Sammlung von Aufsätzen*, p.356–418 (397, 399).

71. "Es bestätigt zwar, die Erfahrung, daß eine Schrift, wenn sie verbothen und confisciert wird, um destomehren Abgang aus Reitz zur Neuigkeit findet: dem ohngeachtet aber kann die Fürstl. Regierung bey Erscheinung dieser boshaften Schrift wohl nicht sich leiden und gleichgültig verhalten" (Landesarchiv Saxony-Anhalt, DE, Z 90, I S Nr. 803, f.24*r*).

72. Beckus, *Land ohne Herr*, p.43–47.

73. Schmohl, "Briefe," p.259–79.

for a short period, and he moved in Enlightenment circles from Dessau to Strasbourg.[74] During his second stint at the university he applied for employment in Anhalt-Zerbst. However, at an audience granted by Friederike of Anhalt-Zerbst, he was only offered a position as a servant in the princely stables or as a secretary. Schmohl wanted more: He saw himself as an expert in cameralism and a future influential member of the Council of Finance.[75] He refused the offer and wrote his *Collection of essays*.

Another reason for Schmohl's critique of the Anhalt-Zerbst government was litigation of his father, Johann Andreas Schmohl. Schmohl senior had been one of the first farmers who participated in the partitioning of common pastures. Because of the supplementary agricultural law of 1775, he had to compensate other peasants. He refused to do so and filed a suit against the Council of Finance before the superior court of the principality. The trial ended in 1781 with a compromise. A large section in Schmohl's account focused on this lawsuit, and all the persons whom he criticized were involved in it.[76] Schmohl's critique of the situation in Anhalt-Zerbst may have been well grounded, but one cannot ignore that his criticisms were shaped by his own grudges and interests. He criticized Frederick August and his government mainly because he could not be a part of it, and, simultaneously, he tried to display his own expertise in this way. In doing so, agricultural reforms, which were a typical interest of Enlightenment authors, could become an object of criticism. It is worth mentioning that Schmohl barely criticized anything in Anhalt-Dessau, although Prince Franz's agricultural reforms created similar problems. Thus, it is not surprising that Prince Franz impeded the arrest of Schmohl and provided an opportunity for Schmohl to defend himself in writing.[77]

Posterity remembered only the severe problems created by the implementation of the reforms in Anhalt-Zerbst; the successes in various sectors such as fruit cultivation, education, or relief for the poor were largely forgotten. In the long run, Frederick August's image was shaped by Schmohl's account, as well as two other accounts, by Christian Frederick Sintenis (1750–1820)

---

74. Niedermeier, "Thu Recht," p.129–30.
75. Niedermeier, "Der anhaltische Philanthrop," p.241.
76. Beckus, *Land ohne Herr*, p.37–38.
77. Beckus, *Land ohne Herr*, p.44–45; Niedermeier, "Der anhaltische Philanthrop," p.245.

and Carl Frederic Ittig (d.1812). Both were officials of Frederick August who had conflicts with the privy council because of their positions and claims.[78] These were the primary sources on which Stenzel based his *Handbuch der Anhaltischen Geschichte*, and which established the historiography about Frederick August. Ultimately, these problematic accounts decided whether he would be considered an enlightened prince or not.

Conclusion

Frederick August of Anhalt-Zerbst has not been perceived as a *prince éclairé*, because he made no effort to appear enlightened, even though he was interested in Enlightenment thought and put reform projects into practice. The most important factor was self-representation.

The same can be said of Prince Franz. If Franz has been considered a *prince éclairé*, then it is not because he imposed reforms in education, art, and agriculture, or because he tolerated religious minorities. The reason is that he cultivated his image as a fervent supporter of the Enlightenment. In order to establish such a public image, he sponsored Enlightenment philosophers. Whoever wanted to be seen as a *prince éclairé* had to be recognized by Enlightenment writers, as happened in the case of Franz. A large number of German Enlightenment authors, for example Johann Joachim Winckelmann (1717–1768), Johann Wolfgang Goethe (1749–1832), and Christoph Martin Wieland (1733–1813), praised and glorified Franz as the model of an enlightened prince.[79] Franz was seen as a modest and caring father to his land and subjects, and a court did not fit into this view. Their focus was on Wörlitz, which was reduced to a symbol of Enlightenment and was seen as a manifestation of Franz's rejection of the court. Although Franz pursued a courtly lifestyle at Wörlitz, the "garden kingdom" was interpreted only as proof of his personal commitment to the Enlightenment and of his modernity. This made Franz a positive figure for future generations of historians. As a consequence, in the historiography, the image of Prince Franz has been remarkably constant over time. Local historians buttressed this perspective and chose Prince Franz as *the* major protagonist in Anhalt's history. The same local historiography also labeled Frederick

---

78. Beckus, *Land ohne Herr*, p.46–47.
79. Erhard Hirsch exhaustively lists who praised Prince Franz. See Hirsch, *Frühklassik*, passim, e.g., p.64, 67–68, 71.

August a villain in the early nineteenth century. Only retrospectively can we deduce that it was the representational strategies of princes, and what was written about them by authors with their own agendas, that determined whether princes were "enlightened" or not.

Enlightenment in courtly garden art: ideas and anti-court sociability in the Sanspareil rock garden of Wilhelmine of Bayreuth

Luise Maslow

Introduction

Stylistic classifications of historic gardens, in particular the dichotomy between picturesque and formal gardens, have been considered critically in recent years, mostly because of inherent, undeclared, judgmental, moral, and political implications.[1] Politically liberal-oriented British authors developed a historiography in the course of anti-French propaganda to legitimize the so-called English landscape garden by assigning a power-political dimension to the French garden.[2] Still following this historiography, the term "Enlightenment," with the exception of a few specific examples, still refers only to landscape gardens.[3] This ongoing narrative[4]

---

1. About this problem see, for example, John Dixon Hunt, "Approaches (new and old) to garden history," in *Perspectives on garden histories*, ed. Michel Conan (Washington, DC, 1999), p.77–90; Michael Leslie, "History and historiography in the English landscape garden," in *Perspectives*, ed. M. Conan, p.91–106; Reinhard Zimmermann, "Freiheit gegen Unfreiheit, Natur gegen Kunst? Der Gegensatz des formalen Gartens und des Landschaftsgartens als Denkfigur," in *Revolution in Arkadien*, ed. Berthold Heinecke and Harald Blanke (Hundisburg, 2007), p.59–82; Stefan Schweizer, "Raumformen, Ornamentik, Stile: der Garten als Kunstwerk im System der bildenden Künste," in *Gartenkunst in Deutschland von der Frühen Neuzeit bis heute: Geschichte–Themen–Perspektiven*, ed. Stefan Schweizer and Sascha Winter (Regensburg, 2012), p.103–21.
2. Above all Horace Walpole in his *Essay on modern gardening*, first published in 1771.
3. See Michael Niedermeier, "Landschaft/Garten," in *Handbuch europäische Aufklärung: Begriffe, Konzepte, Wirkung*, ed. Heinz Thoma (Stuttgart, 2015), p.323–34. While mentioning earlier examples, Niedermeier concentrates on landscape gardens. His article represents the state of the field today.
4. See, for example, Marie Luise Gothein, *Geschichte der Gartenkunst* (Jena, 1914); Dieter Hennebo and Alfred Hoffmann, *Geschichte der deutschen Gartenkunst*,

of the "natural" landscape garden as a moral symbol of republicanism and liberalism in opposition to the Continental baroque garden, identified with absolutist tyranny, luxury, and superficiality, ignores the fact that the protagonists of the Enlightenment usually maintained geometric gardens and that the first landscape gardens, which were only established on the Continent in the last decades of the eighteenth century, remained representational ones and thus instruments of power reserved mainly for the aristocracy. It also appears problematic that purely stylistic considerations are used to prove claims about sociohistorical and political processes.[5]

This chapter addresses the issue by examining how ideas of the Enlightenment could be presented by means of courtly garden art in late baroque gardens, specifically through the example of the Sanspareil rock garden of Wilhelmine of Prussia, margravine of Bayreuth. The Sanspareil rock garden was created in the short time of only four years (1744–1748) and before the triumph of the picturesque English garden with its moral and political associations.[6]

---

3 vols. (Hamburg, 1962–1965); Nikolaus Pevsner, "Von der Entstehung des Malerischen als Kunstprinzip," in Nikolaus Pevsner, *Architektur und Design von der Romantik zur Sachlichkeit* (Munich, 1971), p.11–39; Rudolf Wittkower, "Englischer Neopalladianismus, Landschaftsgärten, China und die Aufklärung," in *Politische Architektur in Europa vom Mittelalter bis heute: Repräsentation und Gemeinschaft*, ed. Martin Warnke (Cologne, 1984), p.309–35; Adrian von Buttlar, *Der Landschaftsgarten: Gartenkunst des Klassizismus und der Romantik* (Cologne, 1989). Up to now this narrative has particularly dominated the presentation of general ideas and chronological overviews of garden history.

5.   This problem is addressed in *Politische Gartenkunst? Landschaftsgestaltung und Herrschaftsrepräsentation des Fürsten Franz von Anhalt-Dessau in vergleichender Perspektive: Wörlitz, Sanssouci und Schwetzingen*, ed. Andreas Pečar and Holger Zaunstöck (Halle, 2015).

6.   For Wilhelmine's role in the creative process with a particular focus on the problem of stylistic classification, see Luise Maslow, "'Die Natur selbst war die Baumeisterin': der Felsengarten Sanspareil der Wilhelmine von Bayreuth als Ergebnis kultureller Austauschprozesse," *Die Gartenkunst* 29:2 (2017), p.250–61. The most important studies about Sanspareil are Erich Bachmann, "Anfänge des Landschaftsgartens in Deutschland," *Zeitschrift für Kunstwissenschaft* 5:3–4 (1951), p.203–28; Klaus Merten, *Der Bayreuther Hofarchitekt Joseph Saint-Pierre (1708/9–1754)* (Bayreuth, 1964); Gerhard Pfeiffer, "Markgräfin Wilhelmine und die Eremitagen bei Bayreuth und Sanspareil," in *Archive und Geschichtsforschung: Studien zur fränkischen und bayrischen Geschichte, Fridolin Solleder zum 80. Geburtstag dargebracht*, ed. Horst Heldmann (Neustadt an der Aisch, 1966), p.209–21; Sylvia Habermann, *Bayreuther Gartenkunst: die Gärten der Markgrafen von Brandenburg-Culmbach im 17. und 18. Jahrhundert* (Worms, 1982), p.147–72.

Without significant subsequent changes or anglicization, Sanspareil is a rare testimony of the independent Continental development of garden art in the course of the eighteenth century. With irregular pathways, the garden integrates the landscape around the medieval castle Zwernitz with its natural, bizarrely shaped rock formations. Because of this Sanspareil, still basically a formal garden, seems to withdraw from a clear stylistic classification. It is probably because of Wilhelmine that this garden appears unique in a lot of ways. Her amateur take on garden design, without the contributions of any famous garden artists, produced an intellectual artwork that cannot be described sufficiently using traditional stylistic models.

Garden design was seldom perceived as the realization or imitation of a stylistic concept, but involved a multitude of artistic, horticultural, functional, and personal contexts. By concentrating on Wilhelmine, whose amateur approach used her knowledge and imagination to inscribe numerous meanings onto the natural beech grove, and understanding her as a junction of cultural exchange processes, this chapter presents a methodically less biased analysis that uses the contemporary perspectives of garden owners and visitors.

Wilhelmine of Bayreuth: a *princesse-philosophe* and her gardens

Wilhelmine of Bayreuth, favorite sister of Frederick II, was raised and educated to be the consort of the future British king. Eventually married to her Hohenzollern kinsman Frederick of Brandenburg-Bayreuth, she tried, still having royal ambitions, to make the small principality one of the main intellectual centers of the Holy Roman Empire, comparable to her brother's court in Potsdam. Wilhelmine took an active interest in all the arts. In various ambitious projects, such as the building of palaces, theaters, gardens, and the founding of universities, the margravine was involved as a layperson. Her privately as well as publicly propagated image emphasized, alongside her social status, her moral notions and her scientific and artistic talents.

In the portrait by the official Prussian court painter Antoine Pesne (1750), she represents herself not only as a dilettante in the arts but also as a *philosophe*. The margravine is seated in a cave with her favorite dog, Folichon, in her lap. Painting material, musical works, and books remind us of her many activities. The pilgrim costume corresponds to

184 *Enlightenment at court*

her self-representation as the abbess of Bayreuth.[7] Caves, as seen in the picture, really exist in Wilhelmine's garden in Sanspareil. According to contemporary reports, she liked reading there.[8] This portrait already indicates the function of this garden as a place for arts, education, and philosophy, away from the more formal aspects of court life. Finally, the self-representation as a dilettante in the arts and, above all, as a *philosophe* ensured Wilhelmine's acceptance in the corresponding social circles. Her self-fashioning as a *philosophe*, as well as her vision of her garden as a place of scholarly education and moral edification, outside the bounds of courtly representation, was similar to that of her brother, Frederick II of Prussia. At the same time, in the 1740s, he was also laying out a garden at Sanssouci as a royal dilettante and with comparable messages, and the two of them conducted an extensive correspondence and reciprocal visits in which they discussed literary and artistic subjects.[9]

Wilhelmine's personal practice and knowledge of art, sciences, and philosophy created space for social interaction between different social classes. The practice of the amateur therefore enabled a social alternative to the traditional court based on the conventions of princely artistic practice and patronage. Wilhelmine does not appear as the responsible garden artist, but as an example of many royal dilettanti, according to early modern notions.[10] This status is an expression of a specific princely self-understanding that sets itself apart not only from the professional artist but also from the art-loving

7. The *philosophes* often used Christian metaphors to ironically articulate a sense of community; see Jochen Schlobach, "Französische Aufklärung und deutsche Fürsten," *Zeitschrift für historische Forschung* 17:3 (1990), p.327–49.
8. See, for example, Johann Gottfried Köppel, *Die Eremitage zu Sanspareil: nach der Natur gezeichnet und beschrieben von Johann Gottfried Köppel, Nachdruck der Ausgabe Erlangen 1793* (Erlangen, 1997), p.6.
9. See Alexander Rosenbaum, *Der Amateur als Künstler: Studien zur Geschichte und Funktion des Dilettantismus im 18. Jahrhundert* (Berlin, 2010), p.179–93; Adrian von Buttlar and Marcus Köhler, *Tod, Glück und Ruhm in Sanssouci: ein Führer durch die Gartenwelt Friedrichs des Großen* (Ostfildern, 2012).
10. Royal and princely artistic practice has only recently come into research focus, but so far without regard to gardening. See Rosenbaum, *Der Amateur als Künstler*; Charlotte Guichard, "'Amatrice': die Rolle der 'Amateurin' im Europa der Aufklärung," in *Aufgeklärter Kunstdiskurs und höfische Sammelpraxis: Karoline Luise von Baden im europäischen Kontext*, ed. Christoph Frank (Berlin, 2015), p.80–89; *Fürst und Fürstin als Künstler: herrschaftliches Künstlertum zwischen Habitus, Norm und Neigung*, ed. Annette C. Cremer, Matthias Müller, and Klaus Pietschmann (Berlin, 2018); *Die Kunst des Adels in der Frühen Neuzeit*, ed. Claudius Sittig and Christian Wieland (Wiesbaden, 2018).

amateur, and is committed to the political function of the regent as well as to the functions of the philosopher, poet, musician, or architect. This form of dilettantism in the arts had for centuries been an integral part of princely obligations. Accordingly, in the gardens created by amateurish intervention, personal preferences are inseparably linked with representative claims.

Wilhelmine used her gardens to express her personal philosophical models as well as other interests. Therefore, the gardens reflect ideas of the Enlightenment, as do her famous memoirs, full of anti-court stereotypes and scandalous family stories, her enormous library, sorted according to the figurative system of human knowledge from D'Alembert and Diderot's *Encyclopédie*,[11] and her works for the stage.[12] This chapter shows how Wilhelmine created spaces for experimental forms of sociability using topoi of the Enlightenment, and how her practice as an amateur artist created room for the development of her personality. I argue that she made particular use of her hermitages with their gardens to create such spaces within courtly life. Wilhelmine described Sanspareil as a rustic place with unique buildings and good company, but without any constrictions.[13] The natural beech grove with its bizarre rocks inspired Wilhelmine to inscribe numerous meanings onto the natural landscape.[14]

11. On Wilhelmine's library, see Daniela Harbeck-Barthel and Gisela Schlüter, "'Meine Bibliothek ist jetzt geordnet': der Aufbau von Wilhelmines französischer Bibliothek," in *Wilhelmine von Bayreuth heute: das kulturelle Erbe der Markgräfin*, ed. Günter Berger (Bayreuth, 2009), p.151–72.

12. See Ruth Müller-Lindenberg, "Melancholie, Suizid und Herrschaft: Quellen und Kontexte zu einigen Libretti der Wilhelmine," in *Wilhelmine von Bayreuth heute*, ed. G. Berger, p.173–86.

13. "[W]ir [haben] hier ein ziemlich einsames Leben geführt, das jedoch nicht ohne Reiz war. Die Lage des Ortes, an dem wir waren, ist einzig. Die Natur selbst war die Baumeisterin. Die dort aufgeführten Gebäude sind von sonderbarem Geschmack. Alles ist ländlich und bäurisch. Wir hatten eine recht gute Gesellschaft, und aller Zwang war verbannt. Wind und Regen haben uns von dort vertrieben." "Wilhelmine an Friedrich, Eremitage, 15. September 1749," in *Friedrich der Große und Wilhelmine von Bayreuth*, vol.2: *Briefe der Königszeit 1740–1758*, ed. Gustav Berthold Volz (Leipzig, 1926), no.217, p.174–75 (174).

14. For Wilhelmine's method of inscribing meaning into landscape, see Constanze Baum, "Ein Lorbeerzweig für Friedrich den Großen: Wilhelmine von Bayreuth am Grab Vergils (1755)," *Schriften der Winckelmann-Gesellschaft* 25 (2006), p.11–34; Helmut-Eberhard Paulus, "Die 'Römische Ruine' von 1756 in der Eremitage zu Bayreuth: eine Gartenstaffage als Denkmal der Erinnerung an die italienische Reise," *Arx: Burgen und Schlösser in Bayern, Österreich und Südtirol* 31:1–2 (2009), p.53–62.

Sanspareil as a place of commemoration

The garden was created around the medieval castle of Zwernitz that had belonged to the Hohenzollerns since the thirteenth century.[15] The castle was consciously integrated in the layout of the garden.[16] At a time that saw a critical questioning of the dynasty and its powers and privileges, the desire for visible, significant pieces of evidence for an uninterrupted genealogical line increased and led to the invention of an ancient prehistory of the ruling family. Genuine and artificial archaeological findings, landmarks, monuments, and pagan places of worship from Germanic times were placed in the seemingly natural space of the garden to establish the deep rootedness of the dynasty in the landscape.[17] The visible situation of the dynasty in the landscape was to make the legitimacy of the ruling family evident, aiming for stabilization of the status quo. In Sanspareil this happened by integrating the medieval castle and the natural beech grove, which, it was claimed, had been a pagan place of worship for the Germanic deity Lollus.[18] These monuments in the territory of the dynasty suggest regal continuity not only since the Middle Ages, but even since pre-Christian times. Such a reference to the distant past and the melding of dynastic tradition with the history of the territory and nature are a particular feature of Sanspareil. This strategy, that builds on common dynastic

15. About the castle see, for example, *850 Jahre Burg Zwernitz: Beiträge zur Geschichte der Burg und des Felsengartens Sanspareil*, ed. Schloss- und Gartenverwaltung Bayreuth-Eremitage (Bayreuth, 2007). Zwernitz had been in the possession of the Hohenzollerns since the thirteenth century and was a residence of the burgrave of Nürnberg. The title, which was related to high administrative functions and an extended territory, from which the margravates of Brandenburg-Ansbach and Brandenburg-Bayreuth originate, was still kept by the Hohenzollerns in the eighteenth century.
16. See Peter O. Krückmann, "Ein Park, ein Lustschloss und eine Burg: Burg Zwernitz als Teil des Felsengartens Sanspareil," in *Festungen in Gärten–Gärten in Festungen*, ed. Volker Mende (Regensburg, 2015), p.84–93, and image on p.199.
17. See Annette Dorgerloh and Michael Niedermeier, "Desire for origins: Archäologie und inszenierte Abstammung in Gärten des europäischen Adels," in *Mythos Ursprung: Modelle der Arché zwischen Antike und Moderne*, ed. Constanze Baum and Martin Disselkamp (Würzburg, 2011), p.95–122.
18. This legend is mentioned in several descriptions of Sanspareil. See for example Johann Michael Füssel, "1784: Johann Michael Füssel," in *Lustgärten um Bayreuth: Eremitage, Sanspareil und Fantaisie in Beschreibungen aus dem 18. und 19. Jahrhundert*, ed. Ingo Toussaint (Hildesheim, 1998), p.164–68 (166): "In der That soll auch dieser Wald ehemals ein Hain gewesen seyn, worinnen der Lollus der alten Deutschen verehrt wurde."

patterns to show political legitimacy, appeared in the European garden culture for the first time in the 1720s. However, only at the end of the eighteenth century was the combination of the dynastic and prehistoric references widespread in German garden design.[19]

The integration of the castle was a conscious choice, as can be seen in the series of copper engravings commissioned on the occasion of the inauguration of the garden (Figure 1). The prominent role of the castle is not restricted to these images. The access road from Bayreuth, designed as an *allée*, leads directly to the castle (Figure 2). None of the later erected buildings was axially integrated in the structure of the garden in such a way. Therefore, the main axis that is most significant ceremonially leads to the old castle. During the necessary overhaul and renovation of the castle, the *donjon* was crowned by a structure that served as an observation deck and was equipped with bells and a clock. The tower totally lost its function as a military watchtower, and instead called court society to the table. The view over the landscape that rolled out across the surrounding countryside was an expression of ownership. Integrated in Sanspareil as both a viewpoint and a scenic backdrop, the so-called "old castle" was a typical display of regal continuity and political legitimacy. The garden was maintained by the descendants to commemorate their ancestors.[20] Morally the castle embodies the traditional ideal of princely chivalry.[21]

19. See Dorgerloh and Niedermeier, "Desire for origins," p.95; Michael Niedermeier, "Germanen in den Gärten: 'altdeutsche Heldengräber,' 'gotische' Denkmäler und die patriotische Gedächtniskultur," in *Revolutio Germanica: die Sehnsucht nach der "alten Freiheit" der Germanen 1750–1820*, ed. Jost Hermand and Michael Niedermeier (Frankfurt am Main, 2003), p.21–116.

20. "Solchemnach haben sich vier durchlauchtigste Friedriche um dieses Schloß und Amt höchst verdient gemacht. Friedrich der IIIte Burggraf, der es an das hochfürstl. Haus Brandenburg käuflich gebracht; Friedrich der Iste Churfürst zu Brandenburg, und Marggraf dieses Namens der VIte, der die Hofkapelle und das Hofdiakonat gestiftet; Georg Friedrich Carl, welcher den seit dem 30jährigen Krieg in seinen Ruinen gelegenen hohen festen runden Thurm wieder aufbauen lassen; Friedrich der holde und gütige, welcher das alte Schloß und den Thurm verschönern und mit seiner königlichen Gemahlin diese natürlichschöne und unvergleichliche Einsiedeley [...] hat einrichten, und welche Se. jetzt glorwürdigstregierende Hochfürstl. Durchl. Herr Marggraf Friedrich Christian, noch immer, als ein unvergeßliches Denkmaal Dero Durchlauchtigsten Regimentsvorfahrer, in baulichen Würden erhalten lassen." Markus Friedrich Hedenus, "1768: Markus Friedrich Hedenus," in *Lustgärten um Bayreuth*, ed. I. Toussaint, p.159–62 (159–60).

21. The suit of armour, in which the margrave was often portrayed, was in the eighteenth century just as much an anachronism as the medieval castle, which

Figure 1: Johann Thomas Köppel, "Vue du vieux chateau de Sanspareil du côté du Römersberg / Prospect von dem alten Schloß zu Sanspareil nach dem Römersberg," copper engraving, 1748, Bamberg State Library, V Ec 66. Photo: Gerald Raab.

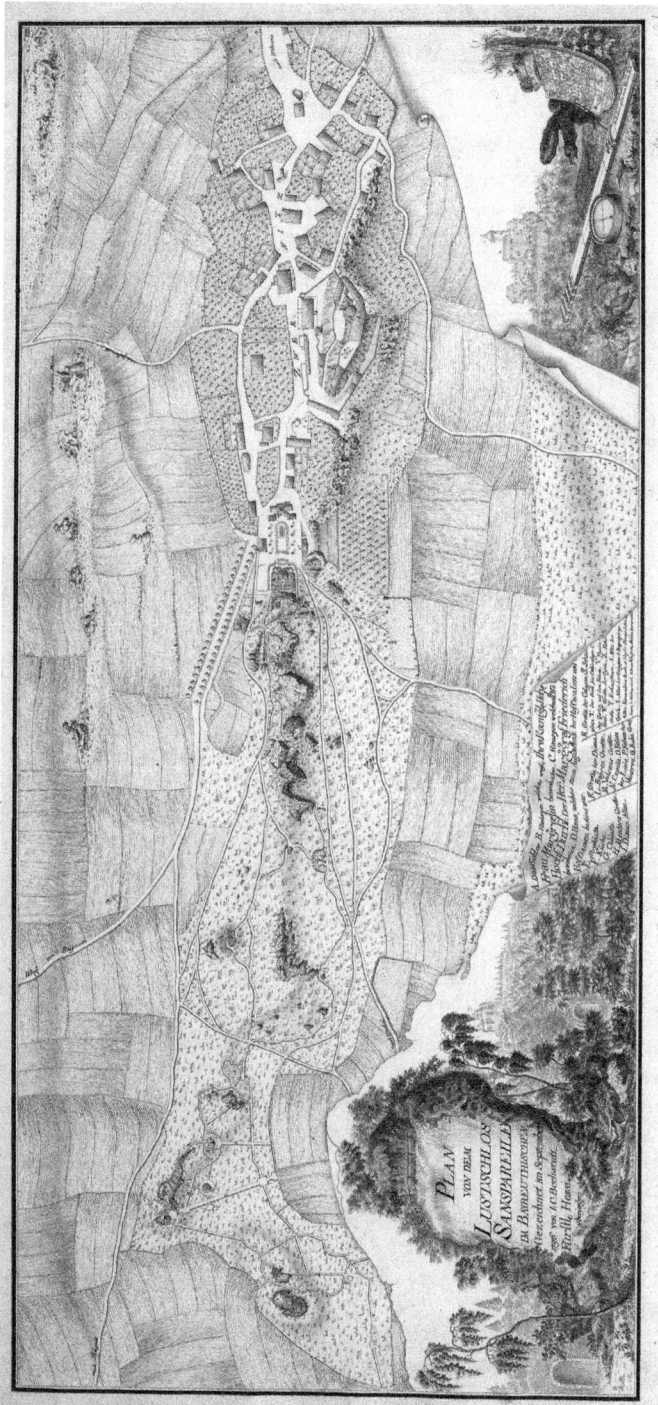

Figure 2: Johann Christoph Bechstatt, "Plan von dem Lustschlos Sanspareile im Bayreuthischen," drawing, 1796, University and State Library of Darmstadt, Collection of historical maps, Mappe006_14.

Sanspareil as a work of nature

Wilhelmine in her memoirs and letters always depicts natural landscapes as wild, strange, uncomfortable, and dangerous.[22] Nevertheless, the natural landscape and in particular the rocks around the castle were the starting point of the creation of the garden and therefore an important garden feature.

With the creation of her *Eremitage* Wilhelmine followed a long Western tradition. Inspired by religious practices, *Eremitage* buildings found their way into gardens as a pseudo-religious form of renunciation of the baneful city or court in favor of a morally better life in the countryside, in the sense of the retreat into nature of the hermit or the classical poet, philosopher, or scholar.[23] Isolation allows for concentration on life's essentials in the solitude of nature. Since the Renaissance these notions had been appearing in gardens in the form of irregular wooded areas or garden sections that were kept completely natural.[24] The inclusion of the natural grove in Sanspareil followed these precursors.

Wilhelmine describes the place as follows: "The location [...] is unique. Nature herself was the architect."[25] By doing so she formulated

---

by then did not serve any military purpose. Both were related to virtues of chivalry that were kept alive by the staging of hunting and tournaments as well as the newly founded knightly orders (in Bayreuth in 1705 the Ordre de la Sincérité, since 1734 the Order of the Red Eagle). See Krückmann, "Ein Park, ein Lustschloss und eine Burg."

22. See Ralph-Rainer Wuthenow, "Fürstliches Elend: die Memoiren der Wilhelmine, Markgräfin von Bayreuth," in *Das Bild und der Spiegel: europäische Literatur im 18. Jahrhundert*, ed. Ralph-Rainer Wuthenow (Munich, 1984), p.114–28 (125).

23. See Annette Dorgerloh, "Love, pilgrims and merry hermits: hermitage as a place of conviviality in the eighteenth century," in *Le tentazioni dell' "ermitage": ideali ascetici e invenzioni architettoniche dal medioevo all'illuminismo*, ed. Paola Zanardi (Milan, 2011), p.137–46.

24. The building tradition of the *Eremitage* still requires systematic research. For an overview see Luisa Hager, "Eremitage," in *Reallexikon zur Deutschen Kunstgeschichte*, ed. Zentralinstitut für Kunstgeschichte München (Munich, 1937–), vol.5, col.1203–29; Nadja Horsch, "Otium religiosum: die Gartener-emitage im Barchetto von Pesaro als christlich konnotierter Rückzugsort," in *Gärten und Parks als Lebens- und Erlebnisraum: funktions- und nutzungsgeschichtliche Aspekte der Gartenkunst in Früher Neuzeit und Moderne*, ed. Stefan Schweizer (Worms, 2008), p.65–80.

25. "Die Lage des Ortes [...] ist einzig. Die Natur selbst war die Baumeisterin." "Wilhelmine an Friedrich, Eremitage, 15. September 1749," in Volz, *Friedrich der Große*, no.217, p.174–75.

her mechanistic worldview.[26] Similar wording can be found in contemporary philosophical texts and geographical descriptions.[27] Nature was understood as having been designed according to mathematical, in particular geometric, rules. This rational notion of nature was influenced by Deism. Nature was the result of the highest reason of God, and natural laws were at the same time divine laws. This perception not only equated nature and morality, but also emphasized the moral power of nature, guided by divine (i.e., natural) laws. The inclusion of nature in the artwork of the garden was legitimized by its dimensions of meaning.[28]

Wilhelmine expands on the then-dominant physico-theological worldview with notions of sensualism and associationism. These ideas were much discussed, for example in the contemporary moral weeklies. Joseph Addison's essay *On the pleasures of the imagination*, published in separate volumes of *The Spectator* in 1712, had an especially lasting effect on the development of garden design. These ideas led to a greater appreciation of the imagination and of the individual experience of nature, and allowed for a more imaginative and associative approach to garden design. They might have contributed to the imaginative and playful way in which Wilhelmine inscribed numerous meanings into the landscape of Sanspareil.[29]

At the end of the grove a theater in the form of a ruin (Figure 3) links natural rocks and man-made architecture. The theater, probably the most prominent feature of the garden, is mostly hidden by trees or rocks. The view does not open up until one passes the big natural cave that serves as an auditorium. The architectural structure of the artificial ruin continues the natural grotto, imitates a grotto itself, and is meant to actually serve as a theater. At this point the conjunction of nature and art is most palpable: Nature, which was created by God and

---

26. See Joachim Kröll, "Naturbegriff und Naturgefühl im 18. Jahrhundert im Hinblick auf die Markgräfin Wilhelmine von Bayreuth," in *Im Glanz des Rokoko: Markgräfin Wilhelmine von Bayreuth, Gedenken zu ihrem 200. Todestag*, ed. Wilhelm Müller (Bayreuth, 1958), p.28–50.

27. See Maslow, "Die Natur selbst war die Baumeisterin," p.253.

28. About the integration of nature into gardens and the strategies of legitimization with special attention to rocks and mountains, see Géza Hajós, "Der Berg und der Garten: mythisches Abbild—künstliche Natürlichkeit—Promenadennatur," in *Garten–Kunst–Geschichte*, ed. Erika Schmidt, Wilfried Hansmann, and Jörg Gamer (Worms, 1994), p.116–24.

29. Wilhelmine's correspondence and her library prove that she had a sound grasp of contemporary developments and discourses.

Figure 3: Johann Thomas Köppel, "Vue du theatre de Sanspareil / Prospect von dem Theatro zu Sanspareil," copper engraving, 1748, Bamberg State Library, V Ec 69. Photo: Gerald Raab.

ruled by geometry and mechanics, combined with reason, which was the higher human nature, resulted in the "third nature" of the garden.[30] On another level the theater also shows that the integration of nature in this garden serves as an attraction for visitors. The experience of nature, only possible at some distance from the court, was something extraordinary.

For Wilhelmine the moral teaching of the Enlightenment was of the upmost importance. Nature as an "architect" was the outcome of mechanistic, divine laws, the expression of moral teaching, and an effective means to exhibit virtue. When nature and reason coincided, the rocky landscape of Sanspareil was an expression of the admirable moral teachings of China.

Sanspareil as chinoiserie

Inspired by the prominent rocks, reminiscent of foreign landscapes, Sanspareil was created as an imitation of a Chinese landscape in miniature.[31] In the eighteenth century rocks were considered a main feature of Asian gardens. The first garden buildings in Sanspareil were pavilions in exotic and Asian styles on top of some of the rocks (Figures 4 and 5), reminiscent of illustrations that could be found in reports about China and on Chinese artworks. These first projects established the stylistic direction of the garden. Not a single building conformed to European architectural forms.

Appearing as a Chinese landscape, Sanspareil was an expression of Chinese moral philosophy, which was admired by the European Enlightenment.[32] China, as a utopian counterpoint of the contemporary European social order, seemed to have solved social conflicts still involving the classical feudal hierarchy. The Chinese fashion in Europe aimed to incorporate features of the ideal society in a playful way.

A so-called oriental building (Figure 6) was erected as the central building of the new palace in Sanspareil. The palace buildings were situated in the geometrical part of the garden. In Sanspareil the

30. See John Dixon Hunt, "The idea of a garden and the three natures," in John Dixon Hunt, *Greater perfections: the practice of garden theory* (Philadelphia, PA, 2000), p.32–75.

31. See Erich Bachmann, *Felsengarten Sanspareil: Burg Zwernitz, amtlicher Führer* (Munich, 1954), p.4; Habermann, *Bayreuther Gartenkunst*, p.169–72.

32. On chinoiserie at the court of Wilhelmine and her siblings, see Gerd-Helge Vogel, "Konfuzianismus und chinoise Architekturen im Zeitalter der Aufklärung," *Die Gartenkunst* 8:2 (1996), p.188–212.

Figure 4: Johann Thomas Köppel, "Vue du cabinet sur le roc de la grotte de Calypse avec une partie du theatre batie a la rocaille á Sanspareil / Prospect des Lust Cabinets auf dem Felsen und bei der Höhle Calypse samt einem Theil des Theatri zu Sanspareil," copper engraving, 1748, Bamberg State Library; V Ec 68. Photo: Gerald Raab.

Figure 5: Johann Gottfried Köppel, "Die Aeolusgrotte zu Sanspareil," colored copper engraving, 1793, Bamberg State Library, JH.Top.q.60#2. Photo: Gerald Raab.

Figure 6: Johann Thomas Köppel, "Vue du batiment principal eremite a Sanspareil / Prospect von dem haupt-Eremite Gebaeude zu Sanspareil," copper engraving, 1748, Bamberg State Library, V Ec 67. Photo: Gerald Raab.

arrangement of the new buildings around one courtyard mimicked contemporary French models in imitation of the layout of Chinese imperial palaces.[33] Thus the arrangement avoids more hierarchical structures by removing the residential buildings of the ruling couple from the center to the sides of the courtyard. This was indeed associated with a critical look at one's own way of living[34] and could only be possible at a court open to Enlightenment ideas.[35] Louis XIV commissioned buildings in the Chinese fashion but endowed with European comforts to demonstrate the superiority of the European Roi Soleil versus the Middle Kingdom.[36] Neither this nor the reproduction of authentic Chinese forms was the aim in Bayreuth. The fusion of the role model with European building traditions can be understood as an attempt to merge the advantages of both cultures in the hope of creating the premises for an ideal harmony in the world.[37] The reference to Chinese forms evoked the ideal role model.

Sanspareil as a *Telemachy*

It was not until the completion of the garden that Sanspareil received an additional level of meaning. Probably on the occasion of the wedding of Wilhelmine's daughter Elisabeth Friederike Sophie with Karl Eugen of Württemberg, during which the garden was intended to be one venue for the wedding ceremony and festivities,[38] Wilhelmine initiated a literary program.[39] The program was based on François

33. See Carsten Neumann, "Das Trianon de Porcelaine im Park von Versailles als erster chinoiser Bau in Europa," in *China in Schloss und Garten: Chinoise Architekturen und Innenräume*, ed. Dirk Welich (Dresden, 2010), p.75–81.
34. See Habermann, *Bayreuther Gartenkunst*, p.170.
35. See Peter O. Krückmann, *Sanspareil: Burg Zwernitz und Felsengarten, amtlicher Führer* (Munich, 2012), p.72–73.
36. See Gerd-Helge Vogel, "Die Anfänge chinoiser Architekturen in Deutschland: Prototypen und ihr soziokultureller Hintergrund," in *China in Schloss und Garten*, ed. D. Welich, p.13–30.
37. See Vogel, "Konfuzianismus."
38. This plan was not realized for unknown reasons. See Karl Müssel, "Die große Bayreuther Fürstenhochzeit 1748—Vorgeschichte, Vorbereitungen und Verlauf: ein Beitrag zum Jubiläum des Markgräflichen Opernhauses," *Archiv für Geschichte von Oberfranken* 77 (1997), p.7–118 (100–101).
39. A contemporary source regarding the literary program is Markus Friedrich Hedenus, "1749: Markus Friedrich Hedenus," in *Lustgärten um Bayreuth*, ed. I. Toussaint, p.149–57. On the literary program, see Luise Maslow, "'…den Vorschriften der Natur folgend, zugleich so weise und so glücklich': Fénelons *Les Aventures de Télémaque* als literarisches Gartenprogramm der Wilhelmine von

Fénelon's *Adventures of Telemachus,* one of the most popular literary works of the eighteenth century. The didactic novel, a destructive attack on the perceived deficiencies of the French monarchy,[40] portrays the moral ideal of a ruler who does not give into the temptations of sensuality, flattery, and violence. Buildings, grottos, and places in the rock garden were subsequently interpreted according to the literary program. The story was visualized by means of pictures and sculptures. The plot could be memorized, told, or even played while walking through the garden. By means of the utopian travels of the son of Ulysses, the garden visitor was able to experience an alternative idea of an ideal society.

The story also had another representational function. By means of the mythological program, a fictional and playful genealogical derivation of the Brandenburg-Bayreuth dynasty from classical mythology was created through the shared possession of the landscape.[41] A sepulchral monument for Odysseus in combination with the artificial ruin of the theater made their fictional genealogy reaching back to the heroes of antiquity real, at least within the garden. The claim gained credibility not only through the tangible artifacts but also in the continuation of a local literary tradition. In the sixteenth century the poet Friedrich Taubmann had already compared Zwernitz with Ithaca, the home of Odysseus.[42]

The reinterpretation of the dry, rocky plateau near Bayreuth as the Mediterranean island gained persuasive power through the festive character of the visits of court society. Wilhelmine's biggest passion was the opera. For theatrical and musical performances parts of the gardens were often completely reinterpreted.[43] Comparable to this theatricalization, the literary program in Sanspareil helped to call

Bayreuth," in *Europäische Utopien–Utopien Europas,* ed. Oliver Victor and Laura Weiß (Berlin, 2021), p.123–47; Mechthild Habiger and Helke Kammerer-Grothaus, "'Les aventures de Télémaque': ein literarisches Programm für den markgräflichen Felsengarten in Sanspareil und die klassizistische Bildtapete von Dufour, Paris 1823," *Zeitschrift des Deutschen Vereins für Kunstwissenschaft* 51 (1997), p.179–94; Arniko F. Schilling, "Telemach und der Felsengarten," in *850 Jahre Burg Zwernitz,* ed. Schloss- und Gartenverwaltung Bayreuth-Eremitage, p.84–89; Krückmann, *Sanspareil.*

40. Marivaux attacked Louis XIV of France. In Sanspareil the program was probably aimed at the future husband of Wilhelmine's daughter, Karl Eugen of Württemberg. See Müssel, "Die große Bayreuther Fürstenhochzeit," p.101.

41. See Dorgerloh and Niedermeier, "Desire for origins."

42. See Hedenus, "1749: Markus Friedrich Hedenus," p.152.

43. See Helena Langewitz, "Der Garten in der Oper—die Oper im Garten:

aesthetic standards of garden forms and designs into question. The story sensitized the garden visitor to a perception of nature that did not follow the usual practice and to the perception of stories that could only be told in an artistic way.

From today's perspective, the connection between chinoiserie and an ancient mythological program seems strange. However, in the eighteenth century this combination was not unusual. Wilhelmine was familiar with the theses of the comte de Caylus.[44] According to his writings the art of antiquity goes back to a common starting point in Egypt, and from there influenced cultures from classical Roman and Greek antiquity through to China. This made it possible to identify with Chinese as well as with classical models. As a distant but related descendant of ancient culture, the Chinese landscape garden could logically be combined with classical myths.

Sanspareil as a space of reduced court ceremonial

In Sanspareil the Chinese and the literary programs, which presented alternative ideals of a state and a sovereign, must be seen as a way of criticizing the court culture of the eighteenth century. The escape from the bothersome court ceremonial was also revealed in structural aspects. The aversion to axiality and formality found in this garden made ceremonial movement practically impossible.[45]

The smaller scale of country chateaus, garden buildings, and hermitages with their surrounding grounds enabled creative experiments. The detached and sometimes remote quality of these sites, away from the binding ceremonial, the constraints, and the business of the main court center, allowed them to become an escape, where the otherwise constricting social norms did not apply in the same ways. They offered possibilities for conviviality based upon an artificially simple life in the artful nature of the garden, and thus created unique opportunities for social encounters and the experience of nature.[46] This can be observed in British country houses as well

---

Theatralisierung von Gärten im Musiktheater des 17. und 18. Jahrhunderts," *Die Gartenkunst* 27:2 (2015), p.329–46.

44. See Saskia Hüneke, "Die Sammlung Bayreuth," in *Kurfürstliche und königliche Erwerbungen für die Schlösser Brandenburg-Preußens vom 17. bis zum 19. Jahrhundert: Antiken I*, ed. Astrid Dostert (Oldenburg, 2008), p.329–94 (330).

45. See Merten, *Der Bayreuther Hofarchitekt*, p.39.

46. See Dorgerloh, "Hermitage."

as in the model of the *maison de plaisance* on the Continent. They cultivated some form of privacy—either in solitude, or in shared intimacies and conversations. Only in the setting of the garden could the hosts and their guests temporarily become the protagonists of a simpler life: a shepherd, a hermit, or a philosopher.[47]

It is no coincidence that the starting point of this layout was a piece of chinoiserie situated in an intimate private retreat at some distance from official court centers. Chinoiserie often served as a field for experiments that provided more creative freedom, because it rejected traditional theoretical principles of art, architecture, and gardening.[48] The oriental building in Sanspareil was planned and erected around an already existing beech tree in the grove. The tree protruding from the roof of the building is a reference to this starting point of the garden layout.[49] A counterpart can be found in another tree on the same axis in front of the kitchen building. From the banquet hall the view leads up to a small inner courtyard with the beech and then through a gateway directly into the rocks of the beech grove. The otherwise important central axis of the baroque seems to be lost, but nevertheless shoulders the task of emphasizing the tree as a meaningful feature. The framed view to the single tree in front of the rock, comparable to a landscape painting, introduces the more natural garden part behind it.[50] The rock garden is presented as a mythological landscape that could be entered by the visitor.

Ceremonial movement was hindered or prevented in several ways, and unusual patterns of movement turn out to be necessary to move through the garden. Since known forms of ceremonial movement and of social hierarchy were suspended, the garden demanded initiative, improvisation of action, and personal, bodily engagement from its users, leading to new garden rituals.[51]

47. Dorgerloh, "Hermitage," p.137.
48. Hans Wernher von Kittlitz, "Ernst und Spiel: Anmerkungen zur kunsthier-archischen und kulturphänomenologischen Stellung der Chinoiserie: das 'Chinesische' als Antithese zum 'Klassischen'?," in *China in Schloss und Garten*, ed. D. Welich, p.31–47.
49. See Merten, *Der Bayreuther Hofarchitekt*, p.39.
50. See Günter Hartmann, *Die Ruine im Landschaftsgarten: ihre Bedeutung für den frühen Historismus und die Landschaftsmalerei der Romantik* (Worms, 1981), p.82–83.
51. See Michel Conan, "Introduction: the significance of bodily engagement with nature," in *Performance and appropriation: profane rituals in gardens and landscapes*, ed. Michel Conan (Washington, DC, 2007), p.3–16.

There is, for example, no specific place in Sanspareil that could be identified as an entrance.[52] Anywhere between the buildings one could enter the courtyard and the grove. Many paths in the garden were laid out in irregular ways. They could be walked in groups at a leisurely pace, in pairs, or alone, and in conversation or in silence. There were places in the woods and rocks, and tables made out of stone in humid caves, that could be used for eating and drinking, for conversation, or for reading and thinking in solitude.[53] Probably the guests could, for the most part, spend their day as they wished, but they came together when summoned by the bell for shared meals. This was common at the courts of Wilhelmine's brother in Rheinsberg and Sanssouci. In Sanspareil visitors had to climb up narrow stairs, carved out of the rocks. The most unusual form of bodily engagement was stimulated by the so-called *Hühnerloch* ("chicken hole") (Figure 7), where guests crawled through a hole in the rock on all fours.[54] A garden description from the end of the eighteenth century reports on this experience, as do several travel descriptions:

> At the end of the walk the guide or steward usually brings those who are here for the first time to this place. In that one approaches the shadow of the boulder, one climbs the steps without thinking... Soon the guide tells the group that there is no way out... other than that one slips through the hole. In such a manner the ladies and gentlemen must commit to slide over a stone which has rolled in front of the hole and then crawl through, very bent over, with quite some effort. Because of this kind of passage, over a long time the stone has become quite smooth and polished.[55]

Imagine people doing that in the rococo clothing of the time!

52. See Merten, *Der Bayreuther Hofarchitekt*, p.39.
53. Unfortunately, there are no known sources with regard to specific details about life under Margravine Wilhelmine in Sanspareil, probably because the garden was not used as often as the other gardens in and around Bayreuth. See Maslow, "Die Natur selbst war die Baumeisterin," p.256–57.
54. "Unter der Grotte von Friedrichschloß, wo zur Seite schon eine solche Gattung von Felsen erscheinet, wodurch die künstliche Natur vermittelst einer geräumigen Oeffnung den Weg selbst gebahnet und Seine Hochfürstliche Durchlaucht den Hinaufgang mit einer Treppe steinernen Treppe und eisernem Gitter erleichtern lassen." Hedenus, "1749: Markus Friedrich Hedenus," p.153.
55. "Der Führer oder Kastellan bringt gemeiniglich diejenigen, welche zum ersten Male hier waren, am Ende der Wanderung an diesen Ort, und indem man sich den umschatteten Fels nähert, steigt man ohne Bedenken de Treppen hinauf [...]. Allein bald gibt der Cicerone der Gesellschaft lächelnd zu verstehen,

Figure 7: Johann Gottfried Köppel, "Das Sogenannte Hühnerloch zu Sanspareil," colored copper engraving, 1793, Bamberg State Library, JH.Top.q.60#2. Photo: Gerald Raab.

Alternative forms of conviviality and reduction of ceremonial were not possible without an alternative set of rules. The garden did not prescribe these new forms but triggered them by framing the actions with the aforementioned semantic programs. Michel Conan has suggested that these references should not be understood as the meaning of the garden, and proposed instead to see them as "the horizons of understanding within which participants in garden rituals could make sense of their own situation and of the actions in which they engaged."[56] Imagining themselves moving through a pastoral world or the ideal state of China or taking part in a reenactment of the adventures of Telemach compelled garden visitors to engage in some otherwise unusual performances, comparable to the hermit's plays in the Eremitage St. Johannis in Bayreuth, performed in a castle laid out like a monastery, or the pastorals performed in the nearby small estate Monplaisir.[57]

Typical for the *Eremitage* in the age of Enlightenment is the secularization of the experience of solitude. The "temporary isolation or a retreat with a small circle of like-minded people was seen as a consciously chosen contrast to the superficial world, above all, the court society... Religious spiritualism, in the tradition of mysticism, was replaced with a notion of an active and creative solitude."[58] Religious devotion and contemplation were replaced with secularized alternatives, as in the Eremitage St. Johannis, where Wilhelmine transformed the quasi-religious hermit's play, already initiated under the previous Margrave Georg Wilhelm of Bayreuth, into a cult of philosophy, art, and literature and a culture of conversation and friendship.

In Sanspareil this practice contributed to a means of social communication deriving expressive power from bodily engagement in the natural setting. Garden visitors "interact with one another in

---

dass hier mein anderer Ausweg sey, [...] als wenn man sich bequeme; durch das Loch zu schlüpfen; und solchergestalt müssen denn Damen und Herren sich entschliessen, über einen vor dem Loche gleichsam hingewälzten [...] Stein zu rutschen, sonach nicht ohne Mühe und sehr gebückt hindurch kriechen. Der Stein ist wegen der auf solche Art oft ausgehaltene Passage durch die Länge der Zeit gleichsam geglättet und polirt worden." Köppel, *Die Eremitage zu Sanspareil,* p.14.

56. Conan, "Introduction," p.14.
57. About the quasi-religious hermit's play in Bayreuth, see Dorgerloh, "Hermitage," p.139–40.
58. Dorgerloh, "Hermitage," p.138.

ways that stimulate a sense of sharing an experience, being active in the development of that experience rather than passive bystanders, and being part of some meaningful activities. So a certain kind of communication is established between them... Performers and audience interact, and they may even exchange roles."[59] In the garden, Enlightenment ideas were thus put into practice: All people are equal before nature, walking upright just as bending over befits all, the ruler just like the courtier, the traveling bourgeoisie just like the rural villagers. The *Hühnerloch* can be understood as the naturalistic philosophical posit of equality inscribed into nature.[60] That the addressees were partly the creators of the message they received would have made it only harder to contest the message.[61] Thus the garden can be seen as an educational trail motivated by the experience of equality before nature. It forced the mighty to experience bending over, an action that was all too familiar to the bourgeois and the rural population, and to appreciate the freedom of walking upright.[62] Sanspareil is an example of how gardening as an art form can enable cultural change by inventing new ways of perceiving and moving through nature:

> [B]odily engagement with nature through ritualized practices of gardens contributes to slow cultural changes, transforming categories of perception of natural spaces, self, and legitimate actions. It may establish a new metonymic or metaphoric understanding of nature in a particular place, and endow it with a sense that one is called there to particular types of action, thus demanding improvisation on the part of the users. Over time, this may lead to large numbers of people being engaged in the acquisition of new gestures that seem to issue from Nature herself.[63]

59. Conan, "Introduction," p.13.
60. Only in the last decade of the century could structures like this and with this meaning be found in gardens without the need for corresponding semantic programs. See for example Karl Braun, *Luisenburg: ein vergessener Landschaftsgarten der Frühromantik* (Marburg, 2005). Sanspareil suggests that this idea had already entered gardens in a courtly context.
61. See Conan, "Introduction," p.14.
62. See Braun, *Luisenburg*, p.55, 98–89. In his *Beantwortung der Frage: was ist Aufklärung?* (1783), Immanuel Kant formulates his discourse on Enlightenment as a discourse on walking.
63. Conan, "Introduction," p.16.

Sanspareil as an Enlightenment garden

Due to the combination of nature—created by God, geometrical, and ruled by laws—and reason—the higher nature of mankind—the "third nature" of Sanspareil has been described in the history of ideas as the perfect park.[64] In Sanspareil semantic and structural elements as well as stylistic choices were used to communicate ideas of the Enlightenment. The natural landscape around Bayreuth appears to be transformed into Wilhelmine's own Tusculum, Arcadia, Golden Age, or China. She was responsible for semantic aspects, which were communicated via sculptural and architectural decoration and literary programs. She inscribed meaning into structural features, by handling established elements of garden design personally or even neglecting them. Furthermore, she used stylistic choices, such as chinoiserie or Roman classicism, and functional aspects of the garden, dedicated to scholarly and musical activities far from court ceremonial, to express her ideas about the ideal society and sovereign.

The idea of progress, central to the Enlightenment, was not shown through the confidence in modern design but more by accentuating local traditions, admiring classical greatness, and condemning modern corruption.[65] This account is diametrically opposed to the master narrative of the English garden, which effectively dismisses all gardens before the landscape garden as "baroque."

The example of Sanspareil sheds new light on connections between courtly gardens and the Enlightenment that have been neglected mostly because of the unstated moral and political implications inherent in stylistic concepts. The garden reveals numerous aspects that are commonly used to prove the influence of the Enlightenment on landscape gardens.[66] The garden is directly available for the creative imagination of the owner, in this instance Wilhelmine of Bayreuth. The garden consciously includes the natural landscape, and there is no demarcation line between garden and surrounding landscape. Garden and landscape commemorate the history of the dynasty. The garden was used as an experiential field for the perception of nature. By means of a symbolic journey it conveys the aesthetic concept of the

---

64. Kröll, "Naturbegriff."
65. See Stephen Bending, "Introduction," in *A Cultural history of gardens in the age of Enlightenment*, ed. Stephen Bending (London, 2016), p.1–27 (11).
66. See, for example, Niedermeier, "Landschaft/Garten."

virtuous education of a good ruler. The garden is a walkable space that reflects Enlightenment ideas and enables one to visualize utopian fantasies.

Conclusion

The exclusive link between landscape garden and Enlightenment appears problematic. Eighteenth-century gardens prove to be a complex entanglement of partly contradictory cultural phenomena. The garden casts a cynical view on the same contemporary social conditions and ways of ruling that the garden ultimately supports and tries to legitimize. The courtly garden, no matter how far from the center of the court and how unusual in design it may have been, remained a place of courtly ceremonial and princely representation. Reading the garden only as a place of retreat, indulgence, and escapism does not do the political scope of the ruler justice. The garden was a public space created to have an effect on its addressees in a specific way, by stimulating associations and presenting the ruler in a specific light. The audience—the entourage of the ruler, her subordinates, or visitors from other parts of the Holy Roman Empire or Europe—could also be addressed by means of the series of copper engravings and published garden descriptions. Imperial princes, whose position became precarious, used their gardens to demonstrate political autonomy. The creation of Sanspareil took place during the time of estrangement between Wilhelmine and her brother Frederick II, a time Wilhelmine used to show independence and to gather a circle of like-minded people.

However, the garden serves more personal needs as well. In several instances Margravine Wilhelmine of Bayreuth describes her own character as unsuitable for court life: "I have always been some sort of philosopher. I am not ambitious; I prefer happiness and a calm life to all glories; discomfort and constraints are odious to me; I appreciate worldly life and pleasures, but I hate dissipation. My character, as I have just described it, is unsuitable for court life."[67] At least her

---

67. "J'ai toujours été un peu philosophe, l'ambition n'est pas mon défaut; je préfère le bonheur et le repos de la vie à toutes les grandeurs; toute gène et toute contrainte m'est odieuse; j'aime le monde et les plaisiers, mais je hais la dissipation. Mon caractère, tel que je viens de le décrire, ne convenoit point à la cour." Wilhelmine Friederike Sophie of Bayreuth, *Mémoires de Frédérique Sophie Wilhelmine, margrave de Bareith, soeur de Frédéric le Grand, depuis l'année 1706*

hermitages allowed her to live in a setting, albeit only for a time, that supported her natural character. By means of her personal artistic practice Wilhelmine was able to create an atmosphere comparable to that of the French salon. Eventually it may have been the ultimate goal of Wilhelmine with her practice of the arts and drawing of Enlightenment topoi to assemble a circle of intellectuals comparable to her brother's Round Table in Sanssouci. While this never succeeded, she did transform Bayreuth into a place about which Voltaire would write: "Bayreuth is a delicious retreat where people enjoy every agreeable aspect of court life without suffering the inconveniences of grandeur."[68] By using her own imagination Wilhelmine secured her court's position in the *république des lettres*.

In Sanspareil, numerous European and global role models and influences come together, just as in the contemporary early English landscape gardens. The unique creation is, as the name says, without parallel, and it stood for an independent development of Continental gardening. That such a highly representative art form, only affordable to the social elites and thus a popular metaphor in anti-court writings, was used to reflect anti-court ideas and to demonstrate an aversion to court ceremonial is part of the paradox of the Enlightenment at court.

jusqu'à 1742, écrits de sa main, 2nd ed., 2 vols. (Leipzig, 1888), vol.1, p.111–12. Similar statements appear in her correspondence.

68. "Bareith est une retraitte délicieuse où on jouit de tout ce qu'une cour a d'agréable sans les incommoditez de la grandeur." Voltaire to Maupertuis (October 16, 1743), *Correspondence and related documents*, ed. Theodore Besterman, in *The Complete works of Voltaire*, vol.85–135 (Oxford, 1968–1977), D2866, p.483.

Clemency in the boudoir: favoritism and imperial virtues at the Russian court (1740s–1790s)

Alexei Evstratov

In 1828, Aleksandr Shishkov (1754–1841), a Russian admiral and an important author, published in the magazine *Saint Petersburg spectator* a short text with a rather uninventive title, *Something about the Russian empress, Catherine the Second*.[1] According to the anecdote from the annals of the Russian imperial court featured in this vignette, a favorite of the empress fell in love with one of the sovereign's maids of honor and Catherine II (r.1762–1796), instead of disgracing the man, granted him permission to marry her rival. In his account, Shishkov emphasizes how offensive this situation would be to any woman, and stresses the fact that the empress could easily have punished those who had offended or embarrassed her. However, Catherine's internal struggle pictured by Shishkov culminates in moderation triumphing over her passions. The author concludes enthusiastically: "This is Catherine! Try as they may, they will never find an example like this in the histories of all times and peoples!"[2]

Shishkov does not specify when the affair happened, but states that many people know about this incident (*prikliuchenie*). Indeed, (auto)biographical narratives of some of Catherine's contemporaries mention a love triangle that left the great empress broken-hearted. A French dramatic actor, Pierre-Jean-Baptiste Choudard, known as Desforges (1746–1806), touches upon a similar episode in his memoir,

1. Aleksandr S. Shishkov, "Nechto o rossiiskoi imperatritse Ekaterine Vtoroi," in Aleksandr S. Shishkov, *Zapiski, mneniia i perepiska admirala A. S. Shishkova*, 2 vols. (Berlin, 1870), vol.2, p.298–303 (302). (All translations are mine, unless otherwise stated.) See also a collection of anecdotes about Catherine II: Aleksandr S. Shishkov, "Dostopamiatnye skazaniia ob Imperatritse Ekaterine Velikoi," ed. Konstantin Bolenko and Ekaterina Liamina, in *Reka vremion: kniga istorii i kul'tury*, 5 vols. (Moscow, 1996), vol.4, p.20–56.
2. Shishkov, "Nechto o rossiiskoi imperatritse Ekaterine Vtoroi," p.302.

which recounts a stay in Russia around 1780 and was published shortly after Catherine's death.[3] Unlike Shishkov, who focuses on the internal and silent moral struggle of the offended empress, Desforges presents a monologue from Catherine that deplores the paradoxical status of sovereigns: "They can do as they please with men and they can do nothing with hearts. [...] They have all the treasures of the world; but the most precious of all, a real friend, they do not have; they have never had, and will never have."[4]

Both Shishkov and Desforges's accounts could be mere anecdotes about a glorious period in the history of the Russian monarchy in general and of the court in particular.[5] Indeed it would hardly be surprising if an actor, who was also a prolific writer, romanticized his narrative of what comes across in his memoir as an uneventful stay in Russia.[6] Moreover, one could wonder whether the two sources tell the same story. While Desforges's version features Countess Praskov'ia Brius (1729–1786) and Ivan Korsakov (1754–1831), the editors of Shishkov's writings maintain that the protagonists of the anecdote were Count Aleksandr Dmitriev-Mamonov (1758–1803) and Princess Dar'ia Shcherbatova (1762–1801), which would situate it in the late 1780s, after Desforges's sojourn in the country had ended.[7] These inconsistencies between different posthumous accounts may

3.   P.-J.-B. Choudard, known as Desforges, *Le Poète, ou Mémoires d'un homme de lettres, écrits par lui-même*, 4 vols. (Hamburg, n.n., 1798), esp. vol.4.
4.   Desforges, *Le Poète, ou Mémoires d'un homme de lettres*, vol.4, p.415.
5.   A shorter version of a similar account also appears in the autobiographical notes of Prince Fiodor N. Golitsyn (1751–1827) edited by Piotr Bartenev. Golitsyn, too, praises the empress's temperance. Fiodor N. Golitsyn, "Zapiski kniazia Fiodora Nikolaevicha Golitsyna," ed. Piotr Bartenev, *Russkii arkhiv* 24:5 (1874), col.1271–1336 (1328). On the memory of Catherine II in the early nineteenth century, see Simon Dixon, "The posthumous reputation of Catherine II in Russia 1797–1837," *The Slavonic and East European review* 77:4 (1999), p.646–79.
6.   On Desforges's stay in Russia (between 1779 and 1782), see Piotr R. Zaborov, "Frantsuzskii aktior v Peterburge i o Peterburge," in *Obraz Peterburga v mirovoi kul'ture: materialy mezhdunarodnoi konferentsii (30 iiunia–3 iiulia 2003 goda)*, ed. Vsevolod E. Bagno (St. Petersburg, 2003), p.286–97.
7.   Shishkov, "Nechto o rossiiskoi imperatritse Ekaterine Vtoroi"; Shishkov, "Dostopamiatnye skazaniia ob Imperatritse Ekaterine Velikoi," p.53–54. Some historians support Desforges's version: Kazimir Waliszewski, *Autour d'un trône, Catherine II de Russie: ses collaborateurs–ses amis–ses favoris*, 4th ed. (Paris, 1894), p.394. According to others, Korsakov had an affair with Baroness Ekaterina Petrovna Stroganova (née Trubeckaia). See, for instance, N. M. Kolmakov, "Dom i familiia Strogonovykh: 1752–1887," *Russkaia starina* 53:3 (1887), p.575–602 (595–96).

raise suspicions regarding the documentary value of these narratives, but the testimonies of those close to Catherine II's court during her lifetime confirm that the stories about the ruler's misfortunes in love circulated well before her death.

Thus comte Valentin Esterhazy (1740–1805), who represented the French crown at the Russian court, wrote to his wife in 1791 about Catherine's reaction to Dmitriev-Mamonov's infidelity: "The next day, the despairing empress announces his marriage, gives a dowry to the maid of honor and organizes the wedding at court, as was customary for maids of honor: she herself does her rival's hair and dresses her."[8] An informed witness's report to Prince Grigorii Potemkin, a former favorite himself, helps to establish the exact moment when the scandal occurs or, rather, the date of the denouement:

> On the July 1, [1789], the wedding of the count [Dmitriev-Mamonov] took place here, at the court church, where, as per his wish, nobody was admitted during the marriage ceremony, except for a small number of people invited to the wedding and to the dinner afterwards. It can now be said with confidence that no event like it has ever met with a happier ending, and that the magnanimity shown to the count on this occasion has surpassed everybody's and any possible expectation.[9]

This praise is striking, given the typical tensions around the ruler's favorite in court culture in general and at the Russian court in particular. Potemkin's informant links the event with the outstanding moral qualities of the sovereign, such as clemency, magnanimity, or exceptional temperance, and locates the illustration of them in the inner rooms of the palace. The accounts that appeared at later dates, such as Shishkov's or Desforges's, take some liberties and report on Catherine's emotions and thoughts, exposing a suffering ruler to the public eye and thus uncovering what, in the first instance, perhaps disappeared behind the empress's magnanimous act of pardon.

This chapter argues that Catherine II was aware of the tensions related to her imperial body. It explores exactly how and why the ruler proceeded to open her carefully staged affective realm to a select

---

8. Valentin Esterhazy, *Lettres du c[om]te Esterhazy à sa femme: 1784–1792*, ed. Ernest Daudet (Paris, 1907), p.348.
9. Mikhail Garnovskii, "Zapiski: 1786–1790," *Russkaia starina* 15:7 (1876), p.399–440 (402). The court journal confirms that the marriage took place on this date. *Kamer-fur'erskie tseremonial'nye zhurnaly za 1789 g.* ([St. Petersburg], n.n., n.d.), p.7, 288–90.

public. Drawing on one specific cluster of motifs from the numerous
narratives shaping imperial representations, this study demonstrates
that discourses and practices of power, law, and art underpinned the
construction of the myth of the enlightened ruler. Here, Catherine's
clemency, highlighted by Shishkov and others, constituted an
important theme. A virtue already associated with ancient rulers,
such as Julius Caesar, it gained renewed relevance in eighteenth-
century Russia when Catherine styled herself "enlightened" while her
power was (at least in theory) not limited by any of the political bodies
many enlightened writers considered central to the prevention of
arbitrary rule. Montesquieu thus discusses clemency as a key virtue of
monarchs who wish to gain respect among both contemporaries and
historians (see below). In many regards, the empress was the author
of her own staging, as were her European peers.[10] However, this does
not necessarily imply either a cynical approach to the narratives
that shaped it, or full control over the myth's semantic workings, as
theatrical metaphors often seem to imply. In order to reach beyond
the ideal scenarios of the imperial self, this chapter focuses on a corpus
of dramatic literature, bound together by one theme, and confronts it
with a variety of other writings, published and personal, commenting
on the same topic. Despite the general semantic coherence, the
dramatic corpus under study here generates ambivalent representations of sovereign *grandeur*. And the social environment in which
the latter circulated had a decisive effect on their potential workings.
The multiple examples of clemency, departing from a single episode
involving an ungrateful and disloyal favorite, broadcast through
various media, which we find in the reign of Catherine II, significantly broaden the context of our analysis.

The playhouse was the only space where most local and foreign
nobles could see the fictional inner space of the palace, which in
reality was protected by elite military regiments. Besides, Catherine II
used the fictional schemes available in the stock of famous dramatic
plots to expose what could appear as deviations from her "legal
monarchy."[11] As my reconstruction of the semantic clusters built

10. Richard Wortman, *Scenarios of power: myth and ceremony in Russian monarchy*,
    2 vols. (Princeton, NJ, 1995), esp. vol.1; Peter Burke, *The Fabrication of Louis XIV*
    (New Haven, CT, 1992); Andreas Pečar, *Die Masken des Königs: Friedrich II. von
    Preußen als Schriftsteller* (Frankfurt am Main, 2016).
11. Oleg A. Omelchenko, *"Zakonnaia monarkhiia" Ekateriny II: prosveshchënnyi
    absoliutizm v Rossii* (Moscow, 1993).

around the relationship between the ruler and her favorite suggests, rather than being a residue of an archaic practice, the public dramatization of this relationship helped to articulate a humanized persona of the absolutist monarch. Thus, attempts were made to transform a customary emblem of aristocratic degradation, especially problematic in the case of a female ruler, into a sentimental narrative fused with *imitatio dei*.

"A woman among women": the Russian court and favoritism

When Princess Sophie Auguste Friederike of Anhalt-Zerbst, the future Catherine II, came to Russia in the early 1740s, the Russian Empire sought to become a legitimate part of the world's political map, on equal terms with leading European powers.[12] These ambitions provoked both close diplomatic surveillance of the St. Petersburg court and attentive self-examination. As elsewhere in Europe, parallel, unofficial hierarchies, favorite courtiers in particular, generated endless gossip, attracted jealous comments, and provoked the most violent of criticism.[13] The court of Catherine is among the most famous cases of institutionalized favoritism—a phenomenon that outraged her contemporaries, inspired adult movies, and made historians wonder if she was a nymphomaniac.[14]

Catherine's affiliation with the Russian throne was enabled by her relation to two male representatives of the Romanov dynasty—first, her husband Peter III (r.1761–1762) and, after his assassination, their son, Grand Duke Paul Petrovitch (1754–1801; r.1796–1801). Another man, Grigorii Orlov, a guards officer who had been Catherine's lover before the palace revolution of June 1762, was instrumental in

12. See Francine-Dominique Liechtenhan, *La Russie entre en Europe: Elisabeth Ire et la succession d'Autriche, 1740–1750* (Paris, 1997).

13. John T. Alexander, "Favorites, favouritism and female rule in Russia: 1725–1796," in *Russia in the age of the Enlightenment*, ed. Roger Bartlett and Janet Hartley (London, 1990), p.106–24. For a broader and comparative study, see *The World of the favorite*, ed. John H. Elliott and Laurence W. B. Brockliss (New Haven, CT, 1999); *Der zweite Mann im Staat: Oberste Amtsträger und Favoriten im Umkreis der Reichsfürsten in der Frühen Neuzeit*, ed. Michael Kaiser and Andreas Pečar (Berlin, 2003).

14. John T. Alexander, *Catherine the Great: life and legend* (New York, 1989), p.201–26; John T. Alexander, "Politics, passions, patronage: Catherine II and Petr Zavadovskii," in *Russia and the world of the eighteenth century*, ed. Roger P. Bartlett *et al.* (Columbus, OH, 1988), p.616–33; Isabel de Madariaga, *Russia in the age of Catherine the Great* (New Haven, CT, 1981), p.343–58.

the coup and afterward became the empress's first official favorite. He thus began the series of the empress's public *liubimtsy* (one of the Russian terms for "favorite"), and attracted the first wave of criticism. This criticism could not, of course, be public, but it is visible in diplomatic correspondence. The French ambassador, the baron de Breteuil, was particularly dismissive and predicted a quick fall for Orlov, whom he found obscure in respect of social origin and generally not very bright.[15]

The mysterious death of her husband, to which the Orlov brothers actively contributed, exposed the empress to criticism in Russia and abroad, further problematizing the conjunction of absolute power with the female gender. Sometimes this criticism targeted the individual fulfilling the role of favorite, as in the case of Breteuil's correspondence. In other cases, the institution was declared unacceptable as such, usually for moral reasons.[16] On the side of the local elite, Prince Mikhail Shcherbatov's pamphlet *On the corruption of morals in Russia* is probably the most famous contemporary diatribe directed against the phenomenon. In this reflection on Russian autocrats, written in the late 1780s (and first published abroad in the mid-nineteenth century), Shcherbatov notes on Catherine II:

> To add to the corruption of women's manners and of all decency, she has set other women the example of the possession of a long and frequent succession of lovers, each equally honoured and enriched, thus advertising the cause of their ascendancy. [...] Generally speaking, women are more prone to despotism than men, and as far as she is concerned, it can justly be averred that she is in this particular a woman among women.[17]

The revealing tendencies of these writings are often echoed in the scholarship, which struggles to reconcile the encomiastic images of

---

15. See his reports in *Sbornik imperatorskago russkago istoricheskago obshchestva* 140 (1912).
16. A prominent French freemason, Louis-Claude de Saint-Martin, refused to visit the country while it was governed by the notoriously immoral empress (Georgii V. Vernadskii, *Russkoe masonstvo v tsarstvovanie Ekateriny II*, St. Petersburg, 1999, p.295).
17. Mikhail M. Shcherbatov, *On the corruption of morals in Russia*, ed. and translated by A. Lentin (New York, 1969), p.245, 247. On representations of Catherine II, see John T. Alexander, "Amazon autocratrixes: images of female rule in the eighteenth century," in *Gender and sexuality in Russian civilisation*, ed. Peter I. Barta (London, 2001), p.33–54.

imperial grandeur that depict Catherine as Astrea, Dido, or, indeed, Augustus, with the everyday life of what one pamphleteer called "gynecocracy."[18] Thus, while the British ambassador James Harris affirmed that "the Gratification of this disgraceful Passion" had become for Catherine II a "Distemper rooted in the Blood,"[19] a contemporary historian writes: "Her urge to dominate, coupled with her fear of domination by another, made for unstable romantic affairs."[20]

In this context, the episodes with the unfaithful favorites look like an anomaly—as if those who sympathized with the empress simply used the anecdote to glorify her. Thus, when the French envoy the comte de Ségur reported on the retirement of Aleksandr Dmitriev-Mamonov from his role as Catherine II's favorite in July 1789, he concluded his dispatch with a paragraph revealing his fascination with the Russian ruler. In his message, he expresses regret about the necessity to recount these circumstances, but invites the Royal Council to admire the qualities of a "great woman," who even in her weaknesses demonstrates outstanding self-restraint by mastering her jealousy.[21] In a private letter to his spouse, Ségur hints at the incident with the following comment: "It is fortunate for humankind that the great men are not put off from beneficence by the frivolity and ingratitude of their friends."[22]

What appear in some writings to be "private" matters had, in fact, broader significance in the eighteenth-century theory of power. In addition to the love triangle story, comte Esterhazy, in the letter to his wife quoted above, mentions another instance of the empress's clemency in her treatment of the Vorontsov family, who did not suffer after Catherine came to power for the fact that Elizaveta Vorontsova held the position of Peter III's favorite.[23] This new episode, from

18. Vera Proskurina, *Creating the empress: politics and poetry in the age of Catherine II* (Boston, MA, 2011), p.14–48; Michael Schippan, *Die Aufklärung in Russland im 18. Jahrhundert* (Wiesbaden, 2012), p.100–16.

19. Quoted in Alexander, *Catherine the Great*, p.203.

20. Alexander, *Catherine the Great*, p.215.

21. Archives des Affaires étrangères (Paris), *Correspondance Ségur*, May–August 1789, no.44, July 1789, p.146–50. Quoted in translation in *Vremia smet,' ili Sushchaia sluzhitel'nitsa Fiva: Khroniki vremën imperatritsy Ekateriny Velikoi*, ed. Piotr Stegnii (Moscow, 2002), p.151–52; for more on the favorite and his affair, see p.129–35.

22. Stegnii, *Vremia smet,' ili Sushchaia sluzhitel'nitsa Fiva*, p.397.

23. Esterhazy, *Lettres du c[om]te Esterhazy à sa femme*, p.348. See Ronald Vroon, "'Ekaterina plachet iavno...': k predystorii perevorota 1762 goda," in *I vremia i mesto: istoriko-filologicheskii sbornik k shestidesiatiletiiu Aleksandra L'vovicha Ospovata*, ed. R. Vroon *et al.* (Moscow, 2008), p.40–54.

the early 1760s, not only magnifies the ruler's forgiving character, but also makes this quality appear a constant feature for the whole of her reign.[24] Thus, what some sources present as an exceptional circumstance and a sublime gesture appears, in other writings, as a feature of Catherine's character. In any event, it evoked a major attribute of the sovereign deployed across early modern narratives and in different genres—clemency.

Clemency comes to Russia

Three spheres are fundamental for the reconstruction of the phenomenon of imperial clemency in early modern Europe: (1) legal theory and practice, (2) the imperial title and references to that title, (3) historical and fictional representations, which organized both legal idioms and the imperial title into narratives. Long before Catherine II demonstrated a generous attitude toward her lover(s), these three components of the imperial myth were closely interwoven and sometimes manifested themselves in what Richard Wortman calls a "scenario of power."[25] Catherine's case, however, suggests that in the eighteenth century the notion of "theater of power" should be expanded beyond public ceremonies and celebrations, and that existing modes of the sacralization of the ruler were complemented by new practices.

In the domain of public rituals in early modern Europe, clemency acted as a reference to the virtues of Roman emperors and, more specifically, to the *imitatio dei*, the imitation of God. From the point of view of power mechanics, it contributed to the formation of the state in the legal sphere and in the sphere of social discipline.[26] Stories of Alexander and the family of Darius, Scipio Africanus, and other rulers whose names resonated with the narrative of clemency were broadly disseminated in the form of paintings, sculptures, and, of course, staged drama, which in eighteenth-century Europe was a distinctive feature of courtly socializing and drew on a stock of

24. This early episode, however, was much more problematic because of Peter III's death that followed his destitution.
25. Wortman, *Scenarios of power.*
26. See Veronika Pokorny, "Clementia Austriaca: Studien zur Bedeutung der clementia Principis für die Habsburger im 16. und 17. Jh.," *Mitteilungen des Instituts für österreichische Geschichtsforschung* 86 (1978), p.310–64.

allegories reconciling absolutist domination with new visions of the polity.

Desforges compares the act of Catherine II's forgiveness to the scene in Pierre Corneille's tragedy *Cinna, or the Clemency of Augustus* (1642), written for the court of Louis XIII. In this play, the Roman emperor discovers that his closest friend has conspired against him, but, rather than punishing him, Augustus places greater trust in his friend and offers him important state responsibilities. This dramatic text was a canonical representation of imperial clemency and a political tragedy *par excellence* with an almost 200-year-long history of highly symbolic performances, ranging from one at the court of Louis XIV, where the prince de Condé wept, to others attended by Napoleon at least twelve times. In 1760, the young Swedish king Gustav III confessed to his instructor that the tragedy made him feel ecstatic, and that he dreamed of an opportunity to say some of the famous lines spoken by Augustus in the play.[27] Catherine II, whose lack of enthusiasm for tragedy as a genre is well known, referred to *Cinna* as "the only tragedy I like."[28]

Corneille's drama was one text among many, dramatic and not, that circulated in the European realm of political representations addressing the topic of clemency. It is customary to connect them to Seneca's seminal treatise *On clemency* (*De clementia*, 55–56 CE), highlighting *Cinna* and Mozart's opera *La Clemenza di Tito* (1791) as the most significant manifestations of this tradition.[29]

In Russia, Empress Elisabeth Petrovna (r.1741–1761), Peter I's daughter, who came to power through a palace revolution at the end of 1741, had already systematically used the language of clemency for the shaping of her own imperial persona. She famously chose Pietro Metastasio's opera *The Clemency of Titus* (*La Clemenza di Tito*, 1734) to be performed during the coronation festival in Moscow in the spring of 1742.[30] The action of this operatic remake of Corneille's *Cinna*

27. Matthew H. Wikander, *Princes to act: royal audience and royal performance, 1578–1792* (Baltimore, MD, 1993), p.265.
28. In her letter to Grimm from August 10, 1785, *Sbornik imperatorskago russkago istoricheskago obshchestva* 23 (1878), p.358–59 (358).
29. Franz Giegling, "'La Clemenza di Tito': Metastasio—Mazzolà—Mozart," *Österreichische Musikschrift* 31:7–8 (1976), p.321–29; R. B. Moberly, "The influence of French classical drama on Mozart's 'La clemenza di Tito,'" *Music & letters* 55:3 (1974), p.286–98.
30. Vsevolod N. Vsevolodskii-Gerngross, *Teatr v Rossii pri imperatritse Elizavete Petrovne* (St. Petersburg, 2003), p.19–25. Metastasio, the court poet of the

glorified the merciful Roman emperor Titus.[31] The prologue to the Russian version performed in 1742, composed on this occasion by Jacob Stählin and titled *Russia rejoicing again after sorrow* (*Rossiia po pechali paki obradovannaia*), emphasized the encomiastic function of the opera and provided a key to the allegorical reading of the plot. Its finale featured a monument on stage with the inscription: "Long live Elisabeth, the most worthy, the most desired crowned Empress of All Russia, the mother of the fatherland, the delight of mankind, the Titus of our time 1742."[32] This use of the dramatic idiom in the staging of the new rule was noticed in Europe. The French newspaper *Mercure de France* published a short report on the performance and commented on the prologue: "The author recalls here many of the circumstances that had preceded the accession of H[er] Ts[arian] M[ajesty] to the throne, & those that followed; & the clemency of the tsarina, compared to that of Titus, makes a link between this prologue and the opera."[33]

As if to demonstrate the consistency between her legal policies and their symbolic representation, Elisabeth suspended, by a 1744 decree, capital punishment in her empire.[34] Later in her reign, during the

---

Habsburgs in Vienna, wrote a libretto that inspired more than ninety musical compositions and was considered a literary masterpiece. See Tatiana Korneeva, "*Refracting translation* zwischen Wien, Dresden und Moskau: Pietro Metastasios *Clemenza di Tito* im deutsch-russischen Kulturtransfer," in *Kreative Praktiken des literarischen Übersetzens um 1800: Übersetzungshistorische und literaturwissen-schaftliche Studien*, ed. Alexander Nebrig and Daniele Vecchiato (Berlin, 2019), p.51–74.

31. Titus occupied a place among the model rulers of Roman history, despite the fact that his rule was very short: His personal reign lasted two years, two months, and twenty days after the death of his father Vespasian in 79 CE. "Ideal figure of benevolent and peaceable ruler during a politically and culturally advanced epoch in history," he was proclaimed to be the "love and delight of the human race" (Werner Wunderlich *et al.*, "Tradition and reception of Roman imperial ethics in the opera *La Clemenzo di Tito*," *The Comparatist* 25, 2001, p.5–21, 8).

32. *Teatral'naia zhizn' Rossii v epokhu Elizavety Petrovny: dokumental'naia khronika, 1740–1750*, ed. Liudmila M. Starikova, vol.2 (Moscow, 2003), part 1, p.60.

33. *Mercure de France* (July 1742), p.1626. On the political trial conducted by the empress that culminated in the pardon and exile of its main protagonists, see Kirill Ospovat, *Terror and pity: Aleksandr Sumarokov and the theater of power in Elizabethan Russia* (Boston, MA, 2016), p.217–19.

34. More on this moratorium, see Elena Marasinova, "The prayer of an empress and the death penalty moratorium in eighteenth-century Russia," *The Journal of religious history, literature and culture* 3:2 (2017), p.36–55.

Seven Years War, the abbé Faure authored a pamphlet celebrating the diplomatic alliance of Russia with France and Austria, where he inscribed the motif of clemency in the theme of moral transformation by the monarch of a hitherto barbarous nation. Faure praises the qualities of Elisabeth, such as "excessive kindness," and affirms that justice directed by clemency is more efficient than one might think: "The excess of kindness in a prince rarely causes licentiousness; almost always it invites repentance, gives remorse, acts as a reminder of one's duty."[35]

The opposition between "clemency" and "justice," which underpins the monologues of the sovereign in *La Clemenza di Tito* and which Faure presents as resolved in Elisabeth's rule, originates from Seneca's treatise and its later interpretations. It was current, in particular, in seventeenth-century French legal rhetoric.[36] In 1748, Montesquieu's major political work *The Spirit of laws* (*De l'esprit des lois*) used these notions to illustrate his theory of political regimes. In chapter 21 of book 6 Montesquieu discusses the prince's clemency:

> CLEMENCY is the characteristic of monarchs. [...] It is more necessary in monarchies, where they [the "great men"] are governed by honor, which frequently requires what the very law forbids. [...] So many are the advantages which monarchs gain by clemency, so greatly does it raise their fame and endear them to their subjects, that it is generally happy for them to have an opportunity of displaying it.[37]

In other words, according to Montesquieu, the very nature of monarchy introduces and maintains a gap between institutional justice and the way the monarch oversees interactions within the nobility and between himself and the nobility. The difference between monarchy and despotism is crystallized in the ruler's use of clemency and disgrace instead of severity and punishment.[38]

35. Otto-Anne Faure, *Discours sur le progrès des beaux arts en Russie* (n.p., n.n., 1760), p.26.
36. Maria Nekliudova, "'Milost' i 'pravosudie': o frantsuzskom kontekste pushkinskoi temy," in *Pushkinskie chteniia v Tartu 2*, ed. Liubov' N. Kisileva (Tartu, 2000), p.204–15 (204–209).
37. Charles-Louis de Montesquieu, *The Spirit of laws*, in *The Complete works of M. de Montesquieu*, 4 vols. (London, printed for T. Evans and W. Davis, 1777), vol.1, p.121.
38. Yvon Le Gall, "Les Lumières et le droit de grâce," *Littératures classiques* 60:2 (2006), p.269–312.

References to imperial virtues were particularly important in the context of the slow process of official acknowledgment of Russia as a modern Western empire (by such countries as France). Catherine II's acute attention to Montesquieu's ideas was demonstrated just after the coup that brought her to power. In summer 1762, the entire court was preparing for the coronation, which would take place in Moscow in September of the same year. In the wake of the recent palace revolution, the empress needed to anticipate reactions to political transformations and changes in patronage networks. Aleksandr Sumarokov, in his capacity as court poet, composed a *Discourse* (*Slovo*) for the coronation and dedicated a part of it to the topic of justice. He insisted on the systematic application of justice, reinterpreting the figure of Titus. In Sumarokov's view, the merciful ruler must act by changing laws and not by changing the punishment prescribed by laws: "Titus wept when he signed sentences for the unrighteous, he wept, but signed them; as if he did not, he would become an accomplice to their crimes. [...] Villains do not deserve any mercy: Politics prescribes punishment for them, in order to prevent others from similar crimes, and the truth requires revenge."[39] The *Discourse* was not published, however, and Catherine II preferred to see *Semira*, a tragedy by Sumarokov, staged at her court by amateur actors, including her current favorite Grigorii Orlov, and the representatives of different clans of the Russian nobility. This performance, inscribed in the ceremonies and celebrations of the Russian court, gave very tangible expression to the idea of reconciliation between noble families after a violent change of rule.[40] In addition, following an established tradition, Catherine II celebrated her coronation day by pardoning a certain number of convicts.[41] One of the empress's maids of honor

39. Aleksandr Sumarokov, *Polnoe sobranie vsekh sochinenii, v stihah i proze*, 2nd ed., 10 vols. (Moscow, Universitetskaia tipografiia u N. Novikova, 1787), vol.1, p.230–31.
40. On this performance, see Alexei Evstratov, "La mise en scène de la cour: la scène et la salle dans le théâtre de cour—étude du théâtre russe à l'aube du règne de Catherine II," in *La Scène, la salle et les coulisses dans le théâtre du XVIIIe siècle en France*, ed. Pierre Frantz and Thomas Wynn (Paris, 2011), p.235–46.
41. *Polnoe sobranie zakonov Rossiiskoi Imperii*, vol.16 (St. Petersburg, 1830), p.69. This fact did not escape the attention of foreign diplomats; see the dispatch of Bérenger from September 27, 1762: "M. Bérenger to duc de Praslin [September 27, 1762]," *Sbornik imperatorskago russkago istoricheskago obshchestva* 140 (1912), p.237–39 (238).

wrote from Moscow to an acquaintance at the imperial court in Vienna: "I have the good fortune to serve a sovereign who, like a second Titus, delights mankind, worshipped and adored by all the nations of her vast empire."[42]

Almost thirty years after the coup that had brought her to the Russian throne and some two years after the storming of the Bastille, in May 1791, Catherine II shared with the French writer Gabriel Sénac de Meilhan her self-perception as a ruler:

> I generally like justice, but my opinion is that strict justice is not justice and that equity alone can be bearable for the weakness of the man. However, in all circumstances I preferred humanity and an indulging attitude toward human nature to the rules of severity, which often seemed wrongly understood to me; I had been guided to this [conclusion] by my own heart, which I believe to be mild and good.[43]

The principle of justice mediated by the mild heart of the ruler thus underpins Catherine's vision of the history of her reign. In November 1788, some months before the scandal with Dmitriev-Mamonov's infidelity, Catherine II's secretary recorded in his diary a conversation that had taken place between himself and the empress: "I talked about the time of Elisabeth Petrovna's reign and about the rule of grandees. I told her a humorous saying, that I used to go to Prince Trubetskoi first, then to Count Shuvalov, and if they did not help, let God's will be. They [Catherine II] grinned. [Catherine responded] I think I improved that *without exiles and executions*."[44] Thus, Catherine II saw in moderation and mildness, which she demonstrated while successfully improving the style of government, a key component of her policy. She believed that she became a real political decision-maker independent from the networks of powerful families and political advisors without resorting to terror. To both stage and reenact the historically emblematic moments of her imperial

42. Letter of Anastasia Sokolova from December 31, 1762, in Valentin Jamerai Duval, *Oeuvres de Valentin Jamerai Duval: précédées des mémoires sur sa vie* (St. Petersburg, n.n., 1784), p.128–29.

43. "Catherine II to Gabriel Sénac de Meilhan [July 1791]," *Sbornik imperatorskago russkago istoricheskago obshchestva* 42 (1885), p.166-67 (167).

44. Aleksandr Hrapovitskii, *Dnevnik A. V. Hrapovitskogo: 1782–1793* (St. Petersburg, 1874), p.196 (original emphasis).

clemency, Catherine used theatrical performances in French, Italian, and Russian.

Clemency and the "happy ending" in tragedy

The new theatrical culture implemented in imperial Russia appropriated narratives and techniques of representation that were circulating in the realm of European courts. Aleksandr Sumarokov was the first Russian writer to compose five-act tragedies in Russian verse for the court. His plays created a vernacular version of the symbolic idiom of dramatic representations, imported via the foreign companies at the service of the Russian monarch—the French dramatic troupe and the Italian opera.[45] In most of his plays, Sumarokov altered this language to suit the local political circumstances and simultaneously adapted narratives from medieval Russian history to fit into a dramatic plot. Performed on particular ceremonial occasions, such as the monarch's birthday or the anniversary of a coup, the tragedy was designed to shape collective political emotion and to provide authoritative models of absolutist kinship and patriotism.[46]

Sumarokov's tragedy *Semira*, first performed in St. Petersburg in 1751, stages a key episode in the history of the Russian monarchy. The play depicts the aftermath of the overthrow of the ruling dynasty in Kiev. The conqueror, prince-regent of Novgorod Oleg, allows the children of the overthrown princes to remain in his court, offering them paternal care. Oleg's generosity notwithstanding, Oskol'd and his sister Semira are determined to take revenge for their father and uncle. Oskol'd prepares an assault on the city with what remains of his army, but the project is discovered and he is imprisoned. Oleg's son Rostislav, hero of the previous war, is in love with Semira and agrees to free her brother, thus committing state treason. As a result, Oleg has to sentence both betrayers: the first of whom he treated *as* his own son, and the second who actually *is* his son. After a dramatic internal struggle, Oleg chooses not to sign Oskol'd's death sentence (act 2, scene 10). By contrast, when Rostislav confesses his crime, his

---

45. See Alexei Evstratov, *Les Spectacles francophones à la cour de Russie (1743–1796): l'invention d'une société*, Oxford University Studies in the Enlightenment (Oxford, Voltaire Foundation, 2016); Robert-Aloys Mooser, *Annales de la musique et des musiciens en Russie au XVIIIᵉ siècle*, 3 vols. (Geneva, 1948–1951).
46. See Ospovat, *Terror and pity. Semira* is not a part of the corpus studied by Ospovat.

father asks him what kind of punishment he deserves, and, when Rostislav names painful death, validates his response.

The court poet's dramatic rendition of the events of the ninth century is not particularly reflective of any of the historical accounts with which he might have been familiar. Instead *Semira*'s action carries references to a handful of French tragedies, most of which were performed by the prestigious company of French actors hired by the Russian court in the early 1740s.[47] Corneille's *Cinna* and Voltaire's *Brutus* (1730), Sumarokov's main models, treat the subject of the uncovered conspiracy in diametrically opposed ways. Whereas Corneille stages an act of imperial clemency, in *Brutus*, the Roman consul Junius Brutus condemns his own son to death. In the Russian play, which could be viewed as the hybrid from the two tragedies, the prince's son, though guilty of treason and sentenced to death by his father, does not die, because he is called to defend the city against an assault led by Oskol'd. The latter, by contrast, although pardoned by Oleg, eventually commits suicide. The fate or, rather, the dramatic narrative establishes the moral justice while maintaining the prince's charisma as guarantor of legality.

This is where Sumarokov's tragedy takes some liberty with its neoclassical models. There are two very similar situations where the prince must pronounce a sentence upon those close to him—a doubling, which contradicts a requirement of Aristotelian poetics, the unity of action. Besides, *Semira* is a tragedy whose protagonists are not destroyed by the terrifying antagonism between their duty and their feelings. The last cue of the play suggests, indeed, a sort of offstage happy ending, an optimistic prospect for the new ruling family. Rostislav summarizes the plot, asking the heavens: "Put an end to these sad days when we suffered, and let us enjoy merry days."[48] The reason for these artistic liberties lies, I contend, in Sumarokov's aim of creating a complex portrait of the sovereign embodying justice unrestrained by family ties, very much in the spirit of his later *Discourse*.[49]

---

47. Eveline Vetter, "Studien zu Sumarokov," doctoral dissertation, University of Berlin, 1961, p.94–104.
48. "Skonchai pechal'ny dni v kotory my terpeli / I zdelai chto by my dni radostny imeli." I quote a manuscript version of the tragedy published only in 1768 (Aleksandr Sumarokov, "Semira," Rossiiskaia Natsional'naia biblioteka: Otdel rukopisei: fonds 588, Pogodinskie avtografy, MS 2044, f.33). See also Ospovat, *Terror and pity*, p.224–27.
49. See Ospovat, *Terror and pity*, p.221–22.

The moral portrait of the ruler that results from the dramatic action is a combination of two conflicting and yet closely linked hypostases: that of the omnipotent and glorious sovereign and that of the suffering prince, subjected to the law whose guarantor he is. An ambiguity of a different sort is to be found at the center of Augustus's monologue in one of the key scenes of *Cinna* (act 4, scene 2). The emperor discovers his friend's betrayal, and, in order to decide how he will react to it, he reflects on the dialectics of violence and power. He recalls the streams of blood in which he bathed his arms while making his way to power, and he finds it only logical that now his absolute power must be challenged. How should he respond? A new execution, that of Cinna, would certainly provoke further conspiracies: "One cut head revives a thousand new ones" (act 4, scene 2).[50] However, a pardon too easily granted would certainly lead to new offenses. Ultimately, he decides to be merciful, but it is the moment of hesitation rather than the decision itself that is central to the dramatic construction of the sovereign's charisma, that of a superior human.

In the equivalent episode of *Semira*, the scene of Oleg's internal struggle at the moment when he signs Oskol'd's death sentence, Sumarokov directly addresses the operatic rendition of the subject, Metastasio's *La Clemenza di Tito*. A parallel reading of two texts, *Semira* and the 1742 Russian translation of the *opera seria*, establishes their intertextual links and helps to highlight the shifts made by Sumarokov's play.

The Italian text of the prince's monologue is clearly structured and rhetorically orchestrated. Before Titus approaches the small table on which lies the decree with the death sentence, his speech traces the logical path from his friend's "infedeltà" (betrayal) to the intention of revenge, "vendetta." Then, before he sits down, from "vendetta" to "leggi" (laws). And, finally, the monologue performs a shift from the "rigore" (severity) associated with laws, which appears when he signs the decree, to "pietà" (pity), when he tears it apart.[51] All of these categories and the logical progression they frame are important to Oleg's monologues in *Semira*.[52] However, they do not reflect the well-organized

50. "Une tête coupée en fait renaître mille." Pierre Corneille, *Cinna*, in *Œuvres complètes: Corneille*, ed. Georges Couton, 3 vols. (Paris, 1980–1987), vol.1, p.905–69 (949).
51. Pietro Metastasio, *La Clemenza di Tito*, in *Drammi per musica*, ed. A. L. Bellina, 3 vols. (Venice, 2000–2004), vol.2, p.433–34.
52. Sumarokov, *Polnoe sobranie vsekh sochinenii*, vol.3, p.285–86. He begins his

complexity of relations between the categories of "vengeance," "justice," and "mercy" which we observe in the Italian libretto. The Russian tragedy exposes the process of how the decision is made, but its logic is merely hinted at. Where Titus compares monarchs to gods, as they are capable of granting pardon, Oleg's only maxim is: "Although my anger is rightful, [the verdict] would satisfy cruelty."[53] This change in vocabulary and accentuation notwithstanding, both sovereigns are conventionally locked in the choice between two versions of authority: a prince supporting justice and a prince providing clemency.[54]

According to a study dedicated to this subject, *clementia* is not merely a sovereign virtue, but an important notion in the process of "humanization" of the exercise of power in early modern Europe.[55] Indeed, the scene from Metastasio's libretto reveals what I am tempted to consider as the roots of the psychologized self in drama of that period: It emerges from the juxtaposition of abstract notions in an inner dialogue occurring in the face of suspended action. The result of this dramatic depiction is a suffering prince, but also a prince who demonstrates a stoic capacity for self-discipline. Humanized power acquires a superlative quality, and very human doubts somewhat unexpectedly lead to the deification of the prince.

Female rule: a lover or a mother?

Milost', the Russian equivalent for "clemency," has two meanings, both of which are relevant for Catherine's treatment of her favorite and his lover. The first and perhaps more common meaning of *milost'* refers to magnanimity, generosity in granting favors (*milosti*) to subjects. The second meaning is the one scrutinized in the previous analysis: It is both general clemency and mercy, *miloserdie*, as it is

---

reflection in an earlier scene, by stating Oskold's ingratitude: "Here is the reward for my kindness towards him" (act 2, scene 7). "Anger" ("gnev") here corresponds to the "vendetta" of the Italian text. Oleg also appeals to justice, to see the conflict between ideas resolved: "Oh justice! Strengthen my soul / And reconcile different views in one."

53. Sumarokov, *Polnoe sobranie vsekh sochinenii*, vol.3, p.285.
54. See Vadim E. Vatsuro, "Iz istoriko-literaturnogo kommentariia k stikhotvoreniiam Pushkina: 4: 'Milost'' i 'pravosudie' v sisteme sotsial'no-eticheskikh predstavlenii Pushkina," *Pushkin: issledovania i materialy* 12 (1986), p.305–23.
55. Rudolf Behrens, "Die Macht der Milde: Konfigurationen der *clemetia* als Herrschertugend bei Seneca, Montaigne, Corneille und Metastasio," *Romanistisches Jahrbuch* 52:1 (2001), p.96–132 (98–99).

demonstrated through specific interventions in juridical cases. These connotations resonate with biblical themes that had to be left out of the present analysis due to space constraints.[56] Both connotations, with their religious associations, were distinctive in the unofficial form of address to Russian empresses—*matushka* (mother, in a respectful diminutive form, "dear mother").

Very early in her reign, Catherine II had acquired the designation of "mother of the fatherland" (*mat' otechestva*), tailored after the imperial epithet *pater patriae*. As we have seen, Empress Elisabeth had already been glorified under this name; still, even if Catherine II inherited it from her female predecessors, she used this title in the public realm in order to convey to it a connotation consistent with her roles. In 1767, after the publication of her *Instruction to the legislative commission* (*Nakaz* [...] *dannyi komissii o sochinenii proekta novogo Ulozheniia*), a public act was staged in which the proposal to name the empress "Catherine the Great, the Wise, Mother of the Fatherland" was submitted by the members of the Commission to the Senate. The empress expressed her gratitude, but did not accept the title, pointing out that an authentic and mutual link existed between her and her subjects, making its symbolic stagings superfluous: "I consider it the duty of my office to love my God-given subjects; to be loved by them is my wish."[57] However, as a historian observes, a great number of artifacts kept insisting on this epithet. Thus, a prominent playwright of Catherine's reign, Iakov Kniazhnin, authored a dramatic reenactment of this episode in 1777. His *Titus's clemency* (*Titovo miloserdie*), the first musical tragedy performed in Russian, draws both on Metastasio's *La Clemenza di Tito* and on Pierre-Laurent de Belloy's tragedy *Titus* (1760). In Kniazhnin's rendition, the play opens with a public ceremony of acclamation in front of the Capitol. The Senate, following the sentiments of the entire population, has proclaimed Titus *pater patriae*, and the senators seek to clarify the exact parameters of deification of the

---

56. Nataliia D. Kochetkova, "Bibleiskii motiv 'milost'' i sud' v russkoi literature XVIII veka," *Trudy Otdela Drevnerusskoi Literatury* 50 (1997), p.155–59; Aleksei Nadezhdin [Nadezhda Alekseeva], "K vorposu o teme *milosti* v russkoi literature XVIII veka," in *Von Wenigen–Ot nemnogikh: Sbornik k 70-letiiu N. D. Kochetkovoi* (St. Petersburg, 2008), p.8–17.

57. Quoted in Ingrid Schierle, "Patriotism and emotions: love of the fatherland in Catherinian Russia," *Ab Imperio* 3 (2009), p.65–93 (74).

emperor. Refusing the acclamations, Titus wishes to be called a "human" on the throne.[58]

Thus, in the studied narratives, "human" appears as an exceptional quality, at least when it comes to princes. It negatively refers not only to the control over one's own affects, but also to the disruption of social links and the resulting isolation from the immediate environment, especially from family. This solitude is what enables the bonds of affection to spread from the ruler to each of the imperial subjects. In the first version of Belloy's encomiastic tragedy *Titus*, written for the Russian court in 1759 under the title *The Triumph of friendship* (*Le Triomphe de l'amitié*), Titus concludes the dramatic action with an act of clemency and self-resignation: "You, tell the conspirators that Titus pardons them. And you, gods protecting the throne, second me. Titus will not choose [...] but Rome for spouse and his people for son."[59] This symbolic arrangement usefully resonated with the charisma of unmarried female rulers on the Russian throne, who either were officially childless, as Elisabeth, or distanced their children from the exercise of power, as Catherine II did with her son Paul.

In the dramatic texts discussed so far, the type of relation between the sovereign exercising justice and the criminal is one of subordination. Typically, as in *Brutus* and *Semira*, the ruler sentences his own son. In all cases, the action submitted to judgment is an actual crime, conspiracy against the sovereign. The human sympathies of the latter are either praised as leading to the apotheosis of imperial clemency or overcome in order for justice to triumph. At this point, the story of Catherine's treatment of her unfaithful favorites deviates from the existing set of narrative themes. First of all, the empress and her favorites were not officially married, and the uncovered infidelity therefore had no legal implications. The ruler did not have to become an agent of justice; moreover, the relocation of this act of imperial justice to the boudoir could look somewhat grotesque.

The zest of the story lies, it seems, in the contradiction between the romantic hierarchy grounded in the patriarchal social order and the political power hierarchy: Dmitriev-Mamonov preferred another woman to the empress, and the latter is therefore considered scorned. The implication is that, thus humiliated as a woman, she

---

58. Iakov Kniazhnin, "Titovo miloserdie," in Iakov Kniazhnin, *Sochineniia Kniazhnina* (St. Petersburg, 1847), p.75–140 (75–76, 78).

59. Pierre Laurent de Belloy, "Le triomphe de l'amitié," Bibliothèque nationale de France (Paris), Département des manuscrits, NAF 1685, p.98.

could easily deploy her absolutist authority to punish those who had humiliated her. A similar shift from a public figure of authority to an offended human is a constant feature of the tragic action. What is praised in the ruler's behavior is that her hurt pride does not provoke persecution, and that her feelings do not interfere with the manifestation of customary generosity—she follows the established practice by serving as a proxy mother of the bride, helping the latter to dress and bestowing jewelry on her.[60] Thus, Catherine performs a double metamorphosis: from a widowed ruler to a party in a morganatic union, and then from lover of a favorite to mother of the fatherland and of her subjects.

Throughout fictional transformations, rulers' inability to completely eliminate their own humanity only adds to their charisma. When represented in dramatic performances, the sovereign's position between justice and an alternative moral order appears to be the source of agonizing hesitations, with no room for error. In Metastasio's poetic variation on the theme, there are no saints on earth: Everybody has sinned, and systematic justice would be devastating.[61] Only the sovereign finds himself excluded from the multitudes of casual and forgivable sinners: "What an unhappy fate, then, does he who rules have! One denies us what is given to the lowliest" (act 3, scene 8).[62] Thus, unlike gods, the sovereign cannot punish, and, unlike humans, he cannot commit sins.

When commenting on the 1789 incident in a letter to Prince Potemkin, Catherine II complained that she had been kept ignorant about the affair between Dmitriev-Mamonov and Shcherbatova that had lasted about a year: "I have never been anybody's tyrant and I hate compulsion [*prinuzhdenie*], *is it possible that you misjudged me to this point! and that the generosity of my character escaped from your attention and that you thought I am an awful egoist, you would have healed me at once by telling me the truth.*"[63] A few months later, in December of the same year, the audience of the empress's more select and intimate

60. Here, *clementia* becomes synonymous with *constantia*, another virtue included by Justus Lipsius in his theory of power (Behrens, "Die Macht der Milde," p.120).
61. "Were justice carried out in its full severity, the earth would be a waste land. Where is someone found who has no guilt whatsoever, be it large or small" (act 1, scene 8), quoted in Wunderlich *et al.*, "Tradition and reception," p.7.
62. Wunderlich *et al.*, "Tradition and reception."
63. Letter from July 14, 1789, "Catherine II to Potemkin [July 14, 1789]," *Sbornik imperatorskago russkago istoricheskago obshchestva* 42 (1885), p.21–23 (22). I italicize

Hermitage theater saw a performance of *Cinna*, played by the French actors upon Catherine's special request.[64]

Conclusion

The empress's two bodies were a source of constant tension in a patriarchal society, where the diffused male domination was barely disguised in the rituals of the *culture galante* performed by the educated members of the ruling class. One instance, in which an imperial guardsman considered breaking into the private chambers of Empress Elisabeth to kill her official favorite on the grounds that her lover "commits fornication" with her, is quite telling of the conflict between imperial bodies.[65] Yet, the new cultural idiom, introduced and adapted first and foremost at the imperial court, provided the possibility for the elaboration of a highly functional, and to some extent original, set of interrelated narratives and representations in which conflicting notions could be exposed without endangering the absolutist status quo. Moreover, the somewhat slippery topic of favoritism could become an integral part of the encomiastic vocabulary, designed to enhance the legitimacy of the usurper to the Russian throne. The texts under investigation here demonstrate that this transformation of the potentially inglorious inclination toward younger lovers into a sign of the personal *grandeur* of the empress was successful in more than one case.[66]

Thus, the political virtue of clemency was given new currency in the age of "enlightened" monarchs, as it was considered a check on the potentially despotic rule of a female monarch whose legitimacy was not uncontested. Catherine II was keen to be seen as in touch with both Russian traditions and the latest Western European enlightened innovations, and court writers were central for establishing complex

---

the fragment that is in French in the original. Compare with an earlier letter to another favorite cited in Alexander, *Catherine the Great*, p.210.

64. Hrapovitskii, *Dnevnik*, p.320.
65. Evgenii Anisimov, *Dyba i knut: politicheskii sysk v Rossii v XVIII veke* (Moscow, 1999), p.64–65.
66. This was despite an emphasis on nuclear family in the nineteenth century that made the previous century in general and Catherine II in particular a much criticized negative example. See Richard Wortman, "The Russian empress as mother" and "The Russian imperial family as symbol," in Richard Wortman, *Russian monarchy: representation and rule, collected articles* (Boston, MA, 2013), p.89–105 and 106–34.

narratives of Catherine's clemency, which were then promoted through theatrical performances as well as through correspondences and other writings emanating from the court. Thus, while the empress disseminated her views in the European "public sphere," the court remained important for constructing and spreading absolutist idiom through several levels of communication. The efficiency of the narrative of clemency was grounded, as in the case of other "scenarios of power," in an extensive production of artistic and other discursive material, encompassing church sermons, poetry, staged drama, and opera. The cases studied in this chapter reveal the abundance of reenactments of this aspect of imperial *grandeur* and the ease with which this theme was appropriated by the Russian court in its performance of enlightened rule, addressed both to a public of local elites and to a broader Russian and international audience.

Fraternal kingdom? Freemasonry at the court of Gustav III of Sweden (1772–1792)

ANDREAS ÖNNERFORS

For two centuries after Adolf Frederick, king of Sweden (1710–1771), started presiding over a masonic lodge that carried his own name in 1753, the position of freemasonry at the Swedish court remained exceptionally strong. His sons Gustav (1746–1792, later Gustav III), Charles (1748–1818, later Charles XIII), and Frederick Adolf (1750–1803) were all initiated as freemasons. As an adolescent, Gustav was consecutively placed under the tutorship of three of the most prominent Swedish freemasons, Carl Gustaf Tessin (1695–1770), Olof von Dalin (1708–1763), and Carl Friedrich Scheffer (1715–1786). Already on the occasion of his birth in 1746, Swedish freemasons had struck a medal and hailed the crown prince in the most elaborate manner. In the context of both Gustav's 'revolution' of 1772 and his assassination in 1792, claims have been made of active masonic involvement. In a sense, the life of Gustav III is thus enframed by the question of the role freemasonry played at the royal court. How far did fraternal visions overlap with the political program of the king? Who were the key masonic actors surrounding the king and the court? It is well known that Gustav III was obsessed with theater, the performance of ceremonies, and what we today would call advanced role play. However, the position of freemasonry at the court of Gustav III remains disputed. Some researchers have not acknowledged his masonic involvement at all, while others have reduced the masonic influence to his brother Duke Charles, who was deeply immersed in the esoteric worldviews and politics of fraternalism. Starting with an overview of the current state of research and then exploring sources that have been made accessible only recently, this chapter aims to elucidate the position of freemasonry at the court of Gustav III as an integrated part of court sociability and the dominant cultural current of the era, "Gustavianism." The overarching aim of this ideology was to promote a modern form of patriotism under the leadership of the enlightened monarch, who styled himself and was styled as the ultimate savior and the fulfillment of Swedish historical development: starting with the establishment of the realm under Gustav (I) Vasa in 1523, continuing with the illustrious reign of Gustav II Adolf, who changed the course of the Thirty Years War on the Continent, and now reaching its pinnacle with the third Gustav.

Another overarching aim of this chapter is to locate the topic within the growing body of scholarship elaborating the relationship of freemasonry and other secret forms of sociability with Enlightenment culture and philosophy in general.[1] Over the last decades and due to new accessibility of sources, new avenues of research have been opened up. Spearheaded by scholars such as Helmut Reinalter, Margaret C. Jacob, and Pierre-Yves Beaurepaire, the research has treated freemasonry as a vanguard of (radical) Enlightenment values and sociability. These scholars highlight rationalized patterns of self-organization, philosophical self-design, and their importance for the formation of a modern public sphere and political culture.

Other scholars, such as Monika Neugebauer-Wölk, Jan Snoek, or Martin Mulsow, underline instead the role of freemasonry as a laboratory of alternative ideas, shaped by esoteric imagination, ritual dynamics, and secrecy as epistemological categories. This inclination toward mysticism was stigmatized in previous scholarship as an anti-Enlightenment Romantic undercurrent of rationality. In the case of Sweden, this position was pushed by literary scholar Martin Lamm, who saw little if any value in the esoteric activities among the elites of the Gustavian age (1771–1818). The tension between these opposite poles—Enlightenment versus Romanticism—is described by Dan Edelstein as an oscillation between transparency and opacity in an attempt to inquisitively wade beyond Locke's narrowly defined "limits of human understanding," beyond Enlightenment and toward the "Super-Enlightenment."[2] All these rather theoretical (and at times contradictory) approaches toward the subject are, however, confirmed

1. The growing trend of academic research into freemasonry is comprehensively represented in *Handbook of freemasonry*, ed. Henrik Bogdan and Jan A. M. Snoek (Leiden, 2014).
2. Dan Edelstein, "Introduction to the Super-Enlightenment," in *The Super-Enlightenment: daring to know too much*, ed. Dan Edelstein (Oxford, 2010), p.1–34.

by a steady stream of recent empirical works such as the five-volume Routledge source edition, edited by Róbert Péter.[3] Koselleck and Habermas have proposed that freemasonry represented a clear-cut division between secret and public space in Enlightenment culture. However, based upon hitherto unedited or very rare masonic printed works from the eighteenth century, as well as a comprehensive analysis of the manifold press references to freemasonry in the Burney collection, Péter and his coeditors are able to demonstrate that this conceptualization is open to challenge. Given the vast prominence of freemasonry in Enlightenment print culture and the press, it is indeed challenging to grasp the exact significance of secrecy as an organizational and epistemological category. Edelstein's proposed oscillation between transparency and opacity emerges particularly well when applied to hundreds if not thousands of individual Enlightenment biographies, such as that of Johann Carl Dähnert (1719–1785), professor of Swedish public law and librarian at the University of Greifswald in Swedish Pomerania. By day, Dähnert would edit his scholarly journal *Critische Nachrichten* (1771–1805) and, in the evening, dress up in his knightly garment and lead lodge assemblies for the masonic Knights Templar and Alchemists. Such supposed tensions cannot be grasped by essentialist understandings of "the Enlightenment" as a monolithic phenomenon.[4]

Foundations of fraternal politics in eighteenth-century Sweden

For the case of Swedish freemasonry and royal involvement in it, it is possible to detect a pattern of coexistence of exoteric reforms and esoteric reflection. Around 1800, at the peak of the masonic craze for elaborate chivalric and deeply arcane rituals, an anonymous author argued for the introduction of a general pension scheme in a publication of the Swedish Order of Freemasons. The masonic orphanage in Stockholm, a forerunner in pediatric care, educational innovation, and inoculation against smallpox, was inaugurated in 1753 with royal acclaim, only three years before the introduction of new masonic degrees linking freemasonry to the esoteric history of the Knights Templar. This tension between the introverted content of freemasonry and its extroverted actions was inherited, as we will see in this chapter, by Gustav III.

3.   *British freemasonry 1717–1813*, ed. Róbert Péter (Abingdon, 2015).
4.   Andreas Önnerfors, *Freemasonry: a very short introduction* (Oxford, 2017), p.17.

However, before returning to royal involvement in the fraternity, it is worth exploring the concepts of social, political, and moral reform in Swedish freemasonry further. With almost 4300 members of Swedish masonic lodges throughout the eighteenth century, freemasonry most certainly represents one of the largest organizations within which values often associated with the Enlightenment, such as that of self-improvement, cosmopolitan philanthropy, and perfection, were disseminated throughout the Swedish realm.[5] At the time it included Finland as well as Swedish Pomerania, a trading post in Canton, and the tiny island of St. Bartholomew in the Caribbean, and masonic lodges were established at all these locations. Sweden represents an exceptional case in its governmental endorsement of this educational program through the involvement of the royal court and substantial parts of the functional elites. In this sense, Swedish freemasonry was never opposed to official politics, but potentially instilled a shared ethos for the governing elites outside the narrow ideological boundaries of the Lutheran state church. The relationship to Lutheranism is complex. A number of leading clerics also occupied high offices within the Swedish Order of Freemasons, which retained a distinctly Christian character, albeit saturated with alternative spiritual elements and "crypto-Catholic" leanings. In this sense, Swedish freemasonry offered space for heterogeneous and complementary practices of Christianity rather than developing into a Deist or secular antagonist of established religion, as frequently was the case on the Continent.

It appears that Swedish freemasons adopted an approach toward religiosity that Jan Assmann has called "religio duplex" (inspired by the conceptualization of ancient Egyptian religion that was cherished by Gustav III and the circles around him): one religion and ideology for the initiated elites, and another religion and ideology for the uninitiated people.[6] By upholding such an elitist dual approach, Swedish freemasons could indulge in elaborate esoteric rituals largely separated from mainstream religiosity, and at the same time identify state religion as a tool for the exoteric education

5. See Andreas Önnerfors, *Mystiskt brödraskap, mäktigt nätverk: studier i det svenska 1700-talsfrimureriet* (Lund, 2006), p.40–93, in which I analyze "the moral realm" and ethos of Swedish freemasonry through a close reading of its rituals, rules, and regulations.
6. Jan Assmann, *Religio duplex: how the Enlightenment reinvented Egyptian religion* (London, 2014).

of the masses (for instance through reforms of hymnbooks, liturgy, and religious education and festivals), a peculiar form of secularization *à la suédoise*. Although never occupying a visible political role in Swedish politics, the politics of fraternalism potentially paved the way for incremental changes in Swedish society in the spirit of cameralistic reforms rather than radical revolution, even during such systematic national crises as the loss of Finland (the eastern part of the realm) and royal abdication and constitutional reform in 1809. Moreover, the language of fraternalism, with its stress on mutual aid, solidarity, charity, and compassion, could be translated into political vocabulary through the actions of civil society. Not only within freemasonry, but also within a host of other fraternal orders during the period, "welfare" turned into a key objective of extroverted and proactive charity, eventually placing pressure upon the state to deliver distributive justice.[7]

The conventional reading of Gustav III's relationship with freemasonry is that it only occupied a minor and relatively negligible role at his court, an expression of a temporary preoccupation with the occult and mysticism.[8] Leif Landen, who in 2004 published the latest authoritative biography of Gustav III, treats freemasonry only as a marginal phenomenon over the course of a few pages and relates freemasonry to a sudden inclination toward religion.[9] It appears that freemasonry was mainly the domain of his brother, Duke Charles, and that Gustav quickly lost interest in the brotherhood and its ideas once he realized it could not fulfill the political ambitions he might have projected onto it. Landen based his judgment mainly on outdated literature. By then, the extent to which social elites in Sweden were engaged in organized freemasonry had not yet emerged. As mentioned previously, an evaluation of an eighteenth-century membership record proves the involvement of more than 4300 members in masonic lodges throughout the realm.[10] Thus, freemasonry during the Gustavian era played a significant role as an expression of enlightened sociability and as sociocultural glue in

---

7.   Andreas Önnerfors, "1803 års statliga reglering av ordenssällskapen," in *Svenskt frimureri under 1800-talet*, ed. Marcus Willén (Uppsala, 2018), p.16–40.

8.   Tore Frängsmyr, *Svensk Idéhistoria* (Stockholm, 2004), p.394.

9.   Leif Landen, *Gustaf III: en biografi* (Stockholm, 2004), p.179–82.

10. Andreas Önnerfors, "'Position or profession in the profane world': 4300 Swedish freemasons from 1731 to 1800," in *Masonic and esoteric heritage: new perspectives for art and heritage policies*, ed. Andrea Kroon (The Hague, 2005), p.194–210.

Swedish society. To address the shortcomings in Swedish historiography, Göran Anderberg in 2009 published a monograph dedicated
to Gustav III and freemasonry.[11] A year later, an edited volume
appeared, bringing together new sources and insights into the history
of the fraternity under the leadership of Duke Charles.[12] Kjell Lekeby
has furthermore assembled and edited hitherto inaccessible source
material related to mysticism and freemasonry during the Gustavian
era.[13] In 2015, My Hellsing published her dissertation dedicated to
Hedvig Elisabeth Charlotte (1759–1818), wife of Duke Charles, who
extensively documented social life at court and was deeply involved
in female freemasonry and other forms of mixed-gender fraternal
orders.[14]

From time to time, new sources emerge that allow us to question,
to amend, and to correct the conventional image of freemasonry as
a supposedly marginal phenomenon at the court of Gustav III. Only
recently has it been discovered that Tessin suggested to Crown
Prince Gustav (prior to his ascension to the throne) that there was an
analogy between the Egyptian mysteries and freemasonry.[15] In what
sense Tessin's ideas potentially played into Gustav III's significant

11. Göran Anderberg, *Frimuraren Gustaf III: bakgrund, visioner, konspirationer,
    traditioner* (Partille, 2009).

12. *Hertig Carl och det svenska frimureriet*, ed. Henrik Berg (Uppsala, 2010).

13. Kjell Lekeby, *Gustaviansk mystik: alkemister, kabbalister, magiker, andeskådare,
    astrologer och skattgrävare i den esoteriska kretsen kring G. A. Reuterholm, hertig Carl
    och hertiginnan Charlotta 1776–1803* (Stockholm, 2010); Kjell Lekeby, *Gustaf
    Adolf Reuterholms hemliga arkiv från 1780-talet* (Stockholm, 2011); Kjell Lekeby,
    Esoterica i Svenska Frimurarordens arkiv 1776–1803 (Stockholm, 2011).

14. My Hellsing, *Hedvig Elisabeth Charlotte: hertiginna vid det gustavianska hovet*
    (Stockholm, 2015).

15. "Anteckningar ur frimurare-synpunkt om egypternas sinnebilder m.m. (med
    anledning av Comte de Caylus' Recueil d'antiquités égyptiennes, étrusques…),"
    Uppsala Universitetsbibliotek F 422.21 Gustavianska Samlingen. Thanks to
    Tim Berndtsson who made the discovery and kindly shared it with me. See
    also Tim Berndtsson's dissertation *The Order and the archive* (Uppsala, 2020), in
    which the emerging practices of masonic archiving are compared to national
    archiving in Sweden in the period. In 2022, a new project started at Uppsala
    University, creating digital access to the enormous collection of Gustav III's
    papers, "Av Gustavs hand: Digitalisering, digital berikning och förmedling av
    Gustav III:s arkiv"; see https://www.rj.se/anslag/2021/av-gustavs-hand-digital-
    isering-digital-berikning-och-formedling-av-gustav-iiis-arkiv/ (last accessed
    February 21, 2022). It is entirely possible that this digitization project will
    reveal more aspects of Gustav's involvement in freemasonry and other fraternal
    orders, their ideas, and cultural practices.

Egyptomania has hitherto not been analyzed.[16] Thus, this chapter attempts to align our insights into freemasonry at the court of Gustav III with the state of the field. However, it is important to address briefly how freemasonry in Sweden became a royal affair in the first place, since this helps to explain longer lines of development that have also been neglected in research about Gustav III and his court. Since freemasonry originated in Britain in the late 1710s and was quickly embraced by a number of royals, princes, and high aristocrats around Europe, it would be rewarding to compare the Swedish case to that of other countries.

How freemasonry in Sweden became a royal affair

Introduced to Sweden from France in 1735, freemasonry did not emerge as a major phenomenon of sociability until the early 1750s.[17] On the occasion of the birth of Crown Prince Gustav, on January 13, 1746, Swedish freemasons struck a medal full of masonic symbolism.[18] The front side displays Minerva on a cloud carrying a shield with the initial "G" (which in masonic circles could also have symbolic associations) above a globe that is surrounded by documents and masonic symbols such as a trowel, a level, a square, and a pair of compasses. The motto on the front side, "Tanto Numine," alluded to the classical quotation "tanto nomine, tanto numine" ("the greater the name, the greater the majesty"). Prince Gustav was thereby placed on a par with the Swedish "nation-builder" Gustav (I) Vasa of the sixteenth century and "the Defender of True Protestantism" Gustav II Adolf of the seventeenth century. On the reverse, a rising sun disperses the darkness over a floor made of equilateral squares (a reference to the

16. In his dissertation Sven Delblanc outlines how Gustav III himself, inspired by imagined Egyptian tradition, promoted the ideal of a "doctrine of posteriority" (*eftervärldsdoktrionen*) in honoring the life of the deceased. This literary development marks a radical shift from religious ideas of punishment and rewards toward the verdict of future generations. See Sven Delblanc, *Ära och minne: studier kring ett motivkomplex i 1700-taletslitteratur* (Stockholm, 1965), p.15–59 and 73; and Andreas Önnerfors, "'Död är liv': iscensättning av döden i det europeiska 1700-talsfrimureriet," *Historisk Tidskrift* 131:3 (2011), p.459–90.

17. The historical overview that follows is based on Anderberg, *Frimuraren Gustaf III*, p.30–48, and Carl Ludwig Henning Thulstrup, *Anteckningar till svenska frimureriets historia*, 2 vols. (Stockholm, 1892–1898), who compiled the first trustworthy historiography of Swedish freemasonry based upon his access to primary sources.

18. Anderberg, *Frimuraren Gustaf III*, p.36–38.

floor design in masonic lodges and the Temple of Solomon) under a quotation from Genesis, "et extitit lux" ("and there was light").

The presentation of the medal was reported in the German journal *Europäischer Staats-Secretarius* in 1746 with a translation of the speech delivered on this occasion.[19] Anders von Höpken (1712–1789), freemason, prominent politician, and an employee of the Office of Foreign Affairs, here described the expectations directed toward the young prince. It was his task to push back the clouds of ignorance and disunion and to restore a sparkling light of glory for himself and the Swedish dynasty. Höpken concluded: "With one word, and using the language that is peculiar to the secrets of the freemasons, you will bring the great building of our felicity and its glory to perfection."[20]

However, it was only in 1753, when Count Scheffer was appointed Grand Master of the Swedish freemasons, that organizational development accelerated. That was the same year King Adolf Frederick established a lodge in his own name (possibly approving one that had previously formed among his royal guard), declared himself protector of all masonic lodges in Sweden, and officially endorsed Scheffer in his office.[21] Also in 1753, on the occasion of the birth of Princess Sophia Albertina, in Stockholm a masonic orphanage was established with royal acclaim. To commemorate the occasion, another masonic medal was struck with the motto "Servavit Regia Nata" ("He was rescued by the royal daughter"), likening the princess to the daughter of Pharaoh who rescued Moses from the Nile. These events mark the tight nexus between freemasonry and state which has been a characteristic trait of freemasonry in Scandinavia for more than two centuries.[22]

There is no clear explanation as to why Adolf Frederick joined the fraternity, but he might have had political considerations we will return to. It is also not certain whether he underwent a proper

19. *Europäischer Staats-Secretarius* 117 (1746), p.828–30.
20. *Europäischer Staats-Secretarius* 117 (1746), p.830. All translations are my own unless otherwise stated.
21. Roger de Robelin, "Johannesfrimureriet i Sverige under 1700-talet," in *I guld och himmelsblått: frimureri, ett ideal i tiden*, ed. Tom C. Bergroth (Åbo, 1992), p.29–92.
22. Whereas the symbolism of the medal dedicated to the birth of Crown Prince Gustav clearly has masonic references, the medal commemorating the birth of Sophia Albertina is more difficult to place within masonic imagery. The reference to the daughter/wife of Pharaoh potentially points, however, to an Egyptian gamut of themes beyond the Old Testament.

initiation into freemasonry (as did his brother-in-law, Frederick II of Prussia) or was simply accepted as a member. Since 1738 Sweden had in practice been a parliamentary monarchy, where the political role of the king was extremely reduced. This "age of liberty" lasted until Gustav's coup d'état in 1772, which reinstated royal power and abolished the rule of the parties that had been formed across all four estates of the realm, the "hats" and "caps." However, on the eve of the Seven Years War, in 1756, Gustav's parents had already attempted to strengthen the might of the monarchy through a failed coup. In this context it is revealing that two of the royalist rebels, leading members of the king's lodge, were publicly executed for treason. The lodge appears to have gathered at the royal castle and existed quite separately from Swedish mainstream freemasonry, which was organized into a proper national Grand Lodge in 1760.[23] One year later, Adolf Frederick joined the Swedish Army's Lodge that had been formed in Swedish Pomerania during the war, and which directed its charity toward pensions for wounded soldiers, widows, and orphans. The king endorsed this charitable initiative and assumed the position of protector of the pension fund, the first of its kind in Sweden. In the membership record, listing no fewer than 4300 freemasons in Swedish lodges during the eighteenth century, King Adolf Frederick was number 704. It is assumed that his lodge Adolph Fredric ceased to exist in 1775. Around one hundred members are identifiable in the membership record, and their occupations already say something about the prevalence of freemasonry at the royal court.[24] Margaret C. Jacob states: "In Sweden the entire court from the king and his ministers on down joined lodges that were feted at the royal palace" and, moreover, "[i]n the second half of the century, the Swedish king and court were deeply masonic, and the palace served as the setting for many feasts organized by the Swedish Grand Lodge. The fit between membership in the leading Stockholm lodges and proximity to king and court could not have been tighter."[25]

23. Robelin, "Johannesfrimureriet," p.59–62.
24. The information is extracted from Önnerfors, *Mystiskt brödraskap*, p.158–265; the transcribed source material has been published by the Forschungszentrum Gotha of the Universität Erfurt, and is accessible at https://tinyurl.com/y39z7ev6 (last accessed January 28, 2022).
25. Margaret C. Jacob, *The Origins of freemasonry: facts and fictions* (Philadelphia, PA, 2006), p.20, 59. It is not entirely clear on which empiricism Jacob rests her conclusions, however, a closer look at the membership structure of the Adolph Fredric lodge indeed reveals intimate connections.

Among a host of decorated officers from the royal regiments of mainly high noble origin, we find court officials (such as the Master of Ceremonies, a royal governor, the governess of Princess Sophia Albertina, lord stewarts, chamberlains, secretaries, the librarian of Queen Lovisa Ulrika, royal musicians, master builders of the royal castle, cavaliers of the royal stable, and so forth), members of the diplomatic corps, but also privileged commoners such as aldermen, skilled craftsmen, lawyers, and a bookseller. Adolph Fredric had the highest concentration of members related to the royal court, but other Stockholm lodges also recruited members from the royal regiment and the royal household (in particular this appears to apply to court musicians who joined the lodges St. Jean Auxiliaire and L'Union). Hence, it is no exaggeration to state that freemasonry was an omnipresent phenomenon not only in the royal family and the close circle of high nobility surrounding it, but also within court culture at large.

A Christian esoteric twist was introduced into Swedish freemasonry with the establishment of a higher degree system, which was built on chivalric imagination in general and the supposedly continued and occult existence of the Knights Templar in particular.[26] Continuing legends that informed the three lower degrees of freemasonry common across Europe, these higher degrees suggested that the Order of the Knights Templar had not been disbanded in 1314 but had secretly withdrawn to Scotland. From here, it was said, the Knights Templar united with the craft lodges of freemasonry and reappeared during the eighteenth century. Research is divided concerning the origin and significance of these ideas, but they quickly gathered enormous attraction throughout Europe between 1760 and 1780. A rival masonic system on the Continent, the so-called Strict Observance, organized no fewer than 1600 masonic Knights Templar in its inner circle and divided Europe into different provinces of the order.[27]

When the crown prince was aged twelve, in 1758, Scheffer gave him the task of designing rules and regulations for three different fraternal orders.[28] Such orders, in vogue across Europe and inspired by freemasonry, were a typical feature of court culture. Continuing an earlier seventeenth-century tradition of *preciosité*, these role plays were modeled on classical literature and the Bible, frequently with a

26. Önnerfors, *Freemasonry*, p.39–42.
27. Önnerfors, *Freemasonry*, p.41, 62, 78, 79, 85, 96, 109.
28. Anderberg, *Frimuraren Gustaf III*, p.53.

pastoral theme. There is a potential overlap between these aristocratic and court orders and fraternal rituals in their character of social play and performance. In the Swedish case, the mixed-gender Order of the Pug (*Mopsorden*) (the ritual of which was published in 1745) was introduced to Sweden by Carl Gustaf Tessin and established at the court of Adolf Fredrik and Lovisa Ulrika.[29] Outside the court, but in close proximity, other orders were established, such as La Resemblance of female poet Hedvig Charlotta Nordenflycht in 1747 or the literary Order of Thought-Builders (1753–1756). The rituals of fraternal orders can be likened to classical music: Set within a fixed framework of ceremonies of initiation and a progression in different degrees with little variation in form and symbolism, the content could vary almost infinitely.[30] From here, freemasonry itself was only a step away, and, at least in the case of Sweden, there is proof of overlapping membership in different fraternal orders. Another interesting parallel and potential overlap is the introduction to Sweden of orders of merit.[31] The state honors system was established in Sweden in 1748 and comprised of the Order of the Seraphim, the Order of the Sword, and the Order of the Polar Star (in 1772, a fourth order designated for non-nobles, the Order of Vasa, was introduced). The royal court was deeply involved in formulating the symbolism, rituals, and content of these orders, and Gustav III later made plans to reactivate the mixed-gender Order of the Amaranth, which had already been established by Queen Christina in 1653. Beyond rewarding outstanding performances and loyalty, the honors system symbolizes the idea of unselfish and patriotic service for the common good of the political community. It is possible to argue that freemasonry and other fraternal orders operated along similar lines of thought, albeit translated into individual perfectibility and local communities. A further potential parallel lies in the function of the orders of merit in foreign politics and diplomacy as tools of mutual recognition, symbolic bonds, and symbolic capital. Once freemasonry

29. Andreas Önnerfors, *Svenska Pommern: kulturmöten och identifikation 1720–1815* (Lund, 2003), p.157–62; Robelin, "Johannesfrimureriet," p.51.
30. Already during the seventeenth century, Queen Christina of Sweden established the mixed-gender Order of the Amaranth, which can be interpreted as a precursor of such court orders in the northern kingdom. See Andreas Önnerfors, "La sociabilité féminine en Suède au XVIIIᵉ siècle," *La Pensée et les hommes* 82–83 (2011), p.77–96.
31. Antti Matikkala and Staffan Rosén, *Perspectives on the honours system* (Stockholm, 2015).

turned into an international affair (arguably after 1760), it is possible to observe a conflation between this function of the orders of merit and orders/degree systems of freemasonry.

Gustav III and freemasonry

In 1770 or 1771, we do not know exactly when or where, the three royal princes Gustav, Charles, and Frederick Adolf were initiated into freemasonry. Thulstrup, who based his historiography of Swedish freemasonry upon direct access to primary source material, states that it happened in 1771, since the Swedish lodges were informed that Gustav III had declared himself protector of the masonic order in October of the same year. Furthermore, Charles and Frederick Adolf attended a meeting of the military lodge in December, which the latter presided over from this time until 1788.[32] Formally, Gustav III is listed as member no.1896 in the general membership record of Swedish freemasonry, together with other members initiated in April 1775. However, this was the date when the supreme degree of Swedish freemasonry at the time, the so-called Ruby Cross, was conferred on him. Also for Duke Charles (no.1832), it is his initiation to the same degree in 1773 that is his first recorded masonic affiliation, and the same applies to Prince Frederick Adolf (no.1842).[33] The absence of a formal date of initiation might indicate that the royal princes were initiated either in a private lodge meeting (possibly by Scheffer) or abroad (most likely in France). Among the three, it was Duke Charles who was the most industrious, and who founded a lodge in the higher degrees in 1774 among a circle closely related to the royal court (the lord stewart of Princess Sophia Albertina, the adjutants of Charles and Frederick Adolf, the royal physician of Charles, a royal secretary, and two chamberlains).[34] It was also in 1774 that Duke Charles took over the leadership of Swedish freemasonry, the masonic chapter L'Innocente (with responsibility for the higher degrees), and the Swedish Grand Lodge (counting twelve lodges across the Swedish realm). By uniting

---

32. Thulstrup, *Anteckningar*, p.53. Robelin, "Johannesfrimureriet," p.67–70, states that Charles and Frederick Adolf were initiated while traveling in France, and Gustav in a private lodge during the autumn of 1771.

33. Önnerfors, *Mystiskt brödraskap*, p.175, 192, 197, and the transcribed source material in the possession of the author. Thulstrup suggests that all three were initiated into the chivalric chapter degrees in 1773.

34. Thulstrup, *Anteckningar*, p.53.

these two offices, Duke Charles created a unique organization of Swedish freemasonry in a unified system from the lowest to the highest degrees. It is also noteworthy that his wife Hedvig Elisabeth Charlotte in 1776 established a female lodge with a constitution signed by the duchess of Bourbon in Paris. Unfortunately, the membership record remains inaccessible; however, given later developments in female and mixed-gender fraternalism in Sweden, it is very probable that the involvement of women attached to the royal court was high.[35]

According to Anderberg, Gustav III himself claimed that he joined freemasonry because his father had been a member (initiation took place either in 1770 or in autumn 1771, after Gustav's journey to France).[36] It is also not unrealistic to imagine that his masonic governors Tessin, Dalin, and Scheffer substantially influenced his decision. In any case there is a striking parallel between political developments and the royal initiations in Sweden. During the 1760s, the Swedish political system of the "age of liberty" had run into a series of systematic crises. One option that started to appeal more and more among the governing elites was a royal coup d'état, followed by a series of fundamental reforms in the spirit of Enlightenment, such as physiocracy, legal reform, and cultural politics. It appears that the Swedish Grand Master of freemasonry and royal governor Scheffer also played the role of an eminence grise during this decisive period. During his time as ambassador in Paris, Scheffer had established close contacts with French physiocrats (and freemasons) and encouraged Crown Prince Gustav to read the works of Le Mercier de La Rivière, who advocated enlightened despotism.[37] When Scheffer traveled to Paris together with Gustav in 1770–1771, one of the main aims was to gain support for a substantial regime change in Sweden. This accelerated when Adolf Frederick suddenly died in February 1771: The plans for a royal revolution materialized in August 1772. All of the leading figures involved in the coup were freemasons, and the royal regiments in Stockholm, where the degree of affiliation was high, played a decisive role in the political overthrow.

It cannot be ruled out that Scheffer's masonic affiliation opened up contacts in the French capital, and that Gustav was impressed by the informal function of freemasonry as a zone of sociopolitical and

35. Önnerfors, "La sociabilité féminine," p.85–90.
36. Anderberg, *Frimuraren Gustaf III*, p.50.
37. Charlotta Wolff, *Vänskap och makt: den svenska politiska eliten och upplysningstidens Frankrike* (Helsingfors, 2004), p.236–42 and 271–75.

cultural contacts among educated elites. Scheffer had in any case achieved that the legacy of harmony between freemasonry and state in Sweden be continued, and that Gustav declare himself protector of the brotherhood.

Studying the social composition of membership, both in Swedish freemasonry at large and in the Stockholm chapter lodge, it can be observed that the high nobility increasingly made way for a new class of wealthy merchants and civil servants. Thus, freemasonry under the protection of Gustav III expanded its social remit horizontally, relieving a tension between the ideal of brotherly equality and vertical societal hierarchies. These hierarchies were only preserved in the chivalric masonic degrees, which until the early nineteenth century were reserved for members of the nobility. However, without delving too deeply into the issue, the Swedish nobility was socially divided between old landed nobility and ennobled commoners. Adolf Frederick was prolific in using ennoblement as a tool for shaping a loyal political elite (and the establishment of the Order of Vasa for commoners in 1772 can also be interpreted as one of these tools). Furthermore, during the last years of his reign, Gustav III actively sought political support among the burghers, intentionally sidestepping the nobility. As I have argued elsewhere, Gustavian involvement in freemasonry might have contributed to a shift toward the creation of (the ethos of) a new service elite.[38]

How immersed court culture was in freemasonry can be illustrated by the birth of Crown Prince Gustav Adolf on November 1, 1778 (d.1837, Gustav IV Adolf 1792–1809). Already the next day, a masonic delegation headed by Duke Charles and Prince Frederick Adolf invited the newborn crown prince to become a member of the Order of Freemasons. Gustav III, who "very graciously" welcomed the delegation to the royal castle, promised to give his son the necessary education in order to "fulfil the obligations that have been conferred on him already on this occasion."[39] This ceremony was repeated when in 1782 Prince Charles Gustav (son of Duke Charles) was born (he died a year later).[40] State secretary Elis Schröderheim (1747–1795)

---

38. Andreas Önnerfors, "From Jacobite support to a part of the state apparatus: Swedish freemasonry between reform and revolution," in *Franc-maçonnerie et politique au siècle des Lumières: Europe–Amériques*, ed. Cécile Révauger (Bordeaux, 2006), p.203–25.
39. Thulstrup, *Anteckningar*, p.105.
40. Thulstrup, *Anteckningar*, p.154.

wrote in his memoirs that Gustav III "with great attendance embraced [freemasonry] and from time to time even followed [it] with a true ardor [...] but I am convinced that he thought it was possible to unite true political purposes with freemasonry."[41] Schröderheim was also convinced that a true description of freemasonry in Sweden during the reign of Gustav III had to be extended to vast fields like "religion, politics, alchemy; it was practiced by some with the best intentions, by others with dirty tricks, and finally it suited all kinds of purposes."[42]

Freemasonry as a platform for international relations

The commitment of the royals to freemasonry can be interpreted as a means to achieve philosophical/moral consensus (and diminish opposition) among the domestic functional elites in Sweden in order to promote a top-down project of social reforms that aimed at the perfection and rationalization of political power and of national wealth paired with national welfare.[43] Gustav III envisioned a northern equivalent of Prussia (ruled by his uncle Frederick II "the Great"), reconnecting with its imagined Gothic past and recovering its former status as a European great power.

In this vein, there are also clear indications that Gustav III and his brother Charles intended to use the masonic order as a platform for international relations. As mentioned before, Swedish freemasonry imagined itself as the continuation of the chivalric tradition of the Knights Templar. Although Swedish freemasonry in the mid-1750s had received its rituals and constitution from another origin (most likely Florence, communicated via Switzerland), the similarities with the system of the Strict Observance (SO) were obvious. The

41. Elis Schröderheim, *Statssekreteraren Elis Schröderheims Anteckningar till Konung Gustaf III's historia; jemte brefvexling emellan Konungen och honom*, ed. Karl Vilhelm Lilljecrona (Örebro, 1851), p.80. Schröderheim was a member of the Swedish Academy and at least two further fraternal orders, the Ordre des Charpentiers and Par Bricole.
42. Schröderheim, *Statssekreteraren Elis Schröderheims Anteckningar*, p.80.
43. Elite consensus is understood as a way to commit members of the elites to a shared framework of voluntarily agreed values. In the Swedish case, royal involvement in freemasonry must have appeared as a strong inducement to join. Service elites are understood as elites in politics, government, the church, military, and administration with decision-making power, and in the Swedish case comprised both high and low nobility (in government and military), as well as merchants, clerics, skilled craftsmen, and government officials of common origin.

development on the Continent had commenced with the German Carl Gotthelf von Hund (1722–1776). With great confidence, Hund established his variant of Knights Templar freemasonry during the 1750s. Despite or even accelerated by the Seven Years War, he managed to attract huge swaths of German aristocrats to his system, which eventually branched off to Italy, France, Poland, and Russia. Europe was divided into different (not always geographically accurate and mostly imagined) provinces of the Order; Lower Germany (where the Strict Observance had its headquarters) was classified as number VII. After Hund's death in 1776, the leadership of this most significant province was contested, and Sweden saw an opportunity to assume power and to unite the two branches of Templar freemasonry.[44] For this purpose, Duke Charles in 1777 sent envoys to the court of Ferdinand of Brunswick-Lüneburg (1721–1792, at this point in time governing the SO), who handed over a letter by (Ferdinand's cousin) Gustav III endorsing Duke Charles's candidature.[45] One of the envoys was the young chamberlain of the king, Count Johan Gabriel Oxenstierna (1750–1818), who would make an exceptional career in Swedish cultural and political circles. Over the next three years, a complex process of diplomacy took place, in which the Swedish king intervened directly on several occasions. Initially, the Swedish initiative was fruitful and Duke Charles was nominated (but not yet formally elected) as the successor of Hund. Gustav III even issued a warrant of protection for the members of the seventh province in his states. His commitment increased when, in early 1778, he received news that the Holy Roman emperor Joseph II intended to convert the higher (Knights Templar) degrees of freemasonry into an imperial order of merit, endowing this establishment with 4 million guilders.[46] Obviously relying upon his source (the landgrave of Hessen-Darmstadt, who was also involved in the SO), Gustav III quickly gathered a number of Swedish high-ranking freemasons and declared that the move of the emperor clearly aimed to undermine the Swedish union with the SO and thus the honor of the Swedish monarchy. Therefore, Gustav III now intended to grant the masonic

---

44. According to Anderberg, *Frimuraren Gustaf III*, p.68 (and sources quoted therein), it was Gustav III who developed the vision that Swedish involvement within the SO might open the door toward an increased influence in the Holy Roman Empire.
45. The French original is transcribed in Thulstrup, *Anteckningar*, p.92.
46. Thulstrup, *Anteckningar*, p.101–102.

Knights Templar his protection in the Swedish realm and to publicly provide them with their traditional privileges. In his royal bill, foreign brothers moving to Sweden were promised "all the rights, liberties, and securities and property rights of indigenous Swedes [*Swenskmanna Rätt*]."[47] However, in the end the news from Vienna turned out to be unsubstantiated rumors, and the royal regulation was never ratified.

Whereas this chain of events from today's point of view might look futile, in its late-eighteenth-century context, it was not. Imagining themselves as successors of the Templars ignited the idea that there was a shared supra-national European space of values within which a shared imagined spiritual medieval ancestry (that of the contested Order of the Knights Templar) produced significant cultural capital.[48] Pierre Mollier, a leading expert on the ideas of the Knights Templar in eighteenth-century freemasonry, has pointed out two dimensions explaining their attractiveness to European elites: first, that of the occult and myth, according to which the Knights Templar were yet another secret community in which arcane mysteries were kept and transferred over centuries; second, the political dimension, which calls for the restoration of justice and law (due to the persecution of the order by church and crown). The alleged heresy of the order thus provides a link between esotericism and social protest and change.[49] On a less esoteric level, it is possible to argue that Gustav III identified Knights Templar freemasonry as a laboratory for a pan-European order of merit under his command. Schröderheim suggests in his memoirs that Gustav III was already planning for the political landscape of Europe and the time after the death of his uncle Frederick II of Prussia and his cousin Catherine II of Russia. In the case of political turbulence following these events, the Baltic provinces might be willing to return to Swedish rule (under which they had been during the seventeenth century), as a majority of their noble families were still members of the Swedish house of nobles. If the Swedish royal family by then were to

47. Thulstrup, *Anteckningar*, p.102.
48. This imagined shared European past, rooted in the Middle Ages, later turned into a powerful figure of thought, as represented in Novalis's 1799 talk "Christianity or Europe," a call for a religious and spiritual renewal of the human being through the revival of "the holy sense," a sense for invisible dimensions like beauty, harmony, peace, and truth. Andreas Önnerfors, "Between the sacred and the secular: connotations of European space," in *Negotiating Europe: foundations, dynamics, challenges*, ed. Anamaria Dutceac and Andreas Önnerfors (Lund, 2007), p.18–37.
49. Önnerfors, *Freemasonry*, p.42.

be in possession of important offices within the Order of the Knights Templars, the connection to the Teutonic Order might be proven and hence an alliance with Sweden would be a natural step.

The Swedish crown was still convinced that Duke Charles would take over the leadership of the seventh province of the SO, and in May 1778 Gustav III issued a solemn patent in Latin, confirming his protection of the members of the SO and the donation of royal estates to the order, as well as a renewed endorsement of his brother. Leading Swedish freemasons (and the king himself) suggested at the same time that Sweden should establish its own province of Templar masonry before merging entirely with Lower Germany. Meanwhile, Swedish negotiations with Brunswick met resistance among Danish freemasons, who (belonging to the seventh province) did not accept the idea of being placed under the leadership of their political adversary, Sweden. Although Gustav III, Duke Ferdinand of Brunswick, and Duke Charles had met in person in southern Sweden shortly thereafter in order to sort out the deal, the nomination of Duke Charles was suddenly questioned by a convention of the SO later during the year. The new terms of engagement were unacceptable to Gustav III and Charles, and thus the idea of an independent Swedish province gained new ground. To complicate the matter, negotiations were resumed and a year later it seems that Duke Charles was finally elected and installed into his office. However, the division of power between Stockholm and Brunswick emerged as a major obstacle for the union to materialize properly. Duke Charles was convinced that his new position allowed him to establish new provinces of the order, and, thus, the formation of a new, so-called IXth, province (or "Archipelago"), covering Sweden, Finland, and the Russian empire (into which the Swedish rite of freemasonry was successfully introduced during the previous years), was envisaged to take place in March 1780.[50]

In the presence of more than 400 freemasons assembled in the Stockholm Stock Exchange, Duke Charles was installed as the master of the ninth province of Templar freemasonry by his own brother, Gustav III.[51] The establishment of this new province was a completely unilateral move and not coordinated with the rest of the SO. When

50. Anderberg, *Frimuraren Gustaf III*, p.65–66. Robelin, "Johannesfrimureriet," p.71–72.
51. Anderberg argues that it was Gustav III who designed the ceremony to contain the power of his brother, Duke Charles; see Anderberg, *Frimuraren Gustaf III*, p.65–66.

informed about the grandiose ceremonies, the Brunswick government of the SO reacted sharply, also in the light of press reports that claimed international support for and submission to Duke Charles. What is interesting to highlight in all these very complex exchanges of opinions is that Sweden had obviously misjudged the spirit of Continental freemasonry, suggesting a more equal division of power and that Swedish masonic leaders were unaware of the trends of the time, which erupted in the impending collapse of the SO in 1782. In one of the letters to Duke Charles, he was accused of confusing his position as a royal and as a brother in the order of freemasons:

> Your Royal Highness is at the same time a prince and a brother in the order. It is only natural, Monseigneur, that you had difficulties to separate these two concepts and positions so that the one would not influence the other. The seventh province does make the sharpest distinction in this regard and has the honor to negotiate with Your Royal Highness as a brother of the order. [During the previous negotiations] your envoys frequently made reference to your dignity outside the order. The laws of our province, excluding princes from the position of being master of the order, follow the same principle and cannot be circumvented. In Sweden, however, the commands given by the head of the order are always to a certain extent the commands of the king's brother.[52]

Sweden had at this point evidently failed to adapt to the more egalitarian form of freemasonry that was steadily gaining ground on the Continent. Also, the relationship with the Russian lodges was damaged, partly due to the impression communicated in the press that Sweden had used its new masonic province to subdue the political elites in the Baltic Sea region (as suggested by Schröderheim). Thus, the course was set for Swedish freemasonry to fail to gain more international influence. Duke Charles abdicated in 1781 from his position (with Gustav III's consent) and, in 1782, the entire SO (formerly a platform of fraternal collaboration across Europe) disintegrated into different branches and systems of freemasonry, many of them advocating less elaborate and more secular forms of freemasonry as had been practiced at the beginning of the century. Some central ideas expressed in Duke Charles's letter of resignation suggest that Swedish involvement within the SO was to be considered a continuation of Swedish foreign policy in the Holy Roman Empire,

52. Thulstrup, *Anteckningar*, p.134–35.

when the Swedish kings of the past had "perpetuated the laws and liberties of the German princes and estates":

> Such would have been the benefits for the Order, since we in a king and as a brother of a Swedish king have found the most noble inclination toward an order, which under his high scepter enjoyed a mighty protection, to be a member of which he was not ashamed, the workings of which he attended, the rules and regulations of which he observed. Moreover, such times might have come [in the future] when the German brothers might have needed both support and asylum, and such protection they could have expected only from the king of Sweden.[53]

One might think that the failure to unite with the SO as much as the collapse of the system in 1782 would have prevented Gustav III from further exploring freemasonry as a part of foreign policy. However, his Italian travels in 1783 prove that this was not the case at all. One of the major issues related to the negotiations with the SO, as much as within the SO itself, was the idea of the existence of so-called unknown superiors and a secret Grand Master who had not (yet) revealed himself. When establishing his system during the 1750s and 1760s, Hund claimed that he had met with this secret leadership and that they had promised to keep in contact. However, strongly questioned by leading members of the SO, he was eventually forced to confess that he was in total ignorance of the true leaders of the masonic Knights Templar and that, since the 1740s, they had never reached out to him again. During the negotiations with the SO, Swedish envoys persistently maintained that the secret superiors were known to them. Many rumors circulated, one of them being that the position of the Grand Master was a hereditary dignity of the Jacobite house of Stuart, ousted from the British throne. Residing in his Florentine exile, it was believed that Charles Edward Stuart (1720–1788) was the secret leader of the masonic Knights Templar. Contemporary sources suggest that one of the main reasons why Gustav III traveled to Italy at this point in time was his plan to ask Charles Edward Stuart to transfer the supposed dignity of leadership to the Swedish monarchy. Schröderheim tells us, among many anecdotes of that visit, that the main motive was "the reestablishment of the sanctuary" and that the "king worked on mysteries with the

---

53. Thulstrup, *Anteckningar*, p.147–48.

Pretender in order to raise the temple of Jerusalem."[54] Throughout the eighteenth century, there is an unlikely line of support for the Jacobite cause in Swedish foreign policy, to which Gustav's initiative adds yet another piece.[55] Moreover, he was successful in his attempts, and in a personal meeting convinced Charles Edward to will the position as Grand Master to the Swedish monarch and his heirs.[56] When Charles Edward died in 1788, Swedish freemasons accepted the transfer of power as entirely legal. Gustav III was at the zenith of his influence in the masonic movement and now imagined himself as its international leader.

Gustavian mysticism? The esoteric aspects of court culture under Gustav III

Whereas royal Swedish involvement with the masonic Knights Templar appears as a projection of fraternal fantasies upon the realities of foreign relations (and a continuation of the idea of orders of merit on the international level), there is yet another aspect of freemasonry at the court of Gustav III that remains to be addressed. During the final decades of the eighteenth century, what we perceive as rational Enlightenment ideas were blended with more esoteric elements. In what sense it is possible to label these ideas as Counter-Enlightenment or pre-Romantic, sentimental, or occult subversive undercurrents is, as outlined extensively at the outset of this chapter, a disputed issue in the scholarship. Rather, it has been suggested that we understand the development as the emergence of two poles between which the Enlightenment continuously oscillated.[57] In any case, at the court of Gustav III, the phenomena associated with esoteric practices are well documented and did to a certain degree overlap with the position of freemasonry, or as Schröderheim put it: "Within a small circle of those brethren, gathered around the king and the duke, we were engaged in more refined aspects of our

---

54. Schröderheim, *Statssekreteraren Elis Schröderheims Anteckningar*, p.84.
55. Anderberg, *Frimuraren Gustaf III*, p.74–80. See also Önnerfors, "From Jacobite support," p.203–25.
56. Schröderheim, *Statssekreteraren Elis Schröderheims Anteckningar*, p.84. There is a full translation into Swedish, based on a contemporary transcription of the original that has disappeared, most likely in connection with the forced exile of Gustav IV Adolf, in Anderberg, *Frimuraren Gustaf III*, p.156–57.
57. Edelstein, "Introduction to the Super-Enlightenment," p.31.

workings. They comprised of religion, union with the underworld, with spirits, politics, morality, and alchemy."[58] A series of people claiming to possess magical powers quickly made their careers at court and within freemasonry, such as Lieutenant Henrik Gustaf Ulvenklou (1756–1819), posing as a necromantic fortune-teller mainly by conjuring the spirits of the deceased.[59] In 1784, Ulvenklou even anointed Duke Charles as king of Sweden, Norway, and Russia in a magic séance in the royal castle of Stockholm.[60] During a Continental journey with the above-mentioned Count Scheffer, Carl Göran Silfverhielm (1754–1808) explored magnetic somnambulism as a therapeutic method, which he imported to Sweden. He attracted large numbers of followers among court officials, and even Gustav III attended Mesmeric séances. Gustav Adolf Reuterholm (1756–1813) was another prominent figure who waded deeply into the occult sciences and carefully documented magic events among the Swedish elites.[61] In 1783, Reuterholm composed a diary titled "Collection of masonic events," which narrates in detail his observations in the realm of spirits. Kjell Lekeby, who has meticulously studied esoteric circles at court, describes how Duke Charles furnished a secret room at the castle in Stockholm, the "Sanctuary," where magical workings took place.[62] Altogether, the esoteric circle at court counted up to fifty people, including women. Remember that, in 1776, the wife of Duke Charles, Hedvig Elisabeth Charlotte, established a lodge of female freemasons at court. She also noted in her diary that Gustav III, on the occasion of his mother Louise Ulrika's death, allowed Hedvig to unbutton his clothes in case he fainted. He told her that he carried a masonic amulet. Since he knew that she was also a (female) freemason, then it would not break any masonic oath of secrecy, if she were to see the amulet.

58. Anderberg, *Frimuraren Gustaf III*, p.84, and Schröderheim quoted therein. Önnerfors, *Mystiskt brödraskap*, p.251. The transcribed source material, published by the Forschungszentrum Gotha of the Universität Erfurt, is accessible at https://tinyurl.com/y39z7ev6 (last accessed January 28, 2022).
59. Lekeby, *Gustaviansk mystik*, p.34–59. On pages 63–65, Lekeby lists about fifty names that can be associated with esoteric circles at court.
60. Andreas Önnerfors, "Norge 1814: den svenska politiken mellan vision och verklighet," in *Overgangstid: forargelse og forsoning høsten 1814*, ed. Ruth Hemstad and Bjørn Arne Steine (Oslo, 2016), p.82–98.
61. Lekeby, *Gustaviansk mystik*, p.9–15.
62. Lekeby, *Gustaviansk mystik*, p.24–28.

Was the assassination of Gustav III in 1792 a masonic plot?

Throughout the 1780s, Gustav III's popularity as an enlightened despot decreased considerably. When, in 1788, he unconstitutionally and unilaterally declared war against Russia, open opposition was expressed in the so-called Anjala mutiny.[63] Huge numbers of (mostly noble) officers refused orders and started peace negotiations with the Russian empress. Eventually, the uprising among the officers was crushed and, after an indecisive war, Gustav III hailed himself victorious. However, when at the diet in Gävle in 1789 he attempted to unite the estate of peasants with the bourgeoisie against the noblemen and passed legislation placing almost unrestricted power into his own hands, the opposition among the aristocracy radicalized considerably. It was in these circles that plans for his assassination were drawn up and put into effect.

On March 16, 1792 Gustav III was shot during a masked ball at the Stockholm Opera by captain Jacob Johan Anckarström.[64] The projectile hit slightly above the king's left hip and next to his spine; it was a mixture of a bullet and small spikes, which caused tremendous pain. Thirteen days later the king died of his infected wounds. The police investigation, which commenced immediately after the shooting at the opera, was carried out with meticulous effectiveness. It revealed a huge political plot among the Swedish aristocracy, who for multiple reasons were opposed to the king and his growing abuse of power. Although the criminal investigation and court procedures were conducted with remarkable transparency and their results publicized across Europe, the assassination fired the imagination of those who identified a greater evil in it. For instance, Anckarström (the assassin) alone was executed. Almost immediately, rumors started to circulate that the assassination and the supposed leniency for the culprits were somehow connected to freemasonry and Duke Charles, to whom power was transferred during the regency

---

63. Andreas Önnerfors, "Knights of freedom? The Swedish 'Order of Wallhall' as a secret network of officers and the Anjala-Mutiny in 1788," in *Geheime Netzwerke im Militär 1700–1945*, ed. Gundula Gahlen, Daniel M. Segesser, and Carmen Winkel (Paderborn, 2016), p.66–84.

64. For a comprehensive overview of the events, see Landen, *Gustaf III*, p.340–53, and Herman Lindqvist, *Historien om Sverige: Gustavs dagar* (Stockholm, 1997), p.460–540. See also Ernst Brunner, *Anckarström och kungamordet: historien i sin helhet* (Stockholm, 2010).

of Crown Prince Gustav Adolf.[65] Shortly after the French Revolution there appeared a brochure titled *Le Tombeau de Jacques Molai*, in which it was claimed that the masonic Knights Templar were in reality a secret organization of criminal cosmopolitans attempting to overthrow the traditional order of crown and church. Since, according to the book, one of the major hubs was in Stockholm, it was claimed that Duke Charles, as one of the leaders of the masonic Knights Templar, had ordered the assassination of his own brother.[66]

Although these fictitious accounts can be disregarded (but serve as a good example of the post-revolutionary craze for conspiracy theories), scholarship has for a long time assumed active involvement of freemasons in the plot to assassinate Gustav III. Anderberg has proven that these claims cannot be substantiated whatsoever. However, it is possible to trace some of the leading representatives of the opposition against Gustav III to another fraternal order, the Order of Walhall, active among regiments deployed to Finland. Nothing suggests that this fraternal order promoted a proto-Finnish agenda of separatism and national independence. On the contrary, the preserved rituals and writings of the order display a thoroughly loyal and royalist attitude with almost hagiographic tendencies. Enormous hopes were projected upon Gustav III as the savior and redeemer of Swedish political order. Why some of the most ardent critics of Gustav III emerged among its members is difficult to explain; however, it might be that, as unrealistic projections of hope increasingly remained unfulfilled, frustration intensified, turning into violent resistance against his rule and finally regicide.

The many facets of freemasonry at the court of Gustav III

As a legacy from the reign of Adolf Frederick, freemasonry at the court of Gustav III initially represented a continuation of sophisticated fraternal sociability which included a number of high-ranking officers and court officials in the immediate proximity of the royal family. Freemasons educated Gustav, his brothers, and his sister, and the initiation of the three princes appears as a natural continuation

65. Andreas Önnerfors, "Criminal cosmopolitans: conspiracy theories surrounding the assassination of Gustav III of Sweden in 1792," in *Höllische Ingenieure: Kriminalitätsgeschichte der Attentate und Verschwörungen zwischen Spätmittelalter und Moderne*, ed. André Krischer and Tilman Haug (Konstanz, 2021), p.135–50.
66. Önnerfors, "Criminal cosmopolitans."

of the masonic presence at court. However, the level of engagement dramatically increased when Duke Charles took over the leadership of Swedish freemasonry and effectively created one of the first European voluntary organizations on a national level. The fraternity turned into a royal affair, perfectly catering to Gustav III's efforts toward self-representation. These manifested in intricate court ceremonies, an elaborate taste for opera, theater, music, chivalric tournaments, and Gustav III's grandiose image of Sweden's historical past, sometimes focusing more on form than on content. Against the backdrop of these political visions, it is clear that freemasonry could serve a purpose in creating shared sociocultural capital among the traditional and new (and continuously socially expanding) service elites. Membership in the fraternity and its increasingly centralized national bureaucracy promised and created an immediate link to the Gustavian monarchy for thousands of members in the local lodges around the Swedish realm.

However, a substantial part of the fraternal visions at court were also projected upon a new role for Sweden in foreign affairs, ending the relative international isolation of Swedish freemasonry during previous decades. With most of Sweden's military might having vanished since the glorious days of Gustav II Adolf and Charles XII, freemasonry was identified as a means to promote Swedish interests through soft politics. Heavy involvement in the Continental masonic Knights Templar tradition aimed to boost Sweden's reputation among European elites, to enlarge the legitimacy and prestige of the Swedish monarchy, and potentially to work toward a strategic goal of foreign politics: the reestablishment of Swedish rule around the Baltic Sea.

On a deeper level, connected to and connecting immediate court circles, freemasonry and other esoteric practices represented a form of psychology avant la lettre, the quest for an alternative form of spirituality that, while not unreligious, challenged established beliefs and searched for answers far beyond the Lockean limits of human understanding. It is this undogmatic intellectual curiosity that characterized the Swedish royal court and its relationship with freemasonry during the reign of Gustav III and after, manifested by the Order of Charles XIII, which was established in 1811 as a semi-official order of merit awarded only to freemasons and still in existence. Freemasonry continued to be intertwined with the Swedish monarchy well into the twentieth century.

The eighteenth century is generally characterized as the "convivial century" in which clubs, associations, and fraternal orders organized large segments of the Enlightenment elites. Emerging from the associational culture of coffeehouses and pubs in urban London, freemasonry occupies a particular place in this development since it attracted the interest and protection of the European high nobility and ruling dynasties early on. But in contrast to other more intimate and internal phenomena of court culture, freemasonry during the Gustavian era created and provided a platform for public (yet "secret") encounters and interaction between the court and a wider circle of the service elites. The ritual practices of freemasonry, encouraging self-mastery, philanthropy, and perfection, could be productively paired with more political visions of the internal cultivation of Sweden and its place in Europe. In this sense, court culture in Sweden extended from being an exclusive practice burdened by ceremonial etiquette to an inclusive idea of participation, preparing the ground for the emergence of a more emancipative associational culture in the following century.

IV

Projects and reforms

Sovereignty and the politics of knowledge: Royal Society, Leibniz, Wolff, and Peter the Great's Academy of Sciences

KIRILL OSPOVAT

Shortly before his death in 1725, Russia's emperor Peter I "the Great" authorized the establishment of a royal Academy of Sciences. Based on the designs developed by Leibniz and officially inaugurated in 1726, the academy represented the culmination of Peter's decades-long effort to reshape his realm according to Western concepts of reformist political reason. After his return from a second trip to Central and Western Europe in 1717, Peter sponsored a series of publications outlining a comprehensive vision of the renewed political order. At its core were three major pieces of administrative legislation—the Naval Statute (1720), the General Regulation (1720), and the Ecclesiastical Regulation (1721). These were accompanied by explanatory works expounding visions of sovereignty and the ethics of service and obedience: *The Justice of the monarch's right*, composed by Peter's ideologist, the bishop of Novgorod Feofan Prokopovich (who also authored the Ecclesiastical Regulation); Prokopovich's 1722 *Exegesis of Christ's sermon on the beatitudes*, personally supervised by the monarch; and a translation of Pufendorf's *On the duty of man and citizen* (1682), which was also ordered by Peter but appeared in 1726 after his death. Central to this reformist vision was the idea that the flourishing of the imperial polity depended on knowledge, learning, and reason. Thus, the Ecclesiastical Regulation argues for the political necessity of the education of subjects as an element of the overall "discipline" introduced to Russia by Peter:

> It is manifest to the whole World, that whatever was the Degeneracy and Feebleness of the Russian Soldiery, whilst it was under no regular discipline, it is now improved exceedingly, and become beyond expectation, great and formidable from the time our Potent Monarch, his Imperial Majesty Peter the Ist, instructed it in the

Principles and Art of War by his excellent Rules and Regulations. The same Observation holds also good, with Regard to Architecture, Physick, Political Institution, and all other Arts and Sciences. [...] Many people talk foolishly that Learning is the Cause of Heresies [...] nevertheless he that foolishly ascribes this Mischief to Learning, will be constrain'd to confess that when a Physician administers Poison to the Patient, the Knowledge of Physick was the Cause of it [...] For Learning is good and fundamental, and as it were the Root, the Seed, and first Principle of all that is good and useful in Church and State; but care must be taken strictly, that it be really good and fundamental learning.[1]

This alignment of "fundamental learning" with imperial reform, invoked by Petrine ideologists and Western thinkers such as Leibniz alike, underlay the institutional design and political functions of the Academy of Sciences. According to Leibniz's plan, it was to function as one of several government ministries, or "colleges"—specifically, as a "college of learning" (*Gelehrt-Collegium*) responsible for producing, applying, disseminating, and controlling knowledge of the sciences and the arts.[2] Besides its core research body, the early academy included a previously established museum of curiosities, the Kunstkamera, as well as a university with a gymnasium, a division for applied arts such as engraving, and a press with a royal monopoly over secular publications in the empire. Along with royal panegyrics, translated works of history and conduct manuals, the academy published its own journal, *Primechaniia na vedomosti (Supplements to news)*, the first in Russia, largely filled with popular science.

Older if still indispensable positivist accounts of the Academy's early history have been recently complemented by revisionist studies by Marc Raeff, Michael Gordin, and Simon Werrett, who situate it within the social framework of the court and the general scheme of Petrine cultural reforms.[3] In particular, Raeff emphasizes the

1. Thomas Consett, "The present state and regulations of the Church of Russia (1729)," in *For God and Peter the Great: the works of Thomas Consett, 1723–1729*, ed. James Cracraft (Boulder, CO, 1962), p.61–63.

2. W. Guerrier, *Leibniz in seinen Beziehungen zu Russland und Peter dem Grossen* (St. Petersburg, 1873), p.365. This edition includes a publication of Leibniz's voluminous correspondence addressed or relating to the Russian court.

3. P. Pekarskii, *Istoriia Imperatorskoi Akademii nauk v Peterburge*, 2 vols. (Saint-Petersburg, 1870–1873); Iu. Kopelevich, *Osnovanie Peterburgskoi akademii nauk* (Leningrad, 1977); Marc Raeff, "Transfiguration and modernization: the paradoxes of social disciplining, paedagogical leadership, and the Enlightenment

crucial link between the Academy's function as the imperial press "entrusted with the selection and production of books" and "the Petrine didactic legacy" which saw the "printed word" as "one of the more significant tools" for the refashioning of elites: "The reorientation of behavior patterns initiated in the reign of Peter I, first for the monarch's servitors (others will follow), had to be rooted and consolidated by dint of great effort: it required disciplining in the literal sense, threatening punishment and promising rewards, and systematic inculcation from an early age."[4] In a similar vein, Gordin demonstrates that the introduction of "new science," the Academy's core task, was inseparable from Peter's "educational projects and new manners reforms designed to transform Russia into a 'Western' state."[5] As a Saxon representative in Petersburg remarked in 1743, the academy had been established "for the propagation of foreign manners."[6]

On the basis of these important conclusions, I will revisit the conceptual frameworks which provided the setting for the academy, underwrote its design, and informed its early activity. I will explore the alignment of scientific knowledge and royal authority which shaped the institutional setup of the academy and was common to courtly learned societies across Europe. While the Royal Society in London, the Académie des sciences in Paris, and the newer learned society in Berlin, the Kurfürstlich-Brandenburgische Societät der Wissenschaften (conceived of earlier by Leibniz along similar lines to the academy in St. Petersburg), all occupied different positions within the social and political structure of their respective monarchies, they all relied on a broadly Baconian agenda associating scientific progress with political rationality of statehood. In what follows, I will trace this interplay of knowledge and politics from Peter and Leibniz's early plans for the academy and their broad Western resonances with

in 18th-century Russia," in *Alteuropa, Ancien Régime, frühe Neuzeit: Probleme und Methoden der Forschung*, ed. Hans-Erich Bödeker and Ernst Hinrichs (Stuttgart, 1991), p.99–115; Michael Gordin, "The importation of being earnest: the early St. Petersburg Academy of Sciences," *Isis* 91:1 (2000), p.1–31; Simon Werrett, *Fireworks: pyrotechnic arts and sciences in European history* (Chicago, IL, 2010), p.103–32.

4. Raeff, "Transfiguration and modernization," p.101–102, 107.
5. Gordin, "The importation of being earnest," p.1.
6. "Zur Fortpflanzung fremder Sitten," "Pezold to Brühl [March 2, 1743]," *Sbornik imperatorskago russkago istoricheskago obshchestva* 6 (1871), p.479–83 (480). All translations are my own unless otherwise stated.

the immediate contexts of Peter's decision to establish the academy, and further through the Academy's own publications in its first two decades.

Reason of state: God, knowledge, and government

Located on the margins of Europe's mental map, Russia's academy was nonetheless intrinsically linked to Western intellectual and institutional patterns. Not only was its design developed by Leibniz, who personally met with Peter I on several occasions and extensively corresponded with his court, but the tsar himself had stayed in London and Paris, visited the Royal Society, might have met with Newton, and was elected a member of the French Académie des sciences. His own academy, originally manned and governed mostly by Germans, was tasked with the transfer and dissemination of Western knowledge in various forms and modes, through books and lectures.

The Academy's central role in Peter's visions of political renovation corresponded to the general functions of "new science" within the emergence of what Michel Foucault defines as "governmental reason." Along with the shift in philosophical and cosmological reasoning "associated with Kepler, Galileo, Descartes, and so on," Foucault discerns "at the end of the sixteenth and in the course of the seventeenth century" the appearance of a "different way of thinking power, the kingdom, the fact of ruling and governing; a different way of thinking the relations between the kingdom of Heaven and the kingdom on Earth. This heterodoxy was identified and called politics; politics would be to the art of government something like what *mathesis* was to the science of nature in the same period."[7] Designated by the contemporary notion of reason of state, "governmental reason delineated the state as both its principle and its objective, as both its foundation and its aim."[8] The state functions both as "a schema of intelligibility for a whole set of already established institutions" and as "an objective in this political reason in the sense that it is that which must result from the active interventions of this reason or rationality."[9] Giovanni Botero, one of the founders of the theory of reason of state,

7. Michel Foucault, *Security, territory, population: lectures at the Collège de France 1977–1978* (Basingstoke, 2007), p.285–86

8. Foucault, *Security, territory, population*, p.286

9. Foucault, *Security, territory, population*, p.286–87.

wrote in 1589: "State is a stable rule over a people and Reason of State is the knowledge of the means by which such dominion may be founded, preserved, and extended."[10]

Over the last decades scholarship has consistently uncovered the fundamental connection between early modern "new science" and the emerging visions and practices of sovereignty and statehood.[11] Unfolding during the century of religious wars, this relationship was indeed underwritten by the shifting politico-theological attitudes toward "the relations between the kingdom of Heaven and the kingdom on Earth." This issue lay at the core of Leibniz's projects for the academy in St. Petersburg. As Werner Schneiders has shown, this institutional utopia was designed to amalgamate sacerdotal monarchy, Christian orthodoxy, scientific rationality, and administrative statehood in a coherent vision of what Leibniz himself called "an empire of reason."[12] Accordingly, one of Leibniz's last and most important memoranda to Peter from 1716 starts with God: "God as a God of order rules over all things with his invisible hand, wisely and orderly. The gods of this world, or the likenesses of the divine power, and I mean sovereign monarchs, must establish the model of their government after that example."[13] God emerges here as the ultimate trope of sovereign order, which requires religious and secular learning as its medium. Much more than a figure of speech, the parallel between the divine and earthly kingdom was fundamental for the emerging idea of constant and all-pervasive governance, both distinct from and correlated with the initial sovereign act of the establishment,

10. Giovanni Botero, *The Reason of state*, translated by P. J. Waley and D. P. Waley (New Haven, CT, 1956), p.3.

11. Margaret C. Jacob, *The Newtonians and the English revolution 1689–1720* (New York, 1990); Margaret C. Jacob, *The Cultural meaning of the Scientific Revolution* (Philadelphia, PA, 1988); Steven Shapin and Simon Schaffer, *Leviathan and the air-pump: Hobbes, Boyle, and the experimental life* (Princeton, NJ, 2011); G. Matthew Adkins, *The Idea of the sciences in the French Enlightenment: a reinterpretation* (Newark, DE, 2013).

12. Werner Schneiders, "Sozietätspläne und Sozialutopie bei Leibniz," *Studia Leibnitiana* 7:1 (1975), p.58–80. On the history of Leibniz's dealings with Russia see Guerrier, *Leibniz in seinen Beziehungen*; Christine Roll, "Barbaren? *Tabula rasa*? Wie Leibniz sein neues Wissen über Russland auf den Begriff brachte: eine Studie über die Bedeutung der Vernetzung gelehrter Korrespondenzen für die Ermöglichung aufgeklärter Diskurse," in *Umwelt und Weltgestaltung: Leibniz' politisches Denken in seiner Zeit*, ed. Friedrich Beiderbeck, Irene Dingel, and Wenchao Li (Göttingen, 2015), p.307–58.

13. Guerrier, *Leibniz in seinen Beziehungen*, p.364.

or "creation," of authority.[14] In a speech which accompanied Peter's assumption of the imperial title in 1721, he was praised for having "transformed us from non-existence into being, bringing us into the society of political nations."[15] Leibniz's earlier memorandum complements this political fiat with a vision of a stable order of governance, a comprehensive system of state administration carried out by a system of colleges which included the Academy of Sciences.

In fact, political theology of governance was intrinsic to the European "new science" as a form of knowledge practiced by Leibniz and observed by Peter in Paris and London. In his classic reading of the Leibniz–Clarke disputes of 1714–1716, Steven Shapin demonstrates that "the 'world natural' and the 'world politick' were connected by a web of religious meaning" in a culture which constantly renegotiated the outlines of divine and earthly monarchy: "The cultures of theology, politics, and natural philosophy overlapped because they were connected in legitimations, justifications, and criticisms, especially in the use of conceptions of God and nature to comment upon political order."[16] Beyond constitutional issues of a limited monarchy central for Leibniz's English opponents but largely irrelevant for him or the Russians, at stake were the theological outlines of an order where, to quote Clarke, a monarch's "arbitrary Power," that is "a Power of doing all things absolutely without controul," could be seen as inseparable from "an Idea of infinite Reason, Wisdom, and Goodness. [...] For in God, Will and Reason are one and the same thing."[17] Leibniz's own formula for this unity, "the empire of reason," stems from his 1698 comments on the modes of rule in England under William of Orange, whom Peter I viewed as a model monarch, preceded by praise for Newtonian science as a contribution to the "public good."[18]

Leibniz's plans for a Russian Academy of Sciences built on a similar understanding of reason as both a politico-theological principle of an all-embracing administrative rule, and a capacity for

---

14. Foucault, *Security, territory, population*, p.238; Giorgio Agamben, *The Kingdom and the glory: for a theological genealogy of economy and government*, translated by Lorenzo Chiesa (Stanford, CA, 2011), p.92.
15. Lindsey Hughes, *Peter the Great: a biography* (New Haven, CT, 2004), p.146.
16. Steven Shapin, "Of gods and kings: natural philosophy and politics in the Leibniz–Clarke disputes," *Isis* 72:2 (1981), p.187–215 (202).
17. Shapin, "Of gods and kings," p.212–13.
18. Gottfried Wilhelm Leibniz, *Political writings*, ed. Patrick Riley, 2nd ed. (Cambridge, 1988), p.191–93.

learning and formal knowledge expected from the subjects of such a state. During his stay in London in 1698, Peter could personally observe the complex alliance between royal prerogative, a state-bound church, and the natural philosophy of the Royal Society.[19] In lengthy conversations with Gilbert Burnet, the clerical apologist of William's reign and a Leibniz correspondent, Peter revealed an interest in the "authority that the Christian Emperours assumed in matters of religion" and in the "great designs of Christianity in reforming men's hearts and lives."[20] Accordingly, in Peter's own Ecclesiastical Regulation of 1721, visions of reforming knowledge were set forth within a framework of an English-type religious settlement that made faith and the church into subordinate institutions of political sovereignty. Vehemently opposed as heretical by Russia's religious conservatives, the imported "new science" was "often regarded as an alternate faith. This in fact is what it eventually came to represent once the revolutionary implications of the Petrine reforms were realized."[21]

The politics of learning and subjecthood

Unlike its Western models, the Royal Society and the Paris Académie, the academy in St. Petersburg was designed to include a teaching division. Easily understood as a local necessity, this novelty derived nonetheless from a theoretical vision of a centralized state-run educational system that Peter came to share with Leibniz. This vision was rooted in English Baconianism as well as in German debates where civil philosophy and metaphysics mounted competing efforts to offer philosophical legitimations of the secular state and develop modes of selfhood appropriate for its subjects.[22] Though in this polemic Leibniz and Samuel Pufendorf stood on opposing sides, a royal reformer could see them as pursuing the same goals. Indeed, Leibniz's plans for the academy perfectly corresponded to visions of education outlined in Pufendorf's *On the duty of man and citizen*,

19. Jacob, *The Newtonians and the English revolution*. On Peter's contacts with English science and church politics see Valentin Boss, *Newton and Russia: the early influence, 1698–1796* (Cambridge, 1972); James Cracraft, *The Church reform of Peter the Great* (London, 1971).
20. Cracraft, *The Church reform of Peter the Great*, p.36–37.
21. Boss, *Newton and Russia*, p.6.
22. Ian Hunter, *Rival Enlightenments: civil and metaphysical philosophy in early modern Germany* (Cambridge, 2001).

translated into Russian on Peter's orders. Pufendorf lists regulating
public education among the immediate duties of sovereigns:

> [E]ach man governs his actions by his own opinion, but most men
> usually judge matters as they have been accustomed, and as they see
> them commonly judged. Very few can discern what is true and good
> by their own intelligence. It is therefore appropriate for the state
> that it universally resound with such doctrines as are consistent with
> the right purpose and usage of states, and that the citizens' minds
> be steeped in them from childhood. It is a function of sovereignty,
> therefore, to appoint public teachers of such doctrines [...] The
> internal peace of the state requires that the wills of the citizens
> be governed and directed as the safety of the state requires. It is
> therefore a duty of sovereigns not only to lay down laws appropriate
> to that purpose, but also to lend authority to public discipline so that
> citizens conform to the precepts of the laws not so much through fear
> of punishment as by habituation. It also contributes to this need to
> ensure that the pure and sincere Christian dogma flourishes in the
> state, and that the public schools teach dogmas consistent with the
> purpose of the state.[23]

Public education appears as a point of assembly of the political order,
instilling obedience with the joined forces of faith and reason, custom
and instruction. Political functions of schooling are designated by the
notion of "discipline," which reappears in Thomas Consett's 1729
translation of the Ecclesiastical Regulation quoted earlier. In both
cases, its Russian equivalent is *uchenie*, "learning."[24] Through public
education the apparatus of sovereignty with its laws and punishments
embeds itself in the interiority of its subjects. Both a theory and a tool
of this procedure, Pufendorf's civil philosophy entails a particular
anthropology of the political subject built around the dialectics
of action and control. In the first pages of his treatise, Pufendorf
dissects the moral structure of man from the standpoint of civic duty:

> By "duty" I mean human action in conformity with the commands
> of the law on the grounds of obligation. To explain this, one must
> first discuss the nature of human action and the nature of laws in

23. Samuel Pufendorf, *On the duty of man and citizen according to natural law*, ed.
    James Tully (Cambridge, 1991), p.141, 151–52.
24. On the concept of discipline in Petrine education see Igor Fedyukin, "Shaping
    up the stubborn: school building and 'discipline' in early modern Russia," *The
    Russian review* 77:2 (2018), p.200–18.

general. By "human action" [...] I mean motion initiated in the light of understanding and at the command of will [...] The faculty of comprehension and judgement is called understanding. It must be taken as certain that any adult of sound mind has natural light enough to enable him, with instruction and proper reflection, to achieve adequate comprehension of at least the general precepts which make for a good and peaceful life in this world; and to recognize their conformity with human nature.[25]

Thus, obedience to civil law is grounded within human nature in the faculty of comprehension and judgment—*razum*, in the Russian translation—which is called upon to control and direct the actions of will and must be trained through "instruction." This vision radically dissociated conformity from blind custom, political or religious, and based it on an intellectual empowerment of the subject. At times suspicious of this approach, Peter seems to have appropriated it in an undated note, possibly linked to the tsar's reading of Pufendorf:

Those who do not know for themselves should very much be instructed. Judgment stands above all virtues, for all virtue is void without reason [...] It is true one should preserve innocence, in the words of St. Paul: Wilt thou then not be afraid of the power? Do that which is good. But this innocence should be steeped in reason, not in foolishness, in the words of Christ: Be ye therefore wise as serpents, and harmless as doves.[26]

Here, Peter summarizes his program of secular, politically steered public education as a central element of governmental reason. A complex interplay of religious orthodoxy and civil philosophy unfolds around an imperative of civic duty, at once biblical and Pufend-orfian: "Wilt thou then not be afraid of the power? Do that which is good" (Romans 13.3).[27] In this maxim, scriptural authority, political coercion, and secular knowledge converge as modes of regulating the subjects' inner selves. *Reason* is both fostered through institutionalized education as a particular ethos of civic zeal and obedience, and represented as a God-given inner faculty of (self-)government.

25. Pufendorf, *On the duty of man*, p.17–18.

26. N. A. Voskresenskii, *Zakonodatel'nye akty Petra I*, vol.1: *Akty o vysšikh gosudarst-vennykh ustanovleniiakh* (Moscow, 1945), p.151–52.

27. On the political theology of duty from Cicero to Pufendorf, see Giorgio Agamben, *Opus Dei: an archaeology of duty*, translated by Adam Kotsko (Stanford, CA, 2013).

This model of political subjecthood shaped by the overlapping of religious and civic duty was common to Pufendorf's treatise, Leibniz's projects for the academy, and Petrine discourses of political obligation. Pufendorf derives the threefold duties of man toward God, oneself, and others from a double foundation of "religion and fear of Deity" and the principle of sociability, which together make man "an agreeable and useful member of human society."[28] Similarly, Leibniz, in his critical engagement with Pufendorf, "by providing a metaphysical grounding for political obligation in rational self-governance [...] provides a metaphysical rationale for the exercise of political coercion."[29] This operation underwrites his vision of Russia's subjects as educated by the future academy:

> The true aim of learning is human happiness, that is constant satisfaction, as far as it is possible among human beings, which implies that they do not spend their lives in leisure and abundance but contribute to the glory of God and the common good by unblemished virtue and righteous consciousness, according to their respective talents.[30]

> That which the youth have to learn consists in the following, namely: in the knowledge of God and creation. In order to comprehend both we must make use of the divine light revealed to us in the Holy Scripture, from which proceeds [...] Theology [...] This, however, consists not in useless squabble and disputations over empty ceremonies, because in this fashion God is not served, but in sincere love for God and your neighbor.[31]

"The true aim of learning" is understood to lie in an ethics of service to the "common good," identified with the "glory of God" but explicitly detached from religious ceremony. Alluding to experience of violent confessional strife common to Western Europe and Russia, Leibniz envisions secular learning as a civic religion. As a theory of proper political subjecthood, his projects for the academy resonated with the political theology of service and obedience developed in Russia by Feofan Prokopovich.

An erudite theologian with Protestant leanings, Prokopovich won Peter's favor in 1716 and was called upon to articulate the theological

28. Pufendorf, *On the duty of man*, p.37–38.
29. Hunter, *Rival Enlightenments*, p.144.
30. Guerrier, *Leibniz in seinen Beziehungen*, p.95.
31. Guerrier, *Leibniz in seinen Beziehungen*, p.367.

foundations of the emperor's reforms. In the treatises and sermons that followed, Prokopovich used the concept of salvation by faith which privileged sincere piety over ceremonial observance as a basis for an ethics of civic service.[32] In a sermon on the name day of the princely saint Alexander Nevsky, delivered in Petersburg in 1718, Prokopovich contrasted true piety to ceremony, and associated it with zealous service and civic obligation:

> Do we think that only a man is angry with a servant who acts contrary to his will, and God loves it when we act against his? This would be error not reason to think so. This makes clear how insane are those who think to please God by abandoning their business and doing something other than what they ought: A judge, for example, who is in church singing while the oppressed await his judgment.

In a language reminiscent of both Pufendorf and Leibniz, Prokopovich identifies one's duty toward God and one's neighbor with the functions and obligations of civil rank:

> Though we must do everything we can to promote the well-being of our neighbor, first and foremost we ought to perform that which befits our rank as an occupation assigned to each of us by God [...] Since all rank comes from God [...] the task most helpful to us and most pleasing to God is that which each of our ranks requires from me, you, and others. If you are a king, rule and provide prosperity for your people, and justice in administration [...] If you are a senator, devote yourself to delivering useful advice and verdicts free of corruption and blind to personality but right and just.[33]

In this context, Leibniz's imagined academy appears as an appropriate institution for the religious and secular education of state servants. In fact, since Francis Bacon's extremely influential *Advancement of learning* (1605), institutional propagation of knowledge was seen as a powerful tool of political discipline. Peter's note, which emphasizes the importance of reasoning and learning for instilling obedience, relied on a Baconian convention. Just as Peter after him, Bacon quoted Solomon and St. Paul to refute religious scruples against formal learning and establish its civic value. Specifically, he argued against the claim that learning makes minds indisposed "for policy

---

32. Ernest Zitser, *The Transfigured kingdom: sacred parody and charismatic authority at the court of Peter the Great* (Ithaca, NY, 2004), p.146–54.

33. Feofan Prokopovich, *Sochineniia*, ed. I. P. Eremin (Moscow, 1961), p.95–98.

and government" and inclined "to leisure and privateness." On the contrary, he insisted, "it may be truly affirmed that no kind of men love business for itself but those that are learned." Amalgamating a theory of knowledge with a theory of government, Bacon understood learning as a source of civic zeal:

> For to say that a blind custom of obedience should be a surer obligation than duty taught and understood, it is to affirm that a blind man may tread surer by a guide than a seeing man can by a light. And it is without all controversy that learning doth make the minds of men gentle, generous, manageable, and pliant to government; whereas ignorance makes them churlish, thwart, and mutinous.[34]

Bacon's vision of the role of knowledge in the political order was integrated into the institutional ideology of the Royal Society, one of Europe's most successful and influential academies. Its ethos of scientific inquiry famously emerged from intensive negotiations regarding the proper modes of political submission in Restoration England.[35] Thomas Sprat's *History of the Royal Society* (1667) declared that a premise of the Society's scientific work was "that in our veneration of God's almighty power we ought to imitate the manner of our respect to Earthly Kings." Accordingly, scientific inquiry "teaches men humility [...] and so removes all overweening haughtiness of mind, and swelling imaginations, that they are better able to manage Kingdoms than those who possess them."[36] Similar assumptions (directly linked to English debates) paved the way for the Paris Académie.[37]

In Russia, a related view of the moral and political workings of natural knowledge was propagated in a publication which Michael Gordin has identified as a "cultural document demonstrating to the small Russian reading public the natural philosophical form of life": Christiaan Huygens's *Cosmotheoros* (1698), published in 1717 and again in 1724 in the royally sponsored Russian translation.[38] This exposition

34. Francis Bacon, *The Major works*, ed. Brian Vickers (Oxford, 2008), p.130; Julian Martin, *Francis Bacon, the state and the reform of natural philosophy* (Cambridge, 2007).
35. Shapin and Schaffer, *Leviathan and the air-pump*.
36. Thomas Sprat, *History of the Royal Society* (St. Louis, MO, 1958), p.132–33, 429–30.
37. Adkins, *The Idea of the sciences*, p.9–26.
38. Gordin, "The importation of being earnest," p.22–26.

of Copernican astronomy was preceded by a short preface by the book's translator, Peter's Newtonian courtier James Bruce:

> If we consider […] that this visible sky and the heavens of all heaven (according to the words of the wisest King Solomon) could not contain the almighty creator of all those immeasurably great things, it will necessarily come that a holy sense of wonder and a terrible horror will usefully augment our knowledge of God and additionally animate us to his honor, glory, and praise. Similarly, we will be forced to inquire into these glorious miracles and their movements which since the beginning of creation invariably follow the laws imposed upon them, as well as to follow obediently God's commands and accomplish good deeds.[39]

Here, physico-theological piety is linked to the royal figure of King Solomon, seen by both Bacon and Petrine encomiasts as a biblical prototype for the alliance between government and science. Natural knowledge is associated with admiration for the divine creation, a deeply felt personal emotion that shapes one's subjectivity and produces an imperative of "good deeds," that is civic action, under the double authority of God and monarch. The idea that the natural sciences provided an incentive for proper political behavior within the sovereign order underlay Petrine visions of learning elaborated in the Ecclesiastical Regulation and in Leibniz's designs for the academy, and permeated the academy's early publications.

Early academy and the ideology of science

During the first decades of the Academy's existence, its publications, alongside its teaching division and public assemblies, were a major means of attracting public interest and the support of the court. Among a variety of genres linked to the court's social existence and political agenda, the academy published works of popular science, such as Fontenelle's *Conversations on the plurality of worlds*, translated by one of its alumni, Prince Antiokh Kantemir.

Besides book editions, between 1728 and 1742 the academy issued Russia's only scholarly periodical. It simultaneously appeared in German and Russian as *Primechaniia na vedomosti* and *Anmerckungen über die Zeitungen*, a supplement to the official newspaper *Sankt-Peterburgskie*

---

39. Christiaan Huygens, *Kniga mirozreniia, ili Mnenie O nebesnozemnykh globusakh, i ikh ukrasheniiakh* (Moscow, n.n., 1724), p.8.

Vedomosti.[40] An editorial preface to the 1731 volume situated scientific knowledge within the divine and royal sovereign order:

> Almighty God who has in his supreme power all earthly occurrences and the inventions of the arts and sciences! Direct the former so that we would remain in peace and tranquility and allow us to learn from the latter as much as is useful for the protection and delight of our short and unfortunate existence! [...] This is the felicity that we in Russia have been enjoying for some time.[41]

Very cautiously, the preface refers to the political crisis of 1730 when a group of magnates attempted to impose limitations of the absolutist rule of the new empress Anna. The preface celebrates the restoration of absolute royal authority as the proper framework for scientific inquiry. Contrasting science and sedition, it amalgamates the "natural philosophical form of life" with a royalist admiration for the person of the monarch and a conformist compliance with one's civic obligations:

> [S]upreme rulers of the earth have such an effect on time that it becomes benevolent and fortunate for their subjects. We ourselves can see and recognize well enough to whom our gratitude is due, so that a ploughman on his field, an artisan in his workshop, a merchant in his office, a scholar by his books, a judge in his chamber can pursue their occupations in calm and joy.[42]

In this context, the preface explained the peculiar conjunction of political and scientific knowledge in the journal:

> In our notes we have so far demonstrated efforts of a double kind. The first is that we inform you about political acts and noteworthy occurrences, as if proceeding by these steps through the whole world. The second is that we reveal and sufficiently explain to you things most useful to humankind in the arts and sciences. The former may lead you to reason, and the latter to the sciences. The former serves for your information, and the latter for your education, but both contribute to your pleasure.[43]

40. Alla Keuten, "K istorii russkikh i nemetskikh Primechanii k Vedomostiam (1728–1742)," *Russian literature* 75:1–4 (2014), p.265–303.
41. *Primechaniia v Vedomostiakh* 1 (1731), p.3.
42. *Primechaniia v Vedomostiakh* 1 (1731), p.3–4.
43. *Primechaniia v Vedomostiakh* 1 (1731), p.2.

This editorial strategy comes with a specific vision of a reading subject equally interested in politics and sciences, in combining political "reason" with scientific learning. In this vision of subjecthood a politico-theological interdependence between outward duty and inner zeal is mirrored and duplicated by a division of time between business and leisure. The 1731 volume of *Primechaniia* inaugurated by this preface was explicitly devoted to the issue of time, and included a translation of Joseph Addisson's essay from *The Spectator* 93 (1711) on its uses.[44] Here, readers were told that, instead of playing cards during their "retired hours," they should maintain an "Intercourse and Communication [...] with the great Author of his Being," cultivate their friends, engage in arts such as "Musick, Painting, or Architecture," but first of all in "the reading of useful and entertaining Authors" and, more generally, in "the Pursuit of Knowledge."[45] All of these prescriptions are derived from a doctrine of "virtue," more precisely identified as "social virtue" which provides a common ethical foundation for business and leisure.

Addison's vision of knowledge and virtue fits well with the ideological tasks of the academy in St. Petersburg and its Western counterparts. This vision was itself rooted in the "Newtonian" consensus which informed the activities of the Royal Society.[46] Feofan Prokopovich summarized his doctrine of civic duty in the image of man as God's servant, adopted from the Gospel, while Addison's essay translated into Russian included an oblique reference to the parable of the talents, where this image unfolds, in its portrayal of virtuous life in business and leisure: "When a Man has but a little Stock to improve, and has opportunities of turning it all to good Account, what shall we think of him if he suffers nineteen Parts of it to lie dead, and perhaps employs even the twentieth to his Ruin or Disadvantage?"[47] The importation of popular natural-philosophical knowledge and the concept of leisure to Russia was made possible by their intrinsic links to the politico-theological ethics of duty and discipline shared across early modern Europe.

44. V. M. Zhivov, "Vremia i ego sobstvennik v Rossii rannego Novogo vremeni (XVII–XVIII veka)," in *Ocherki istoricheskoi semantiki russkogo iazyka rannego novogo vremeni*, ed. V. M. Zhivov *et al.* (Moscow, 2009), p.64–66.
45. John Addison, "Proper methods of employing time," *Addison's spectator* 93 (June 16, 1711), ed. George Washington Greene (New York, 1858), p.257–61.
46. Jacob, *The Newtonians and the English revolution*, p.19.
47. Addison, "Proper methods of employing time," p.260.

In fact, the association of scientific knowledge with obedient fulfillment of the duties of one's rank, which might appear as an ad hoc political conceit in the editorial preface of 1731, was a common theme of popular natural philosophy translated and propagated in Russia by the academy. Thus, in Fontenelle's *Conversations* the cosmic equilibrium of the solar system was explicitly compared to the social hierarchy which must be preserved from disturbances: "[T]hese different gravities will very well regulate their [the planets'] several ranks; I wish there was something similar amongst us to regulate ours, and which would fix people in those spheres of life that are natural to them!"[48] The Marquise who says these words boasts afterwards that she herself is "easily satisfied" with her position, giving a lesson of morality proper to any subject and reader of popular science.

A similar lesson is delivered at length in the essay *On philosophy* which extended over several issues of *Primechaniia* in 1738. Here, a survey of different areas of scientific study was framed by a general exposition of the usefulness of knowledge. Once again paraphrasing the parable of the talents and comparing the subject to a servant in God's garden, the essay sets out a Baconian vision of reason and philosophy as pivotal elements of diligent service: "[A] philosopher is always a good citizen or a good member of the society where he lives. For he only strives to fulfill with utmost diligence the duties imposed on us by God and nature."[49] This general formula is elucidated by concrete examples which link philosophical duty to the obligations of specific social ranks: "If a nobleman wishes to act reasonably according to his God-given rank, he must know not only the number and wealth of his subjects [serfs] but also their mores, so that the industrious would not be overloaded with work and the idle encouraged in their sloth. The same is required in all other ranks."[50] Philosophical knowledge is explicitly identified with the requirements of one's social function, and is limited by its boundaries:

> Who will thus survey and examine all the ranks of the world, will see the truth of the words that anyone who has any business in the world must have a perfect knowledge of the matters of his rank if he wishes to perform his business reasonably. [...] someone who wishes to fulfill *in his fashion* and with diligence both these main duties imposed on us

48. Bernard de Fontenelle, *Conversations on the plurality of worlds* (London, n.n., 1760), p.202; Jacob, *The Cultural meaning of the Scientific Revolution*, p.64–65.
49. *Primechaniia na Vedomosti* 53 (1738), p.199.
50. *Primechaniia na Vedomosti* 53 (1738), p.197.

by God must be a philosopher. I say purposely *in his fashion* because a
man ought not to know more than relates to his rank.[51]

In an empire where higher education was only gradually imposed
on the political class as a service duty, this was the officially sponsored
blueprint for any knowledge and learning, as well as for selfhood
and leisure. Indeed, for several decades the Academy's relatively
scarce publications, and *Primechaniia* in particular, remained the only
printed sources of secular knowledge available to the wider Russian
public. At the same time, this politicized approach to knowledge
which linked it to politico-theological visions of duty and governance
was shared by royal administrations and academies across Europe,
making the Petersburg academy a vivid example of pan-European
interplay between knowledge and power.

Science at court, or what is Enlightenment?

Inaugurated after Peter's death by his widow Catherine I, the Petersburg
Academy of Sciences emerged as an "auxiliary institution" to the
royal court.[52] Its very survival, as Simon Werrett has demonstrated,
depended on court patronage that largely determined the direction of
its efforts. On the wishes of Peter and Catherine's powerful favorite
Alexander Menshikov and the influential Jena-educated courtier and
diplomat Heinrich Johann Friedrich (Andrei Ivanovich) Ostermann,
the academy played a central part in the education of the heir to the
throne, who in 1727 became Peter II. In Simon Werrett's words, "On
Ostermann's prompting, academicians began a new project to print a
range of textbooks dedicated to Peter II, but produced for circulation
at court. This was the Academy's first major publishing project, and
likely the spur for a government edict granting academicians their
first imprimatur to publish books through their own press."[53] Its next
German patron, the engineer and general Burkhard Christoph von
Münnich, found the academy useful for devising fireworks for court
festivities.[54] Of course, the Academy's links to the court were not

51. *Primechaniia na Vedomosti* 53 (1738), p.197 (original emphasis).
52. G. A. Gukovskii, *Ocherki po istorii russkoi literatury XVIII veka* (Moscow, 1936),
    p.13.
53. Simon Werrett, "An odd sort of exhibition: the St. Petersburg Academy of
    Sciences in enlightened Russia," doctoral dissertation, University of Cambridge,
    2000, p.76.
54. Werrett, *Fireworks*, p.111–36.

limited to pyrotechnical expertise: It was responsible for publishing translated manuals of courtly conduct—such as *La Véritable Politique des personnes de qualité* (1737) ascribed to Fénelon, and Gracian's *Homme de cour* (1741)—alongside libretti for opera performances at court, panegyrics on dynastic occasions, and Empress Elizabeth's coronation album (1745). As a press and employer for secular authors, the academy was a central site for the emergence of court literature by the mid-1740s.[55]

The academy's intricate ties with ceremonies and political visions of an unlimited monarchy, and the emphasis of its publications on the ethics of conformity and compliance, place it outside of the all-too-common vision of Enlightenment as a movement of emancipated reason toward British liberalism and French revolution. This contradiction was succinctly articulated by a contemporary who was himself an important Enlightenment figure. Francesco Algarotti, the cosmopolitan man of letters and best-selling popularizer of Newtonian science, visited Petersburg in 1739 and remarked on the academy:

> Everything concerning the arts and sciences is assembled here at the academy; one could say that the Russians have so far made little or no progress in this field. [...] But how could letters strive in such a militarized country [...]? If a Russian has some ability he is forced to serve in a government office [*Collegio*] or to become a secretary or a miserable subordinate, thus losing his freedom [...]
>
> From tyrants and [from] priests the muses fly,
> Daughters of reason, and of liberty.[56]

This concise assessment of the academy, confirmed by a later first-hand account by August Ludwig Schlözer,[57] presupposes a fundamental link between the state of knowledge and the political regime. Quoting

55. Gukovskii, *Ocherki*; L. V. Pumpianskii, "Lomonosov i nemetskaia shkola razuma," *XVIII vek* 14 (1983), p.3–44; Kirill Ospovat, "Mikhail Lomonosov writes to his patron: professional ethos, literary rhetoric and social ambition," *Jahrbücher für Geschichte Osteuropas* 59:2 (2011), p.240–66.

56. Francesco Algarotti, *Giornale del viaggio da Londra a Petersbourg (1739)*, ed. Anna Maria dè Salva (Rome, 2015), p.71. Russian translation: Francesco Algarotti, *"Okno v Evropu": Dnevnik puteshestviia iz Londona v Peterburg v 1739 godu*, ed. and translated by M. G. Talalaj (Moscow, 2016), p.75.

57. August Ludwig Schlözer, *August Ludwig Schlözers öffentliches und Privatleben, von ihm selbst berschrieben: erstes Fragment* (Göttingen, 1802); August Ludwig Schlözer, *Obshchestvennaia i chastnaia zhizn' Avgusta Ludviga Shletsera, im samim opisannaia* (St. Petersburg, 1875).

(in original English) verses by George Lyttelton, by then a Whig opponent of Walpole and a member of the Royal Society, Algarotti measures the Petersburg academy against the conceptual background of English liberalism, which associated the progress of the sciences and "reason" with political liberty and the disempowerment of the church.

A blueprint for an understanding of Enlightenment still widely shared today, this vision of knowledge was nonetheless distinctly different from the one encountered by Peter I in London in 1698, propagated by Leibniz, and enacted in Russia's academy. Indeed, students of eighteenth-century Germany, from Werner Schneiders to Steffen Martus, have uncovered the alignment of the Enlightenment's reforming reason with visions of absolute sovereignty and coercive governance.[58] Similar to Foucault, they have discerned in eighteenth-century thought a philosophy of governmentality. A central figure for this strain of Enlightenment is Christian Wolff, a follower of Leibniz who became Germany's most influential philosopher just as he succeeded his deceased teacher and patron in Peter I's graces. At the moment of his famous exile from Prussia in 1723 Wolff was courted by the Russian government to move to Petersburg and supervise the establishment of the future academy.[59] While he eventually declined, in the course of his negotiations with the Russian court Wolff began to articulate a relationship between knowledge and power which appealed to Peter, came to inform the ideology of the Petersburg academy (which Wolff helped staff), and attracted "politic" audiences in Germany.

This relationship was strategically voiced in the specific medium of courtly literature: Wolff's dedication to Peter of his 1723 German treatise on physics, *Vernünfftige Gedancken von den Würckungen der Natur.* Adopting the language of courtly praise, Wolff used the dedication to

58. Schneiders, "Sozietätspläne und Sozialutopie bei Leibniz"; Werner Schneiders, "Die Philosophie des aufgeklärten Absolutismus: zum Verhältnis von Philosophie und Politik, nicht nur im 18. Jahrhundert," in *Aufklärung als Politisierung–Politisierung der Aufklärung*, ed. Hans Erich Bödeker and Ulrich Herrmann (Hamburg, 1987), p.32–52; Steffen Martus, *Aufklärung: das deutsche 18. Jahrhundert–ein Epochenbild* (Berlin, 2015); Marc Raeff, *The Well-ordered police state: social and institutional change through law in the Germanies and Russia, 1600–1800* (New Haven, CT, 1983).

59. Christian Wolff, *Briefe von Christian Wolff aus den Jahren 1719–1753: ein Beitrag zur Geschichte der Kaiserlichen Academie der Wissenschaften zu St. Petersburg* (St. Petersburg, 1860).

publicize Peter's ambitious goals to educated audiences and assert his own role in the emperor's reforms. Wolff addressed Peter with the title of emperor, which the tsar had only claimed for the Russian monarchy two years earlier, and praised the "higher dignity" achieved by Peter for his realm. As a part of this *renovatio imperii*, Wolff announced Peter's plans for establishing scientific institutions in Russia and his choice of Wolff himself as the trusted advisor in the matter. Much more than "mere" encomiastic tropes, Wolff's compliments to Russia's first emperor outline an alliance between "wisdom" and "power" which inverts Algarotti's liberal vision:

> Your Imperial Majesty has extended the Russian Empire through wisdom and power, raised it to a higher dignity and brought it to astonishing prosperity [...] The whole world narrates these feats, and it has recently resounded everywhere how much your Imperial Majesty is feared by nations for your might, just as you are loved and venerated for your wisdom and justice.[60]

> [A] wise man among the Greeks said: A country will only prosper when either kings learn philosophy or philosophers rule. Nowadays we can confirm that not only by examples taken from the old chronicles of the Chinese whose ancient emperors and kings were at the same time their greatest philosophers; that is to say, had the most knowledge. Now we can go to Russia and see a monarch who [...] can judge with his own most enlightened reason [*nach seinem hocher-leuchteten Verstande*] which arts and sciences are useful for a country.[61]

For Wolff, royal encouragement of knowledge does not contradict the new empire's military ambition, reinforced by a comparison of Peter to Alexander the Great. Peter's "wisdom" is an attribute of his unlimited and violent sovereignty, and the respect it evokes among conquered nations only magnifies the awe inspired by his conquering arms. Comparing Peter to Chinese emperors, Wolff references his recent speech on Chinese political wisdom which occasioned his banishment from Prussia at the instigation of the Pietist theologians.[62] Thus, Wolff's vision of Russia's monarch and his reforms is manifestly grounded in his influential political philosophy.

60. Wolff, *Briefe von Christian Wolff*, p.9.
60. Wolff, *Briefe von Christian Wolff*, p.9.
61. Wolff, *Briefe von Christian Wolff*, p.11.
62. *Die Causa Christian Wolff: ein epochemachender Skandal und seine Hintergründe*, ed. Andreas Pečar, Holger Zaunstöck, and Thomas Müller-Bahlke (Wiesbaden, 2015).

As if to confirm this link, in 1730 Wolff drew on the phrasing of his dedication to Peter in another essay, translated into English in 1750 as *The Real happiness of a people under a philosophical king demonstrated.*[63] Here, he tackled the question which Foucault later identified as the central question of Enlightenment: "the relationship of power, truth, and the subject."[64] Departing from Kant's famous 1784 essay, Foucault derived his vision of Enlightenment (*Aufklärung*) from the centuries-long "great process of the governmentalization of society," which gives birth to its counterpart—critique as the "art of not being governed like that."[65] Writing before Kant but within the same constellation of "enlightened absolutism," Wolff demonstrated this intrinsic connection between Enlightenment reasoning and what Foucault would call "the arts of governing." While he shares with Algarotti and Kant a "critical" mistrust of religious authority, Wolff proclaims "the indispensable Necessity of Philosophy no less in governing than in forming a Commonwealth."[66] "The Things therefore, which depend on the Form of a Common-Wealth [...] are all of them to be laid to the Score of Philosophy."[67] This logic culminates in the proposed personal union between sovereignty and philosophy, whose example Wolff had already found in Peter I.[68]

If Foucault finds in Kant's definition of the Enlightenment a vision of critique as an "art of voluntary inservitude, of reflective indocility,"[69] Wolff proposes an opposite political role to the enlightened subject. He reflects on "how the Mind be disposed towards Philosophy, so as always to act by Truth," because "If any one be well stored with a sufficiency of Philosophy, such a one clearly sees, what makes either for or against the publick Welfare."[70] In Baconian fashion, knowledge provided by the sciences is identified with the principles of top-down

63. Christian Wolff, *The Real happiness of a people under a philosophical king demonstrated* (London, n.n., 1750).
64. Michel Foucault, "What is critique?," in *What is Enlightenment? Eighteenth-century answers and twentieth-century questions*, ed. James Schmidt (Berkeley, CA, 1996), p.382–98 (397).
65. Foucault, "What is critique?," p.384.
66. Wolff, *The Real happiness*, p.31.
67. Wolff, *The Real happiness*, p.84.
68. On Wolff's ideas and their uses at the Prussian court, see Johannes Bronisch, *Der Mäzen der Aufklärung: Ernst Christoph von Manteuffel und das Netzwerk des Wolffianismus* (Berlin, 2010), p.106–11.
69. Foucault, "What is critique?," p.386.
70. Wolff, *The Real happiness*, p.71.

governance of the whole body politic and disciplined submission of the individual.[71] Not surprisingly, Wolff anticipates the arguments of the Petersburg *Primechaniia* on the limits of personal knowledge: "It therefore suffices an Individual to be wise in these things, which are within his proper Province to manage."[72] It would, however, be an oversimplification to see the vision of knowledge shared by Peter "the Great," Wolff, and the Petersburg Academy of Sciences of the 1730s as a mere inversion or negation of Kant's *Aufklärung*. Indeed, encouraging freedom for "the public use of reason," Kant immediately limits it to publications of "scholars," *Gelehrte*, addressing the "reading world." The scholars themselves, as well as their readers, "must conduct themselves passively in order that the government may direct them, through an artificial unanimity, to public ends." At the core of Kant's essay we famously find a compliment to the model ruler who says: "*Argue*, as much as you want and about whatever you want, but *obey!*"[73]

71. Christoph Böhr, "Erkenntnisgewißheit und politische Philosophie: zu Christian Wolffs Postulat des philosophus regnans," *Zeitschrift für philosophische Forschung* 36:4 (1982), p.579–98.
72. Wolff, *The Real happiness*, p.8.
73. Immanuel Kant, "An answer to the question: what is Enlightenment?," in *What is Enlightenment?*, ed. J. Schmidt, p.58–64 (59), original emphasis.

Continuity and change in courtly and Enlightenment discourse on education in Spain: Gaspar Melchor de Jovellanos and the moral regeneration of the nobility

GIJS VERSTEEGEN

Gaspar Melchor de Jovellanos (1744–1811), considered to be one of the leading thinkers of the Spanish Enlightenment,[1] has been the subject of widely divergent historiographical interpretations, as have his ideas on education. Historians who have described his pedagogical reflections as part of the educational tradition of the Old Regime have emphasized that Jovellanos recommended educating each of the social estates in a way appropriate to their duties in society. Conversely, others have attached particular importance to "genuine" Enlightenment aspects of his thinking: a free public education that was patriotic and universal as the road to moral happiness, virtue, and prosperity.[2]

The research for this chapter was possible thanks to the support of the projects "Del Patrimonio Dinástico al Patrimonio Nacional: los Sitios Reales" (HAR2015-68946-C3-3-P), funded by the Ministerio de Economía y Competitividad-FEDER, and "La Herencia de los Reales sitios. Madrid, de Corte a capital (Historia, Patrimonio y Turismo)" (H2015/HUM3415) of the Call for R&D Programmes in Social Sciences and Humanities 2015 of the Community of Madrid, funded by the European Social Fund.
1. See below for the distinctive traits of the Spanish Enlightenment.
2. Regarding Jovellanos's educational ideas as an instrument for social change, see José Luis Abellán, *Historia crítica del pensamiento español*, vol.3: *Del Barroco a la Ilustración (Siglos XVII y XVIII)* (Madrid, 1988), p.537. On his educational ideas as a step toward a more egalitarian society, but emphasizing their Christian humanistic character, see José Luis Fernández Fernández, *Jovellanos: Antropología y teoría de la Sociedad* (Madrid, 1991). p.391. Vicent Llombart regards Jovellanos as a precursor of the modern welfare state: *Jovellanos y el otoño de las luces: educación, economia, politica y felicidad* (Gijón, 2012), p.254. Fernando Baras Escolá places Jovellanos's educational ideas in the context of

The interpretation of "moral happiness" and "virtue" in Jovellanos's writings is one of the main reasons why these perspectives are so contradictory. His moral education has been understood as contributing to a conservative, conformist attitude that accepted the social status quo,[3] but also as contributing to the enlightened ideal of achieving a morally regenerated society through free and utilitarian public education. The aim of such an education would have been a more egalitarian society.[4] This question is related to the role, in the opinion of Jovellanos, that the nobility was supposed to fulfill in the Spanish monarchy. While some historians have portrayed him as defending the privileges of the nobles, who had to act as a model for the rest of society,[5] others have highlighted his criticism of the moral decadence of the aristocracy and the superficiality of its manners.[6]

One dimension that has received little or no attention is the way his ideas on moral education formed part of a critical reflection on the long tradition of courtly aristocratic ethics, which is also discussed in Clarissa Campbell Orr's chapter in this volume. That tradition interpreted virtue and excellence as being expressed in refined and elegant manners, with an appropriate display of luxury in accordance with the decorum of the nobility.[7] In early modern anti-court discourses, this aristocratic behavior and display of luxury was frequently criticized as outward appearance, and contrasted with Christian virtues based on *contemptus mundi*.[8] Jovellanos echoed this critical tradition, but did not place the display of luxury and decadent

the Old Regime: *El reformismo político de Jovellanos: nobleza y poder en la España del Siglo XVIII* (Zaragoza, 1993), p.268. Antonio Viñao Frago highlights the complexity of and contradictions in Jovellanos's different educational plans written in different moments and with different objectives: *Política y educación en los orígenes de la España contemporánea: examen especial de sus relaciones en la enseñanza secundaria* (Madrid, 1982), p.156. Regarding his ambiguity, see also Francisco Sánchez Blanco, *La ilustración goyesca: la cultura en España durante el reinado de Carlos IV, 1788–1808* (Madrid, 2007), p.239.

3.   Baras Escolá, *El reformismo político*, p.177; Sánchez Blanco, *La ilustración goyesca*, p.253.

4.   Llombart, *Jovellanos*, p.252–54.

5.   Baras Escolá, *El reformismo político*, p.191–92.

6.   Llombart, *Jovellanos*, p.252; Antonio Elorza, *La ideología liberal en la ilustración española* (Madrid, 1970), p.109.

7.   Amedeo Quondam, *Forma del vivere: l'etica del gentiluomo e i moralisti italiani* (Bologna, 2010).

8.   For example, in the work of Antonio de Guevara, see Amedeo Quondam, *El discurso cortesano*, ed. Eduardo Torres Corominas (Madrid, 2013), p.72.

manners in opposition to a life of renunciation. According to him, the aristocracy had to fulfill its duties in society by contributing to moral regeneration through exemplary behavior, and by contributing to public prosperity through increasing economic productivity. In this way, Jovellanos introduced Enlightenment ideas into the critical discourse on the moral decadence of the aristocracy.

Jovellanos in historiography

The fact that Jovellanos remains a somewhat enigmatic figure for historians is partly the consequence of his resilience as an enlightened nobleman and courtier. He was the son of the well-situated Asturian nobleman Francisco Gregorio de Jovellanos, and was appointed as magistrate in Seville in 1767, where he moved in the Enlightenment circles of Pablo de Olavide. Then, in 1778, he became a magistrate in Madrid and, from 1780, a member of the Council of Military Orders. Jovellanos was banished from court in 1790, after Charles IV took the throne, and he was sent to Gijón, where he founded the Royal Asturian Nautical and Mineralogical Institute in 1794. He returned to Madrid and served as minister of Grace and Justice for nine months between 1797 and 1798. He was accused by a powerful clerical faction of heresy and of insulting the Church and nobility, leading to his arrest in 1801 and imprisonment in Mallorca until 1808. After the outbreak of the Peninsular War, Jovellanos became a member of the Junta Central, the alternative patriotic government to the Napoleonic administration, which prepared the ground for convening the Cortes de Cádiz, the legislative body that approved a new constitution for Spain. Finally, in 1812, two months after his death, he was declared a national hero by the Cortes de Cádiz for his Enlightenment educational efforts and firm resistance to "the cruel hand of despotism."[9]

During this long period of political activity, Jovellanos wrote many reports, recommendations, essays, and literary texts on a wide range of topics, from theater and education, to tariffs, to agricultural and consti-tutional politics. Jovellanos, therefore, developed and expressed his ideas in diverse political contexts, starting with the enlightened court of Charles III and ending with the revolutionary period that gave way to the liberal constitutional project for Spain. This explains why it is so

9.   For biographical notes on Jovellanos, see Javier Varela, *Jovellanos* (Madrid, 1988); Baras Escolá, *El reformismo político*, p.21–47; Llombart, *Jovellanos*, p.50.

difficult to give a comprehensive and coherent historical interpretation of his writings: Was he an Enlightenment thinker whose aspirations did not go beyond limited social, economic, and political reform of the Old Regime, or did his ideas already point toward a society based on equal opportunity, to be accomplished through free public education?

Nineteenth-century historiographical discussions of national identity have also been a source of polemics surrounding the nature of Jovellanos's political and educational ideas. In the second half of the nineteenth century, the degree to which Spain's national identity was linked to Catholic orthodoxy became a subject of debate between conservative Catholic thinkers and liberals. This also affected the interpretations of the nation's most prominent intellectuals, such as Jovellanos, whose work was valued by some for its Catholic orthodoxy, while for others his religious ideas were of secondary importance.

The debate on Spain's national identity developed primarily after the regime of Ferdinand VII. This king returned to Spain in 1814 after the Peninsular War, disappointed liberal expectations by abolishing the Constitution that the Cortes de Cadiz had promulgated and imposing an absolutist regime. From the perspective of the counter-revolutionary supporters of his regime, the Peninsular War had been a crusade against the freemason conspiracy of rationalist sects who wanted to destroy Catholic civilization. Only an absolutist regime based on the union of the altar and the throne could save the Spaniards from apocalyptic disaster. To them, even the concept of "nation" was a suspiciously liberal idea.[10] When the liberals returned to power after the death of Ferdinand VII in 1833, they split into a minor progressive current and a movement of conservative liberalism, which shared a secular attitude toward politics. The reactionary sectors that finally embraced nationalism and parliamentary politics formed the neo-Catholic movement in the second half of the nineteenth century.[11]

These diverse political currents all claimed Jovellanos as one of their illustrious precursors.[12] While the incorporation of Jovellanos into the gallery of eminent liberals was understandable, if we bear in

10. José Álvarez Junco, *Mater dolorosa: la idea de España en el siglo XIX* (Madrid, 2016), p.343–57.
11. Pedro Carlos González Cuevas, *Historia de las derechas españolas: de la Ilustración a nuestros días* (Madrid, 2000), p.92–103, 164–75; Eric Storm, *La perspectiva del progreso: pensamiento político en la España del cambio de siglo, 1890–1914* (Madrid, 2001), p.42–44.
12. Silverio Sánchez Corredera, *Jovellanos y el jovellanismo, una perspectiva filosófica* (Oviedo, 2004); Llombart, *Jovellanos*, p.207–37.

mind his membership of the Junta Central, the neo-Catholics' claim on him required rather more intellectual flexibility. Nevertheless, the assimilation of a nationalist discourse by the neo-Catholics required a broader intellectual background that went beyond the absolutists and the counter-revolutionary clergy who had backed Ferdinand VII.[13] Jovellanos's varied and extensive works left enough room for interpretation to enable him to be included in the pantheon of orthodox Catholic thinkers.

This effort started in 1858–1859 with an edition of his work by the neo-Catholic parliamentary deputy Cándido Nocedal, and was continued by Marcelino Menéndez Pelayo, who, in his ambitious *Historia de los heterodoxos españoles* (1880–1882), divided the Spaniards into orthodox and heterodox Catholics and—which for him was the same thing—into good citizens and disloyal Spaniards.[14] This Manichean intellectual history, though certainly impressive, devoted extensive attention to Jovellanos, who was portrayed as a person of high moral integrity, which meant, according to Menéndez Pelayo, that his orthodoxy was beyond question. The strategy of the neo-Catholics was to focus on his moralism, his piety, and his rejection of the French Revolution, while downplaying important publications, such as the *Informe de ley agraria (Report on agrarian law)*, which had been on the Index since 1825 and proposed, or merely suggested, the voluntary and gradual sale of the property of the Church. These texts were seen as "mistakes," although understandable ones, given the omnipresence of Enlightenment thinking from which hardly anyone at the time could escape.[15]

To make his claim more convincing, Menéndez Pelayo harshly criticized liberal admiration for Jovellanos as intellectually questionable. He particularly attacked the essay on Jovellanos by a "certain German called [Hermann] Baumgarten [...] considered to be a vulgar Protestant propagandist in his country,"[16] which was published in Spanish in the *Revista Contemporánea* in 1877, and was highly praised by the progressive liberal thinker and politician

---

13. On the assimilation of nationalist thinking by reactionary Catholic thinkers, see Álvarez Junco, *Mater dolorosa*, p.433–57.
14. Marcelino Menéndez Pelayo, *Historia de los heterodoxos españoles*, 8 vols. (Madrid, 1880–1882), esp. vol.3.
15. Pelayo, *Historia de los heterodoxos españoles*, vol.3, p.288.
16. Joaquín Álvarez Barrientos, "El siglo XVIII, según Menéndez Pelayo," *Boletín de la Biblioteca de Menéndez Pelayo* 82 (2006), p.297–329 (308); Sánchez Corredera, *Jovellanos*, p.310–11.

Gumersindo de Azcárate. Azcárate belonged to the Institución Libre de Enseñanza (Free Educational Institution), which promoted a new form of education designed to stimulate tolerance and independent thinking among children.

These ideological polemics now belong to the historiographical past. An effort has recently been made to give Jovellanos his place within the broader context of the European Enlightenment, by studying his reception of English, French, and Italian Enlightenment philosophers.[17] The same can be said, broadly speaking, of recent approaches to the Spanish Enlightenment. Nowadays, an attempt is being made to see how Spanish intellectuals and reformers used Enlightenment ideas to reflect on the causes of Spain's "backwardness" in the eighteenth century—in relation to its past and to other European monarchies— and to address its social, economic, and political problems through scholarly development, legal-political reform, or political economy. The Spanish Enlightenment is difficult to understand within the dichotomy of a radical and a moderate Enlightenment. Rather than being characterized by the development of philosophical systems, it was essentially pragmatic and utilitarian.[18] This approach connects well to Jovellanos, who was not a systematic philosopher, but rather a writer of reports, recommendations, and essays: in short, a pragmatic thinker who emphasized the importance of educational reform to achieve prosperity and happiness.

Nevertheless, this approach does not entirely overcome the contradictions regarding the conservative, enlightened, or liberal nature of his ideas either, especially when the focus is on his proposals for moral and educational reform. If backwardness was essentially to be remedied by scientific and economic progress and constitutional reform, the question remains as to why Jovellanos devoted so much attention to the moral decadence that allegedly depressed Spanish society. A new perspective on the ideas of Jovellanos can be developed if the focus is placed on the significance of the court as the political center of the early modern monarchy. Jovellanos formed part of the court society that was gradually losing its political hegemony after

17. For example: María del Carmen Lara Nieto, *Ilustración española y pensamiento inglés: Jovellanos* (Granada, 2008).
18. For a recent reflection on the Spanish Enlightenment, see Jesús Astigarraga, "Introduction: *admirer, rougir, imiter*–Spain and the European Enlightenment," in *The Spanish Enlightenment revisited*, ed. Jesús Astigarraga, Oxford University Studies in the Enlightenment (Oxford, Voltaire Foundation, 2015), p.1–17.

the Peninsular War and the construction of the nation-state. The courtly context makes it easier to understand why Jovellanos attached so much importance to the moral integrity of the nobility, and how his focus on the nobility might be compatible with his enlightened, liberal, and patriotic ideas.[19]

The moral criticism of the nobility

From the second half of the fifteenth century until the first decades of the nineteenth century, the Spanish court enjoyed indisputable political preeminence among the various agencies of power that characterized the Old Regime. It was a space for political negotiation between the nobles and the kings, and it determined the values and way of life of the elites of the Spanish monarchy.[20] At court, it was difficult to separate politics from morals or the exercise of power from lifestyle: "[G]ood manners, etiquette and ceremonial, conversation strategies, the art of observation, concealment and pretense were social rules of behavior developed in a space of competition between families and factions to conserve or increase their levels of power."[21]

Courtly ethics were based on the idea that the moral excellence of the aristocracy was expressed through decorum, which meant that the appearance and actions of the nobility reflected their moral qualities. Good manners revealed the dignity of noblemen and, at the same time, indicated esteem for others, via courtliness expressed in conversation. Courtly manners had to be expressed with *sprezzatura*, a graceful, seemingly natural behavior that concealed all signs of effort and studiedness and avoided affectation. The effortless display of good manners showed that they had taken firm root and formed part of the person's second nature, which was the opposite of primary instinctive behavior.[22]

19. On the court in enlightened Spain, see María Victoria López-Cordón Cortezo, "The merits of good *gobierno*: culture and politics in the Bourbon court," in *The Spanish Enlightenment revisited*, ed. J. Astigarraga, p.19–39.

20. Antonio Álvarez-Ossorio, "Corte y cortesanos en la monarquía de España," in *Educare il corpo, educare la parola nella trattatistica del Rinascimento*, ed. Giorgio Patrizi and Amedeo Quondam (Rome, 1998), p.297–365.

21. Álvarez-Ossorio, "Corte y cortesanos," p.298. All translations are my own unless otherwise stated.

22. Regarding the ideal of *sprezzatura* in eighteenth-century Spain, see Diana Campóo, "Danza y educación nobiliaria en el siglo XVIII: el método de la

In the hierarchical, highly competitive world of the court, good education referred to the ability not only to follow the more or less fixed rules of etiquette, but also to adapt one's behavior to circumstances. This was part of the art of conversation; depending on the rank of the person and the place or the topic of conversation, the courtier had to adapt his speech and gestures.[23] Graceful behavior allowed the courtier to establish a respectful relationship with the king and queen, to avoid adulation, gain their confidence, and eventually participate in the political decision-making process. The field of *otium*, including theater, balls, jousts, and tournaments, was an important part of courtly life. In the refined atmosphere of play and sociability, courtiers confirmed their aristocratic identity, practiced their conversational skills, and established political relationships.

Despite the growing bureaucratization of political practice in eighteenth-century Spain,[24] these courtly practices remained intact in the time of Jovellanos. This was most clearly seen in the spectacular career at court of Manuel Godoy, who belonged to the minor nobility and managed to rise to become a member of the royal bodyguard. After an incident when he had fallen off his horse, he attracted the attention of the future king and queen, Charles IV and his wife María Luisa de Parma. He was invited to their private apartments at the royal palace, where he participated in festive soirées with music and games, thus gaining their trust. When Charles became king, Godoy was soon honored with distinctions and offices, and eventually became the favorite of the king and queen. His position as favorite was certainly questioned in anti-court literature and aroused the hostility of the higher aristocracy, who felt displaced. However, the criticism, typically in the context of the court, essentially acquired a moral character in the form of gossip about the supposed sexual relationship between Godoy and María Luisa.[25]

Forming part of the inner circle of courtiers or being excluded was arbitrary. After all, judgments about affectation and immoral behavior depended on the opinions of others. It was perhaps precisely

escuela de baile en el Real Seminario de Nobles de Madrid," *Ars bilduma* 5 (2015), p.157–73.

23. Amedeo Quondam, *La conversazione: un modello italiano* (Rome, 2007), p.19–20.
24. María Victoria López-Cordón Cortezo, "Burocracia y erudición en la España del siglo XVIII," in *L'Espagne, l'Etat, les Lumières: mélanges en l'honneur de Didier Ozanam*, ed. Jean-Pierre Dedieu and Bernard Vincent (Madrid, 2004), p.155–72.
25. Emilio La Parra, *Manuel Godoy: la aventura del poder* (Barcelona, 2005), p.68–69.

this subjectivity that led to the constant stream of treatises on courtliness that set out to make explicit the codes of behavior at court. Moreover, as morals and politics were difficult to separate at court, moral discourse always had a political dimension, which was particularly useful for attacking opponents in a more or less veiled way. As Jovellanos would find out, public demonstrations of disapproval, gossip, satires, and denunciations to the Inquisition all belonged to the courtly arsenal of political weapons.[26] Finally, the idea of second nature, as opposed to primary impulses, raised the question of sincerity. The question of whether good manners really reflected virtues or merely concealed immoral objectives explains the anti-court satires that had, nonetheless, formed an intrinsic part of discourse about the court since the late Middle Ages.[27]

Jovellanos was the author of two famous satirical poems, *Sátira I a Arnesto* and *Sátira II a Arnesto* (1786, 1787), in which he portrayed the vices that supposedly typified the Castilian aristocracy of his time. He criticized their addiction to luxury and their custom of mimicking the dress and behavior of the *majos*, flashily dressed lower-class men and women characterized by a defiant attitude, the use of coarse language, and provocative behavior. This fashion was interpreted in the nineteenth and twentieth centuries by authors such as Menéndez Pelayo and Ortega y Gasset as an idealization of popular autochthonous culture reacting to French Enlightenment influences. Nevertheless, the *majos* did not initially emerge as authentic portraits of lower-class types, but were originally literary creations of the successful playwright Ramón de la Cruz, who introduced them into his comic operas as counter-figures to the *petimetres* (petits-maîtres), extravagantly dressed pretentious characters obsessed with following French courtly customs. Between the two extremes appeared the well-educated nobleman who was not seduced by lascivious or pretentious female behavior, and the modest noble ladies who were in control of their passions.[28]

The objective of the plays was moral edification, especially for the upper classes, whose manners had to serve as a model for the

26. On satires at the court of Charles IV, see Nigel Glendinning, "La sátira en el arte y la literatura en la época de Carlos IV," in *La época de Carlos IV (1788–1808)*, ed. Elena de Lorenzo Álvarez (Oviedo, 2009), p.17–39.
27. Álvarez-Ossorio, "Corte y cortesanos," p.327.
28. Xavier Andreu, "Figuras modernas del deseo: las majas de Ramón de la Cruz y los orígenes del majismo," *Ayer* 78:2 (2010), p.25–34. Also, Julio Caro Baroja, "Los Majos," *Cuadernos Hispanoamericanos* 299 (May 1975), p.281–349.

rest of society. Nevertheless, the *majos* took on a life of their own and started to be imitated outside the theater in real life, as a playful twist on decorum practiced mainly, though not exclusively, by the higher aristocracy. Whereas the minor nobility felt the need to demonstrate their status with fine courtly manners, many grandees did not worry about their noble rank, and allowed themselves to adopt the popular lifestyle in dress, language, manners, and leisure.[29] It seemed that the attractiveness and daring of the female *majas*, expressed in their dancing, movements, gestures, and clothing, turned them into objects of desire for men, including nobles, who by dressing up as *majos* adopted the role of their suitors. Instead of the *majos* serving as an instrument of moral edification, imitating them became a transgressive custom, which allowed the higher aristocracy to parody themselves and the role they were supposed to play in society.[30] This was the opposite of what Jovellanos expected of the nobility.

The moral regeneration of the nobility

In his *Memoria sobre las diversiones públicas*, a report on the history of spectacle and public entertainment, read to the Royal Academy of History in 1796, and published in 1812, Jovellanos reflects on the role of leisure in the education of the nobility and the Third Estate in the Spanish monarchy. According to him, historically significant Spanish spectacles and public entertainments started in the Middle Ages with hunting, jousting, tournaments, and balls. He distinguished these from private "sedentary" entertainments, such as chess, draughts, and dice. Jovellanos used his descriptions of medieval leisure and play as a commentary on the educational value of public spectacle in his own day. The cultural phenomena described are set in a courtly context, with the nobles as the main actors, while the role of the Third Estate was essentially reduced to that of spectator. Jovellanos considered that the court should continue to be a major point of reference for culture and education. Therefore, he reflects on the historical change in courtly cultural practices, which, despite their decadence in his day, could again have educational value if the necessary reforms were applied.[31]

29. La Parra, *Manuel Godoy*, p.68.
30. Andreu, "Figuras modernas," p.41–45.
31. Gaspar Melchor de Jovellanos, *Espectáculos y diversiones públicas: informe sobre la ley agraria*, ed. Guillermo Carnero (Madrid, 1998), p.113–222.

This view was widespread in the traditions of courtly discourse that often set the learning of moral values within the context of play. As had been expressed in exemplary fashion by Baldassare Castiglione in his *Book of the courtier* (1528), courtly nobles expressed their moral qualities in conversation, especially with the ladies. As a matter of fact, the conversations in the evenings at the court of Urbino described by Castiglione took place in the presence of and were conducted by Duchess Elisabetta Gonzaga and her court ladies. Courtly leisure included playful expressions of sociability, such as the chivalric sports of tournaments and jousting, but also dancing, music, and witty dialogue. Courtly conversation, which referred in a broad sense to "all aspects of the fact of being together, of social and sociable cooperation,"[32] was practiced in untroubled moments of peace, when the nobleman relaxed in the company of others and their interaction delighted reason and the senses through the arts. According to Castiglione's Aristotelian reflection, moderate leisure and good manners guaranteed social harmony in times of peace. The prince therefore should give his subjects the laws that would allow them to "live safe and dignified lives in peace and quiet and enjoy in a worthy manner the tranquility for which they actively strive."[33]

Jovellanos's historical overview and proposal regarding the reform of public spectacle and entertainment were a reinterpretation of this discourse on the moral value of *otium*. He describes medieval tournaments as the "most important entertainments for the court and the big cities," celebrated on the occasion of special "public" events, such as coronations, princely weddings, and the signing of peace treaties.[34] In time, these events, which gave noblemen the opportunity to show their courage, became part of the aristocratic way of life and were celebrated more regularly, while their magnificence increased. They were not only about the display of courage and military skills. According to Jovellanos, the most admirable aspect of the tournament was the spirit of gallantry caused by the presence of the ladies. They did not merely attend as spectators, but granted awards; knights tried to attract their attention by displaying their bravery and dedicating their victories to them. However, it was mainly in the evening, when the tournaments, jousting, and hunting activities were over, that

32. Marc Fumaroli, *La República de las Letras* (Barcelona, 2013), p.194.
33. Baldassare Castiglione, *The Courtier*, ed. and translated by George Bull (London, 2003), p.302.
34. Jovellanos, *Espectáculos*, p.143–44.

courtly festivities acquired a more peaceful character. When the knights and ladies returned to the palace, they enjoyed a splendid banquet, and alternated dancing and music with conversation. In this pleasant light-hearted atmosphere, the knights, forgetting their ferocity and the stress of battle, cultivated their sociable qualities, elevating wit and gallantry to higher levels. Wealth and luxury were sustained by urbanity, while female beauty was accompanied by wit and humor.[35]

In summary, the knights cultivated their moral qualities in a playful environment to impress the ladies, which also happened in Castiglione's version at the court of Urbino. Of course, the historical context of the end of the eighteenth century, in which Jovellanos reflects on courtly culture, was entirely different. Jovellanos describes the late medieval courts as a distant world from the perspective of the moral decay of his own times, which provides him with the justification for a project of moral regeneration through education.

The moral corruption of the nobility was expressed precisely in its ludic culture. The theater of his time was a disgrace. It lacked the expression of lofty ideals, and seemed to stimulate disobedience, and uncouth and disrespectful behavior, all encapsulated in the magic of theater, the language of poetry, and the excitement of music. Spectators watched dancing *manolos* and *verduleras*, figures from popular urban culture, instead of gods and nymphs. The corrupting effect of these plays was apparent because of the aristocratic custom of dressing up and behaving like *majos*.[36]

Different educational institutions could restore to the nobility their lost splendor and prestige. Jovellanos mentions that the *maestranzas de caballería*, aristocratic corporations that taught horse-riding and skill in the use of arms, would restore noble manliness and elegance in harmony with the ideas of a more "enlightened century." Academies of drama, which should be established in the cities, but above all at court, could teach the young noblemen "to carry themselves with confidence, to walk and move with assurance, to speak and gesture with propriety, to articulate clearly and in a well-modulated voice, and to give their expression the feelings and tone of sincerity that is the soul of conversation, and which is as necessary to please and persuade as it is rare among us."[37] Legislation could also help create (neoclassical) theater

35. Jovellanos, *Espectáculos*, p.156–57.
36. Jovellanos, *Espectáculos*, p.210.
37. Jovellanos, *Espectáculos*, p.194.

that would fulfill moral requirements by inspiring love for God, for one's country, for the king and the constitution, as well as respect for hierarchy and authority, and matrimonial fidelity and paternal love. This edifying drama should be performed in a suitably magnificent environment: splendid, beautifully ornate theaters.[38]

In this way, Jovellanos continued the tradition of teaching good manners and morals within the ludic framework of theater, balls, and chivalric exercises, but reinserted it into a context of patriotism. The lower estate was entitled to its own particular leisure with festivities in villages, to be organized under the supervision of magistrates. Theater, however, was "a school for educating the rich and the comfortably wealthy." Educating the elites would improve the moral state of society in general, since they set an example for the rest of society: "From whom do [the common people] receive their principles but from those who always shine in their eyes, whose fortune they envy, whose example they observe and whose customs they seek to imitate, even when they criticize and condemn them?"[39] The aristocratic *habitus*, fine manners, and elegance would embody the moral superiority that was to regenerate the Spanish monarchy.

Educating the nobility

A practical example of this effort was the Real Seminario de Nobles de Madrid, known as a model for Spanish enlightened education. Jovellanos was responsible for the college when he was minister of Grace and Justice between 1797 and 1798. An educational plan for the reform of the college found among his papers was for a long time wrongly attributed to him, but turns out to have been written by his friend José de Vargas Ponce (1760–1821), with whom he corresponded on different topics, among them education. Possibly Jovellanos came to be in possession of this paper because new regulations had to be adopted for the college, which finally occurred in 1799. In addition, Jovellanos considered Vargas Ponce as the future director of the college.[40]

---

38. Jovellanos, *Espectáculos*, p.209–10.
39. Jovellanos, *Espectáculos*, p.202.
40. José de Vargas Ponce, "Plan para la educación de la nobleza y clases pudientes españolas," in *Obras completas de Gaspar Melchor Jovellanos*, vol.14: *Escritos pedagógicos, 2°*, ed. Olegario Negrín Fajardo (Gijón, 2010), p.1181–1240 (p.1181, editor's n.1).

The Real Seminario de Nobles de Madrid, founded by Philip V along the lines of the Collège Louis-le-Grand in Paris, opened its doors on September 21, 1725 and was a model for the education of the nobility until its closure in 1808 after the outbreak of the Peninsular War. According to its original regulations, published in 1730, the college welcomed sons of the hereditary nobility between the ages of eight and fifteen, excluding the offspring of those who merely enjoyed privileges.[41] The college was run by the Society of Jesus until its expulsion in 1767. Three years later it was reopened and acquired a more military character under the coordination of the scientist and seafarer Jorge Juan y Santacilia (1713–1773). In spite of an increasing emphasis on a secular educational approach, with an attempt to strengthen scientific education related to the military arts, the influence of the Jesuits was discernible until the final years in the handbooks on history, morals, and religion.[42] From 1790 onward, the institution lost something of its elitist character when sons of the "well-off classes" were also allowed to study at the college.[43]

The regulations of 1730 state that its most important objective was to raise Christian gentlemen so that later, as fathers of families, they would be able to serve as a model of virtue, piety, and modesty. A secondary ("less important, but also important") objective was to teach the sons of gentlemen the "faculties and sciences that most embellish them," which were grammar, rhetoric, poetry, languages (French, Italian, and Greek), logic, philosophy, metaphysics, and canon law. Furthermore, since the aim was that "nothing should be lacking that could contribute to the education of a perfect gentleman," mathematics and geography were also taught. Finally, the regulations mention that "secular masters" would be appointed to teach the skills and exercises appropriate to gentlemen, which were dancing, music, fencing, and horse-riding.[44]

Apart from its educational purpose, the institution had to provide "luster" to the Spanish nation and be of "general usefulness" to the

41. Francisco Aguilar Piñal, "Los Reales Seminarios de Nobles en la política ilustrada española," *Cuadernos Hispanoamericanos* 356 (February 1980), p.329–49.

42. Regarding scholarly education at the college, see José Luis Peset, "Ciencia, nobleza y ejército en el Seminario de Nobles de Madrid (1770–1788)," in *Mayans y la Ilustración*, ed. Salvador Cardona Miralles (Valencia, 1981), p.519–35.

43. Francisco Andújar Castillo, "El Seminario de Nobles de Madrid en el siglo XVIII: un estudio social," *Cuadernos de Historia Moderna: Anejos* 3 (2004), p.201–25 (208).

44. *Constituciones de El Real Seminario de Nobles* (Madrid, Gabriel del Barrio, 1730).

kingdom, which meant alumni would be able to take up positions in the king's service. This entailed good manners that were practiced discreetly and in accordance with the circumstances. The sons of gentlemen in the college were supposed to behave in the first place in a Christian way, that is, to be modest and silent, and have a solemn, serious demeanor. Nevertheless, since the students belonged to the nobility, graceful behavior was also necessary. Teaching this was the task of the "secular masters." After all, religious discipline might be suitable for students in a Jesuit college, but it was not becoming for noblemen at court, where their behavior was not to be confused with that of the clergy.

At the end of the eighteenth century, the institution was especially attractive to the minor nobility from the provinces and sons of wealthy families anxious to acquire the prestige of the aristocracy and gain access to their networks. Being a noble, in the end, meant living like one, and that included the acquisition of an aristocratic *habitus*. Besides, the college was a space of sociability that provided fruitful contacts with nobles linked to the court, and where important information about future career opportunities circulated. The old titled nobility, who did not need to confirm their noble status, and could even afford to flirt with *majismo*, took less interest in the institution. Though technical education was an instrument for social promotion, family background and networks were more important to gain access to the inner circles of the court where the display of conversational skills was essential.[45]

The educational plan of 1798 drawn up by José de Vargas Ponce emphasized the importance of useful knowledge, but also included the traditional training in conversational abilities and activities like dancing, playing music, fencing, and horse-riding. There are many similarities between this plan and Jovellanos's ideas on education, although Jovellanos himself would no longer have been in favor of special educational institutions for the nobility.[46] In his famous "Memoria sobre educación pública" ("Report on public education"), written in 1802 for the Real Sociedad Mallorquina de Amigos del País (Royal Majorcan Society of Friends of the Country), which called for the establishment of a college for the nobility on the island,

45. Andújar Castillo, "El Seminario," p.220–22.
46. Gaspar Melchor de Jovellanos, "Memoria sobre educación pública," in *Obras completas de Gaspar Melchor Jovellanos*, vol.13: *Escritos pedagógicos, 1º*, ed. Olegario Negrín Fajardo (Gijón, 2010), p.435–532 (p.435, editor's n.2).

Jovellanos advised founding a free public educational institution that was accessible to all classes. He even seemed to criticize the education that was offered at colleges for the nobility, stating that "education," in the sense of knowing the codes of social intercourse, had often been confused with "instruction," which referred to useful technical knowledge. Moreover, he stated in the same report that "urbanity is a beautiful veneer for instruction and is its best ornament, but without instruction it has no value and is mere outward appearance. Urbanity gilds the statue, instruction gives it shape."[47]

The fact that Jovellanos advised against setting up a college for the nobility in Majorca, however, does not mean that he rejected this kind of education. He thought that a free public institution was more useful for achieving prosperity in a relatively small territory, since not only the nobility, but also the Third Estate would benefit from it. This did not mean that all estates should receive the same education. A close reading reveals that Jovellanos made a distinction between an "absolutely necessary" basic education that was accessible to all, and a higher level of "necessary education" for the nobility, the well-off, and "all those who could pay for it."[48] In the report's extensive section on ethics, Jovellanos emphasized that reforms should not overthrow the existing social order but improve it, adding that human beings were not born free, but subject to authority: "[S]ociety [cannot exist] without hierarchy, nor hierarchy without a progressive order of distinction and superiority; inequality is not only necessary, but essential in civil society."[49]

To be sure, Jovellanos criticized self-interested nobles living in excessive luxury who concealed their vices behind good manners and a hypocritical discourse of virtue and honor. This was, however, a topic with a long tradition that criticized not so much good manners in themselves, but the moral emptiness and scholarly ignorance behind them. This discourse often interpreted morality in the tradition of Christian ethics. Jovellanos did the same, but with the addition of an Enlightenment discourse that emphasized that it was the patriotic duty of the nobility to contribute to the prosperity and happiness of Spanish society.

The divergent historiographical interpretations regarding the educational ideas of Jovellanos seem to be the consequence of an all

47. Jovellanos, "Memoria sobre educación pública," p.445.
48. Baras Escolá, *El reformismo político*, p.172.
49. Jovellanos, "Memoria sobre educación pública," p.507.

too simplified division between the courtly ethics of good manners associated with the Old Regime and absolutism on the one hand, and the enlightened patriotic ideals of free and utilitarian public education embraced by liberals on the other. For Jovellanos, however, critical courtly discourse was a vehicle that enabled him to propose his enlightened educational ideas. Concepts such as good manners, virtue, moral happiness, and patriotic love of one's country should be understood in relation to each other: The aristocracy could fulfill its role as a moral example in society if its good manners were backed by an Enlightenment commitment to the regeneration of society. After the outbreak of the Peninsular War, Jovellanos once more adapted his ideas to the new political circumstances. As a member of the Junta Central, he drew up a new plan for "national instruction" in 1809, which included teaching how to handle weapons for personal defense and for the defense of the "nation." Jovellanos's concern for the exemplary good manners of the aristocracy disappeared, though he still foresaw special educational institutions for the sons of "wealthy families" who aspired to a career in the Church, the law, or the military. Jovellanos died two years later on November 27, 1811, a few months before the promulgation of the Constitution of Cádiz on March 19, 1812.

The king is dead—long live the Enlightenment? Viennese court culture, networks, and enlightened reforms in periods of transition (1765–1795)

SIMON KARSTENS

It is conventional wisdom to understand the court as the central place for political resources, especially prestige and connections in early modern monarchies. Therefore, in the age of Enlightenment, anybody interested in influencing policy and politics—anybody who wanted to turn their ideas into reality—had to cultivate connections with the court. It was also the most important place for rulers to employ and patronize reformers or traditionalists who supported their rule, and to represent their own attitude toward politics for the court elites and an ever-growing public audience. All in all, the court was the place where princes established the kind of balance between reform and tradition which they considered appropriate for the welfare of their territory.

Just like the solar system, the famous analogy used to describe Versailles, each court had an obvious center: the ruler. However, what happened if the central star of this system died and a new sun arose? The basic assumption of this chapter is that analyzing such periods of transition can be used as a focus to better understand the connection between the Enlightenment and court in general. This leads to further questions: How could a new monarch make his own political agenda visible and change or maintain the established balance of reform and tradition? Did he choose to present himself openly as a man of reform or tradition (a question also discussed in this volume by Paul Beckus)? How did reformers and their networks react to the situation? And how did the outcome of such moments of transition influence the construction of contemporary or historiographic characterizations of a monarch and of his rule as "enlightened" or "conservative"?

To answer these questions, this chapter will look to the Austrian monarchy of the late eighteenth century. Historians have often characterized this as a time of drastic changes between conservative and reform-oriented, enlightened sovereigns. This chapter will examine the establishment of the reign of Joseph II (1765–1790), who is commonly characterized as an almost furiously enlightened monarch; the short and rather ambiguous rule of his brother Leopold II (1790–1792); and the early years of his nephew Francis II (1792–1835), who has often been described as a man of conservative reaction.[1]

To put these categorizations to the test, the early years of each monarch's reign will be examined more closely with a focus on two fields of reform policy: first, the organization of court life and the emperor's attitude toward court elites. Second, the networks of two distinct police reformers and their success or failure in implementing their policy at court.

The first approach will focus primarily on how, when they came to power, the monarchs changed personnel, raised or cut the numbers of court officials, and changed or confirmed the established rules of access. This information is especially important since access to the court was a power asset controlled by the monarch and sought after by people who wanted to influence politics. Any change in this field would indicate a shift in power, and was therefore watched very closely by the rulers' contemporaries, who all advocated for gradual changes but not for major, structural ones.

This scrutiny of the actual policy of the monarchs will be supported by an examination of how they publicly staged their attitude toward tradition by participation or non-participation in court rituals. This will allow us to analyze to what extent their proclaimed position toward court life, their actual policy of change or continuity, and the role historiography has attributed to each of them are in accordance. Concerning this question, this chapter benefits especially from research on the most prominent political advisor of the time, State Chancellor (*Staatskanzler*) Clemens Wenzel Anton

1.   For a first impression on the historiographical traditions, compare the respective articles in the German national biography: Hans Wagner, "Joseph II.," *Neue Deutsche Biographie* 10 (1974), p.617–22; Adam Wandruszka, "Leopold II.," *Neue Deutsche Biographie* 14 (1985), p.260–66; Hugo Hantsch, "Franz II.," *Neue Deutsche Biographie* 5 (1961), p.358–61. See also the following articles: Peter Baumgart, "Joseph II. und Maria Theresia 1765–1790," in *Die Kaiser der Neuzeit 1519–1918*, ed. Anton Schindling and Walter Ziegler (Munich, 1990), p.249–76; Lorenz Mikoletzky, "Leopold II. 1790–1792," in *Kaiser*, ed. A. Schindling and W. Ziegler, p.277–87; Walter Ziegler, "Franz II. 1792–1806," in *Kaiser*, ed. A. Schindling and W. Ziegler, p.289–306.

von Kaunitz-Rietberg (1711–1794), who has often been studied as an example of continuity despite the three successions he experienced in office.[2] It remains to be shown if this was actually exceptional or, rather, normal.

The second approach focuses on the reform of the Austrian police, and builds upon the analysis of court networks and rules of access. This field has been of special importance in the historiography to argue for a categorization of the three monarchs as "reformers" or "conservatives." Francis II especially has been cast in a bad light because of his police regime.[3] The basis for this historiographical tradition was laid by liberal historians of the nineteenth century who focused on this aspect, drawing a connection to their own present and using it as an analogy in public debates. Even authors of biographical articles who attempted to give a positive impression of Francis II severely criticized his police regime.[4] In his case, then, a strict police regime was presented as the epitome of an anti-enlightened policy.

These short impressions make the three monarchs' approaches to police reform a very interesting example for a comparative study, even more so, since Francis himself did not implement a completely new policy but rather followed in the footsteps of his uncle Joseph II.[5] To understand why and how he did this, the present chapter takes a closer look at two men who fought, with varying success, to convince the monarchs to follow their recommendations. The first was Johann Anton von Pergen (1725–1814), a protégé of State Chancellor Kaunitz. He argued for a secret police, whose mandate was to be the

2.   On his career, compare Grete Klingenstein, *Der Aufstieg des Hauses Kaunitz: Studien zur Herkunft und Bildung des Staatskanzlers Wenzel Anton* (Göttingen, 1975); Franz A. J. Szabo, *Kaunitz and enlightened absolutism 1753–1780* (Cambridge, 1994); Karl Otmar Freiherr von Aretin, "Kaunitz, Wenzel Anton Fürst," *Neue Deutsche Biographie* 11 (1977), p.363–69; Franz A. J. Szabo, "Favorit, Premierminister oder drittes Staatsoberhaupt?," in *Der zweite Mann im Staat: Oberste Amtsträger und Favoriten im Umkreis der Reichsfürsten in der Frühen Neuzeit*, ed. Michael Kaiser and Andreas Pečar (Berlin, 2003), p.345–62.

3.   Ziegler, "Franz II.," p.289. These attacks by contemporary critics and later historians were mostly focused on Franz's later head of government, Klemens Wenzel Lothar von Metternich, who has been stigmatized as a figurehead of conservatism and anti-liberalism; see Wolfram Siemann, *Metternich: Staatsmann zwischen Restauration und Moderne* (Munich, 2010), p.8–17.

4.   Anton Victor Felgel, "Franz II.," *Allgemeine Deutsche Biographie* 7 (1878/1968), p.285–90. See also Ziegler, "Franz II.," p.289.

5.   Wagner, "Joseph II."; Simon Karstens, *Lehrer–Schriftsteller–Staatsreformer: Die Karriere des Joseph von Sonnenfels 1733–1817* (Vienna, 2011), p.364–69.

surveillance of the populace and crime fighting. His counterpart was Professor Joseph von Sonnenfels (1733–1817), who, through letters and publications, was well connected to those who identified themselves as part of the Enlightenment. He advocated for a public welfare police which, instead of just fighting crime, would take on what he perceived to be the causes of criminal behavior.[6]

Retracing the efforts and networks of these influential courtiers will provide a deeper understanding of the connection between court and Enlightenment reform. It will also show that different conclusions by T. C. Blanning, who wrote that under Joseph II power was personal, and Frank Szabo, who stressed the interdependency of the monarch and the elites, may seem contradictory, but actually complement each other.[7] This is because, as will be shown, policies that contemporaries and historians considered to be enlightened reforms or conservative rollbacks were enacted by much the same personnel—people who could not completely change, but could (and did) influence the rulers' policies. Testing this hypothesis with the examples of court culture and police reform will not only allow us to answer the questions stated above, but also offer suggestions for a better understanding of contemporary and historiographical characterizations such as "conservative" or "enlightened" with respect to sovereigns, their courts, and their policy.

Everything changes? The court of Joseph II (1765–1790)

The autobiography of the successful poet and author Caroline Pichler (1769–1843), published in 1844, describes the transition after the deaths of Maria Theresa, Joseph II, and Leopold II.[8] Pilcher's views are important because they are based on contemporary insights as well as on the nineteenth century's common memory. Since Pichler's parents were a court councilor and a lady-in-waiting of the empress herself, with the special duty of reading to her mistress, it is hardly a surprise that Pichler described the first succession as a transition

6. On the different contemporary concepts of police or *Polizey* of these two men, compare Karstens, *Sonnenfels*, p.345–46 with further references; Karl-Heinz Osterloh, *Joseph von Sonnenfels und die österreichische Reformbewegung im Zeitalter des aufgeklärten Absolutismus: eine Studie zum Zusammenhang von Kameralwissenschaft und Verwaltungspraxis* (Lübeck, 1970), p.136–40.
7. T. C. Blanning, *Joseph II* (London, 1994), p.60; Szabo, *Kaunitz*, p.347.
8. Caroline Pichler, *Denkwürdigkeiten aus meinem Leben* (Vienna, 1844). Compare Stefan Jordan, "Pichler, Caroline," *Neue Deutsche Biographie* 20 (2001), p.411–12.

awaited with hope by some but with fear by her own family. She described the dying empress as a setting star with "mild, soothing warmth," and her successor as a rising star with a "fiery shine."[9] The fear of drastic changes seems to have been justified, considering the way Joseph had acted when his mother made him her co-regent and placed him in charge of the royal and imperial court after his father's death in 1765.[10]

Almost every biographer describes how Joseph drastically reduced court personnel, closed sections of the Hofburg palace, and broke radically with the traditional system of ceremonies.[11] Joseph immediately combined his and his mother's households, and opened the nearby imperial hunting grounds and gardens to the public. There, as many popular anecdotes published under his newly granted freedom of the press claimed, he took public walks and encountered lowborn subjects. Joseph also abolished the Spanish court dress and ceremonial hand-kissing and kneeling, and reduced the number of secular and sacral court events. The number of official religious services at court, not considering Sunday mass, diminished from eighty-seven in 1765 to thirty-three in 1774.[12] With this course of action, Joseph distanced himself from his ancestors' famous virtue

9.   Pichler, *Denkwürdigkeiten*, p.67: "in allen Familien regten sich [...], je nachdem sie mehr der milden wohltätigen Wärme des sinkenden Gestirnes, oder dem feurigen Glanze des aufsteigenden zugewendet waren, verschiedene aber lebhafte Besorgnisse, Hoffnungen, Erwartungen." All translations are my own unless otherwise stated.

10. For an overview of the ranks at the Austrian court, see Martin Scheutz and Jakob Wühner, "Dienst, Pflicht, Ordnung und gute policey," in *Der Wiener Hof im Spiegel der Zeremonialprotokolle (1652–1800)*, ed. Irmgard Pangerl, Martin Scheutz, and Thomas Winkelbauer (Innsbruck, 2007), p.15–94. Compare Robert John Evans, "The Austrian Habsburgs: the dynasty as a political institution," in *The Courts of Europe*, ed. Arthur Dickens (New York, 1984), p.121–47.

11. Karl Gutkas, *Joseph II* (Vienna, 1989), p.81–88; Helmut Reinalter, *Joseph II.: Reformer auf dem Kaiserthron* (Munich, 2011), p.45, 56; Hanns Mikoletzky, *Österreich: das große 18. Jahrhundert* (Vienna, 1967), p.324; François Fejtö, *Joseph II.: Kaiser und Revolutionär* (Stuttgart, 1956), p.108–109, 232–34; Humbert Fink, *Joseph II.: Kaiser, König und Reformer* (Düsseldorf, 1990), p.90–98, 165–67; Derek Beales, *Joseph II*, 2 vols. (Cambridge, 1987–2009), vol.1, p.154–73, vol.2, p.20, 49–56, 437; compare Irmgart Pangerl, "Höfische Öffentlichkeit," in *Wiener Hof*, ed. I. Pangerl, M. Scheutz, and T. Winkelbauer, p.255–87 (257–77).

12. Ines Lang, "Die Marienfeste und Pfingstfeiern am Wiener Hof im 17. und 18. Jahrhundert," in *Wiener Hof*, ed. I. Pangerl, M. Scheutz, and T. Winkelbauer, p.463–92. See Beales, *Joseph II*, vol.2, p.426, and vol.1, p.157–58.

of *pietas Austriaca*, which they had used to legitimize their claim to rule.[13] Several noble courtiers complained about these developments, especially about the loss of exclusive spaces like the Augarten, a former secluded baroque park in Vienna's Leopoldstadt district, and the lack of opportunities to interact with each other and the emperor.[14]

After his mother's death in 1780, Joseph made even more changes. He dismissed some of her courtiers and forced those of his siblings who still resided in Vienna to leave the capital and mostly to take residence in clerical institutions. The most consequential of his ceremonial reforms was his refusal to be crowned in Hungary and Bohemia, and his decision therefore not to perform the ceremonies that traditionally made the composite nature of the monarchy manifest. Joseph openly despised this as a sign of backwardness and ordered that the crown of Hungary simply be sent to Vienna and stored in the treasury.[15] Many Hungarian nobles saw this as an insult to the kingdom, but Joseph seemed indifferent about whether his behavior provoked the traditional elites or not. To give another example: He once commanded all nobles to come to his New Year's reception in simple, plain dress, giving them only two days' warning.[16] This was widely considered shockingly rude, because many courtiers had already invested heavily in new dresses, jewelry, and other items to show their status.

Joseph's reforms were certainly dramatic, considering how important court life and ceremony were for the elites. He reduced the number of important opportunities to represent and therefore create or stabilize hierarchies and prestige. However, and especially in a composite monarchy like the Habsburg Empire, a central court was of highest importance to bind nobles from different lands together and to harness their power and connections for the benefit of the central authority. This is why, though he certainly changed a lot, Joseph also abided by a number of traditional elements. As the ceremonial protocols show, although he simplified dress code and procedures, he kept quite a number of ceremonies and court events in place, especially

13. Evans, "Habsburgs," p.136.
14. Frank Huss, *Der Wiener Kaiserhof, eine Kulturgeschichte von Leopold I. bis Leopold II.* (Gernsbach, 2008), p.198–99; Jeroen Duindam, *Vienna and Versailles: the courts of Europe's dynastic rivals, 1550–1780* (Cambridge, 2003), p.211.
15. Beales, *Joseph II*, vol.2, p.57–63.
16. Beales, *Joseph II*, vol.2, p.437.

those of the Order of the Golden Fleece.[17] Just like his predecessors, he used the order as an instrument to bestow special honor upon a selected few of his highborn subjects. And sometimes even Joseph had to compromise. In 1767, for example, he tried to abandon the ritual of washing poor men's feet, yet his mother convinced him to perform it again the next year and he continued the ritual until 1786, long after her death.[18]

It is also readily apparent when looking at the numbers that Joseph did not make many changes in personnel.[19] This is rather remarkable considering that it was common in Austria to initially dismiss all courtiers of one's predecessor and to decide later who would be reinstated and who would not.[20] Instead, when Joseph unified his and his mother's courts after his father's death in 1765, he filled the highest positions twice so that the Austrian court included more than 2000 people in 1780—the highest number to date.[21]

After his mother's death, he again confirmed all the highest court officials, department heads, and members of the Council of State (Staatsrat) in their positions.[22] There was no need for change, as Joseph had already installed his Lord Chamberlain (*Obersthofmeister*) Johann Karl, prince of Dietrichstein-Proskau-Leslie, and his favorite general Franz Moritz, count of Lacy.[23] Together with Franz Xavier Wolf, prince of Orsini-Rosenberg as Lord High Treasurer (*Oberstkämmerer*), these men built a circle of close confidants around the monarch, especially on his many journeys.[24] When in Vienna, Joseph

17. Astrid Wielach, "Die Ordensfeste der Ritter vom goldenen Vlies im Spiegel der Zeremonialprotokolle," in *Wiener Hof*, ed. I. Pangerl, M. Scheutz, and T. Winkelbauer, p.287–308; Anna-Katharina Stacher-Gfall, "Das Andreasfest des Ordens vom Goldenen Vlies im Spiegel der Zeremonialprotokolle des Wiener Hofes der Jahre 1712–1800," in *Wiener Hof*, ed. I. Pangerl, M. Scheutz, and T. Winkelbauer, p.309–36.
18. Beales, *Joseph II*, vol.1, p.157.
19. For a quick overview on the officials at court, see Reinalter, *Joseph II.*, p.38–45.
20. Huss, *Kaiserhof*, p.167–68; Duindam, *Vienna and Versailles*, p.105.
21. Duindam, *Vienna and Versailles*, p.73–74, 78. Honorary positions are excluded. Compare Hubert Ehalt, *Ausdrucksformen absolutistischer Herrschaft: der Wiener Hof im 17. und 18. Jahrhundert* (Munich, 1980), p.39.
22. Joseph changed far fewer personnel than his mother; see Beales, *Joseph II*, vol.2, p.30.
23. Gutkas, *Joseph II*, p.91, 100–101; Huss, *Kaiserhof*, p.227.
24. On Orsini-Rosenberg, see Karl Otmar Freiherr von Aretin, "Orsini und Rosenberg, Franz Xaver Wolf Fürst von," *Neue Deutsche Biographie* 19 (1999), p.596.

spent several hours every other day with a group of noblewomen of ancient, well-established families, who were married to his court nobles. The women were called the "five princesses" (*fünf Fürstinnen*).[25] By occasionally extending this group to encompass other people, he offered an exclusive place of interaction to parts of the traditional elites. Due to a lack of sources, this circle's political influence is still open to debate.[26]

There are other examples of individual nobles whose relationship to the crown simply continued, most prominently Count Kaunitz, Maria Theresa's closest counselor.[27] The reasons for this continuity may seem obvious, since Kaunitz's experience and diplomatic networks were valuable resources to any monarch. However, due to previous confrontations, Joseph must have been wary of Kaunitz's political independence. After Joseph became co-regent in 1765, he, Maria Theresa, and Kaunitz had ruled together in a complex triangle of changing alliances, in which the emperor and the chancellor threatened to withdraw from the government.[28] Despite their previous conflicts, Joseph, when he became single ruler, immediately wrote Kaunitz a personal letter asking for his support.[29] Kaunitz even became the emperor's deputy, with full authority to make decisions in Joseph's absence.[30] While Joseph relied on his chancellor in many ways, he still followed his own agenda, against the older man's advice, for example in speeding up his reforms so much that he provoked uprisings in several provinces, or in waging war against the Ottoman Empire. Joseph's obstinacy finally led to their estrangement, and as a result they never again met in person after 1787.

If the high-ranking nobles at court and government stayed in office, what happened to the common-born or newly ennobled, the middle- and lower-level courtiers? At first, Joseph reduced the number of personnel in these groups by centralizing the branches of government. Soon, however, his state reforms required more officials,

25. Huss, *Kaiserhof*, p.130; Mikoletzky, *Österreich*, p.298; Beales, *Joseph II*, vol.1, p.134–46, 324–35.
26. Beales considers these meetings as important for politics and career networks. Beales, *Joseph II*, vol.2, p.24. Most biographers quoted above mention this circle and state its importance.
27. On his career and position at court, see Klingenstein, *Der Aufstieg*; Szabo, *Kaunitz*; Aretin, "Kaunitz," p.363–69; Szabo, "Favorit," p.345–62.
28. Szabo, *Kaunitz*, p.61–63, 99–111; and Szabo, "Favorit," p.356–60.
29. Gutkas, *Joseph II*, p.222; Szabo, *Kaunitz*, p.70–71.
30. Szabo, "Favorit," p.361.

so their numbers rose again.[31] Considering these observations, it becomes apparent that the only group Joseph considered superfluous were his mother and sisters' female courtiers as well as hunting personnel. The court was thereby reduced to 1676 people in 1781 but soon grew again.[32]

What is more important than numbers is that Joseph ordered that every person's workload and behavior should be monitored and the reports sent to him personally.[33] Joseph also—and more than once—complained publicly about his own officials. His brother Leopold wrote that this sign of distrust offended the officials, so they in return sabotaged his projects.[34] Finally, Joseph irritated the officials at court and in government by establishing a close circle of commoners around him who served as secretaries and personal confidants. Leopold II called them "a bunch of mean and greedy people and lowly schemers" in a letter to his son.[35] They soon became the target of gossip among the nobles at court, who speculated about the influence they might have.[36] By choosing people without a family network, who thus completely depended on him, Joseph presented himself as being independent from the old elites and being the sole head of government.[37] By meeting in closed sessions with these secretaries, he made clear that, even though all his high-ranking officials stayed in office and were still consulted, it was he alone who was making decisions. This was part of his plan to turn the complex composite monarchy into a centralized state under one law and a single authority.

Just as every biographer describes the cutbacks at court, they also mention Joseph's new public accessibility. He granted public audiences to ordinary subjects on a daily basis. On these occasions, people could hand him petitions and talk to him personally in the

31. Duindam, *Vienna and Versailles*, p.82.
32. Duindam, *Vienna and Versailles*, p.83.
33. This was never really applied throughout the monarchy; see Mikoletzky, *Österreich*, p.326–27, 332–33. See also Beales, *Joseph II*, vol.2, p.46–47, 339; Michael Erbe, *Deutsche Geschichte 1713–1790: Dualismus und aufgeklärter Absolutismus* (Stuttgart, 1985), p.135.
34. Beales, *Joseph II*, vol.2, p.351–52.
35. "eine Clique gemeiner und habsüchtiger Personen und niedriger Intriganten," quoted in Hans Wagner, *Wien von Maria Theresia bis zur Franzosenzeit: aus den Tagebüchern des Grafen Karl v. Zinzendorf* (Vienna, 1972), p.48–49.
36. Erbe, *Geschichte*, p.136; Gutkas, *Joseph II*, p.258.
37. Blanning, *Joseph II*, p.61–63.

corridor outside his cabinet. There, he met several hundred people every month. This procedure has been interpreted as a new form of direct interaction between the ruler and his subjects with the potential to seriously weaken the influence of traditional networks.[38] However, a closer look at the effects of these audiences shows that they posed no threat to the established elites.[39] Joseph mostly just handed the petitions over to the proper authorities. He did, however, use them as an empirical background to strengthen his position in debates with his highest officials if these documents supported his previously held opinions. Thus, the public audiences were more a spectacle and an instrument to promote the image of a caring monarch.

His ostentatious approachability and his readiness to ignore traditions show that he deliberately fashioned himself as a "new" monarch, as a prince who lived for the ideals of a reform based on reason, to ensure and improve public welfare.[40] It is remarkable, however, that Joseph did not promote this image of himself by publishing books or keeping in close contact with famous authors, as other monarchs considered to be enlightened reformers had done. What Joseph did was to declare a certain liberty of the press (*Press-Freyheit*) in 1781.[41] This loosening of censorship brought him wide support, and several authors were willing to praise him and his reforms. Many of them were part of pro-reform networks in the monarchy and beyond, and considered themselves to be members of "the" Enlightenment while, in their conversations, they shaped their own idea about what Enlightenment meant and who was and was not part of it. Thus, although censorship was not completely abolished, Joseph won public support, at least at first. Despite his celebrated image as a reformer, he was ready to compromise and to guarantee a level of continuity to members of the high nobility who assured him of their support. Joseph expressed his own opinion on the ambiguity between his real behavior and his publicly proclaimed beliefs in a letter to his brother Leopold, in which he called himself "a charlatan of reason and modesty."[42]

---

38. On the importance of restricting access at the Austrian court, see John Spielman, *The City and the crown: Vienna and the imperial court, 1600–1740* (West Lafayette, IN, 1993), p.57–58.
39. Beales, *Joseph II*, vol.2, p.20, 143–51, 435–36.
40. Joseph followed the example of Peter I of Russia, Charles XII of Sweden, and Frederick William I of Prussia; see Beales, *Joseph II*, vol.2, p.49.
41. On Joseph's approach to censorship, see Karstens, *Sonnenfels*, p.216–26.
42. Beales, *Joseph II*, vol.2, p.312.

Fighting crime instead of preventing crime: the police reforms of Joseph II (1765–1790)

Already during Joseph's co-regency, Joseph von Sonnenfels, professor of cameralism (*Kameralwissenschaft*), promoted the establishment of a welfare police that would reduce the number of criminals in the country by applying public welfare programs such as health care.[43] Sonnenfels was supported by Councilor Greiner, the father of Caroline Pichler, who had a close connection to Maria Theresa. This police system included several decentralized layers of administration to organize the literal enlightenment of the city at night, public safety, health care, housing and building, and traffic. A crime-fighting criminal police was just one of many parts of this vast machine. By 1776, this system was in place (in Vienna, at least), but turned out to be very expensive.

Two years after Joseph became sole ruler, in 1782, the police changed drastically.[44] Johann Anton Pergen, a protégé of Kaunitz, approached the monarch with the help of his wife, who gave him access to the circle of the "five princesses."[45] Pergen argued for a cheaper, centralized police system focused on the surveillance of foreigners and the defense of the state instead of public welfare. In 1782, he convinced Joseph to appoint him head of the police, in addition to his position as head of government (*Landesmarschall*) of Lower Austria. Pergen established a police bureau whose leader was a protégé of his own, concerned solely with matters of security, while the broader aspects of the welfare police were handed over to different branches of the local government on a low budget. Greiner and Sonnenfels argued against these changes, yet their protest was in vain, due to Joseph's open support for Pergen. He even allowed Pergen to present reports directly to him at any time, and made him accountable

43. For further references, see Karstens, *Sonnenfels*, p.345–54. For an overview, see Gutkas, *Joseph II*, p.239–41; Ernst Wangermann, *From Joseph II to the Jacobin trials: government policy and public opinion in the Habsburg dominions in the period of the French Revolution* (London, 1969).

44. Paul Bernard, *From the Enlightenment to the police state: the public life of Johann Anton Pergen* (Urbana, IL, 1991), p.127–71. Compare Karstens, *Sonnenfels*, p.354–59. Beales explicitly takes a position against the works of Wangermann and Reinalter, by stating that the police system was without much effect during Joseph's reign. Beales, *Joseph II*, vol.2, p.552–54.

45. On his wife's networking, see Wagner, *Wien*, p.37; Bernard, *Pergen*, p.124. On his connection to Kaunitz: Bernard, *Pergen*, p.64–68.

to no one but himself. At first, Joseph showed only occasional interest in these reports. However, with tensions rising after his reforms provoked unrest, he took a keen interest in having foreigners and suspicious activities monitored. Taking advantage of this situation, Pergen extended the use of a special procedure for political criminals (*Staatsverbrecher*), who could be incarcerated and interrogated without the involvement of a court of law.[46] It is important to note that Joseph, who had granted the press more liberties than any of his predecessors, supported this violation of his own penal law code. He even expanded Pergen's influence into other cities, especially in Hungary, and gave him authority to limit the much-celebrated freedom of the press after 1786. Whenever Pergen faced resistance, he stated that he answered only to the emperor himself, and that any complaints should be directed to the court. Yet, before Pergen's system was fully established, the emperor fell gravely ill.

Reacting to crisis: court policy and police reforms of Leopold II (1790–1792)

When Joseph died in 1790, the monarchy was in turmoil due to his attempts at centralization: The Southern Netherlands were in open rebellion, and dissension in Hungary was rising so high that some noblemen conspired with Prussia and others publicly celebrated his death.[47] In Vienna especially, his reforms concerning the Church and public religious practice had alienated the local population and were openly criticized.[48]

When Joseph's heir, Grand Duke Leopold of Tuscany, was called to Vienna by his dying brother to ease the transition, he claimed to be sick and refused to travel.[49] He preferred not to be connected to a despised regime, so that he could claim to personify a fresh start once he came to court. After his arrival, he immediately made his own approach to politics visible to his subjects and especially the elites in court life and ceremonies. First, Leopold met with a deputation of the estates and asked for their grievances. Secondly, he invited noblemen who had resigned because of his brother's reform policy to come back

---

46. Bernard, *Pergen*, p.153.
47. Fink, *Joseph II.*, p.298.
48. See for example the pamphlet by Joseph Richter, *Warum wird Kaiser Joseph von seinem Volke nicht geliebt?* (Vienna, Wucherer, 1787).
49. Fejtö, *Joseph II.*, p.398.

to court and into government.[50] In addition, he called for a meeting of the Hungarian Diet, and expressed his wish to swear a solemn oath in a traditional coronation ceremony to uphold the kingdom's liberties and privileges.[51] The reaction was very positive, and the estates even elected a relative of Leopold as his deputy in Hungary. He also arranged for his and his wife's coronation as rulers of Bohemia in Prague. The message was clear: Unlike his brother, he respected the composite nature of the monarchy. In her autobiography, Caroline Pichler described how she and her peers had expected a return to the "good old days" due to the new ruler's respect for the Church and family values.[52] Her description, published in 1844, illustrates the contrast between an overzealous Joseph and a more careful Leopold that was established in the historiography.

Leopold indeed established a more vibrant court life and held a classic, family-centered court. Although he did not fully restore the situation as it had been before 1765, he still celebrated more religious holidays and also invited the nobles to balls and carnival.[53] He also resumed the ritual of washing poor men's feet that his brother had abandoned in 1786.[54] Moreover, Leopold reestablished the classic order of ceremony for the festivities of the Order of the Golden Fleece.[55] On some occasions, he also allowed hand-kissing and the traditional formal dress. On others, however, he kept simplifications in place. The final aspect of returning to the old ways was to reduce public accessibility to his person, for example by planting hedges in the Augarten.[56] At the same time, Leopold denied former accessibility to the nobles by formally separating his private living space and the ceremonial state apartments.[57]

50. Adam Wandruszka, *Leopold II.: Erzherzog von Österreich, Grossherzog von Toskana, König von Ungarn und Böhmen, Römischer Kaiser*, 2 vols. (Vienna, 1965), vol.2, p.255.
51. Wandruszka, *Leopold II.*, vol.2, p.302.
52. "so hoffte ich denn von Kaiser Leopolds Familientugenden, von seiner Achtung für häusliches Glück [...] Wiederherstellung der alten guten Zeit, vermehrte Sittlichkeit, Achtung für Religion." Pichler, *Denkwürdigkeiten*, p.182.
53. Wandruszka, *Leopold II.*, vol.2, p.328; Lang, "Marienfeste," p.482.
54. Johanna Atzmansdorfer *et al.*, "Much of the same? Das Leben am Hof im Spiegel der Zeremonialprotokolle (1652–1800)," in *Wiener Hof*, ed. I. Pangerl, M. Scheutz, and T. Winkelbauer, p.229–54 (248).
55. Stacher-Gfall, "Andreasfest," p.326.
56. Atzmansdorfer *et al.*, "Much of the same," p.248; Wagner, *Wien*, p.45.
57. Duindam, *Vienna and Versailles*, p.212. Pangerl, "Höfische Öffentlichkeit," p.277–78.

Restoring traditional court protocol and practices was made easy by Leopold's decision to refrain from replacing key noble personnel, just like his brother had.[58] He dismissed all of his brother's lowborn personal servants and secretaries right away, though.[59] This decision served a double purpose: It symbolized a fresh start and also satisfied the noblemen. His brother's close confidants of noble birth faced no such treatment, of course. Orsini-Rosenberg, for example, remained Lord High Treasurer (*Oberstkämmerer*), and also took up political duties as a leading member of the Council of State (*Staats- und Konferenzminister*).[60] In fact, Leopold kept all high-ranking officials in office, most prominently his mother's and brother's expert on foreign relations, Kaunitz. Just like his brother Joseph, Leopold appointed Kaunitz his deputy in case of his own absence.[61] However, it soon became obvious that the sovereign and the chancellor pursued different agendas.[62] So, though the chancellor and his network officially stayed in power, they effectively lost influence on the grand design of foreign policy.

A closer look at Leopold's police reforms will further elucidate the balance between tradition and reform that he tried to establish.[63] He kept Pergen in office, but reduced his influence—especially in Hungary—and ordered supervision of his work. Leopold amnestied the political criminals (*Staatsverbrecher*), who had been held without trial, and issued an order to inspect living conditions in prisons. When Pergen's complaints about this interference were ignored, the count asked to be dismissed on the pretense of health issues. Leopold accepted and again installed a revised form of the former welfare-police. He commissioned the old expert Sonnenfels to write a new police law, to establish a system of free health care, and to create a public police force to protect the people.[64]

58. Wandruszka, *Leopold II.*, vol.2, p.249–52.
59. Gutkas, *Joseph II*, p.258, 383; Wandruszka, *Leopold II.*, vol.2, p.253.
60. Aretin, "Orsini," p.596.
61. Szabo, "Favorit," p.361.
62. Ernst Wangermann, "Kaunitz und der Krieg gegen das Revolutionäre Frankreich," in *Staatskanzler Wenzel Anton von Kaunitz Rietberg: neue Perspektiven zu Politik und Kultur der europäischen Aufklärung*, ed. Grete Klingenstein and Franz Szabo (Graz, 1996), p.131–41.
63. Karstens, *Sonnenfels*, p.359–64; Wandruszka, *Leopold II.*, vol.2, p.238, 276–79, 337–41; Bernard, *Pergen*, p.171–80.
64. Wangermann, *Trials*, p.96–97; Osterloh, *Reformbewegung*, p.150–55; Wandruszka, *Leopold II.*, vol.2, p.339.

However, there was a dark side to this reform. Leopold kept several of Pergen's agents in his service and created his own network of secret informants, spying on Hungarian officers but also watching over the activities of freemasons and Illuminati in Vienna. This network included several rather dubious characters, like some of Sonnenfels's academic rivals, who claimed they had seen the sixty-year-old professor climbing the roofs of Vienna at night in a cloak and mask to prepare an Illuminati uprising.[65] Although Leopold never acted on the information he received through this network, he protected and supported his informants. Some of his agents supported their patron in return and published a journal to glorify Leopold's reign and to discredit what they saw as wrong and overzealous Enlightenment.[66] Leopold supported their effort by handing them official documents for publication and publicly shaming authors who acted against his supporters.[67]

A return to the old ways? Court policy and police reforms of Francis II (1792–1835)

All this came to an end when the emperor suddenly died. He left the Habsburg monarchy in a better position than his brother had, but the French Revolution and the aftermath of the uprisings in Belgium and Hungary still made for a very tense political situation. Therefore, as Caroline Pichler wrote, many people were worried about Francis's youth—he was twenty-four—and inexperience.[68] Her description, published in 1844, created the image of a young prince facing hard times, and made it seem natural to her readers that he would look for guidance. Indeed, Francis, confronted with the challenge of war, really did put his trust in experience. Several of his highest courtiers and government officials had been in service since the reign of his grandmother. One reason for this may have been that Joseph had educated his nephew in Vienna and required that Francis participate

---

65. Karstens, *Sonnenfels*, p.123–44.
66. Wandruszka, *Leopold II.*, vol.2, p.377–80; see also Helmut Reinalter, "Gegen die 'Tollwuth der Aufklärungsbarbarei': Leopold Alois Hoffmann und der frühe Konservativismus in Österreich," in *Von "Obscuranten" und "Eudämonisten": Gegenaufklärerische, konservative und antirevolutionäre Publizisten im späten 18. Jahrhundert*, ed. Christoph Weiß and Reiner Wild (St. Ingbert, 1999), p.221–44.
67. Karstens, *Sonnenfels*, p.123–45; compare Gerda Lettner, *Das Rückzugsgefecht der Aufklärung in Wien 1790–1792* (Frankfurt am Main, 1988).
68. Pichler, *Denkwürdigkeiten*, p.184.

in council sessions, so that the young emperor knew the established court elites.[69] Naturally, Francis also kept Kaunitz, with whom he had ruled for a couple of weeks between the death of Joseph and the arrival of Leopold.

In court life, Francis made it obvious that he was a preserver of tradition, although he shared his father's preference for a rather simple family life separated from official ceremonies. He organized a formal coronation in Hungary and his court grew in numbers until, in 1796, it encompassed 1881 people, making it almost as big as the court of Joseph II in 1780.[70] This number is particularly remarkable since Francis's mother died early, so there was no need for a dowager-empress court. Despite the deaths of two emperors and one empress, Francis, like his father, seems to have valued celebrations more than mourning. The ceremonial protocols show only twenty-two events related to mourning, compared to fifty-eight celebrations of inaugurations in from 1790 to 1792.[71]

Just like Joseph, Francis installed a group of very few close confidants in his personal cabinet, though he chose them from among the high nobility. The most interesting of these was his old teacher, Count Colloredo-Waldsee.[72] Because of his direct access to the emperor, he rose to a powerful position outside of the official hierarchy. However, this was just a gradual shift of power, not a change in the established ways in which policy was made. Simultaneously, Kaunitz had to deal with the ambitions of his own assistants and withdrew from office, aged eighty-one, in August 1792.[73] But Francis was not ready to sever all ties. He let Kaunitz keep his apartment in the government building, called the *Staatskanzlei*, and ordered that the pensioner be briefed on all new developments. Therefore, the old chancellor still sent reports and analyses until his death in 1794.[74]

It is well known that Francis's policy concerning the police was guided by a general fear of French agents and a spreading revolution.[75]

---

69. Aretin, "Orsini," p.596.
70. Duindam, *Vienna and Versailles*, p.83.
71. Atzmansdorfer, "Much of the same," p.247.
72. Betrand Buchmann, *Hof, Regierung, Stadtverwaltung: Wien als Sitz der österreichischen Zentralverwaltung von den Anfängen bis zum Untergang der Monarchie* (Munich, 2002), p.82.
73. Michael Hochedlinger, "Das Ende der Ära Kaunitz in der Staatskanzlei," in *Kaunitz*, ed. G. Klingenstein and F. Szabo, p.117–31 (126–27).
74. Hochedlinger, "Ära Kaunitz," p.126.
75. Bernard, *Pergen*, p.180–200; Karstens, *Sonnenfels*, p.364–68.

Therefore, he wanted a strong and well-controlled police force. He disbanded his father's informal network of dubious secret informants and stopped supporting their publications.[76] Thus, instead of using the public sphere to promote policies he considered good for the state, as his father had begun to do, he preferred to strengthen censorship.

Francis's attitude made certain people in the government believe in a window of opportunity. Several officials, mostly former protégés and partners of Pergen, opposed the established welfare police and advocated the return to a secret police under their own control.[77] Confronted with different propositions by Sonnenfels and the former associates of Pergen, Francis turned to the old police expert himself for counsel. Unsurprisingly, Pergen, who had officially kept his distance, favored the reinstitution of his own police regime, which offered to incarcerate more criminals at less cost and supply constant information about potential conspiracies. Francis accepted his proposal and reinstated Pergen as head of the police.[78] The count quickly reestablished his system, and was able to use the rather unspectacular conspiracy of the so-called Vienna Jacobins to further strengthen it.

To understand the reception of the changing directions of the Austrian police, it is important to remember that Sonnenfels was well established as a leading figure of those who considered themselves to embody an Austrian Enlightenment. Pergen instead had a much more court-centered network, and did not publish his writings. When Francis pushed Sonnenfels to the sidelines and promoted Pergen, this was therefore seen as a sign of distancing himself from the Enlightenment, regardless of the actual policy pursued. This led to the process alluded to in the introduction of this chapter: Francis was regarded negatively by those who considered themselves to be men of the Enlightenment and whose works became cornerstones for the liberal historical tradition of the nineteenth century.

However, the fact that Francis's police system was later criticized as an instrument of oppression should not make one forget that efficiency, control, and rationality are core values of enlightened reform.[79] From that perspective, Sonnenfels and Pergen may not have fought a battle between enlightenment and darkness, but rather

---

76. Reinalter, "Tollwuth," p.233.
77. Wangermann, *Trials*, p.97–99; Karstens, *Sonnenfels*, p.364–66.
78. Wandruszka, *Leopold II.*, vol.2, p.341; Wangermann, *Trials*, p.124–25.
79. On the historiographical reception, see Ziegler, "Franz II.," p.289.

argued over the right pace and course for modernizing the state in the early years of Francis's reign.

Conclusion

It has become obvious that court life in the age of Enlightenment was a venue for monarchs to promote themselves either as reformers or as preservers of tradition. The publicity of court events gave this field of reform a certain level of performativity. Even though reducing numbers at court is not genuinely enlightened and had been done long before in the eighteenth century, it could be interpreted in this fashion. However, doing so created frictions with the established elites. Therefore, even Joseph II, who publicly took a radical new approach to court life, had to compromise and faced resistance when he took things too far. This is why he retained a large number of people who had come into office under his mother and who just adapted to the young monarch and his new policies. His reforms aimed at creating a centralized, well-governed monarchy, and, as the reorganization of the police has shown, he was guided by the ideal of utility and efficiency, rather than liberty.

His successor Leopold also employed the (re)organization of court life to create an image, albeit a very different one. By abolishing the most controversial reforms while keeping others in place, Leopold demonstrated that he was living a compromise between reform and tradition. This strategy was probably quite easy to implement, as many officials had been in office since Theresian times. They simply returned to a modernized version of their old values and procedures, as the example of Sonnenfels and the welfare police has proven. However, a closer look at the police system has also shown that Leopold implemented certain (albeit mostly covert) changes to collecting information and approaching the public in order to strengthen the claim that he offered the ideal balance of reform and tradition.

When Francis succeeded his father, he made continuity and tradition his key characteristics. He relied on the same corps of officials and the same noble families as his predecessors. Regarding the danger of revolution expanding from France or uprisings in his own countries, Francis profited from both his father and his uncle's work. Leopold had brought balance to the kingdoms and retied the knot with the elites. Joseph, by contrast, had shown the people that reform could come without a revolution and that too much of it, undertaken too quickly, was not desirable.[80] Joseph also set an example for an efficient and centralized police system that Francis felt he needed in an era of revolution. Thus, remarkably, both the monarch considered to be most inspired by the Enlightenment and the one considered to be most opposed to it in fact favored the same man—Pergen—and the same reform program.

This example shows that, despite all changes, the networks of power kept working and showed remarkable resilience in the face of considerable change. What contemporaries or historians considered to be enlightened reforms or conservative rollbacks was achieved with mostly the same key personnel. These individuals were neither enemies of religion and tradition, nor enemies of reforms per se, but simply well-connected courtiers who seized chances to improve their own (and their families') status and to pursue whatever policy they saw fit to ensure the monarchy's welfare. This political ambiguity of officials and courtiers connects back to the ambivalence of enlightened reform itself. Its basic elements (like statistical knowledge, rationalization, centralization, and the equality of all subjects before the law) could be used to spread liberty and reason, as well as to establish more suppression and control than the *ancien régime* ever knew.

The prevailing descriptions of the reign of Joseph II as "enlightened" and reforming and the reign of Francis II as conservative and reactionary rest on the rulers' own projection of their images. However, if one actually examines their concrete actions, for example the policing strategies presented here, then one can draw conclusions about the relationship of the court and Enlightenment that are applicable even beyond the imperial court:

— Common attributions in the historiography of rulers of the *ancien régime* to Enlightenment (Joseph II) or Counter-Enlightenment (Francis II) are often based on a few cherry-picked statements or events, rather than a comprehensive analysis of rulers' actual governing practices.

— In analyzing the governing practices, not only rulers but also their most important advisors and ministers should be considered. In this empirical case there is astonishing continuity of political personnel between the reigns of the three emperors (Joseph II, Leopold II, and Francis II). This continuity makes it improbable that these emperors pursued different political goals, and this applies for all situations in which the leading officials or figures at court or in the government

80. Blanning, *Joseph II*, p.203–204.

remained in place regardless of the succession of one ruler by another. This does not constitute factionalism along Enlightenment and Counter-Enlightenment lines; as the chapters in this volume by Andreas Pečar and Damien Tricoire show, this seems also true for the court of Versailles.

— To explain the aforementioned continuity, one might think that courtiers and government officials could simply have been opportunistically obeying their sovereigns' instructions and following their initiatives. However, this is not very convincing. The monarch was the one setting the guidelines, but he depended on the cooperation of his officials who therefore could influence his policy, as the example of court policy has shown here. This is why both statements mentioned at the beginning of this chapter, Blanning's "power was personal" and Szabo's remark on the importance of the established elites, are equally true.[81]

— As in the case of the intra-court debates about various policing strategies, Enlightenment and Counter-Enlightenment positions cannot be differentiated. Pergen and Sonnenfels both used the vocabulary of Enlightenment to make their suggestions seem plausible and appealing. These debates therefore were not conflicts between Enlightenment and Counter-Enlightenment positions, or between reform and the status quo, but rather controversies over different concepts of reform and the associated different notions of crime and punishment.[82] These arguments were carried out in the language of Enlightenment. Enlightenment thereby proves to be more of a political language with a specific vocabulary, rather than a political program on which *philosophes*, courtiers, and ministers agreed.

81. Blanning, *Joseph II*, p.60; Szabo, *Kaunitz*, p.347.
82. On the general invalidity of the idea of a "Counter-Enlightenment," see the special issue of *Eighteenth-century studies* 49:1 (2015), especially Jeremy L. Caradonna, "There was no Counter-Enlightenment," p.51–69; Graeme Garrard, "Tilting at Counter-Enlightenment windmills," p.77–81; and James Schmidt, "The Counter-Enlightenment: historical notes on a concept historians should avoid," p.83–86.

Bibliography

Pre-1800 works

Addison, John, "Proper methods of employing time," *Addison's spectator* 93 (June 16, 1711), ed. George Washington Greene (New York, 1858), p.257–61.

Agricola, Johann Friedrich, *Anleitung zur Singkunst* (Berlin, Winter, 1757).

–, *Schreiben an Herrn === in welchem Flavio Anicio Olibrio, sein Schreiben an den critischen Musikus an der Spree vertheidigt, und auf dessen Wiederlegung antwortet* (n.p., n.n., 1749).

–, *Schreiben eines reisenden Liebhabers der Musik von der Tyber, an den critischen Musikus an der Spree* (Berlin, n.n., 1749).

Albert, [Ludwig], "War das Culturgesetz, welches der Fürst Friedrich August 1775 bekannt machte, zweckmäßig?," *Möglinsche Annalen der Landwirtschaft* 20 (1827), p.96–164.

Algarotti, Francesco, *Giornale del viaggio da Londra a Petersbourg (1739)*, ed. Anna Maria dè Salva (Rome, 2015).

–, *"Okno v Evropu": Dnevnik puteshestviia iz Londona v Peterburg v 1739 godu*, ed. and translated by M. G. Talalaj (Moscow, 2016).

Anecdotes sur Madame la comtesse Du Barri (London, n.n., 1775).

Arrest de la cour de parlement qui condamne un imprimé, en dix vol. in-8°, ayant pour titre: Histoire philosophique et politique des etablissemens et du commerce des Européens dans les deux Indes, par Guillaume-Thomas Raynal; [...] à être lacéré et brûlé par l'exécuteur de la haute-justice. Extrait des registres du parlement du 25 mai 1781 (Paris, P. G. Simon, 1781).

Bacon, Francis, *The Major works*, ed. Brian Vickers (Oxford, 2008).

Belloy, Pierre Laurent de, "Le triomphe de l'amitié," Bibliothèque nationale de France (Paris), Département des manuscrits, NAF 1685, p.98.

Béranger, Raymond de, "M. Bérénger to duc de Praslin [September 27, 1762]," *Sbornik imperatorskago russkago istoricheskago obshchestva* 140 (1912), p.237–39.

Betskoy, Ivan Ivanovitch, *Plans et statuts des différents établissements ordonnés par sa majesté impériale Catherine II* (Amsterdam, Marc Michel Rey, 1775).

Botero, Giovanni, *The Reason of state*, translated by P. J. Waley and D. P. Waley (New Haven, CT, 1956).

Burney, Charles, *Memoirs of Dr. Charles Burney 1726–1769*, ed. Slava Klima, Garry Bowers, and Kerry S. Grant (Lincoln, NE, 1989).

–, *The Present state of music in Germany, the Netherlands, and United Provinces*, 2 vols. (London, Becket, 1773).

Burney, Frances, *Court journals and letters*, ed. Peter Sabor *et al.*, 6 vols. (Oxford, 2011–2019).

– (ed.), *Memoirs of Dr. Burney, arranged from his own manuscripts, from family papers and from personal recollections*, 3 vols. (London, 1832).

Castiglione, Baldassare, *The Courtier*, ed. and translated by George Bull (London, 2003).

[Catherine II, tsarina of Russia], "Catherine to Grimm [August 10, 1785]," ed. J. Grot, *Sbornik imperatorskago russkago istoricheskago obshchestva* 23 (1878), p.358–59.

[–], "Catherine II to Potemkin [July 14, 1789]," *Sbornik imperatorskago russkago istoricheskago obshchestva* 42 (1885), p.21–23.

[–], "Catherine II to Gabriel Sénac de Meilhan [July 1791]," *Sbornik imperatorskago russkago istoricheskago obshchestva* 42 (1885), p.166–67.

Caussin, Nicolas, *La Cour sainte, tome second: contenant les vies et les eloges des personnes illustres de la cour, tant du vieil que du nouveau testament, divisées en cinq ordres: les monarques et princes, les reines et dames, les cavaliers, les hommes d'Estat, les hommes de Dieu* (Paris, J. Dubray, 1653).

Consett, Thomas, "The present state and regulations of the Church of Russia (1729)," in *For God and Peter the Great: the works of Thomas Consett, 1723–1729*, ed. James Cracraft (Boulder, CO, 1962).

Constituciones de El Real Seminario de Nobles (Madrid, Gabriel del Barrio, 1730).

Corneille, Pierre, *Cinna*, in *Œuvres complètes: Corneille*, ed. Georges Couton, 3 vols. (Paris, 1980–1987), vol.1, p.905–69.

Desforges, P.-J.-B. Choudard, known as, *Le Poète, ou Mémoires d'un homme de lettres, écrits par lui-même*, 4 vols. (Hamburg, n.n., 1798).

Diderot, Denis, *Correspondance*, ed. Georges Roth and Jean Varloot, 16 vols. (Paris, 1955–1970).

–, *Essai sur les règnes de Claude et de Néron*, in Denis Diderot, *Œuvres complètes*, ed. Jean Deprun and H. Dieckmann, 33 vols. (Paris, 1975–), vol.25 (1986).

–, *Leçons de clavecin et principes d'harmonie*, in Denis Diderot, *Œuvres complètes*, ed. Jean Deprun and H. Dieckmann, 33 vols. (Paris, 1975–), vol.19 (1983).

–, *Œuvres complètes de Diderot*, ed. J. Assézat, 20 vols. (Paris, 1875–1877).

Esterhazy, Valentin, *Lettres du c[om]te Esterhazy à sa femme: 1784–1792*, ed. Ernest Daudet (Paris, 1907).
Europäischer Staats-Secretarius 117 (1746).

Faure, abbé Otto-Anne, *Discours sur le progrès des beaux arts en Russie* (n.p., n.n., 1760).
"Folgendes Schreiben an den Herrn Verfasser des Kritischen Musicus an der Spree ist uns zur Einrückung zugefertiget," *Freye Urtheile u. Nachrichten zum Aufnehmen der Wissenschaften und der Historie überhaupt* 7:38 (May 12, 1750), p.289–95.
Fontenelle, Bernard de, *Conversations on the plurality of worlds* (London, n.n., 1760).
Frederick II, king of Prussia, *Memoirs of the house of Brandenburg: from the earliest accounts, to the death of Frederick I. king of Prussia* (London, J. Nourse, 1751).
Füssel, Johann Michael, "1784: Johann Michael Füssel," in *Lustgärten um Bayreuth: Eremitage, Sanspareil und Fantaisie in Beschreibungen aus dem 18. und 19. Jahrhundert*, ed. Ingo Toussaint (Hildesheim, 1998), p.164–68.

Garnovskii, Mikhail, "Zapiski: 1786–1790," *Russkaia starina* 15:7 (1876), p.399–440.
Golitsyn, Fiodor N., "Zapiski kniazia Fiodora Nikolaevicha Golitsyna," ed. Piotr Bartenev,

Russkii arkhiv 24:5 (1874), col.1271–1336.
Gottsched, Johann Christoph, *Beobachtungen über den Gebrauch und Mißbrauch vieler deutscher Wörter und Redensarten* (Strasbourg and Leipzig, Johann Amandus Königen, 1758).

Harrington, James, *The Commonwealth of Oceana and a system of politics*, ed. John G. A. Pocock (Cambridge, 1992).
Hedenus, Markus Friedrich, "1749: Markus Friedrich Hedenus," in *Lustgärten um Bayreuth: Eremitage, Sanspareil und Fantaisie in Beschreibungen aus dem 18. und 19. Jahrhundert*, ed. Ingo Toussaint (Hildesheim, 1998), p.149–57.
–, "1768: Markus Friedrich Hedenus," in *Lustgärten um Bayreuth: Eremitage, Sanspareil und Fantaisie in Beschreibungen aus dem 18. und 19. Jahrhundert*, ed. Ingo Toussaint (Hildesheim, 1998), p.159–62.
Hrapovitskii, Aleksandr, *Dnevnik A. V. Hrapovitskogo: 1782–1793* (St. Petersburg, 1874).
Huber, Therese (ed.), *Johann Georg Forster's Briefwechsel: nebst einigen Nachrichten von seinem Leben*, 2 vols. (Leipzig, 1929).
Huygens, Christiaan, *Kniga mirozreniia, ili Mnenie O nebesnozemnykh globusakh, i ikh ukrasheniiakh* (Moscow, n.n., 1724).

Jamerai Duval, Valentin, *Oeuvres de Valentin Jamerai Duval: précédées des mémoires sur sa vie* (St. Petersburg, n.n., 1784).

Journal historique de la révolution opérée dans la constitution de la monarchie françoise, par M. de Maupeou, chancelier de France [from vol.6 onward: *Journal historique du rétablissement de la magistrature*], 7 vols. (London, John Adamson, 1774–1776).

Jovellanos, Gaspar Melchor de, *Espectáculos y diversiones públicas: informe sobre la ley agraria*, ed. Guillermo Carnero (Madrid, 1998).

–, "Memoria sobre educación pública," in *Obras completas de Gaspar Melchor Jovellanos*, vol.13: *Escritos pedagógicos, 1º*, ed. Olegario Negrín Fajardo (Gijón, 2010), p.435–532.

Kamer-fur'erskie tseremonial'nye zhurnaly za 1789 g., vol.7 ([St. Petersburg], n.n., n.d.).

Kant, Immanuel, "An answer to the question: what is Enlightenment?" in *What is Enlightenment? Eighteenth-century answers and twentieth-century questions*, ed. James Schmidt (Berkeley, CA, 1996), p.58–64.

La Bruyère, Jean de, *Les Caractères, ou les Mœurs de ce siècle* (1688; Paris, 1994).

Leibniz, Gottfried Wilhelm, *Political writings*, ed. Patrick Riley, 2nd ed. (Cambridge, 1988).

Lettres originales de Madame la comtesse du Barry, avec celles des princes, seigneurs, ministres et autres qui lui ont écrit, et qu'on a pu recueillir (London, John Adamson, 1779).

Llanover, Augusta Hall, Lady (ed.), *The Autobiography and correspondence of Mary Granville, Mrs Delany*, 6 vols. (London, 1860–1861).

Marpurg, Friedrich Wilhelm, *Anleitung zur Singcomposition* (Berlin, Lange, 1758).

–, "Hochzuehrender Herr Criticus," *Der critische Musicus an der Spree* 1:5 (April 1, 1749), p.33–40.

–, "Lebensläufe: Joh. Friedr. Agricola," *Historisch=kritische Beyträge zur Aufname der Musik* 1:2 (1754), p.148–52.

–, *Raccolta delle più nuove composizioni di clavicembalo: di differenti maestri ed autori per l'anno 1756*, 2 vols. (Leipzig, Breitkopf, 1756–1757).

–, "Schreiben aus Paris über den Streit daselbst zwischen den französischen und welschen Tonkünstern: aus dem Französischen übersetzt," *Historisch=kritische Beyträge zur Aufname der Musik* 1:2 (1754), p.160–66.

–, "Schreiben eines reisenden Liebhabers der Musik von der Tyber, an den critischen Musikus an der Spree," *Der critische Musicus an der Spree* 1:4 (March 25, 1749), p.25–32.

–, *Sendschreiben an die Herren Verfasser der freyen Urtheile in Hamburg, das Schreiben an den Herrn Verfasser des kritischen Musikus an der Spree betreffend* (Berlin, n.n., 1750).

–, "Über den Stellenwert deutscher Musik und Musiker," *Der critische*

Musicus an der Spree 1:1 (March 4, 1749), p.1–8.

Mémoires authentiques de la comtesse de Barré, maîtresse de Louis XV, roi de France, extraits d'un manuscrit que possède la duchesse de Villeroy: par le chevalier Fr. N.; traduits de l'anglois (London [Paris?], chez J. Roson, 1772).

Mémoires secrets pour servir a l'histoire de la republique des lettres en France: depuis MDCCLXII jusqu'a nos jours, ou Journal d'un observateur, 36 vols. (London [Amsterdam?], John Adamson, 1777–1789).

Metastasio, Pietro, *La Clemenza di Tito*, in *Drammi per musica*, ed. A. L. Bellina, 3 vols. (Venice, 2000–2004), vol.2, p.433–34.

Montesquieu, Charles-Louis de, *The Spirit of laws*, in *The Complete works of M. de Montesquieu*, 4 vols. (London, printed for T. Evans and W. Davis, 1777).

L'Observateur anglois, ou Correspondance secrete entre milord All'eye et milord Alle'ar, 10 vols. (London [Amsterdam], John Adamson, 1777–1784).

Palissot de Montenoy, Charles, *Les Philosophes: comédie* (Paris, Duchesne, 1760).

Pezold, Johann Sigismund von, "Pezold to Brühl [March 2, 1743]," *Sbornik imperatorskago russkago istoricheskago obshchestva* 6 (1871), p.479–83.

Polnoe sobranie zakonov Rossiiskoi Imperii, vol.16 (St. Petersburg, 1830).

Pufendorf, Samuel, *On the duty of man and citizen according to natural law*, ed. James Tully (Cambridge, 1991).

Raguenet, François, and Johann Mattheson, "Eine Vergleichung zwischen den Italiänern und Franzosen betreffend die Music und Opern: Vorbericht," *Critica musica* 1:4 (August 1722), p.[105]–18, *Critica musica* 1:5 (September 1722), p.[121]–47, and *Critica musica* 1:6 (October 1722), p.[153]–66.

Raynal, Guillaume-Thomas, *Histoire philosophique et politique des établissemens et du commerce des Européens dans les deux Indes*, 10 vols. (Geneva, Pellet, 1780).

Richter, Joseph, *Warum wird Kaiser Joseph von seinem Volke nicht geliebt?* (Vienna, Wucherer, 1787).

Rousseau, Jean-Jacques, *The Social contract and discourses*, ed. G. D. H. Cole (London, 1973).

Saint-Simon, Louis de Rouvroy de, *Mémoires complets et authentiques du duc de Saint-Simon sur le siècle de Louis XIV et la Régence*, 40 vols. (Paris, 1840).

Scheibe, Johann Adolph, "Die Haupteintheilung der Musik wird angezeiget und untersuchet," *Der critische Musicus: neue, vermehrte und verbesserte Auflage* 1:3 (April 2, 1737), p.29–38.

Schlözer, August Ludwig, *August Ludwig Schlözers öffentliches und Privatleben, von ihm selbst berschrieben: erstes Fragment* (Göttingen, 1802).

–, *Obshchestvennaia i chastnaia zhizn' Avgusta Ludviga Shletsera, im samim opisannaia* (St. Petersburg, 1875).

Schmohl, Johann Christian, "Briefe an Herrn Pstlzz [...] über den Zustand der Landwirth-schaft und des Bauerstandes im Fürstenthum Anhalt," in *Sammlung von Aufsätzen verschiedner Verfasser besonders für Freunde der Cameralwissenschaften und der Staatswirthschaft* (Leipzig, Schwickert, 1781), p.199–340.

–, "Kameralische Reise durch das Fürstenthum Anhalt," in *Sammlung von Aufsätzen verschiedner Verfasser besonders für Freunde der Cameralwissenschaften und der Staatswirthschaft* (Leipzig, Schwickert, 1781), p.356–418.

–, *Sammlung von Aufsätzen verschiedner Verfasser besonders für Freunde der Cameralwissenschaften und der Staatswirthschaft* (Leipzig, Schwickert, 1781).

Shaftesbury, Anthony Ashley Cooper, earl of, *Characteristicks of men, manners, opinions, times*, ed. Philip Ayres, 2 vols. (1711; Oxford, 1999).

Shcherbatov, Mikhail M., *On the corruption of morals in Russia*, ed. and translated by A. Lentin (New York, 1969).

Shishkov, Aleksandr S., "Dostopa-miatnye skazaniia ob Imperatritse Ekaterine Velikoi," in *Reka vremion: kniga istorii i kul'tury*, ed. Konstantin Bolenko and Ekaterina Liamina, 5 vols. (Moscow, 1996), vol.4, p.20–56.

–, "Nechto o rossiiskoi imperatritse Ekaterine Vtoroi," in Aleksandr

S. Shishkov, *Zapiski, mneniia i perepiska admirala A. S. Shishkova*, 2 vols. (Berlin, 1870), vol.2, p.298–303.

Sumarokov, Aleksandr, *Polnoe sobranie vsekh sochinenii, v stihah i proze*, 2nd ed., 10 vols. (Moscow, Universitetskaia tipografiia u N. Novikova, 1787).

Vargas Ponce, José de, "Plan para la educación de la nobleza y clases pudientes españolas," in *Obras completas de Gaspar Melchor Jovellanos*, vol.14: *Escritos pedagógicos, 2º*, ed. Olegario Negrín Fajardo (Gijón, 2010), p.1181–1240.

Voltaire, *Correspondence and related documents*, ed. Theodore Besterman, in *The Complete works of Voltaire*, vol.85–135 (Oxford, 1968–1977).

Wagner, Hans, *Wien von Maria Theresia bis zur Franzosenzeit: aus den Tagebüchern des Grafen Karl v. Zinzendorf* (Vienna, 1972).

Wolff, Adolph Friedrich, "Entwurf einer ausführlichen Nachricht von der Musikübenden Gesellschaft zu Berlin," *Historisch-Kritische Beyträge zur Aufnahme der Musik* 1:5 (1755), p.385–413.

Wolff, Christian, *Briefe von Christian Wolff aus den Jahren 1719–1753: ein Beitrag zur Geschichte der Kaiser-lichen Academie der Wissenschaften zu St. Petersburg* (St. Petersburg, 1860).

–, *The Real happiness of a people under a philosophical king demonstrated* (London, n.n., 1750).

Post-1800 works

Abellán, José Luis, *Historia crítica del pensamiento español*, vol.3: *Del Barroco a la Ilustración (Siglos XVII y XVIII)* (Madrid, 1988).

Abrosimov, Kirill, *Aufklärung jenseits der Öffentlichkeit: Friedrich Melchior Grimms Correspondance littéraire (1753–1773) zwischen der "république des lettres" und europäischen Fürstenhöfen* (Ostfildern, 2014).

Adamson, John (ed.), *The Princely courts of Europe: ritual, politics and culture under the ancien régime 1500–1750* (London, 1999).

Adkins, G. Matthew, *The Idea of the sciences in the French Enlightenment: a reinterpretation* (Newark, DE, 2013).

Agamben, Giorgio, *The Kingdom and the glory: for a theological genealogy of economy and government*, translated by Lorenzo Chiesa (Stanford, CA, 2011).

–, *Opus Dei: an archaeology of duty*, translated by Adam Kotsko (Stanford, CA, 2013).

Agnew, Vanessa, *Enlightenment Orpheus: the power of music in other worlds* (New York, 2008).

Aguilar Piñal, Francisco, "Los Reales Seminarios de Nobles en la política ilustrada española," *Cuadernos Hispanoamericanos* 356 (February 1980), p.329–49.

Alexander, John T., "Amazon autocratrixes: images of female rule in the eighteenth century," in *Gender and sexuality in Russian civilisation*, ed. Peter I. Barta (London, 2001), p.33–54.

–, *Catherine the Great: life and legend* (New York, 1989).

–, "Favorites, favouritism and female rule in Russia: 1725–1796," in *Russia in the age of the Enlightenment*, ed. Roger Bartlett and Janet Hartley (London, 1990), p.106–24.

–, "Politics, passions, patronage: Catherine II and Petr Zavadovskii," in *Russia and the world of the eighteenth century*, ed. Roger P. Bartlett et al. (Columbus, OH, 1988), p.616–33.

Álvarez Barrientos, Joaquín, "El siglo XVIII, según Menéndez Pelayo," *Boletín de la Biblioteca de Menéndez Pelayo* 82 (2006), p.297–329.

Álvarez Junco, José, *Mater dolorosa: la idea de España en el siglo XIX* (Madrid, 2016).

Álvarez-Ossorio, Antonio, "Corte y cortesanos en la monarquía de España," in *Educare Il corpo, educare la parola nella trattatistica del Rinascimento*, ed. Giorgio Patrizi and Amedeo Quondam (Rome, 1998), p.297–365.

Anderberg, Göran, *Frimuraren Gustaf III: bakgrund, visioner, konspirationer, traditioner* (Partille, 2009).

Andreu, Xavier, "Figuras modernas del deseo: las majas de Ramón de la Cruz y los orígenes del majismo," *Ayer* 78:2 (2010), p.25–34.

Andrew, Edward G., *Patrons of the Enlightenment* (Toronto, 2006).

Andújar Castillo, Francisco, "El Seminario de Nobles de Madrid en el siglo XVIII: un estudio social," *Cuadernos de Historia Moderna: Anejos* 3 (2004), p.201–25.

Anisimov, Evgenii, *Dyba i knut: politicheskii sysk v Rossii v XVIII veke* (Moscow, 1999).

Arcelli, Clelia (ed.), *I saperi nelle corti: knowledge at the courts* (Florence, 2008).

Aretin, Karl Otmar Freiherr von (ed.), *Der Aufgeklärte Absolutismus* (Cologne, 1974).

–, "Aufgeklärter Herrscher oder aufgeklärter Absolutismus: eine notwendige Begriffserklärung," in *Gesellschaftsgeschichte*, ed. Ferdinand Seibt, 2 vols. (Munich, 1988), vol.1, p.78–87.

–, "Kaunitz, Wenzel Anton Fürst," *Neue Deutsche Biographie* 11 (1977), p.363–69.

–, "Orsini und Rosenberg, Franz Xaver Wolf Fürst von," *Neue Deutsche Biographie* 19 (1999), p.596.

Arndt, Johannes, "Gab es im frühmodernen Heiligen Romischen Reich ein 'Mediensystem der politischen Publizistik'? Einige systemtheoretische Überlegungen," *Jahrbuch für Kommunikationsgeschichte* 6 (2004), p.74–102.

Arndt, Ludwig, *Friedrich der Große und die Askanier seiner Zeit (Dargestellt hauptsächlich aus der "Politischen Korrespondenz" des Königs), Anhaltische Geschichtsblätter* 13 (1937), ed. Verein für Anhaltische Geschichte und Altertumskunde (Dessau, 1938).

Asch, Ronald G., and Adolf M. Birke (ed.), *Princes, patronage, and the nobility: the court at the beginning of the modern age c.1450–1650* (London, 1991).

Assmann, Jan, *Religio duplex: how the Enlightenment reinvented Egyptian religion* (London, 2014).

Astigarraga, Jesús, "Introduction: admirer, rougir, imiter–Spain and the European Enlightenment," in *The Spanish Enlightenment revisited*, ed. Jesús Astigarraga, Oxford University Studies in the Enlightenment (Oxford, Voltaire Foundation, 2015), p.1–17.

Atzmansdorfer, Johanna, *et al.*, "Much of the same? Das Leben am Hof im Spiegel der Zeremonialprotokolle (1652–1800)," in *Der Wiener Hof im Spiegel der Zeremonialprotokolle (1652–1800)*, ed. Irmgard Pangerl, Martin Scheutz, and Thomas Winkelbauer (Innsbruck, 2007), p.229–54.

Bachmann, Erich, "Anfänge des Landschaftsgartens in Deutschland," *Zeitschrift für Kunstwissenschaft* 5:3–4 (1951), p.203–28.

–, *Felsengarten Sanspareil: Burg Zwernitz, amtlicher Führer* (Munich, 1954).

Baker, Keith Michael, *Inventing the French Revolution* (Cambridge, 1990).

–, "Politique et opinion publique sous l'ancien régime," *Annales ESC* 42:1 (1987), p.41–71.

–, and Peter Hanns Reill (ed.), *What's left of Enlightenment? A postmodern question* (Stanford, CA, 2001).

Baras Escolá, Fernando, *El reformismo político de Jovellanos: nobleza y poder en la España del Siglo XVIII* (Zaragoza, 1993).

Baroja, Julio Caro, "Los Majos," *Cuadernos Hispanoamericanos* 299 (May 1975), p.281–349.

Bauer, Volker, *Die höfische Gesellschaft in Deutschland von der Mitte des 17. bis zum Ausgang des 18. Jahrhunderts: Versuch einer Typologie* (Tübingen, 1993).

–, "Strukturwandel der höfischen Öffentlichkeit: zur Medialisierung des Hoflebens vom 16. bis zum 18. Jahrhundert," *Zeitschrift für historische Forschung* 38:4 (2011), p.585–620.

Baum, Constanze, "Ein Lorbeerzweig für Friedrich den Großen: Wilhelmine von Bayreuth am Grab Vergils (1755)," *Schriften der Winckelmann-Gesellschaft* 25 (2006), p.11–34.

Baumgart, Peter, "Absolutismus ein Mythos? Aufgeklärter Absolutismus ein Widerspruch? Reflexionen zu einem kontroversen Thema gegenwärtiger Frühneuzeitforschung," *Zeitschrift für historische Forschung* 27:4 (2000), p.573–89.

–, "Joseph II. und Maria Theresia 1765–1790," in *Die Kaiser der Neuzeit 1519–1918*, ed. Anton Schindling and Walter Ziegler (Munich, 1990), p.249–76.

Beales, Derek, *Joseph II*, 2 vols. (Cambridge, 1987–2009).

Beaurepaire, Pierre-Yves, *Echec au roi: irrespect, contestations et révoltes dans la France des Lumières* (Paris, 2015).

Bechtholdt, Frank-Andreas, and Thomas Weiß (ed.), *Weltbild Wörlitz: Entwurf einer Kulturlandschaft* (Wörlitz, 1996).

Beckus, Paul, "Franz in seiner Stadt: Dessau als Residenz des Fürsten Leopold Friedrich Franz von Anhalt-Dessau," in *Der Fürst in seiner Stadt: Leopold Friedrich Franz und Dessau*, ed. Andreas Pečar and Frank Kreißler (Petersberg, 2017), p.18–29.

–, *Hof und Verwaltung des Fürsten Franz von Anhalt-Dessau (1758–1817): Struktur, Personal, Funktionalität* (Halle, 2015).

–, *Land ohne Herr–Fürst ohne Hof? Friedrich August von Anhalt-Zerbst und sein Fürstentum* (Halle, 2018).

–, "Zwischen Image und Ökonomie: Fürst Franz und die Juden 1758–1817," in *Politische Gartenkunst? Landschaftsgestaltung und Herrschaftsrepräsentation des Fürsten Franz von Anhalt-Dessau in vergleichender Perspektive: Wörlitz, Sanssouci und Schwetzingen*, ed. Andreas Pečar and Holger Zaunstöck (Halle, 2015), p.143–57.

Behrens, Rudolf, "Die Macht der Milde: Konfigurationen der *clemetia* als Herrschertugend bei Seneca, Montaigne, Corneille und Metastasio," *Romanistisches Jahrbuch* 52:1 (2001), p.96–132.

Bending, Stephen, "Introduction," in *A Cultural history of gardens in the age of Enlightenment*, ed. Stephen Bending (London, 2016), p.1–27.

Benharrech, Sarah, "Guerre des farines et dénigrement de l'autorité: l'imaginaire burlesque dans les *Mémoires secrets*," in *Le Règne de la critique: l'imaginaire culturel des Mémoires secrets*, ed. C. Cave (Paris, 2010), p.115–29.

Berg, Henrik (ed.), *Hertig Carl och det svenska frimureriet* (Uppsala, 2010).

Bernard, Paul, *From the Enlightenment to the police state: the public life of Johann Anton Pergen* (Urbana, IL, 1991).

Berndtsson, Tim, *The Order and the archive* (Uppsala, 2020).

Bibby, Andrew Scott, *Montesquieu's political economy* (New York, 2016).

Binoche, Bertrand, "Les historiens, les philosophes et l'opinion publique," in *L'Opinion publique dans l'Europe des Lumières: stratégies et concepts*, ed. Bertrand Binoche and Alain J. Lemaître (Paris, 2013), p.7–14.

Birtsch, Günter, "Aufgeklärter Absolutismus oder Reformabsolutismus?," *Aufklärung* 9:1 (1996), p.101–109.

– (ed.), *Der Idealtyp des aufgeklärten Herrschers* (Hamburg, 1987).

–, "Der Idealtyp des aufgeklärten Herrschers: Friedrich der Große, Karl Friedrich von Baden und Joseph II. im Vergleich," *Aufklärung* 2:1 (1987), p.9–47.

– (ed.), *Patriotismus* (Hamburg, 1991).

– (ed.), *Reformabsolutismus im Vergleich: Staatswirklichkeit–Modernisierungsaspekte–verfassungsstaatliche Positionen* (Hamburg, 1996).

– (ed.), *Reformabsolutismus und ständische Gesellschaft: Zweihundert Jahre Preußisches Allgemeines Landrecht* (Berlin, 1998).

Biskup, Thomas, *Friedrichs Größe: Inszenierungen des Preußenkönigs in Fest und Zeremoniell 1740–1815* (Frankfurt am Main, 2012).

–, "German court and French Revolution: émigrés and the Brunswick court around 1800," *Francia: Forschungen zur westeuropäischen Geschichte* 34:2 (2007), p.61–87.

–, "The University of Göttingen and the personal union 1737–1837," in *The Hanoverian dimension in British history: 1714–1837*, ed. Brendan Simms and Torsten Riotte (Cambridge, 2007), p.128–60.

Blanning, T. C., *The Culture of power and the power of culture* (Oxford, 2006).

–, *Joseph II* (London, 1994).

Blom, Hans, John Christian Laursen, and Luisa Simonutti (ed.), *Monarchisms in the age of Enlightenment: liberty, patriotism, and the common good* (Toronto, 2007).

Bogdan, Henrik, and Jan A. M. Snoek (ed.), *Handbook of freemasonry* (Leiden, 2014).

Böhr, Christoph, "Erkenntnisgewißheit und politische Philosophie: zu Christian Wolffs Postulat des philosophus regnans," *Zeitschrift für philosophische Forschung* 36:4 (1982), p.579–98.

Böning, Holger, *Der Musiker und Komponist Johann Mattheson als Hamburger Publizist: Studie zu den Anfängen der Moralischen Wochenschriften und der deutschen Musikpublizistik*, 2nd ed. (Bremen, 2014).

Borek, Johanna, *Denis Diderot* (Reinbek, 2000).

Borm, Jan, Bernard Cottret, and Monique Cottret (ed.), *Savoir et pouvoir au siècle des Lumières* (Paris, 2011).

Boss, Valentin, *Newton and Russia: the early influence, 1698–1796* (Cambridge, 1972).

Bourdieu, Pierre, *The Field of cultural production: essays on art and literature* (New York, 1993).

–, *Homo academicus*, translated by Peter Collier (Stanford, CA, 1988).

Braun, Karl, *Luisenburg: ein vergessener Landschaftsgarten der Frühromantik* (Marburg, 2005).

Brewer, John, *Party ideology and popular politics at the accession of George III* (Cambridge, 1976).

Brian, Eric, *La Mesure de l'Etat: administrateurs et géomètres au XVIII⁴ siècle* (Paris, 1994).

Bronisch, Johannes, *Der Mäzen der Aufklärung: Ernst Christoph von Manteuffel und das Netzwerk des Wolffianismus* (Berlin, 2010).

Brunner, Ernst, *Anckarström och kungamordet: historien i sin helhet* (Stockholm, 2010).

Buchmann, Betrand, *Hof, Regierung, Stadtverwaltung: Wien als Sitz der österreichischen Zentralverwaltung von den Anfängen bis zum Untergang der Monarchie* (Munich, 2002).

Bucholz, R. O., *The Augustan court: Queen Anne and the decline of court culture* (Stanford, CA, 1993).

–, "The database of court officers: 1660–1837," http://courtofficers. ctsdh.luc.edu./ (last accessed January 21, 2022).

Burke, Peter, *The Fabrication of Louis XIV* (New Haven, CT, 1992).

Burrows, Simon, *Blackmail, scandal, and revolution: London's French libellistes, 1758–1792* (Manchester, 2006).

Buttlar, Adrian von, *Der Landschaftsgarten: Gartenkunst des Klassizismus und der Romantik* (Cologne, 1989).

–, and Marcus Köhler, *Tod, Glück und Ruhm in Sanssouci: ein Führer durch die Gartenwelt Friedrichs des Großen* (Ostfildern, 2012).

Butz, Reinhardt, and Jan Hirschbiegel (ed.), *Informelle Strukturen bei Hof: Dresdener Gespräche III zur Theorie des Hofes* (Berlin, 2009).

Campbell Orr, Clarissa, "The late Hanoverian court and the Christian Enlightenment," in *Monarchy and religion: the transformation of royal culture in eighteenth-century Europe*, ed. Michael Schaich (Oxford, 2007), p.317–44.

–, "Marriage in a global context," in *Queens consort, cultural transfer and European politics, c.1500–1800*, ed. Helen Watanabe-O'Kelly and Adam Morton (Abingdon, 2017), p.109–31.

–, *Mrs. Delany: a life* (New Haven, CT, 2019).

–, "New perspectives on Hanoverian Britain," *Historical journal* 52:2 (2009), p.513–29.

–, "Queen Charlotte as patron: some intellectual and social contexts," *The Court historian* 6:3 (2001), p.183–212.

– (ed.), *Queenship in Britain 1660–1837: royal patronage, court culture and dynastic politics* (Manchester, 2002).

– (ed.), *Queenship in Europe, 1660–1815: the role of the consort* (Cambridge, 2004).

Campóo, Diana, "Danza y educación nobiliaria en el siglo XVIII: el método de la escuela de baile en el Real Seminario de Nobles de Madrid," *Ars bilduma* 5 (2015), p.157–73.

Caradonna, Jeremy L., "There was no Counter-Enlightenment," *Eighteenth-century studies* 49:1 (2015), p.51–69.

Castro, Alexander de, "Enlightened absolutism and legal culture in Portugal: rise and decline of legal Pombalism in the 18th century (1769–1789)," *Zeitschrift der Savigny-Stiftung für Rechtsgeschichte / Germanistische Abteilung* 133:1 (2016), p.296–364.

Cave, Christophe, "Les *Anecdotes* de Pidansat de Mairobert sur Madame du Barry," in *L'Histoire en miettes: anecdotes et temoignages dans l'écriture de l'histoire (XVIᵉ– XIXᵉ siècles)*, ed. Carole Dornier and Claudine Pouloin (Caen, 2004), p.279–98.

–, "Les *Anecdotes sur Madame la comtesse du Barri* et les *Mémoires secrets*," in *Le Règne de la critique: l'imaginaire culturel des Mémoires secrets*, ed. C. Cave (Paris, 2010), p.357–62.

–, "Instrumentalisation politique de l'esthétique et critique de la politique-spectacle," in *Le Règne de la critique: l'imaginaire culturel*

des Mémoires secrets, ed. C. Cave (Paris, 2010), p.95–114.

–, "Préface," in *Le Règne de la critique: l'imaginaire culturel des Mémoires secrets*, ed. Christophe Cave (Paris, 2010), p.7–25.

–, and Suzanne Cornand, "Présentation générale," in *Mémoires secrets pour servir à l'histoire de la république des lettres en France, depuis 1762 jusqu'à nos jours*, ed. Christophe Cave and Suzanne Cornand, 5 vols. (Paris, 2009–2010), vol.1, p.xiii–lxxxviii.

Chalus, Elaine, *Elite women in English political life c.1754–1790* (Oxford, 2005).

Charlton, David, "The melodic language of *Le Devin du village* and the evolution of *opéra-comique*," in *Rousseau on stage: playwright, musician, spectator*, ed. Maria Gullstam and Michael O'Dea (Oxford, 2017), p.179–208.

–, "New light on the Bouffons in Paris (1752–1754)," *Eighteenth-century music* 11:1 (2014), p.31–54.

Chartier, Roger, "Der Gelehrte," in *Der Mensch der Aufklärung*, ed. Michel Vovelle (Frankfurt am Main, 1996), p.122–68.

–, *Les Origines culturelles de la Révolution* (Paris, 1990).

Chaussinand-Nogaret, Guy, *Choiseul: naissance de la gauche* (Paris, 1998).

Christensen, Thomas, "Music theory as scientific propaganda: the case of D'Alembert's *Elémens de musique*," *Journal of the history of ideas* 50:3 (1989), p.409–27.

–, *Rameau and musical thought in the Enlightenment* (Cambridge, 1993).

Clark, William, *Academic charisma and the origins of the research university* (Chicago, IL, 2006).

Conan, Michel, "Introduction: the significance of bodily engagement with nature," in *Performance and appropriation: profane rituals in gardens and landscapes*, ed. Michel Conan (Washington, DC, 2007), p.3–16.

Cowan, Brian, "Rise of the coffeehouse reconsidered," *Historical journal* 47:1 (2004), p.21–46.

Cowart, Georgia, *The Origins of modern musical criticism: French and Italian music, 1600–1750* (Ann Arbor, MI, 1981).

Cracraft, James, *The Church reform of Peter the Great* (London, 1971).

Cremer, Annette C., Matthias Müller, and Klaus Pietschmann (ed.), *Fürst und Fürstin als Künstler: herrschaftliches Künstlertum zwischen Habitus, Norm und Neigung* (Berlin, 2018).

Cust, Richard, "News and politics in early seventeenth-century England," *Past and present* 112:1 (August 1986), p.60–90.

Daniel, Ute, "Höfe und Aufklärung in Deutschland: Plädoyer für eine Begegnung der dritten Art," in *Hofkultur und aufklärerische Reformen in Thüringen: die Bedeutung des Hofes im späten 18. Jahrhundert*, ed. Marcus Ventzke (Cologne, 2002), p.11–31.

Dann, Otto, "Eine höfische Gesellschaft als Lesegesellschaft," *Aufklärung* 6:1 (1991), p.43–57.

Darnton, Robert, *The Business of Enlightenment: a publishing history of the Encyclopédie, 1775–1800* (Cambridge, MA, 1979).

–, *Censors at work: how states shaped literature* (New York, 2014).

–, *The Corpus of clandestine literature in France: 1769–1789* (New York, 1995).

–, *The Devil in the holy water, or the Art of slander from Louis XIV to Napoleon* (Philadelphia, PA, 2010).

–, *The Forbidden best-sellers of pre-revolutionary France* (New York, 1995).

–, "La France, ton café fout le camp!," *Actes de la recherche en sciences sociales* 100 (December 1993), p.16–26.

–, "The Grub Street style of revolution: J.-P. Brissot, police spy," *Journal of modern history* 40:4 (1968), p.301–27.

–, *The Literary underground of the Old Regime* (Cambridge, MA, 1982).

–, "'Philosophical sex': pornography in Old Regime France," in *Enlightenment, passion, modernity: historical essays in European thought and culture*, ed. Mark S. Micale and Robert L. Dietle (Stanford, CA, 2000), p.88–112.

–, *Poetry and the police: communication networks in eighteenth-century Paris* (Cambridge, MA, 2010).

Deflers, Isabelle, "Diderots Auseinandersetzung mit dem 'aufgeklärten Despotismus' Friedrichs II.," in *Denis Diderot und die Macht / Denis Diderot et le pouvoir*, ed. Isabelle Deflers (Berlin, 2015), p.61–82.

Delblanc, Sven, *Ära och minne: studier kring ett motivkomplex i 1700-taletslitteratur* (Stockholm, 1965).

Demuth, Joseph, *Das unbekannte und geheimnisvolle Luxemburg: Chronik eines kleinen, grossen Landes*, 10 vols. (Luxembourg, 1982–1989).

Dennison, Matthew, *The First Iron Lady: a life of Caroline of Ansbach* (London, 2017).

Dieckmann, Herbert, *Inventaire du fond Vandeul et inédits de Denis Diderot* (Geneva, 1951).

Dijn, Annelien de, "The politics of Enlightenment: from Peter Gay to Jonathan Israel," *Historical journal* 55 (2012), p.785–805.

Dilly, Heinrich, and Barry Murnane (ed.), *"Seltsam, abenteuerlich und unbeschreiblich verschwenderisch": gotische Häuser um 1800 in England, Potsdam, Weimar und Dessau-Wörlitz* (Halle, 2014).

Dixon, Simon, "The posthumous reputation of Catherine II in Russia 1797–1837," *The Slavonic and East European review* 77:4 (1999), p.646–79.

Doody, Margaret Anne, *Frances Burney: the life in the works* (Cambridge, 1988).

Dorgerloh, Annette, "Love, pilgrims and merry hermits: hermitage as a place of conviviality in the eighteenth century," in *Le tentazioni dell' "ermitage": ideali ascetici e invenzioni architettoniche dal medioevo all'illuminismo*, ed. Paola Zanardi (Milan, 2011), p.137–46.

–, and Michael Niedermeier, "Desire for origins: Archäologie und inszenierte Abstammung in Gärten des europäischen Adels," in *Mythos Ursprung: Modelle der*

Arché zwischen Antike und Moderne, ed. Constanze Baum and Martin Disselkamp (Würzburg, 2011), p.95–122.

Dubowy, Norbert, "Italienische Instrumentalisten in deutschen Hofkapellen," in *The Eighteenth-century diaspora of Italian music and musicians*, ed. Reinhard Strohm (Turnhout, 2001), p.61–120.

Ducini, Hélène, *Faire voir, faire croire: l'opinion publique sous Louis XIII* (Seyssel, 2003).

Duindam, Jeroen, *Myths of power: Norbert Elias and the early modern court* (Amsterdam, 1995).

–, *Vienna and Versailles: the courts of Europe's dynastic rivals, 1550–1780* (Cambridge, 2003).

Dulac, Georges, "Diderot éditeur des *Plans et statuts* des établissements de Catherine II," *Dix-huitième siècle* 16 (1984), p.323–44.

Edelstein, Dan, *The Enlightenment: a genealogy* (Chicago, IL, 2010).

–, "Introduction to the Super-Enlightenment," in *The Super-Enlightenment: daring to know too much*, ed. Dan Edelstein (Oxford, 2010), p.1–34.

Edmonds, John, and John Eidinow, *Rousseau's dog: a tale of two great thinkers at war in the age of Enlightenment* (London, 2006).

Eger, Elizabeth, and Lucy Peltz (ed.), *Brilliant women: 18th-century bluestockings* (London, 2008).

Ehalt, Hubert, *Ausdrucksformen absolutistischer Herrschaft: der Wiener Hof im 17. und 18. Jahrhundert* (Munich, 1980).

Elias, Norbert, *The Court society* (Oxford, 1983).

Elliott, John H., *History in the making* (New Haven, CT, 2012).

–, and Laurence W. B. Brockliss (ed.), *The World of the favorite* (New Haven, CT, 1999).

Elorza, Antonio, *La ideología liberal en la ilustración española* (Madrid, 1970).

Elton, Geoffrey R., "Tudor government," *Historical journal* 31:2 (1988), p.425–34.

–, "Tudor government: the points of contact," in Geoffrey R. Elton, *Studies in Tudor politics and government*, 4 vols. (Cambridge, 1983), vol.3, p.3–57.

–, *The Tudor revolution in government* (Cambridge, 1953).

Erbe, Michael, *Deutsche Geschichte 1713–1790: Dualismus und aufgeklärter Absolutismus* (Stuttgart, 1985).

Evans, Robert John, "The Austrian Habsburgs: the dynasty as a political institution," in *The Courts of Europe*, ed. Arthur Dickens (New York, 1984), p.121–47.

Evstratov, Alexei, "La mise en scène de la cour: la scène et la salle dans le théâtre de cour— étude du théâtre russe à l'aube du règne de Catherine II," in *La Scène, la salle et les coulisses dans le théâtre du XVIIIe siècle en France*, ed. Pierre Frantz and Thomas Wynn (Paris, 2011), p.235–46.

–, *Les Spectacles francophones à la cour de Russie (1743–1796): l'invention d'une société*, Oxford University Studies in the Enlightenment (Oxford, Voltaire Foundation, 2016).

Faccarello, Gilbert, "Galiani, Necker and Turgot: a debate on economic reform and policy in eighteenth-century France," in *Studies in the history of French political economy: from Bodin to Walras*, ed. Gilbert Faccarello (London, 1998), p.120–95.

Faculty of Medieval & Modern Languages at the University of Oxford, "Marrying cultures: queens consort and European identities 1500–1800," www.marryingcultures.eu (last accessed January 21, 2022).

Farge, Arlette, *Dire et mal dire: l'opinion publique au XVIIIe siècle* (Paris, 1992).

Farguson, Julie, "Enlightenment and modernity? German princesses in Georgian Britain," *The Court historian* 23:1 (2018), p.62–65.

Fedyukin, Igor, "Shaping up the stubborn: school building and 'discipline' in early modern Russia," *The Russian review* 77:2 (2018), p.200–18.

Fejtö, François, *Joseph II.: Kaiser und Revolutionär* (Stuttgart, 1956).

Felgel, Anton Victor, "Franz II.," *Allgemeine Deutsche Biographie* 7 (1878/1968), p.285–90.

Félix, Joël, "L'économie politique et la naissance de l'opinion publique," in *L'Opinion publique dans l'Europe des Lumières: stratégies et concepts*, ed. Bertrand Binoche and Alain J. Lemaître (Paris, 2013), p.87–104.

Fellinger, Imogen, "Mattheson als Begründer der ersten Musikzeitschrift ('Critica Musica')," in *New Mattheson studies*, ed. George J. Buelow and Hans Joachim Marx (Cambridge, 1983), p.179–97.

Fernández Fernández, José Luis, *Jovellanos: Antropología y teoría de la Sociedad* (Madrid, 1991).

Ferret, Olivier, "La vie privée... du duc de Chartres et les *Mémoires secrets*," in *Le Règne de la critique: l'imaginaire culturel des Mémoires secrets*, ed. C. Cave (Paris, 2010), p.397–414.

Fink, Humbert, *Joseph II.: Kaiser, König und Reformer* (Düsseldorf, 1990).

Fischer, Ernst, "'... dem Buchhandel eine andere Richtung zu geben': die Dessauer 'Allgemeine Buchhandlung der Gelehrten' als verlegerisches Avantgardeunternehmen," in *Bücherwelten im Gartenreich Dessau-Wörlitz*, ed. Wilhelm Haefs (Hannover, 2009), p.113–30.

Fort, Bernadette, "Esthétique et imaginaire sexuel: la femme peintre dans les salons," in *Le Règne de la critique: l'imaginaire culturel des Mémoires secrets*, ed. C. Cave (Paris, 2010), p.269–94.

Foucault, Michel, *Security, territory, population: lectures at the Collège de France 1977–1978* (Basingstoke, 2007).

–, "What is critique?," in *What is Enlightenment? Eighteenth-century answers and twentieth-century questions*, ed. James Schmidt (Berkeley, CA, 1996), p.382–98.

Frängsmyr, Tore, *Svensk Idéhistoria* (Stockholm, 2004).

Freist, Dagmar, *Governed by opinion: politics, religion and the dynamics of communication in Stuart London* (London, 1997).

Fumaroli, Marc, *La República de las Letras* (Barcelona, 2013).

Furbank, P. N., *Diderot: a critical biography* (London, 1992).

Füssel, Marian, *Gelehrtenkultur als symbolische Praxis: Rang, Ritual und Konflikt an der Universität der Frühen Neuzeit* (Darmstadt, 2006).

–, Antje Kuhle, and Michael Stolz (ed.), *Höfe und Experten: Relationen von Macht und Wissen in Mittelalter und Früher Neuzeit* (Göttingen, 2018).

Garber, Jörn (ed.), *"Die Stammutter aller guten Schulen": das Dessauer Philanthropinum und der deutsche Philanthropismus 1774–1793* (Tübingen, 2008).

Garrard, Graeme, *Rousseau's Counter-Enlightenment: a republican critique of the philosophes* (Albany, NY, 2003).

–, "Tilting at Counter-Enlightenment windmills," *Eighteenth-century studies* 49:1 (2015), p.77–81.

Gascoigne, John, *Joseph Banks and the English Enlightenment: useful knowledge and polite culture* (Cambridge, 1994).

–, *Science in the service of empire* (Cambridge, 1998).

Gauvard, Claude, "Qu'est-ce que l'opinion avant l'invention de l'imprimerie?," in *L'Opinion: information, rumeur, propagande*, ed. Claude Gauvard (Nantes, 2008), p.21–59.

Gestrich, Andreas, *Absolutismus und Öffentlichkeit: Politische*

Kommunikation in Deutschland zu Beginn des 18. Jahrhunderts (Göttingen, 1994).

Giegling, Franz, "'La Clemenza di Tito': Metastasio—Mazzolà—Mozart," *Österreichische Musikschrift* 31:7–8 (1976), p.321–29.

Glendinning, Nigel, "La sátira en el arte y la literatura en la época de Carlos IV," in *La época de Carlos IV (1788–1808)*, ed. Elena de Lorenzo Álvarez (Oviedo, 2009), p.17–39.

González Cuevas, Pedro Carlos, *Historia de las derechas españolas: de la Ilustración a nuestros días* (Madrid, 2000).

Gordin, Michael, "The importation of being earnest: the early St. Petersburg Academy of Sciences," *Isis* 91:1 (2000), p.1–31.

Gothein, Marie Luise, *Geschichte der Gartenkunst* (Jena, 1914).

Gregory, Jeremy, "Religion: faith in the age of reason," *Eighteenth-century studies* 34:1 (2011), p.435–43.

Grote, Simon, "Review-essay: religion and Enlightenment," *Journal of the history of ideas* 75:1 (2014), p.137–60.

Guenée, Bernard, *L'Opinion publique à la fin du Moyen Age d'après la "Chronique de Charles VI" du Religieux de Saint-Denis* (Paris, 2002).

Guerrier, W., *Leibniz in seinen Beziehungen zu Russland und Peter dem Grossen* (St. Petersburg, 1873).

Guichard, Charlotte, "'Amatrice': die Rolle der 'Amateurin' im Europa der Aufklärung," in *Aufgeklärter Kunstdiskurs und höfische Sammelpraxis: Karoline Luise von Baden im europäischen Kontext*, ed. Christoph Frank (Berlin, 2015), p.80–89.

Gukovskii, G. A., *Ocherki po istorii russkoi literatury XVIII veka* (Moscow, 1936).

Gunn, John W. A., *Queen of the world: opinion in the public life of France from the Renaissance to the Revolution* (Oxford, 1995).

Gutkas, Karl, *Joseph II* (Vienna, 1989).

Habermann, Sylvia, *Bayreuther Gartenkunst: die Gärten der Markgrafen von Brandenburg-Culmbach im 17. und 18. Jahrhundert* (Worms, 1982).

Habermas, Jürgen, *The Structural transformation of the public sphere: an inquiry into a category of bourgeois society*, translated by Thomas Burger (1962; Cambridge, MA, 1989).

Habiger, Mechthild, and Helke Kammerer-Grothaus, "'Les aventures de Télémaque': ein literarisches Programm für den markgräflichen Felsengarten in Sanspareil und die klassizistische Bildtapete von Dufour, Paris 1823," *Zeitschrift des Deutschen Vereins für Kunstwissenschaft* 51 (1997), p.179–94.

Haechler, Jean, *Le Prince de Conti: un cousin embarrassant* (Paris, 2007).

Hager, Luisa, "Eremitage," in *Reallexikon zur Deutschen Kunstgeschichte*, ed. Zentralinstitut für Kunstgeschichte München (Munich, 1937–), vol.5, col.1203–29.

Hajós, Géza, "Der Berg und der Garten: mythisches Abbild—künstliche Natürlichkeit—Promenadennatur," in *Garten–Kunst–Geschichte*, ed. Erika Schmidt, Wilfried Hansmann, and Jörg Gamer (Worms, 1994), p.116–24.

Hanham, Andrew, "'So few facts': Jacobites, Tories and the Pretender," *Parliamentary history* 19:2 (2002), p.233–57.

Hanrahan, James, *Voltaire and the parlements of France* (Oxford, 2009).

Hantsch, Hugo, "Franz II.," *Neue Deutsche Biographie* 5 (1961), p.358–61.

Harbeck-Barthel, Daniela, and Gisela Schlüter, "'Meine Bibliothek ist jetzt geordnet': der Aufbau von Wilhelmines französischer Bibliothek," in *Wilhelmine von Bayreuth heute: das kulturelle Erbe der Markgräfin*, ed. Günter Berger (Bayreuth, 2009), p.151–72.

Harksen, Marie-Luise, *Erdmannsdorff und seine Bauten in Wörlitz* (Wörlitz, 1973).

Hartmann, Günter, *Die Ruine im Landschaftsgarten: ihre Bedeutung für den frühen Historismus und die Landschaftsmalerei der Romantik* (Worms, 1981).

Hatton, Ragnhild, *George I: elector and king* (London, 1978).

Hellsing, My, *Hedvig Elisabeth Charlotte: hertiginna vid det gustavianska hovet* (Stockholm, 2015).

Hengerer, Mark, *Kaiserhof und Adel in der Mitte des 17. Jahrhunderts: eine Kommunikationsgeschichte der Macht in der Vormoderne* (Konstanz, 2004).

Hennebo, Dieter, and Alfred Hoffmann, *Geschichte der deutschen Gartenkunst*, 3 vols. (Hamburg, 1962–1965).

Henshall, Nicholas, *The Myth of absolutism: change and continuity in early modern European monarchy* (London, 1992).

Henze-Döhring, Sabine, *Friedrich der Große: Musiker und Monarch* (Munich, 2012).

Henzel, Christoph, "Die Zeit des Augustus in der Musik: Berliner Klassik, ein Versuch," in *Berliner Aufklärung: Kulturwissenschaftliche Studien*, ed. Ursula Goldenbaum and Alexander Košenina, 7 vols. (Hanover, 1999–), vol.2 (2003), p.7–33.

Hirsch, Erhard, *Dessau-Wörlitz: Aufklärung und Frühklassik*, 2nd ed. (Leipzig, 1987).

–, *Die Dessau-Wörlitzer Reformbewegung im Zeitalter der Aufklärung: Personen–Strukturen–Wirkungen* (Tübingen, 2003).

Hirschbiegel, Jan, Werner Paravicini, and Jörg Wettlaufer (ed.), *Städtisches Bürgertum und Hofgesellschaft: Kulturen integrativer und konkurrierender Beziehungen in Residenz- und Hauptstädten vom 14. bis ins 19. Jahrhundert* (Ostfildern, 2012).

The History of Parliament Trust, "The History of Parliament: British political, social and local history," http://www.historyofparliamentonline.org/ (last accessed January 21, 2022).

Hochedlinger, Michael, "Das Ende der Ära Kaunitz in der

Staatskanzlei," in *Staatskanzler Wenzel Anton von Kaunitz Rietberg: neue Perspektiven zu Politik und Kultur der europäischen Aufklärung*, ed. Grete Klingenstein and Franz Szabo (Graz, 1996), p.117–31.

Hock, Jonas, and Kirill Abrosimov (ed.), *Friedrich Melchior Grimm: pensée, réseaux et génie médiatique du philosophe européen de Ratisbonne* (forthcoming).

–, *Romanische Studien* (2020), special issue: *Friedrich Melchior Grimm, philosophe et homme de réseaux dans l'Europe des Lumières*.

Holenstein, Andre, "Introduction: empowering interactions: looking at statebuilding from below," in *Empowering interactions: political cultures and the emergence of the state in Europe (1300–1900)*, ed. Wim Blockmans *et al.* (Burlington, VT, 2009), p.1–34.

Holmes, Richard, *The Age of wonder* (London, 2009).

Horn, Wolfgang, *Die Dresdner Hofkirchenmusik 1720–1745: Studien zu ihren Voraussetzungen und ihrem Repertoire* (Kassel, 1987).

Horowski, Leonhard, *Die Belagerung des Thrones: Machtstrukturen und Karrieremechanismen am Hof von Frankreich 1661–1789* (Ostfildern, 2012).

–, "Hof und Absolutismus: was bleibt von Norbert Elias' Theorie?," in *Absolutismus, ein unersetzliches Forschungskonzept?*, ed. Lothar Schilling (Munich, 2008), p.143–76.

Horsch, Nadja, "Otium religiosum: die Gartener- emitage im Barchetto von

Pesaro als christlich konnotierter Rückzugsort," in *Gärten und Parks als Lebens- und Erlebnisraum: funktions- und nutzungsgeschichtliche Aspekte der Gartenkunst in Früher Neuzeit und Moderne*, ed. Stefan Schweizer (Worms, 2008), p.65–80.

Hughes, Lindsey, *Peter the Great: a biography* (New Haven, CT, 2004).

Hüneke, Saskia, "Die Sammlung Bayreuth," in *Kurfürstliche und königliche Erwerbungen für die Schlösser Brandenburg-Preußens vom 17. bis zum 19. Jahrhundert: Antiken I*, ed. Astrid Dostert (Oldenburg, 2008), p.329–94.

Hunt, John Dixon, "Approaches (new and old) to garden history," in *Perspectives on garden histories*, ed. Michel Conan (Washington, DC, 1999), p.77–90.

–, "The idea of a garden and the three natures," in John Dixon Hunt, *Greater perfections: the practice of garden theory* (Philadelphia, PA, 2000), p.32–75.

Hunt, Lynn, "Louis XVI wasn't killed by ideas: this is what happens when you ignore the role of politics in intellectual history," *The New Republic*, https:// newrepublic.com/article/118044/ revolutionary-ideas-jonathan- israel-reviewed (last accessed January 19, 2022).

Hunter, Ian, *Rival Enlightenments: civil and metaphysical philosophy in early modern Germany* (Cambridge, 2001).

Huss, Frank, *Der Wiener Kaiserhof, eine Kulturgeschichte von Leopold I. bis Leopold II.* (Gernsbach, 2008).

Israel, Jonathan, *Democratic Enlight-enment: philosophy, revolution, and human rights 1750–1790* (Oxford, 2012).

–, *Enlightenment contested: philosophy, modernity, and the emancipation of man 1670–1752* (Oxford, 2006).

–, *A Revolution of the mind: radical Enlightenment and the intellectual origins of modern democracy* (Princeton, NJ, 2010).

–, *Revolutionary ideas: an intellectual history of the French Revolution from "The Rights of man" to Robespierre* (Princeton, NJ, 2014).

–, and Lynn Hunt, "Was Louis XVI overthrown by ideas?," *The New Republic*, https://newrepublic.com/article/118811/jonathan-israel-response-lynn-hunts-review (last accessed January 19, 2022).

Jablonowski, Ulla, "Wirtschaftliche und soziale Grundlagen der Dessau-Wörlitzer Aufklärung (etwa 1760 bis 1800)," *Mitteilungen des Vereins für Anhaltische Landeskunde* 1 (1992), p.39–75.

Jacob, Christian (ed.), *Lieux de savoir*, vol.1: *Espaces et communautés* (Paris, 2007).

– (ed.), *Lieux de savoir*, vol.2: *Les Mains de l'intellect* (Paris, 2011).

Jacob, J. R., *Robert Boyle and the English revolution: a study in social and intellectual change* (New York, 1977).

Jacob, Margaret C., *The Cultural meaning of the Scientific Revolution* (Philadelphia, PA, 1988).

–, *Living the Enlightenment: freemasonry and politics in*

eighteenth-century Europe (New York, 1991).

–, *The Newtonians and the English revolution: 1689–1720* (New York, 1990).

–, *The Origins of freemasonry: facts and fictions* (Philadelphia, PA, 2006).

Jones, Peter M., *Agricultural Enlight-enment: knowledge, technology, and nature, 1750–1840* (Oxford, 2016).

Jordan, Stefan, "Pichler, Caroline," *Neue Deutsche Biographie* 20 (2001), p.411–12.

Jung, Hans Rudolf, and Hans-Eberhard Dentler, "Briefe von Lorenz Mizler und Zeitgenossen an Meinrad Spiess: mit einigen Konzepten und Notizen," *Studi musicali* 32:1 (2003), p.74–196.

Kaiser, Michael, and Andreas Pečar (ed.), *Der zweite Mann im Staat: Oberste Amtsträger und Favoriten im Umkreis der Reichs-fürsten in der Frühen Neuzeit* (Berlin, 2003).

Karstens, Simon, *Lehrer–Schrift-steller–Staatsreformer: Die Karriere des Joseph von Sonnenfels 1733–1817* (Vienna, 2011).

Kelly, George Armstrong, "The machine of the duc d'Orléans and the new politics," *Journal of modern history* 51 (December 1979), p.667–84.

Kerautret, Michel, "Diderot et la Révolution américaine," in *Denis Diderot und die Macht / Denis Diderot et le pouvoir*, ed. Isabelle Deflers (Berlin, 2015), p.101–19.

Keuten, Alla, "K istorii russkikh i nemetskikh Primechanii k

Vedomostiam (1728–1742)," *Russian literature* 75:1–4 (2014), p.265–303.

Kiesel, Hellmuth, *"Bei Hof, bei Höll": Untersuchungen zur literarischen Hofkritik von Sebastian Brant bis Friedrich Schiller* (Tübingen, 1979).

Kirk, Linda, "The matter of Enlightenment," *Historical journal* 43:4 (2000), p.1129–43.

Kittlitz, Hans Wernher von, "Ernst und Spiel: Anmerkungen zur kunsthierarchischen und kulturphänomenologischen Stellung der Chinoiserie: das 'Chinesische' als Antithese zum 'Klassischen'?," in *China in Schloss und Garten: Chinoise Architekturen und Innenräume*, ed. Dirk Welich (Dresden, 2010), p.31–47.

Klingenstein, Grete, *Der Aufstieg des Hauses Kaunitz: Studien zur Herkunft und Bildung des Staatskanzlers Wenzel Anton* (Göttingen, 1975).

Kniazhnin, Iakov, "Titovo miloserdie," in Iakov Kniazhnin, *Sochineniia Kniazhnina* (St. Petersburg, 1847), p.75–140.

Knott, Sarah, and Barbara Taylor (ed.), *Women, gender and the Enlightenment* (Basingstoke, 2005).

Kochetkova, Nataliia D., "Bibleiskii motiv 'milost' i sud' v russkoi literature XVIII veka," *Trudy Otdela Drevnerusskoi Literatury* 50 (1997), p.155–59.

Kolmakov, N. M., "Dom i familiia Strogonovykh: 1752–1887," *Russkaia starina* 53:3 (1887), p.575–602.

Kontler, László, "What is the (historians') Enlightenment today?," *European review of history / Revue européene d'histoire* 13:3 (2006), p.357–71.

Kopelevich, Iu., *Osnovanie Peterburgskoi akademii nauk* (Leningrad, 1977).

Köppel, Johann Gottfried, *Die Eremitage zu Sanspareil: nach der Natur gezeichnet und beschrieben von Johann Gottfried Köppel, Nachdruck der Ausgabe Erlangen 1793* (Erlangen, 1997).

Korneeva, Tatiana, *"Refracting translation* zwischen Wien, Dresden und Moskau: Pietro Metastasios *Clemenza di Tito* im deutsch-russischen Kulturtransfer," in *Kreative Praktiken des literarischen Übersetzens um 1800: Übersetzungshistorische und literaturwissenschaftliche Studien*, ed. Alexander Nebrig and Daniele Vecchiato (Berlin, 2019), p.51–74.

Koselleck, Reinhart, *Critique and crisis: Enlightenment and the pathogenesis of modern society* (1959; Cambridge, MA, 1988).

Kreißler, Frank, "'Die Toleranz ist in Dessau ganz zu Hause…': Fürst Franz und die jüdische Gemeinde in Dessau im Spiegel der fürstlichen Verordnungen," in *Das Leben des Fürsten: Studien zur Biografie von Leopold III. Friedrich Franz von Anhalt-Dessau (1740–1817)*, ed. Holger Zaunstöck (Halle, 2008), p.82–93.

Kröll, Joachim, "Naturbegriff und Naturgefühl im 18. Jahrhundert im Hinblick auf die Markgräfin

Wilhelmine von Bayreuth," in *Im Glanz des Rokoko: Markgräfin Wilhelmine von Bayreuth, Gedenken zu ihrem 200. Todestag*, ed. Wilhelm Müller (Bayreuth, 1958), p.28–50.

Krückmann, Peter O., "Ein Park, ein Lustschloss und eine Burg: Burg Zwernitz als Teil des Felsengartens Sanspareil," in *Festungen in Gärten–Gärten in Festungen*, ed. Volker Mende (Regensburg, 2015), p.84–93.

–, *Sanspareil: Burg Zwernitz und Felsengarten, amtlicher Führer* (Munich, 2012).

Kühn, Sebastian, *Wissen, Arbeit, Freundschaft: Ökonomien und soziale Beziehungen an den Akademien in London, Paris und Berlin um 1700* (Göttingen, 2011).

Kühner, Christian, *Politische Freundschaft bei Hofe: Repräsentation und Praxis einer sozialen Beziehung im französischen Adel des 17. Jahrhunderts* (Göttingen, 2013).

Kunisch, Johannes, *Absolutismus: Europäische Geschichte vom Westfälischen Frieden bis zur Krise des Ancien Régime* (Göttingen, 1999).

Labourdette, Jean-François, *Vergennes: ministre principal de Louis XVI* (Paris, 1990).

Labrosse, Claude, "Les *Mémoires secrets* et les gazettes," in *Le Règne de la critique: l'imaginaire culturel des Mémoires secrets*, ed. C. Cave (Paris, 2010), p.327–44.

Lake, Peter, and Steve Pincus, "Rethinking the public sphere in early modern England,"

Journal of British studies 45 (2006), p.270–92.

Landen, Leif, *Gustaf III: en biografi* (Stockholm, 2004).

Landes, Joan B., *Women and the public sphere in the age of the French Revolution* (Ithaca, NY, 1988).

Landi, Sandro, "Censure et formation de l'opinion publique dans l'Italie des Habsbourg," in *L'Opinion publique dans l'Europe des Lumières: stratégies et concepts*, ed. Bertrand Binoche and Alain J. Lemaître (Paris, 2013), p.25–39.

Lane, Jeremy F., *Pierre Bourdieu: a critical introduction* (London, 2000).

Lang, Ines, "Die Marienfeste und Pfingstfeiern am Wiener Hof im 17. und 18. Jahrhundert," in *Der Wiener Hof im Spiegel der Zeremonialprotokolle (1652–1800)*, ed. Irmgard Pangerl, Martin Scheutz, and Thomas Winkelbauer (Innsbruck, 2007), p.463–92.

Langewitz, Helena, "Der Garten in der Oper—die Oper im Garten: Theatralisierung von Gärten im Musiktheater des 17. und 18. Jahrhunderts," *Die Gartenkunst* 27:2 (2015), p.329–46.

La Parra, Emilio, *Manuel Godoy: la aventura del poder* (Barcelona, 2005).

Lara Nieto, María del Carmen, *Ilustración española y pensamiento inglés: Jovellanos* (Granada, 2008).

Le Gall, Yvon, "Les Lumières et le droit de grâce," *Littératures classiques* 60:2 (2006), p.269–312.

Lekeby, Kjell, *Esoterica i Svenska Frimurarordens arkiv 1776–1803* (Stockholm, 2011).

–, *Gustaf Adolf Reuterholms hemliga arkiv från 1780-talet* (Stockholm, 2011).

–, *Gustaviansk mystik: alkemister, kabbalister, magiker, andeskådare, astrologer och skattgrävare i den esoteriska kretsen kring G. A. Reuterholm, hertig Carl och hertiginnan Charlotta 1776–1803* (Stockholm, 2010).

Lemaître, Alain J., "Repères historiographiques," in *L'Opinion publique dans l'Europe des Lumières: stratégies et concepts*, ed. Bertrand Binoche and Alain J. Lemaître (Paris, 2013), p.15–22.

Leslie, Michael, "History and historiography in the English landscape garden," in *Perspectives on garden histories*, ed. Michel Conan (Washington, DC, 1999), p.91–106.

Lettner, Gerda, *Das Rückzugsgefecht der Aufklärung in Wien 1790–1792* (Frankfurt am Main, 1988).

Liechtenhan, Francine-Dominique, *La Russie entre en Europe: Elisabeth Iʳᵉ et la succession d'Autriche, 1740–1750* (Paris, 1997).

Lilti, Antoine, *The World of the salons: sociability and worldliness in eighteenth-century Paris*, translated by Lydia G. Cochrane (Oxford, 2015).

Lindqvist, Herman, *Historien om Sverige: Gustavs dagar* (Stockholm, 1997).

Llombart, Vicent, *Jovellanos y el otoño de las luces: educación, economía, política y felicidad* (Gijón, 2012).

Lock, F. P., *The Politics of Gulliver's travels* (Oxford, 1980).

Lonsdale, Roger, *Dr. Charles Burney: a literary biography* (Oxford, 1965).

López-Cordón Cortezo, María Victoria, "Burocracia y erudición en la España del siglo XVIII," in *L'Espagne, l'Etat, les Lumières: mélanges en l'honneur de Didier Ozanam*, ed. Jean-Pierre Dedieu and Bernard Vincent (Madrid, 2004), p.155–72.

–, "The merits of good *gobierno*: culture and politics in the Bourbon court," in *The Spanish Enlightenment revisited*, ed. Jesús Astigarraga, Oxford University Studies in the Enlightenment (Oxford, Voltaire Foundation, 2015), p.19–39.

Luh, Jürgen, *Der Große: Friedrich II. von Preußen* (Munich, 2011).

Machlitt, Ulla, *Die anhaltisch-dessauischen Domänen in der Periode des Übergangs von der feudalen zur kapitalistischen Produktionsweise (etwa 1700 bis 1800)* (Eisleben, 1971).

Madariaga, Isabel de, *Russia in the age of Catherine the Great* (New Haven, CT, 1981).

Marasinova, Elena, "The prayer of an empress and the death penalty moratorium in eighteenth-century Russia," *The Journal of religious history, literature and culture* 3:2 (2017), p.36–55.

Marschke, Benjamin, *Absolutely Pietist: patronage, factionalism, and state-building in the early eighteenth-century Prussian army chaplaincy* (Tübingen, 2005).

–, "Die russische Partei, ein Pietist auf dem Thron, und ein Hof-Komödiant: Wandel und Wendepunkte am Hof Friedrich Wilhelms I.," in *Mehr als Soldatenkönig: neue Schlaglichter auf Lebenswelt und Regierungswerk Friedrich Wilhelms I.*, ed. Frank Göse and Jürgen Kloosterhuis (Berlin, 2020), p.73–86.

Marschner, Joanna, David Bindman, and Lisa L. Ford (ed.), *Enlightened princesses: Caroline, Augusta and Charlotte and the making of the modern world* (New Haven, CT, 2017).

Martin, Julian, *Francis Bacon, the state and the reform of natural philosophy* (Cambridge, 2007).

Martus, Steffen, *Aufklärung: das deutsche 18. Jahrhundert–ein Epochenbild* (Berlin, 2015).

Maslow, Luise, "'Die Natur selbst war die Baumeisterin': der Felsengarten Sanspareil der Wilhelmine von Bayreuth als Ergebnis kultureller Austauschprozesse," *Die Gartenkunst* 29:2 (2017), p.250–61.

–, "'…den Vorschriften der Natur folgend, zugleich so weise und so glücklich': Fénelons *Les Aventures de Télémaque* als literarisches Gartenprogramm der Wilhelmine von Bayreuth," in *Europäische Utopien–Utopien Europas*, ed. Oliver Victor and Laura Weiß (Berlin, 2021), p.123–47.

Mason, Haydn T. (ed.), *The Darnton debate: books and revolution in the eighteenth century* (Oxford, 1998).

Matikkala, Antti, and Staffan Rosén, *Perspectives on the honours system* (Stockholm, 2015).

Mauser, Wolfram, "Von der Hofkritik zur Fürstenschelte: Kritischer Diskurs als Akt politischer Selbstbefreiung von Canitz bis Pfeffel," in *Konzepte aufgeklärter Lebensführung: literarische Kultur im frühmodernen Deutschland*, ed. Wolfram Mauser (Würzburg, 2000), p.80–102.

McMahon, Darrin M., and Samuel Moyn (ed.), *Rethinking modern European intellectual history* (Oxford, 2014).

Menéndez Pelayo, Marcelino, *Historia de los heterodoxos españoles*, 8 vols. (Madrid, 1880–1882).

Merten, Klaus, *Der Bayreuther Hofarchitekt Joseph Saint-Pierre (1708/9–1754)* (Bayreuth, 1964).

Michels, Norbert (ed.), *"... Waren nicht des ersten Bedürfnisses, sondern des Geschmacks und des Luxus": zum 200. Gründungstag der Chalcographischen Gesellschaft Dessau* (Weimar, 1996).

Michon, Cédric, "Du bon usage de l'anachronisme en histoire: l'opinion publique à la Renaissance," in *L'Opinion publique en Europe (1600–1800)*, ed. Lucien Bély (Paris, 2011), p.39–67.

Mikoletzky, Hanns, *Österreich: das große 18. Jahrhundert* (Vienna, 1967).

Mikoletzky, Lorenz, "Leopold II. 1790–1792," in *Die Kaiser der Neuzeit 1519–1918*, ed. Anton Schindling and Walter Ziegler (Munich, 1990), p.277–87.

Mittelstädt, Ina, *Wörlitz, Weimar, Muskau: der Landschaftsgarten als Medium des Hochadels, 1760–1840* (Cologne, 2015).

Moberly, R. B., "The influence of French classical drama on Mozart's 'La clemenza di Tito,'" *Music & letters* 55:3 (1974), p.286–98.

Mooser, Robert-Aloys, *Annales de la musique et des musiciens en Russie au XVIIIᵉ siècle*, 3 vols. (Geneva, 1948–1951).

Mornet, Daniel, *Les Origines intellectuelles de la Révolution: 1715–1787* (Paris, 1933).

Moroney, Davitt, "Couperin, Marpurg and Roeser: a Germanic *Art de toucher le clavecin*, or a French *Wahre Art?*," in *The Keyboard in baroque Europe*, ed. Christopher Hogwood (Cambridge, 2003), p.111–30.

Morrow, Mary Sue, *German music criticism in the late eighteenth century: aesthetic issues in instrumental music* (New York, 1997).

Müller-Lindenberg, Ruth, "Melancholie, Suizid und Herrschaft: Quellen und Kontexte zu einigen Libretti der Wilhelmine," in *Wilhelmine von Bayreuth heute: das kulturelle Erbe der Markgräfin*, ed. Günter Berger (Bayreuth, 2009), p.173–86.

Mulsow, Martin, *Moderne aus dem Untergrund: Radikale Frühaufklärung in Deutschland (1680–1720)* (Hamburg, 2002).

Müssel, Karl, "Die große Bayreuther Fürstenhochzeit 1748—Vorgeschichte, Vorbereitungen und Verlauf: ein Beitrag zum Jubiläum des Markgräflichen Opernhauses," *Archiv für Geschichte von Oberfranken* 77 (1997), p.7–118.

Nadezhdin, Aleksei [Nadezhda Alekseeva], "K vorposu o teme *milosti* v russkoi literature XVIII veka," in *Von Wenigen–Ot nemnogikh: Sbornik k 70-letiiu N. D. Kochetkovoi* (St. Petersburg, 2008), p.8–17.

Nekliudova, Maria, "'Milost' i 'pravosudie': o frantsuzskom kontekste pushkinskoi temy," in *Pushkinskie chteniia v Tartu 2*, ed. Liubov' N. Kisileva (Tartu, 2000), p.204–15.

Neugebauer, Wolfgang, "Aufgeklärter Absolutismus, Reformabsolutismus und struktureller Wandel im Deutschland des 18. Jahrhunderts," in *Ernst II. von Sachsen-Gotha-Altenburg: ein Herrscher im Zeitalter der Aufklärung*, ed. Werner Greiling, Andreas Klinger, and Christoph Köhler (Cologne, 2005), p.23–39.

Neumann, Carsten, "Das Trianon de Porcelaine im Park von Versailles als erster chinoiser Bau in Europa," in *China in Schloss und Garten: Chinoise Architekturen und Innenräume*, ed. Dirk Welich (Dresden, 2010), p.75–81.

Niedermeier, Michael, "Der anhaltische Philanthrop: Schriftsteller und Aufrührer Johann Christian Schmohl und seine spektakuläre Flucht aus Halle im Jahre 1781," in *Europa in der Frühen Neuzeit*, ed. Erich Donnert, 7 vols. (Weimar, 1997–2008), vol.4, p.229–48.

–, "Campe als Direktor des Dessauer Philanthropins," in *Visionäre Lebensklugheit: Joachim Heinrich Campe in seiner Zeit (1746–1818)*, ed. Hanno Schmitt (Wiesbaden, 1996), p.45–65.

–, "Germanen in den Gärten: 'altdeutsche Heldengräber,' 'gotische' Denkmäler und die patriotische Gedächtniskultur," in *Revolutio Germanica: die Sehnsucht nach der "alten Freiheit" der Germanen 1750–1820*, ed. Jost Hermand and Michael Niedermeier (Frankfurt am Main, 2003), p.21–116.

–, "Im Gartenland der Göttin Venus: Dessau-Wörlitz zwischen Aufklärung, Politik und erotisch-kosmologischer Weltanschauung," in *Schauplatz vernünftiger Menschen: Kultur und Geschichte in Anhalt-Dessau*, ed. Hans Wilderotter (Berlin, 2006), p.157–92.

–, "Landschaft/Garten," in *Handbuch europäische Aufklärung: Begriffe, Konzepte, Wirkung*, ed. Heinz Thoma (Stuttgart, 2015), p.323–34.

–, "Macht, Memoria und Mätressen: herrschaftliche Gartenkunst als politische Besetzung der Landschaft in Schwetzingen und Wörlitz," in *Politische Gartenkunst? Landschaftsgestaltung und Herrschaftsrepräsentation des Fürsten Franz von Anhalt-Dessau in vergleichender Perspektive: Wörlitz, Sanssouci und Schwetzingen*, ed. Andreas Pečar and Holger Zaunstöck (Halle, 2015), p.35–81.

–, "'Thu Recht und scheue Niemand': Johann Christian Schmohl: sorbisch-patriotischer Bauernsohn, philanthropischer Radikalaufklärer, 'Hochverräter': erneute Spurensuche," in *Dessau-Wörlitz und Reckahn: Treffpunkte für Aufklärung, Volksaufklärung und Philanthropismus*, ed. Hanno Schmitt (Bremen, 2014), p.123–42.

–, "'Wir waren vor den Hohenzollern da': zur politischen Ikonographie des frühen Landschaftsgartens mit einem Seitenblick auf Fontanes Roman 'Vor dem Sturm,'" in *Gehäuse der Mnemosyne: Architektur als Schriftform der Erinnerung*, ed. Harald Tausch (Göttingen, 2003), p.171–207.

Nussbaum, Felicity, *The Brink of all we hate: English satires on women 1660–1750* (Lexington, KY, 1984).

O'Brien, Karen, "The return of the Enlightenment," *American historical review* 115:5 (2010), p.1426–35.

Oevermann, Ulrich, "Der Intellektuelle: soziologische Strukturbestimmung des Komplementär von Öffentlichkeit," in *Die Macht des Geistes: Soziologische Fallanalysen zum Strukturtyp des Intellektuellen*, ed. Andreas Franzmann, Sascha Liebermann, and Jörg Tykwer (Frankfurt am Main, 2001), p.13–75.

Ohji, Kenta, "Raynal, Necker et la Compagnie des Indes: quelques aspects inconnus de la génèse et de l'évolution de l'*Histoire des deux Indes,*" in *Raynal et ses réseaux,* ed. Gilles Bancarel (Paris, 2011), p.105–82.

Oleskiewicz, Mary, "Music at the court of Brandenburg-Prussia," in *Music at German courts, 1715–1760: changing artistic priorities,* ed. Samantha Owens, Barbara M. Reul, and Janice B. Stockigt (Woodbridge, 2011), p.79–130.

Omelchenko, Oleg A., *"Zakonnaia monarkhiia" Ekateriny II: prosveshchënnyi absoliutizm v Rossii* (Moscow, 1993).

Önnerfors, Andreas, "1803 års statliga reglering av ordenssällskapen," in *Svenskt frimureri under 1800-talet,* ed. Marcus Willén (Uppsala, 2018), p.16–40.

–, "Between the sacred and the secular: connotations of European space," in *Negotiating Europe: foundations, dynamics, challenges,* ed. Anamaria Dutceac and Andreas Önnerfors (Lund, 2007), p.18–37.

–, "Criminal cosmopolitans: conspiracy theories surrounding the assassination of Gustav III of Sweden in 1792," in *Höllische Ingenieure: Kriminalitätsgeschichte der Attentate und Verschwörungen zwischen Spätmittelalter und Moderne,* ed. André Krischer and Tilman Haug (Konstanz, 2021), p.135–50.

–, "'Död är liv': iscensättning av döden i det europeiska 1700-talsfrimureriet," *Historisk Tidskrift* 131:3 (2011), p.459–90.

–, *Freemasonry: a very short introduction* (Oxford, 2017).

–, "From Jacobite support to a part of the state apparatus: Swedish freemasonry between reform and revolution," in *Franc-maçonnerie et politique au siècle des Lumières: Europe–Amériques,* ed. Cécile Révauger (Bordeaux, 2006), p.201–24.

–, "Knights of freedom? The Swedish 'Order of Wallhall' as a secret network of officers and the Anjala-Mutiny in 1788," in *Geheime Netzwerke im Militär 1700–1945,* ed. Gundula Gahlen, Daniel M. Segesser, and Carmen Winkel (Paderborn, 2016), p.66–84.

–, *Mystiskt brödraskap, mäktigt nätverk: studier i det svenska 1700-talsfrimureriet* (Lund, 2006).

–, "Norge 1814: den svenska politiken mellan vision och verklighet," in *Overgangstid: forargelse og forsoning høsten 1814,* ed. Ruth Hemstad and Bjørn Arne Steine (Oslo, 2016), p.82–98.

–, "'Position or profession in the profane world': 4300 Swedish freemasons from 1731 to 1800," in *Masonic and esoteric heritage: new perspectives for art and heritage policies,* ed. Andrea Kroon (The Hague, 2005), p.194–210.

–, "La sociabilité féminine en Suède au XVIIIᵉ siècle," *La Pensée et les hommes* 82–83 (2011), p.77–96.

–, *Svenska Pommern: kulturmöten och identifikation 1720–1815* (Lund, 2003).

Ospovat, Kirill, "Mikhail Lomonosov writes to his patron: professional ethos, literary rhetoric and social ambition," *Jahrbücher für Geschichte Osteuropas* 59:2 (2011), p.240–66.

–, *Terror and pity: Aleksandr Sumarokov and the theater of power in Elizabethan Russia* (Boston, MA, 2016).

Osterloh, Karl-Heinz, *Joseph von Sonnenfels und die österreichische Reformbewegung im Zeitalter des aufgeklärten Absolutismus: eine Studie zum Zusammenhang von Kameralwissenschaft und Verwaltungspraxis* (Lübeck, 1970).

Ozouf, Mona, "L'opinion publique," in *The French Revolution and the creation of modern political culture*, ed. Keith Michael Baker, 4 vols. (Oxford, 1987–1994), vol.1, p.419–34.

Paku, Gillian, "Anonymity in the eighteenth century," *Oxford handbooks online*, http://www.oxfordhandbooks.com/view/10.1093/oxfordhb/9780199935338.001.0001/oxfordhb-9780199935338-e-37 (last accessed January 25, 2022).

Pangerl, Irmgart, "Höfische Öffentlichkeit," in *Der Wiener Hof im Spiegel der Zeremonialprotokolle (1652–1800)*, ed. Irmgard Pangerl, Martin Scheutz, and Thomas Winkelbauer (Innsbruck, 2007), p.255–87.

Paulus, Helmut-Eberhard, "Die 'Römische Ruine' von 1756 in der Eremitage zu Bayreuth: eine Gartenstaffage als Denkmal der Erinnerung an die italienische Reise," *Arx: Burgen und Schlösser in Bayern, Österreich und Südtirol* 31:1–2 (2009), p.53–62.

Pečar, Andreas, "Der Intellektuelle seit der Aufklärung: Rolle und/oder Kulturmuster?," *Das achtzehnte Jahrhundert* 35 (2011), p.187–203.

–, *Die Masken des Königs: Friedrich II. von Preußen als Schriftsteller* (Frankfurt am Main, 2016).

–, *Die Ökonomie der Ehre: Der höfische Adel am Kaiserhof Karls VI. (1713–1740)* (Darmstadt, 2003).

–, "Vater Franz oder Fürst Franz von Anhalt-Dessau? Vorbedingungen zum Verständnis des Fürsten in seiner Residenzstadt Dessau," in *Der Fürst in seiner Stadt: Leopold Friedrich Franz und Dessau*, ed. Andreas Pečar and Frank Kreißler (Petersberg, 2017), p.10–17.

–, and Thomas Müller-Bahlke (ed.), *Die Causa Christian Wolff: ein epochemachender Skandal und seine Hintergründe* (Wiesbaden, 2015).

–, and Damien Tricoire, *Falsche Freunde: War die Aufklärung wirklich die Geburtsstunde der Moderne?* (Frankfurt am Main, 2015).

–, and Holger Zaunstöck (ed.), *Politische Gartenkunst? Landschaftsgestaltung und Herrschaftsrepräsentation des Fürsten Franz von Anhalt-Dessau in vergleichender Perspektive: Wörlitz, Sanssouci und Schwetzingen* (Halle, 2015).

Pekarskii, P., *Istoriia Imperatorskoi Akademii nauk v Peterburge*, 2 vols. (Saint-Petersburg, 1870–1873).

Peset, José Luis, "Ciencia, nobleza y ejército en el Seminario de Nobles de Madrid (1770–1788)," in *Mayans y la Ilustración*, ed. Salvador Cardona Miralles (Valencia, 1981), p.519–35.

Péter, Róbert (ed.), *British freemasonry 1717–1813* (Abingdon, 2015).

Pevsner, Nikolaus, "Von der Entstehung des Malerischen als Kunstprinzip," in Nikolaus Pevsner, *Architektur und Design von der Romantik zur Sachlichkeit* (Munich, 1971), p.11–39.

Pfeifer, Ingo, "Dynastische Repräsentation im Wörlitzer Gartenreich," in *Politische Gartenkunst? Landschaftsgestaltung und Herrschaftsrepräsentation des Fürsten Franz von Anhalt-Dessau in vergleichender Perspektive: Wörlitz, Sanssouci und Schwetzingen*, ed. Andreas Pečar and Holger Zaunstöck (Halle, 2015), p.25–33.

–, *Schloss Wörlitz* (Munich, 2000).

Pfeiffer, Gerhard, "Markgräfin Wilhelmine und die Eremitagen bei Bayreuth und Sanspareil," in *Archive und Geschichtsforschung: Studien zur fränkischen und bayrischen Geschichte, Fridolin Solleder zum 80. Geburtstag dargebracht*, ed. Horst Heldmann (Neustadt an der Aisch, 1966), p.209–21.

Pichler, Caroline, *Denkwürdigkeiten aus meinem Leben* (Vienna, 1844).

Pizer, John, "Lessing and Wieland on music and poetry," *Lessing yearbook* 33 (2001), p.97–114.

Pocock, J. G. A., "Historiography and Enlightenment: a view of their history," *Modern intellectual history* 5:1 (2008), p.83–96.

Poirson, Martial, "Du spectacle de la société à la société de spectacle: la critique théâtrale dans les *Mémoires secrets*," in *Le Règne de la critique: l'imaginaire culturel des Mémoires secrets*, ed. C. Cave (Paris, 2010), p.179–204.

Pokorny, Veronika, "Clementia Austriaca: Studien zur Bedeutung der clementia Principis für die Habsburger im 16. und 17. Jh.," *Mitteilungen des Instituts für österreichische Geschichtsforschung* 86 (1978), p.310–64.

Popkin, Jeremy, "The *Mémoires secrets* and the reading of the Enlightenment," in *The Mémoires secrets and the culture of publicity in eighteenth-century France*, ed. Jeremy Popkin and Bernadette Fort (Oxford, 1998), p.9–35.

–, "Pamphlet journalism at the end of the Old Regime," *Eighteenth-century studies* 22:3 (1989), p.351–67.

Porter, Roy, and Mikuláš Teich (ed.), *The Enlightenment in national context* (Cambridge, 1981).

Prignitz, Christoph, *Vaterlandsliebe und Freiheit: deutscher Patriotismus von 1750 bis 1850* (Wiesbaden, 1981).

Prokopovich, Feofan, *Sochineniia*, ed. I. P. Eremin (Moscow, 1961).

Proskurina, Vera, *Creating the empress: politics and poetry in the age of Catherine II* (Boston, MA, 2011).

Proust, Jacques, "Diderot et l'expérience russe: un exemple de pratique théorique au XVIIIe siècle," *SVEC* 151–55 (1976), p.1777–1800.

Psychoyou, Théodora, "Ancients and Moderns, Italians and French: the seventeenth-century quarrel over music, its status and transformations," in *The Ancients and the Moderns: comparative perspectives*, ed. Paddy Bullard and Alexis Tadié (Oxford, 2016), p.133–54.

Pumpianskii, L. V., "Lomonosov i nemetskaia shkola razuma," *XVIII vek* 14 (1983), p.3–44.

Quintili, Paolo, "Le stoïcisme révolutionnaire de Diderot dans l'*Essai sur Sénèque* par rapport à la contribution à l'*Histoire des deux Indes*," *Recherches sur Diderot et sur l'Encyclopédie* 36 (2004), p.29–42.

Quondam, Amedeo, *La conversazione: un modello italiano* (Rome, 2007).

–, *El discurso cortesano*, ed. Eduardo Torres Corominas (Madrid, 2013).

–, *Forma del vivere: l'etica del gentiluomo e i moralisti italiani* (Bologna, 2010).

Raeff, Marc, "Transfiguration and modernization: the paradoxes of social disciplining, paedagogical leadership, and the Enlightenment in 18th-century Russia," in *Alteuropa, Ancien Régime, frühe Neuzeit: Probleme und Methoden der Forschung*, ed. Hans-Erich Bödeker and Ernst Hinrichs (Stuttgart, 1991), p.99–115.

–, *The Well-ordered police state: social and institutional change through law in the Germanies and Russia,* 1600–1800 (New Haven, CT, 1983).

Rahmede, Stephanie, *Die Buchhandlung der Gelehrten zu Dessau: ein Beitrag zur Schriftstelleremanzipation um 1800* (Wiesbaden, 2008).

Rattner Gelbart, Nina, "The *Journal des dames* and its female editors: politics, censorship and feminism in the Old Regime press," in *Press and politics in pre-revolutionary France*, ed. Jack Censer and Jeremy Popkin (Berkeley, CA, 1987), p.24–73.

Raven, James, *British fiction 1750–1770: a chronological check-list of prose fiction printed in Britain and Ireland* (Newark, DE, 1987).

Raymond, Joad, *Pamphlets and pamphleteering in early modern Britain* (Cambridge, 2003).

Reil, Friedrich, *Leopold Friedrich Franz, Herzog und Fürst von Anhalt-Deßau, ältestregierender Fürst in Anhalt, nach Seinem Wirken und Wesen: mit Hinblick auf merkwürdige Erscheinungen Seiner Zeit* (Dessau, 1845).

Reinalter, Helmut, "Gegen die 'Tollwuth der Aufklärungsbarbarei': Leopold Alois Hoffmann und der frühe Konservativismus in Österreich," in *Von "Obscuranten" und "Eudämonisten": Gegenaufklärerische, konservative und antirevolutionäre Publizisten im späten 18. Jahrhundert*, ed. Christoph Weiß und Reiner Wild (St. Ingbert, 1999), p.221–44.

–, *Joseph II.: Reformer auf dem Kaiserthron* (Munich, 2011).

Reinhard, Wolfgang, *Geschichte der Staatsgewalt: eine vergleichende Verfassungsgeschichte Europas von den Anfängen bis zur Gegenwart* (Munich, 1999).

– (ed.), *Power elites and state building* (Oxford, 1996).

Robbins, Caroline, *The Eighteenth-century Commonwealth man* (Cambridge, MA, 1959).

Robelin, Roger de, "Johannes-frimureriet i Sverige under 1700-talet," in *I guld och himmelsblått: frimureri, ett ideal i tiden*, ed. Tom C. Bergroth (Åbo, 1992), p.29–92.

Robertson, Ritchie, "Religion and the Enlightenment: a review essay," *German history* 25:3 (2007), p.422–32.

Roche, Daniel, *Les Républicains des lettres: gens de culture et Lumières au XVIIIᵉ siècle* (Paris, 1988).

–, *Le Siècle des Lumières en province: académies et académiciens provinciaux, 1680–1789* (Paris, 1978).

Röder, Matthias, "Music, politics, and the public sphere in late eighteenth-century Berlin," doctoral dissertation, Harvard University, 2009.

Rogers, Pat, *Pope and the destiny of the Stuarts* (Oxford, 2005).

Roll, Christine, "Barbaren? *Tabula rasa?* Wie Leibniz sein neues Wissen über Russland auf den Begriff brachte: eine Studie über die Bedeutung der Vernetzung gelehrter Korrespondenzen für die Ermöglichung aufgeklärter Diskurse," in *Umwelt und Weltgestaltung: Leibniz' politisches Denken in seiner Zeit*, ed. Friedrich Beiderbeck, Irene Dingel, and Wenchao Li (Göttingen, 2015), p.307–58.

Rosenbaum, Alexander, *Der Amateur als Künstler: Studien zur Geschichte und Funktion des Dilettantismus im 18. Jahrhundert* (Berlin, 2010).

Sánchez Blanco, Francisco, *La ilustración goyesca: la cultura en España durante el reinado de Carlos IV, 1788–1808* (Madrid, 2007).

Sánchez Corredera, Silverio, *Jovellanos y el jovellanismo, una perspectiva filosófica* (Oviedo, 2004).

Sareil, Jean, *Voltaire et les Grands* (Geneva, 1978).

Sauter, Michael, "The Prussian monarchy and the practices of Enlightenment," in *Monarchisms in the age of Enlightenment: liberty, patriotism, and the common good*, ed. Hans Blom, John Christian Laursen, and Luisa Simonutti (Toronto, 2007), p.217–39.

Sawyer, Jeffrey K., *Printed poison: pamphlet propaganda, faction politics and the public sphere in early seventeenth-century France* (Berkeley, CA, 1990).

Scheutz, Martin, and Jakob Wühner, "Dienst, Pflicht, Ordnung und gute policey," in *Der Wiener Hof im Spiegel der Zeremonialprotokolle (1652–1800)*, ed. Irmgard Pangerl, Martin Scheutz, and Thomas Winkelbauer (Innsbruck, 2007), p.15–94.

Schierle, Ingrid, "Patriotism and emotions: love of the fatherland in Catherinian Russia," *Ab Imperio* 3 (2009), p.65–93.

Schilling, Arniko F., "Telemach und der Felsengarten," in *850 Jahre Burg Zwernitz: Beiträge zur Geschichte der Burg und des Felsengartens Sanspareil*, ed. Schloss- und Gartenverwaltung Bayreuth-Eremitage (Bayreuth, 2007), p.84–89.

Schilling, Lothar, *Kaunitz und das Renversement des alliances: Studien zur außenpolitischen Konzeption Wenzel Antons von Kaunitz* (Berlin, 1994).

–, "Vom Nutzen und Nachteil eines Mythos," in *L'Absolutisme*, ed. Lothar Schilling (Munich, 2008), p.13–31.

Schippan, Michael, *Die Aufklärung in Russland im 18. Jahrhundert* (Wiesbaden, 2012).

Schlobach, Jochen, "Französische Aufklärung und deutsche Fürsten," *Zeitschrift für historische Forschung* 17:3 (1990), p.327–49.

Schloss- und Gartenverwaltung Bayreuth-Eremitage (ed.), *850 Jahre Burg Zwernitz: Beiträge zur Geschichte der Burg und des Felsengartens Sanspareil* (Bayreuth, 2007).

Schmidt, James, "The Counter-Enlightenment: historical notes on a concept historians should avoid," *Eighteenth-century studies* 49:1 (2015), p.83–86.

–, "Enlightenment as concept and context," *Journal of the history of ideas* 75:4 (2014), p.677–85.

– (ed.), *What is Enlightenment? Eighteenth-century answers and twentieth-century questions* (Berkeley, CA, 1996).

Schneiders, Werner, "Die Philosophie des aufgeklärten Absolutismus: zum Verhältnis von Philosophie und Politik, nicht nur im 18. Jahrhundert," in *Aufklärung als Politisierung–Politisierung der Aufklärung*, ed. Hans Erich Bödeker and Ulrich Herrmann (Hamburg, 1987), p.32–52.

–, "Sozietätspläne und Sozialutopie bei Leibniz," *Studia Leibnitiana* 7:1 (1975), p.58–80.

Schröderheim, Elis, *Statssekreteraren Elis Schröderheims Anteckningar till Konung Gustaf III's historia; jemte brefvexling emellan Konungen och honom*, ed. Karl Vilhelm Lilljecrona (Örebro, 1851).

Schulze, Hans-Joachim, "Friedrich Wilhelm Marpurg, Johann Sebastian Bach und die 'Gedanken über die welschen Tonkünstler' (1751)," *Bach-Jahrbuch* 90 (2004), p.121–32.

–, "Johann Friedrich Agricola," in *Die Musik in Geschichte und Gegenwart: Personenteil*, ed. Ludwig Finscher, 2nd ed., 17 vols. (Kassel, 1999), vol.1, p.219.

Schwartz, Michael, "Leviathan oder Lucifer: Reinhart Kosellecks 'Kritik und Krise' revisited," *Zeitschrift für Religions- und Geistesgeschichte* 45:1 (1993), p.33–57.

Schweinitz, Anna-Franziska von, *Waldersee und Vater Franz: vom Unglück der nichtehelichen Geburt* (Wettin-Löbejün, 2017).

Schweizer, Stefan, "Raumformen, Ornamentik, Stile: der Garten als Kunstwerk im System der bildenden Künste," in *Gartenkunst in Deutschland von der Frühen Neuzeit bis heute: Geschichte–Themen–Perspektiven*, ed. Stefan Schweizer and Sascha Winter (Regensburg, 2012), p.103–21.

Scott, Hamish M. (ed.), *Enlightened absolutism: reform and reformers in later eighteenth-century Europe* (London, 1990).

Sellin, Volker, "Friedrich der Große und der aufgeklärte Absolutismus: Ein Beitrag zur Klärung eines umstrittenen Begriffs," in *Soziale Bewegung und politische Verfassung: Beiträge zur Geschichte der modernen Welt*, ed. Ulrich Engelhardt (Stuttgart, 1976), p.83–112.

Sgard, Jean, "Les *Mémoires secrets* et l'*Observateur anglais*," in *Le Règne de la critique: l'imaginaire culturel des Mémoires secrets*, ed. C. Cave (Paris, 2010), p.345–56.

–, "Pidansat de Mairobert: journaliste à deux visages," in *Nouvelles, gazettes, mémoires secrets (1775–1800)*, ed. Birgitta Berglund-Nilsson (Karlstad, 2000), p.15–26.

Shapin, Steven, "Of gods and kings: natural philosophy and politics in the Leibniz–Clarke disputes," *Isis* 72:2 (1981), p.187–215.

–, and Simon Schaffer, *Leviathan and the air-pump: Hobbes, Boyle, and the experimental life* (Princeton, NJ, 2011).

Sharpe, Kevin, *Selling the Tudor monarchy: authority and image in sixteenth-century England* (New Haven, CT, 2009).

Sheehan, Jonathan, "Enlightenment, religion, and the enigma of secularization: a review essay," *American historical review* 108:4 (2003), p.1061–80.

Siemann, Wolfram, *Metternich: Staatsmann zwischen Restauration und Moderne* (Munich, 2010).

Sittig, Claudius, and Christian Wieland (ed.), *Die Kunst des Adels in der Frühen Neuzeit* (Wiesbaden, 2018).

Smith, Hannah, *Georgian monarchy, politics, and culture: 1714–1760* (Cambridge, 2006).

Specht, Reinhold, *Geschichte der Stadt Zerbst*, 2 vols. (Dessau, 1998).

–, "Das unrühmliche Ende des Fürstentums Anhalt-Zerbst: ein Beitrag zur preußischen Kriegspolitik und zu dem Soldatenhandel deutscher Fürsten im 18. Jahrhundert," unpublished manuscript, 1958 (Landesarchiv Saxony-Anhalt, Abt. Dessau: LAO 230).

Spielman, John, *The City and the crown: Vienna and the imperial court, 1600–1740* (West Lafayette, IN, 1993).

Sprat, Thomas, *History of the Royal Society* (St. Louis, MO, 1958).

Stacher-Gfall, Anna-Katharina, "Das Andreasfest des Ordens vom Goldenen Vlies im Spiegel der Zeremonialprotokolle des Wiener Hofes der Jahre 1712–1800," in *Der Wiener Hof im Spiegel der Zeremonialprotokolle (1652–1800)*, ed. Irmgard Pangerl, Martin Scheutz, and Thomas Winkelbauer (Innsbruck, 2007), p.309–36.

Starikova, Liudmila M. (ed.),
*Teatral'naia zhizn' Rossii v epokhu
Elizavety Petrovny: dokumental'naia
khronika, 1740–1750*, vol.2
(Moscow, 2003).

Starkey, David, "Court history
in perspective," in *The English
court from the Wars of the Roses to
the Civil War*, ed. David Starkey
(London, 1987), p.1–24.

–, "A reply: Tudor government:
the facts?," *Historical journal* 31:4
(1988), p.921–31.

Stegnii, Piotr (ed.), *Vremia smet,'
ili Sushchaia sluzhitel'nitsa Fiva:
Khroniki vremën imperatritsy
Ekateriny Velikoi* (Moscow, 2002).

Stenger, Gerhardt, *Diderot: le
combattant de la liberté* (Paris,
2013).

–, "Diderots Beitrag zu Raynals
Geschichte beider Indien:
das erste Donnergrollen der
Französischen Revolution,"
in *Denis Diderot und die Macht
/ Denis Diderot et le pouvoir*,
ed. Isabelle Deflers (Berlin,
2015), p.121–34.

Stenzel, Gustav Adolf Harald,
*Handbuch der Anhaltischen
Geschichte*, 2 vols. (Dessau,
1820–1824).

–, "Leopold Friedrich Franz:
Herzog zu Anhalt-Dessau,"
*Zeitgenossen: ein biographisches
Magazin für die Geschichte unserer
Zeit* 2:3 (1817), p.37–82.

Stewart, Philip, "Critiquer la
politique," in *Le Règne de la
critique: l'imaginaire culturel des
Mémoires secrets*, ed. C. Cave
(Paris, 2010), p.83–94.

Storm, Eric, *La perspectiva del
progreso: pensamiento político en
la España del cambio de siglo,
1890–1914* (Madrid, 2001).

Stroev, Alexandre, and Georges
Dulac, "Diderot en 1775 vu par
Grimm: deux lettres inédites à la
princesse Golitsyna et au comte
Roumiantsev," *Dix-huitième siècle*
25 (1993), p.275–93.

Strohm, Reinhard, "Italian *operisti*
north of the Alps: 1700–1750,"
in *The Eighteenth-century diaspora
of Italian music and musicians*, ed.
Reinhard Strohm (Turnhout,
2001), p.1–60.

Süßmann, Johannes, "Der
Garten als Bauakt: zur
Einrichtung 'natürlicher
Herrschaft' in der Wörlitzer
Landschaftsarchitektur,"
in *Politische Gartenkunst?
Landschaftsgestaltung und
Herrschaftsrepräsentation des
Fürsten Franz von Anhalt-Dessau
in vergleichender Perspektive:
Wörlitz, Sanssouci und
Schwetzingen*, ed. Andreas Pečar
and Holger Zaunstöck (Halle,
2015), p.15–24.

Swann, Julian, "Ministres et
opinion publique," in *L'Opinion
publique dans l'Europe des Lumières:
stratégies et concepts*, ed. Bertrand
Binoche and Alain J. Lemaître
(Paris, 2013), p.41–60.

Szabo, Franz A. J., "Favorit,
Premierminister oder drittes
Staatsoberhaupt?," in *Der zweite
Mann im Staat: Oberste Amtsträger
und Favoriten im Umkreis der
Reichsfürsten in der Frühen Neuzeit*,
ed. Michael Kaiser and Andreas
Pečar (Berlin, 2003), p.345–62.

–, *Kaunitz and enlightened absolutism
1753–1780* (Cambridge, 1994).

Talbot, Michael, "Et in Italia ego: musicians and the experience of Italy, 1650–1750," in *Europäische Musiker in Venedig, Rom und Neapel (1650–1750)*, ed. Anne-Madeleine Foulet and Gesa zur Nieden (Kassel, 2015), p.68–86.

Tarin, René, *Diderot et la Révolution française: controverses et polémique autour d'un philosophe* (Paris, 2001).

Taruskin, Richard, *The Oxford history of Western music*, 6 vols. (Oxford, 2005).

Theis, Robert (ed.), *Die deutsche Aufklärung im Spiegel der neueren französischen Aufklärungsforschung* (Hamburg, 1998).

– (ed.), *Themenschwerpunkt: Religion* (Hamburg, 2009).

Thompson, Andrew, *George II: king and elector* (New Haven, CT, 2011).

Thulstrup, Carl Ludwig Henning, *Anteckningar till svenska frimureriets historia*, 2 vols. (Stockholm, 1892–1898).

Tiller, Elisabeth (ed.), *Bücherwelten–Raumwelten: Zirkulation von Wissen und Macht im Zeitalter des Barock* (Cologne, 2014).

Tricoire, Damien, "Attacking the monarchy's sacrality in late seventeenth-century France: the underground literature against Louis XIV, Jansenism, and the Dauphin court faction," *French history* 31:2 (2017), p.152–73.

–, "D'une Fronde à l'autre: pouvoirs et contestations aristo-cratiques du Grand Condé à Philippe Egalité," in *Etat, pouvoirs et contestations dans les monarchies française et britannique et dans leurs colonies américaines*, ed. Deborah Cohen (Paris, 2018), p.4–22.

–, "The fabrication of the *philosophe*: Catholicism, court culture, and the origins of Enlightenment moralism in France," *Eighteenth-century studies* 51:4 (2018), p.453–77.

–, "Raynal's and Diderot's patriotic history of the two Indies, or the problem of anticolonialism in the eighteenth century," *The Eighteenth century: theory and interpretation* 59:4 (2018), p.429–48.

Trousson, Raymond, *Diderot* (Paris, 2007).

Varela, Javier, *Jovellanos* (Madrid, 1988).

Vatsuro, Vadim E., "Iz istoriko-literaturnogo kommentariia k stikhotvoreniiam Pushkina: 4: 'Milost' i 'pravosudie' v sisteme sotsial'no-eticheskikh predstavlenii Pushkina," *Pushkin: issledovania i materialy* 12 (1986), p.305–23.

Verba, Cynthia, *Music and the French Enlightenment: reconstruction of a dialogue, 1750–1764* (Oxford, 1993).

Vernadskii, Georgii V., *Russkoe masonstvo v tsarstvovanie Ekateriny II* (St. Petersburg, 1999).

Vetter, Eveline, "Studien zu Sumarokov," doctoral disser-tation, University of Berlin, 1961.

Veysman, Nicolas, *Mise en scène de l'opinion publique dans la littérature des Lumières* (Paris, 2004).

Vierhaus, Rudolf, *Deutschland im 18. Jahrhundert: politische Verfassung, soziales Gefüge, geistige Bewegungen* (Göttingen, 1987).

–, *Germany in the age of absolutism*,
translated by Jonathan
B. Knudsen (Cambridge, 1988).

–, "'Patriotismus': Begriff und
Realität einer moralisch-
politischen Haltung," in *Deutsche
Patrioten und gemeinnützige Gesell-
schaften*, ed. Rudolf Vierhaus
(Munich, 1980), p.9–29.

Viñao Frago, Antonio, *Política
y educación en los orígenes de la
España contemporánea: examen
especial de sus relaciones en la
enseñanza secundaria* (Madrid,
1982).

Vogel, Gerd-Helge, "Die Anfänge
chinoiser Architekturen in
Deutschland: Prototypen und ihr
soziokultureller Hintergrund,"
in *China in Schloss und
Garten: Chinoise Architekturen
und Innenräume*, ed. Dirk Welich
(Dresden, 2010), p.13–30.

–, "Konfuzianismus und chinoise
Architekturen im Zeitalter der
Aufklärung," *Die Gartenkunst* 8:2
(1996), p.188–212.

Volz, Gustav Berthold (ed.),
*Friedrich der Große und Wilhelmine
von Bayreuth*, vol.2: *Briefe der
Königszeit 1740–1758* (Leipzig,
1926).

Voskresenskii, N. A., *Zakonodatel'nye
akty Petra I*, vol.1: *Akty o vysšikh
gosudarstvennykh ustanovleniiakh*
(Moscow, 1945).

Vroon, Ronald, "'Ekaterina plachet
iavno…': k predystorii perevorota
1762 goda," in *I vremia i mesto:
istoriko-filologicheskii sbornik
k shestidesiatiletiiu Aleksandra
L'vovicha Ospovata*, ed. R. Vroon
et al. (Moscow, 2008), p.40–54.

Vsevolodskii-Gerngross, Vsevolod
N., *Teatr v Rossii pri imperatritse
Elizavete Petrovne* (St. Petersburg,
2003).

Wagner, Hans, "Joseph II.," *Neue
Deutsche Biographie* 10 (1974),
p.617–22.

Waliszewski, Kazimir, *Autour d'un
trône, Catherine II de Russie: ses
collaborateurs–ses amis–ses favoris*,
4th ed. (Paris, 1894).

Walker, Greg, *Writing under
tyranny: English literature and the
Henrician Reformation* (Oxford,
2005).

Walker, Timothy D., "Enlightened
absolutism and the Lisbon
earthquake: asserting state
dominance over religious
sites and the Church in
eighteenth-century Portugal,"
Eighteenth-century studies 48:3
(2015), p.307–28.

Wandruszka, Adam, "Leopold II.,"
Neue Deutsche Biographie 14 (1985),
p.260–66.

–, *Leopold II.: Erzherzog von
Österreich, Grossherzog von Toskana,
König von Ungarn und Böhmen,
Römischer Kaiser*, 2 vols. (Vienna,
1965).

Wangermann, Ernst, *From Joseph II
to the Jacobin trials: government
policy and public opinion in the
Habsburg dominions in the period
of the French Revolution* (London,
1969).

–, "Kaunitz und der Krieg gegen
das Revolutionäre Frankreich,"
in *Staatskanzler Wenzel Anton von
Kaunitz Rietberg: neue Perspektiven
zu Politik und Kultur der
europäischen Aufklärung*, ed. Grete

Klingenstein and Franz Szabo (Graz, 1996), p.131–41.

Wäschke, Hermann, *Anhaltische Geschichte*, 3 vols. (Köthen, 1912–1913).

Watanabe-O'Kelly, Helen, and Adam Morton (ed.), *Queens consort: cultural transfer and European politics, c. 1500–1800* (Abingdon, 2017).

Werrett, Simon, *Fireworks: pyrotechnic arts and sciences in European history* (Chicago, IL, 2010).

–, "An odd sort of exhibition: the St. Petersburg Academy of Sciences in enlightened Russia," doctoral dissertation, University of Cambridge, 2000.

Wielach, Astrid, "Die Ordensfeste der Ritter vom goldenen Vlies im Spiegel der Zeremonialprotokolle," in *Der Wiener Hof im Spiegel der Zeremonialprotokolle (1652–1800)*, ed. Irmgard Pangerl, Martin Scheutz, and Thomas Winkelbauer (Innsbruck, 2007), p.287–308.

Wikander, Matthew H., *Princes to act: royal audience and royal performance, 1578–1792* (Baltimore, MD, 1993).

Wilhelmine, Friederike Sophie, margravine of Bayreuth, *Mémoires de Frédérique Sophie Wilhelmine, margrave de Bareith, soeur de Frédéric le Grand, depuis l'année 1706 jusqu'à 1742, écrits de sa main*, 2nd ed., 2 vols. (Leipzig, 1888).

Willenberg, Jennifer, *Distribution und Übersetzung englischen Schrifttums im Deutschland des 18. Jahrhunderts* (Munich, 2008).

Wilson, Arthur M., *Diderot* (Oxford, 1957).

Wittkower, Rudolf, "Englischer Neopalladianismus, Landschaftsgärten, China und die Aufklärung," in *Politische Architektur in Europa vom Mittelalter bis heute: Repräsentation und Gemeinschaft*, ed. Martin Warnke (Cologne, 1984), p.309–35.

Wokler, Robert, *Rousseau: a very short introduction* (Oxford, 2001).

Wolff, Charlotta, *Vänskap och makt: den svenska politiska eliten och upplysningstidens Frankrike* (Helsingfors, 2004).

Wollny, Peter, "Introduction," in *C. P. E. Bach: the complete works*, vol.1/8.2: *Miscellaneous keyboard works II*, ed. Peter Wollny (Los Altos, CA, 2005), p.xiii–xxvi.

Woodbridge, John, *Revolt in pre-revolutionary France: the prince de Conti's conspiracy against Louis XV, 1755–1757* (Baltimore, MD, 1995).

Wortman, Richard, "The Russian empress as mother," in Richard Wortman, *Russian monarchy: representation and rule, collected articles* (Boston, MA, 2013), p.89–105.

–, "The Russian imperial family as symbol," in Richard Wortman, *Russian monarchy: representation and rule, collected articles* (Boston, MA, 2013), p.106–34.

–, *Scenarios of power: myth and ceremony in Russian monarchy*, 2 vols. (Princeton, NJ, 1995).

Wunderlich, Werner, *et al.*, "Tradition and reception of Roman imperial ethics in

the opera *La Clemenzo di Tito*,"
The Comparatist 25 (2001),
p.5–21.

Wuthenow, Ralph-Rainer,
"Fürstliches Elend: die Memoiren
der Wilhelmine, Markgräfin von
Bayreuth," in *Das Bild und der
Spiegel: europäische Literatur im 18.
Jahrhundert*, ed. Ralph-Rainer
Wuthenow (Munich, 1984),
p.114–28.

Zaborov, Piotr R., "Frantsuzskii
aktior v Peterburge i o
Peterburge," in *Obraz Peterburga v
mirovoi kul'ture: materialy mezhdunarodnoi konferentsii (30 iiunia–3
iiulia 2003 goda)*, ed. Vsevolod
E. Bagno (St. Petersburg, 2003),
p.286–97.

Zaret, David, *Origins of democratic
culture: printing, petitions, and
the public sphere in early-modern
England* (Princeton, NJ, 2000).

Zaunstöck, Holger, *Sozietätslandschaft und Mitgliederstrukturen:
die mitteldeutschen*

*Aufklärungsgesellschaften im 18.
Jahrhundert* (Tübingen, 1999).

Zhivov, V. M., "Vremia i ego
sobstvennik v Rossii rannego
Novogo vremeni (XVII–XVIII
veka)," in *Ocherki istoricheskoi
semantiki russkogo iazyka rannego
novogo vremeni*, ed. V. M. Zhivov
et al. (Moscow, 2009), p.64–66.

Ziegler, Walter, "Franz II.
1792–1806," in *Die Kaiser der
Neuzeit 1519–1918*, ed. Anton
Schindling and Walter Ziegler
(Munich, 1990), p.289–306.

Zimmermann, Reinhard, "Freiheit
gegen Unfreiheit, Natur
gegen Kunst? Der Gegensatz
des formalen Gartens und
des Landschaftsgartens als
Denkfigur," in *Revolution in
Arkadien*, ed. Berthold Heinecke
and Harald Blanke (Hundisburg,
2007), p.59–82.

Zitser, Ernest, *The Transfigured
kingdom: sacred parody and
charismatic authority at the court of
Peter the Great* (Ithaca, NY, 2004).

Index

Printed and bound by CPI Group (UK) Ltd, Croydon, CR0 4YY

01/02/2023

03186599-0003